*America's Best Day Hiking*

# Hiking
# INDIANA

**Sally McKinney**

**Human Kinetics**

**Library of Congress Cataloging-in-Publication Data**

McKinney, Sally, 1933-
    Hiking Indiana / Sally McKinney.
       p.  cm. -- (America's best day hiking series)
    ISBN 0-88011-901-2
    1. Hiking--Indiana--Guidebooks.   2. Trails--Indiana--Guidebooks.
    3. Indiana--Guidebooks.  I. Title.  II. Series.
    GV199.42.I6M34   1999                  98-55073
    917.7204'43--dc21                  CIP

ISBN: 0-88011-901-2

**Acquisitions Editor:** Patricia Sammann
**Managing Editor:** Coree Schutter
**Assistant Editor:** Jan Feeney
**Copyeditors:** Denelle Eknes and Lisa Satterthwaite
**Graphic Designer:** Robert Reuther
**Graphic Artist:** Francine Hamerski
**Cover Designer:** Jack W. Davis
**Photographer (cover):** DNR photographer, Richard Fields
**Photographer (interior):** Sally McKinney
**Illustrator:** Tim Shedelbower
**Printer:** Versa Press

Maps adapted from—**Indiana Department of Natural Resources:** Parks #2, #4, #8, #9, #10, #13, #15, #16, #19, #21, #22, #23, #26, #27, #29, #31, #32, #36, #37, #41, #42, #43, #45; **National Park Service, U.S. Department of the Interior:** Park #1; **LaPorte County Parks and Recreation:** Park #3; **South Bend Parks and Recreation:** Park #6; **Elkhart Historic & Cultural Preservation Commission, property of Scott Hendrie:** p. 29; **Elkhart County Parks:** pp. 30-32; **ARCH, Inc. (219-426-5117):** Park #11; **Wells County Chamber of Commerce:** Park #12; **United States Government Service:** Park # 14; **Indiana DNR Division of Nature Preserves:** Park #17; **Courtesy of the *Journal and Courier*, Lafayette, IN:** p. 77; **Indy Parks and Recreation:** Park #20; **Cardinal Greenway:** Park #24; **City of Richmond Parks and Recreation Department:** Park #25; **Vincennes/Knox County Convention and Visitors Bureau:** Park #28; **Indiana Department of Fish & Wildlife:** Parks #30, #34; **U.S. Department of Agriculture Forest Service:** Parks #33, #35; **Indiana DNR Division of Forestry:** Parks #38, #40; **Columbus Area Visitors Center:** Park #39; **Historic Madison, Inc.:** Park #44

Bob Ramsbottom hiked and wrote the trail description for Mogan Ridge East (p. 140). Chuck Weis wrote the text for parks #42–45.

Human Kinetics books are available at special discounts for bulk purchase. Special editions or book excerpts can also be created to specification. For details, contact the Special Sales Manager at Human Kinetics.

Printed in the United States of America     10  9  8  7  6  5  4  3  2  1

**Human Kinetics**
Web site: http://www.humankinetics.com/

*United States:* Human Kinetics
P.O. Box 5076
Champaign, IL 61825-5076
1-800-747-4457
e-mail: humank@hkusa.com

*Canada:* Human Kinetics
475 Devonshire Road Unit 100
Windsor, ON N8Y 2:L5
1-800-465-7301 (in Canada only)
e-mail: humank@hkcanada.com

*Europe:* Human Kinetics, P.O. Box IW14
Leeds LS16 6TR, United Kingdom
+44 (0) 113-278 1708
e-mail: humank@hkeurope.com

*Australia:* Human Kinetics
57A Price Avenue
Lower Mitcham, South Australia 5062
(08) 82771555
e-mail: humank@hkaustralia.com

*New Zealand:* Human Kinetics
P.O. Box 105-231, Auckland Central
09-523-3462
e-mail: humank@hknewz.com

*My family has encouraged me all along, beginning when my father, Joseph B. Brown, took me for springtime walks in the woods when I was five years old. Although he called this "hunting for mushrooms," we were actually hiking. Later, my sister, Judy Brown, would often join me on hikes over many state park trails. In many ways, my mother, Hazel E. Brown, has also helped to make this book possible, as have my four adult sons, Brian, Mark, Bruce, and Matt McKinney.*

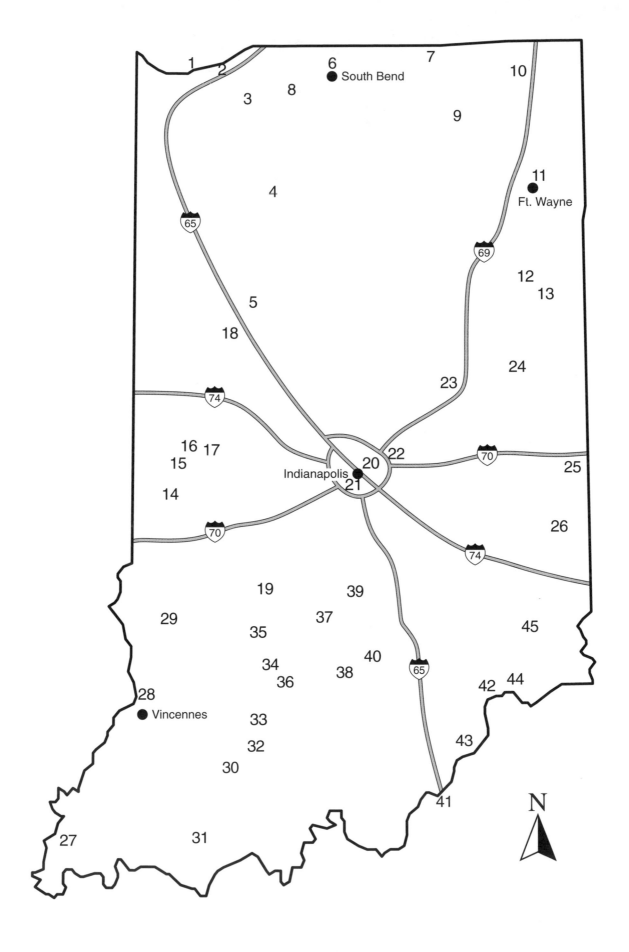

# Contents

# How to Use This Book

Hiking is an antidote to modern life. It gives the body some much-needed (and enjoyable) exercise, and it gives the mind both rest and stimulation. It even lifts the spirit to connect again with this earth that we're a part of but seldom have time to think about. With the America's Best Day Hiking Series, we hope to provide you with an incentive to start or continue hiking, for the pleasure and the challenge of it.

Each book in the series offers information on more than 100 of the most interesting and scenic trails in a particular state, as well as notes about recreational, historical, and sightseeing destinations located near the trails. The assortment of trails ranges from short, easy hikes for occasional hikers and families with young children to longer, more rugged ones for the experienced trailblazer. None of the trails takes more than a day to hike, although some trails may be linked together to create a hike of several days.

The trails in *Hiking Indiana* are divided into three main areas—North, Central, and South. Divider pages signal the beginning of each new area, and those pages include information on the local topography, major rivers and lakes, flora and fauna, weather, and best features of the area.

The innovative format is designed to make exploring new parks and trails easy. Information on each park or other nature area always appears on a right-hand page. It begins with the park's name and a small state map that shows the park's general location. Bulleted highlights then point out the trails' most interesting features. A description of the park's history and terrain comes next, with practical information on how to get to the park and the park's hours, available facilities, permits and rules, and the address and phone number of a contact who can give you more information. The section entitled "Other Areas of Interest" briefly mentions nearby parks and recreational opportunities, with phone numbers to call for more information.

After the general information follows a selected list of trails in the park. The length and difficulty of hiking each is given, along with a brief description of its terrain. The difficulty rating, shown by boot icons, ranges from one (the easiest) to five (the most difficult).

On the other side of the page is a full-sized map of the park. Our book's larger format allows us to provide clear, readable maps that are easy to follow.

easiest  🥾 🥾 🥾 🥾 🥾  most difficult
1    2    3    4    5

The next right- and left-hand pages are usually descriptions of the two best hikes in that park, along with a trail map at the bottom of each page (a few parks have only one hike, with just one map that primarily shows the trail). Each hike begins with information on the length and difficulty of the trail, and the estimated time to walk it, plus cautions to help you avoid possible annoyances or problems. The description of the trail provides more than directions; it's a guided tour of what you will see as you hike along. The scenery, wildlife, and history of the trail are all brought to life. Points of interest along the trail are numbered in brackets within the text, and those numbers are shown on the trail map to guide you. The approximate distance from the trailhead to each point of interest is given.

The park descriptions, maps, and trails are all kept as a unit within an even number of pages. Parks for which only one trail is highlighted take up only two pages; those with the regular two trails cover four pages. We've perforated the book's pages so you can remove them if you like, or you can copy them for your personal use. If you carry the pages with you as you hike, you might want to use a plastic sleeve to protect them from the elements. You also can make notes on these pages to remind you of your favorite parts of the park or trail.

If you want to find a park or trail quickly, use the trail finder that appears on the next pages. It gives essential information about each highlighted trail in the book, including the trail's length, difficulty, special features, and park facilities.

We hope the books in the America's Best Day Hiking Series inspire you to get out and enjoy a wide range of outdoor experiences. We've tried to find interesting trails from all parts of each state. Some are unexpected treasures—places you'd never dream exist in the state. Some may be favorites that you've already hiked and recommended to friends. But whether you live in a city or in the country, are away vacationing or are at home, some of these trails will be near you. Find one you like, strap on your hiking boots, and go!

# Acknowledgments

Hilary McDaniel-Douglas, Becky Weber, Nila Armstrong, Chuck Weis, and editor Pat Sammann all shared their expertise during the planning. Chuck Weis hiked and described trails in southeastern Indiana. Barbara Krause pitched in wonderfully as the book came together, running errands, making copies, organizing files and dot map information, and braving winter winds to do anything needed.

I also want to thank Bruce, Angela, Rhonda, Jonathan, and Alex McKinney, and Judy Brown, Jack Dearhammer, Louise Economides, Bob Ramsbottom, Charlotte Chastain, and Jerry Paeth for hiking beside me while I took notes and photographs. Editor Coree Schutter has the patience of an angel, while Nigel Speirs, who lent me equipment when he hardly knew me, has the faith of one.

Many people statewide helped in various ways, including Kevin Waltman in Indianapolis, Jackie Hughes in Elkhart, Janet Hartsuff, and especially Darla Blazey in Jasper—amazing woman! Ted Winterfield conveyed much information about the Indiana Dunes National Lakeshore, and Wendy Weis-Smith, a naturalist on the Indiana Dunes State Park staff, gave me much-needed counsel. Fred Wooley furnished important background information for Pokagon. Leo Finnerty with the National Park Service gave me wonderful help in Vincennes; and Lou Brainerd, Kara, and "just Bill" at Delaney Park offered valuable perspective on the Knobstone Trail. Sincere thanks as well to Lisa Allen, Diana Peine, Jennifer Lute, and Rob Browning. Appreciation is also due to anyone I've overlooked—I'm sure you'll remember who you are!

# Trail Finder

## KEY

RV camping · tent camping · swimming · canoeing
fishing · boating · picnicking · biking

| Trail Sites and Trails | Park Facilities | Miles | Trail Difficulty Rating | Hills | Prairie/Grass | Forest | Lake | Wetlands | Overlook | River/Stream | Page # |
|---|---|---|---|---|---|---|---|---|---|---|---|
| **1 Indiana Dunes National Lakeshore** | RV camping | | | | | | | | | | |
| Miller Woods | tent camping | 1.1 | 1 boot | ✓ | | ✓ | ✓ | ✓ | ✓ | | 5 |
| West Beach—Dune Succession Loop | swimming | 1 | 3 boots | ✓ | ✓ | ✓ | ✓ | | | | 6 |
| West Beach Loop | picnicking | 1.65 | 3 boots | ✓ | ✓ | | ✓ | ✓ | | | 7 |
| Cowles Bog to Beach | | 2 | 4 boots | ✓ | ✓ | ✓ | ✓ | ✓ | ✓ | | 8 |
| Beach to Cowles Bog | biking | 3.0 | 4 boots | ✓ | ✓ | | ✓ | ✓ | | | 9 |
| Chellberg Farm Loop | | 1.2 | 2 boots | | ✓ | ✓ | | | ✓ | | 10 |
| **2 Indiana Dunes State Park** | RV camping, tent camping, swimming, picnicking | | | | | | | | | | |
| Dune Mountain | | 1.5 | 4 boots | ✓ | ✓ | | ✓ | | ✓ | | 13 |
| Forest to Dune Ridge | | 3.75 | 3 boots | ✓ | | ✓ | ✓ | | ✓ | | 14 |
| **3 LaPorte County Parks** | picnicking | | | | | | | | | | |
| Hickory Hollow | | 0.75 | 1 boot | | ✓ | ✓ | ✓ | | | | 17 |
| Crabapple Corners | | 0.8 | 1 boot | | | ✓ | | | ✓ | | 18 |
| **4 Tippecanoe River State Park** | tent camping, canoeing, fishing, picnicking | | | | | | | | | | |
| Oxbow | | 1.9 | 1 boot | ✓ | ✓ | ✓ | ✓ | | | | 21 |
| Bluestem | | 1.4 | 1 boot | ✓ | ✓ | ✓ | | | | | 22 |
| **5 Historic Delphi** | picnicking | | | | | | | | | | |
| Delphi Towpath | | 1 | 1 boot | | | ✓ | | | | | 24 |
| **6 South Bend Riverside Parks** | picnicking | | | | | | | | | | |
| Howard Park to East Race Waterway | | 1 | 1 boot | | | ✓ | | | | ✓ | 26 |

*Continued* ☞

ix

| Trail Sites and Trails | Park Facilities | Miles | Trail Difficulty Rating | Hills | Prairie/Grass | Forest | Lake | Wetlands | Overlook | River/Stream | Page # |
|---|---|---|---|---|---|---|---|---|---|---|---|
| **7 Elkhart** | 🏕️ | | | | | | | | | | |
| Elkhart Architecture Walk | 🚐 | 3.5 | 🥾 | | | | | | | | 29 |
| Elkhart Riverside Parks | | 3.7 | 🥾 | | | | | | | ✓ | 30 |
| Bonneyville Mill—North Loop | | 1 | 🥾🥾 | | ✓ | ✓ | | | | ✓ | 31 |
| Bonneyville Mill—Lookout Loop | | 0.83 | 🥾🥾 | ✓ | ✓ | ✓ | | | | | 32 |
| **8 Potato Creek State Park** | 🏕️🚐🏕️ | | | | | | | | | | |
| Quaking Aspen Loop | 🏊🛶 | 1 | 🥾🥾 | ✓ | | ✓ | ✓ | ✓ | ✓ | ✓ | 35 |
| Porter Rea Loop | 🚤 🏕️ | 2.5 | 🥾🥾 | | | ✓ | ✓ | ✓ | ✓ | | 36 |
| **9 Chain O'Lakes State Park** | 🏕️🚐🏕️ | | | | | | | | | | |
| Self-Guided Nature | 🏊🛶 | 0.5 | 🥾🥾 | | | ✓ | ✓ | ✓ | | | 39 |
| Sand Lake | 🚤 🏕️ | 1.3 | 🥾🥾 | ✓ | | ✓ | ✓ | ✓ | | | 40 |
| **10 Pokagon State Park** | 🏕️🚐🏕️ | | | | | | | | | | |
| Hell's Point | 🏊🛶 | 2.5 | 🥾🥾🥾 | ✓ | ✓ | ✓ | ✓ | ✓ | | | 43 |
| Bluebird Hills | 🚤 🏕️ | 2 | 🥾🥾 | ✓ | ✓ | ✓ | ✓ | ✓ | | | 44 |
| **11 Fort Wayne** | 🏊 | | | | | | | | | | |
| Central Downtown Heritage | | 1.5 | 🥾 | | | | | | | | 47 |
| Kekionga Heritage | 🏕️ | 2.5 | 🥾 | | | | | | | ✓ | 48 |
| Lawton Park to Main Street Bridge | | 1.45 | 🥾 | | ✓ | | | | | ✓ | 49 |
| Foster Park Loop | | 1.93 | 🥾 | | | ✓ | | | ✓ | ✓ | 50 |
| **12 Bluffton** | All facilities | | | | | | | | | | |
| River Greenway—White's Bridge to Downtown | | 1.42 | 🥾 | | ✓ | | | | | ✓ | 53 |
| White's Bridge to Ouabache State Park | | 1 | 🥾 | | ✓ | | | | | ✓ | 54 |
| **13 Ouabache State Park** | 🏕️🚐🏕️ | | | | | | | | | | |
| Wildlife Exhibit Loop | 🏊🛶🎣 | 1 | 🥾 | | ✓ | ✓ | | | | | 57 |
| Kunkel Lake Loop | 🚤 🏕️ | 1 | 🥾🥾 | | | ✓ | ✓ | ✓ | | | 58 |
| **14 Parke County** | 🏕️ | | | | | | | | | | |
| Mansfield to Ferndale | | 4.8 | 🥾 | ✓ | ✓ | ✓ | | | ✓ | ✓ | 62 |

*Continued* ☞

| # | Trail Sites and Trails | Park Facilities | Miles | Trail Difficulty Rating | Hills | Prairie/Grass | Forest | Lake | Wetlands | Overlook | River/Stream | Page # |
|---|---|---|---|---|---|---|---|---|---|---|---|---|
| 15 | **Turkey Run State Park** | | | | | | | | | | | |
| | Rocky Hollow Loop | | 1.7 | 4 | ✓ | | ✓ | | | ✓ | ✓ | 65 |
| | Turkey Run Hollow Loop | | 1.74 | 3 | ✓ | | | | | ✓ | ✓ | 66 |
| 16 | **Shades State Park** | | | | | | | | | | | |
| | Devil's Punch Bowl Loop | | 0.75 | 2 | ✓ | | ✓ | | | | ✓ | 69 |
| | Pearl Ravine Loop | | 2 | 5 | ✓ | | ✓ | | | ✓ | ✓ | 70 |
| 17 | **Pine Hills Nature Preserve** | | | | | | | | | | | |
| | Clifty Creek Loop | | 1.77 | 2 | ✓ | | ✓ | | | ✓ | ✓ | 73 |
| | Indian Creek Loop | | 0.98 | 5 | ✓ | | ✓ | | | | ✓ | 74 |
| 18 | **Lafayette/West Lafayette** | | | | | | | | | | | |
| | Wabash Heritage | | 8 | 2 | ✓ | ✓ | ✓ | | ✓ | | ✓ | 77 |
| | Celery Bog Nature Area | | 1 | 1 | | | ✓ | | ✓ | | | 78 |
| | Purdue Blue | | 1.75 | 1 | | | | | | | | 79 |
| | Purdue Gold | | 1.5 | 1 | | | | | | | | 80 |
| 19 | **McCormick's Creek State Park** | | | | | | | | | | | |
| | Fire Tower Loop | | 1.9 | 3 | ✓ | | ✓ | | | | ✓ | 83 |
| | Wolf Cave | | 2.5 | 3 | | | ✓ | | | | ✓ | 84 |
| 20 | **Indianapolis Parks and Recreation** | | | | | | | | | | | |
| | Eagle Creek Bird Sanctuary Loop | | 1.24 | 3 | | ✓ | ✓ | ✓ | | ✓ | | 87 |
| | Nature Trail Loop | | 0.3 | 1 | | | ✓ | | | | | 88 |
| | Holliday Park—Trail 8 | | 0.4 | 1 | | | ✓ | | | | ✓ | 89 |
| | Holliday Park—Trails 2 and 1 | | 0.5 | 2 | ✓ | | ✓ | | | | ✓ | 90 |
| 21 | **White River State Park** | | | | | | | | | | | |
| | Riverwalk Promenade | | 1.7 | 1 | | | | | | | ✓ | 93 |
| | Canal Walk | | 2.6 | 1 | | | | | | | ✓ | 94 |
| 22 | **Fort Harrison State Park** | | | | | | | | | | | |
| | Lawrence Creek | | 2 | 2 | ✓ | | ✓ | ✓ | ✓ | | ✓ | 97 |
| | Fall Creek | | 2.12 | 2 | ✓ | ✓ | ✓ | ✓ | ✓ | ✓ | ✓ | 98 |

*Continued* ☞

*Continued* ☞

| Trail Sites and Trails | Park Facilities | Miles | Trail Difficulty Rating | Hills | Prairie/Grass | Forest | Lake | Wetlands | Overlook | River/Stream | Page # |
|---|---|---|---|---|---|---|---|---|---|---|---|
| **32 Patoka Lake** | | | | | | | | | | | |
| Totem Rock | | 2.15 | 3 boots | ✓ | | ✓ | | | | ✓ | 133 |
| Wildlife Management Demonstration | | 1.71 | 2 boots | | ✓ | ✓ | ✓ | | | | 134 |
| **33 Hoosier National Forest** | All facilities | | | | | | | | | | |
| Pioneer Mothers' Memorial Forest | | 1.25 | 2 boots | | ✓ | ✓ | | | | ✓ | 137 |
| Two Lakes Loop | | 4 | 4 boots | ✓ | ✓ | ✓ | ✓ | ✓ | ✓ | ✓ | 138 |
| Hemlock Cliffs | | 1.44 | 3 boots | ✓ | | ✓ | | | | ✓ | 139 |
| Mogan Ridge East | | 5 | 3 boots | ✓ | ✓ | ✓ | | | ✓ | ✓ | 140 |
| **34 Avoca State Fish Hatchery** | | | | | | | | | | | |
| Avoca Fish Hatchery Pond Walk | | 1 | 1 boot | | | | ✓ | ✓ | | ✓ | 142 |
| **35 Bloomington/Monroe County** | | | | | | | | | | | |
| Deam Wilderness—Axom Branch Experience | | 2 | 4 boots | ✓ | ✓ | ✓ | ✓ | | | ✓ | 145 |
| Deam Wilderness—Grubb Ridge | | 4.14 | 2 boots | | | ✓ | | ✓ | | | 146 |
| **36 Spring Mill State Park** | All facilities | | | | | | | | | | |
| Pioneer Village/Donaldson Cave Loop | | 2 | 2 boots | | | ✓ | ✓ | | | ✓ | 149 |
| Donaldson Nature Preserve | | 2 | 2 boots | | | ✓ | | | ✓ | ✓ | 150 |
| **37 Brown County State Park** | | | | | | | | | | | |
| Tulip Tree Loop | | 2.5 | 3 boots | ✓ | ✓ | ✓ | | | | ✓ | 153 |
| Ogle Lake Loop | | 1.5 | 3 boots | | | ✓ | ✓ | ✓ | | | 154 |
| **38 Wyandotte Cave State Recreation Area** | | | | | | | | | | | |
| Monument Mountain Hike | | 1.6 | 3 boots | ✓ | | | | | | | 157 |
| Twigs to Timber | | 0.5 | 2 boots | ✓ | | ✓ | | | | | 158 |
| **39 Columbus** | All facilities | | | | | | | | | | |
| Architecture Walk | | 1 | 1 boot | | | | | | | | 161 |
| Mill Race Loop | | 1.33 | 1 boot | | | ✓ | ✓ | | | ✓ | 162 |

*Continued* ☞

| | Trail Sites and Trails | Park Facilities | Miles | Trail Difficulty Rating | Terrain/Landscape | | | | | | | Page # |
|---|---|---|---|---|---|---|---|---|---|---|---|---|
| | | | | | Hills | Prairie/Grass | Forest | Lake | Wetlands | Overlook | River/Stream | |
| 40 | **Jackson-Washington State Forest** | | | | | | | | | | | |
| | Pinnacle Peak | | 0.73 | 🥾🥾🥾🥾 | ✓ | | ✓ | | | ✓ | | 165 |
| | Tree Identification Loop | | 0.75 | 🥾 | | | ✓ | | | | | 166 |
| | Backcountry Fire | | 0.73 | 🥾🥾🥾 | ✓ | ✓ | ✓ | ✓ | | | ✓ | 167 |
| | Knobstone Trail—Delaney Park to Spurgeon Hollow | | 3 | 🥾🥾🥾 | ✓ | | ✓ | ✓ | ✓ | | ✓ | 168 |
| 41 | **Falls of the Ohio State Park** | | | | | | | | | | | |
| | Goose Island | | 3.5 | 🥾🥾 | | | | | | | ✓ | 171 |
| | Woodland Loop | | 0.75 | 🥾 | | | ✓ | | | | ✓ | 172 |
| 42 | **Clifty Falls State Park** | | | | | | | | | | | |
| | Overlook Loop | | 1.8 | 🥾🥾 | ✓ | | ✓ | | | ✓ | ✓ | 175 |
| | Falls/Clifty Creek | | 3 | 🥾🥾🥾🥾 | | | ✓ | ✓ | | | ✓ | 176 |
| 43 | **Charlestown State Park** | | | | | | | | | | | |
| | Fourteenmile Creek | | 1.8 | 🥾🥾 | ✓ | | ✓ | | | | ✓ | 179 |
| | Oak/Clark Shelter Loop | | 1 | 🥾 | ✓ | ✓ | ✓ | ✓ | | | ✓ | 180 |
| 44 | **Madison** | All facilities | | | | | | | | | | |
| | Historic District Walking Tour | | 1.3 | 🥾 | | | | | | | | 182 |
| 45 | **Versailles State Park** | | | | | | | | | | | |
| | Fallen Timber Creek | | 1.5 | 🥾🥾 | ✓ | | ✓ | ✓ | | | ✓ | 185 |
| | Laughery Creek Canoe | | | 🥾 | | | | | | ✓ | ✓ | 186 |

# North

The northern region of Indiana, made up of 31 counties, stretches across the uppermost third of the state. Bounded by Illinois, Michigan, and Ohio on three sides and the central region to the south, the north also has 14 miles of public access to the Lake Michigan shore.

## Topography

Drive across northern Indiana from the industrial northwest to the agricultural southeast and you'll see mainly flatland. Take a closer look to find terrain broken here and there by lakes, marshes, and patches of woodland, the surface etched by watersheds of rivers and streams.

More than one million years ago, when the North American continent was still linked to other landmasses, what is now northern Indiana was covered by an inland sea. In the northwest corner of this region, the glacial Lake Chicago, formerly much larger than Lake Michigan, left a fascinating, sandy lake bed and a series of moraines when it receded. Over the centuries, wave action by these lakes has formed beaches, shifting sand dunes, and moist valleys.

Study a map of northern Indiana and you'll see scattered, natural lakes that form a dotted, blue crescent curving from the marshland near Lake Michigan to Indiana's northeast corner. Drive across northern Indiana and you'll notice small lakes and gently rolling terrain. Here and there, receding glaciers left boulders and other glacial debris—gravel, dirt, and deposits of sand—to form moraines (long ridges), kames (conical or fan-shaped mounds), and swales (moist depressions). Over time, glacial pockets known as kettle holes have filled with water, and these depressions have become freshwater lakes or ponds.

## Major Rivers and Lakes

The Wabash River, fed by the Tippecanoe, the Mississinewa, and smaller tributaries, dominates this region as it flows southwest past occasional islands; forested hills; and rough, clay embankments. Here and there are limestone cliffs and intriguing sandstone formations. The Wabash, the Hoosier state's official river, has a watershed so extensive it affects most counties in the state. The river travels a total of 475 miles, eventually flowing southwest toward the Illinois state line, into the Ohio, then the Mississippi. However, the Maumee and the Pigeon Rivers flow toward the Great Lakes.

Northern Indiana has soil that ranges from moist peat bogs and fertile loam to patches of sand. Some of Indiana Territory's earliest settlers sent letters home boasting about the soil's fertility. However, these early farmers hesitated to drain, plow, and plant crops in the region's prairie and marshland; after all, if the soil lacked enough fertility to support the growth of trees, then how could it possibly nourish crops?

The northern region of Indiana claims about 50 miles of Lake Michigan shoreline; much of it has public access for recreation. Lake Wawasee, Lake James, and Lake Maxinkuckee are among the largest of the glacial lakes in northern Indiana. There are perhaps 1,000 such natural lakes in the region; most are small lakes that formed in depressions when the glaciers receded. The northern region also has several reservoirs.

## Common Plant Life

Most of northern Indiana was once blanketed by forests; yet, you can find scattered maple-beech and oak-hickory forest communities. In the duneland to the northwest, the sand ridges and valleys support tall white pine trees and sturdy black oaks, as well as jack pine, tulip, and sassafras trees. In the marshlands farther south, bog willow and tamarack trees grow. In the Wabash River Basin, sycamores, cottonwoods, and river birch thrive in the floodplains. In the woodlands of northern Indiana lake country, oak, hickory, maple, or beech may dominate the forest community, but black walnut, ash, and tulip poplar, or tulip tree—the official state tree—also appear.

Northern Indiana's early settlers described myriad wildflowers that bloomed in the marshland, prairies, and forests. In season, wildflowers still flourish in protected habitats or survive among wild grasses that grow beside the roads. In early spring, look for blue and white violets, buttercups, trillium, and wild geranium, as well as Dutchman's breeches and fringed gentian. In late spring, mayapples, jack-in-the-pulpit, lady's slipper, and yellow cinquefoil follow the early wildflower show. During the warm, moist summers, blue and yellow coneflowers; daisies; black-eyed Susans; sweet William; Queen Anne's lace; and tall, violet thistles thrive among tangled grasses. Autumn brings goldenrod, cattails, and Indian paintbrush, harmonizing with the bright, warm colors of autumn leaves.

The self-taught Hoosier botanist Charles Deam grew up in Bluffton, in the upper Wabash River valley. Deam collected 65,000 plant specimens from around Indiana during his lifetime and discovered various new species.

## Common Birds and Mammals

Northern Indiana's earliest inhabitants could feed on the bountiful wildlife that roamed the countryside. Hunters found bison, wolves, and game birds in the tallgrass prairies, and deer, wildcats, and smaller game in the shadowy forests. No longer preyed upon by wolves, white-tailed deer still thrive. Squirrels, chipmunks, raccoons, beaver, rabbits, foxes, muskrats, mink, opossums, and weasels still inhabit northern Indiana's forests, fields, and streams.

In the northwest corner of this region, an intricate duneland ecosystem supports an unusual variety of wildlife. Bird-watchers have checked off more than 300 species of birds from their lists in the area near Lake Michigan. Gulls, swallows, warblers, thrushes, bitterns, egrets, and cranes have all been seen here. Also favoring this habitat are the rare Franklin's ground squirrel; the Karner blue butterfly; and the intriguing ant lion, an insect that catches other insects in traps that it builds.

In the northern Indiana marshlands south of the dunes, wood ducks, Canada geese, kingfishers, herons, and red-tailed hawks prefer this habitat near water. In the region's scattered woodlands, you may also find warblers; woodpeckers; mourning doves; crows; blue jays; owls; and the cardinal, Indiana's official state bird.

## Climate

Northern Indiana has a temperate climate and four distinct seasons. Expect summer daytime temperatures to reach 80 degrees Fahrenheit or more and winter nighttime lows to fall below freezing. The rainfall in this region may average 35 inches a year. In general, the north remains cooler and drier than the central or southern regions of Indiana. Yet, rain may fall during any month of the year, and thunderstorms may occur, especially in spring and summer. During the coldest months, the counties that border Lake Michigan can get up to 100 inches of snowfall, compared with the 30 to 50 or so inches downstate. In the North, cooling breezes from Lake Michigan may also moderate summer heat.

## Best Natural Features

- A surprising variety of habitats for wildlife, such as sand dunes, rocky canyons, marshland, prairies, and forests, laced with a network of rivers, streams, lakes, and ponds
- The shifting duneland sands—fascinating ecosystem—along Lake Michigan
- Scattered wetlands, visited by migrating waterfowl in season, including wood ducks, Canada geese, sandhill cranes, and others
- Picturesque natural lakes, originally formed by glacial action
- The official Hoosier state river, the undammed and unstoppable Wabash
- Wildflower blossoms providing brilliant color— white, yellow, pink, red, blue, violet, or purple—amid the greenery
- Foliage in an array of warm colors

# 1. Indiana Dunes National Lakeshore

- Explore a floral melting pot where desert plants, such as the prickly pear cactus, mingle with others from woodlands, swamps, savannas, and prairies.
- Watch birds along the sandy shore and shifting dunes beside freshwater Lake Michigan.
- Visit the bog where Professor Henry Cowles first formulated theories of plant succession.

## Area Information

During an Ice Age that lasted about one and a half million years, four advancing and receding waves of glaciation formed Lake Michigan, the sixth largest freshwater lake in the world. An earlier, more extensive Lake Chicago, created by glacial activity, once reached much farther inland. As Lake Chicago retreated, it left behind this rare assortment of duneland ridges and moist swales, moraines and marshes, swamps and savannas.

When the Ice Age ended, forests of spruce and fir were typical of this region; bearberry, jack pine, and other plants more typical of a northern climate survive. Approximately 1,400 varieties of plants and 250 species of birds have been noted here, depending on the season.

Dr. Henry Cowles, a botanist from the University of Chicago, used this region as a natural laboratory for 20 years. Younger plants tend to live closer to the lake, and these complex dune communities are always changing. After observing the ways that a later community succeeds an earlier one, Dr. Cowles could better understand the process of succession.

Behind the beach are the shifting sand dunes and behind them the swales, or depressions. Farther back from the lake, there may be forest, then a marsh, then another type of forest, then a stream. Each habitat supports a different mix of mammals, amphibians, reptiles, and other life forms.

**Directions:** The lakeshore is located on the southern shore of Lake Michigan. Take I-94 to Portage; then turn north at Route 249. Drive two miles north to US 12; turn left and go west to County Line Road. Turn right and follow signs to the West Beach Visitor Center.

**Hours Open:** The park is open daily year-round, except Thanksgiving, Christmas, and New Year's Day.

**Facilities:** The national lakeshore has drive-in and walk-in campsites with no electrical hookups. Motels, restaurants, and service stations are located outside the park. You can enjoy summer swimming, picnicking, hiking, bird watching, and winter cross-country skiing here.

**Permits and Rules:** Hike on marked trails. Drive motor vehicles or motorbikes on the roads. Keep any pet on a leash. Do not disturb plants or animals. Ground fires are prohibited; use grates, grills, or portable stoves. Do not trespass on any private property near or within the park. Secure any valuables out of sight, and lock your vehicle. In an emergency call 800-PARK-TIP.

**Further Information:** Indiana Dunes National Lakeshore, 1100 North Mineral Springs Road, Porter, IN 46304-1299; 219-926-7461.

## Other Areas of Interest

**The Paul H. Douglas Center for Environmental Education,** located on Lake Street .5 mile north of downtown Miller, has a variety of programs and methods for teaching ecology and the environmental sciences. Located beside Miller Woods, the center honors a statesman whose leadership helped establish a national park in the duneland area. Call 219-926-7561 for more information.

## Park Trails

Hiking trails within the Indiana Dunes National Lakeshore form interlocking loops. Painted signs show a separate color for each park trail, and trails are identified with color-coded markers.

**Long Lake Loop Trail** 🥾—1.5 miles—This grassy trail begins off the West Beach Loop and roughly follows Long Lake, a popular local fishing site, before returning to the starting point.

**Inland Marsh Trail** 🥾🥾🥾—2.5 miles—This unkempt route begins at a parking lot beside US 12 about 1 mile east of the West Beach entrance. An access spur leads to two loops. The trail leads over ridges of the Tolleston Dunes and follows the edge of the Great Marsh.

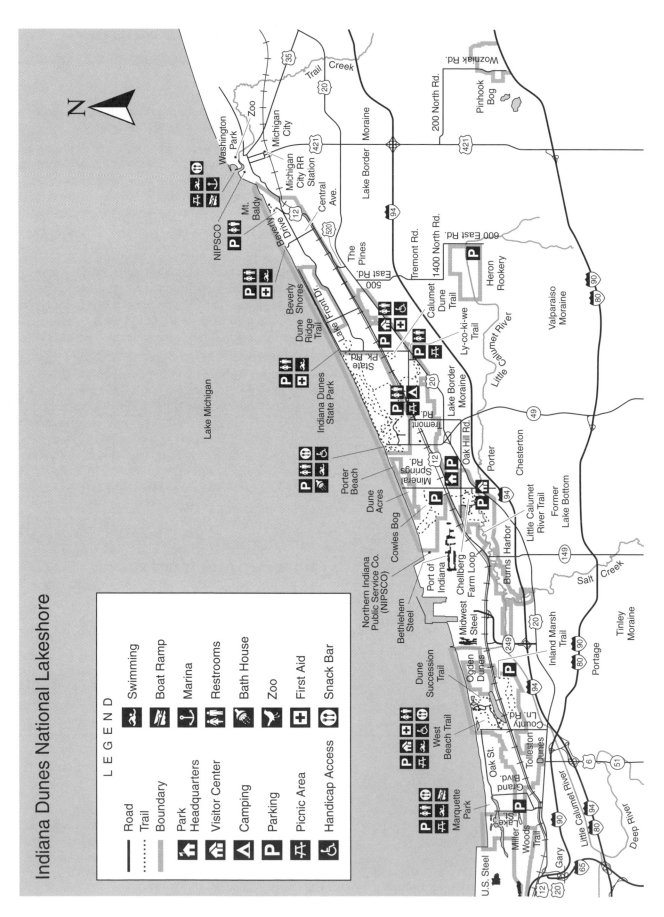

# Indiana Dunes National Lakeshore

**L E G E N D**

- —— Road
- ······· Trail
- Boundary
- Park Headquarters
- Visitor Center
- Camping
- P Parking
- Picnic Area
- Handicap Access
- Swimming
- Boat Ramp
- Marina
- Restrooms
- Bath House
- Zoo
- First Aid
- Snack Bar

Lake Michigan

Washington Park
Michigan City
Michigan City RR Station
Central Ave.
Mt. Baldy
NIPSCO
Beverly Drive
Beverly Shores
Dune Ridge Trail
Lake Front Dr.
State Pk. Rd.
Indiana Dunes State Park
Porter Beach
Dune Acres
Cowles Bog
Mineral Springs Rd.
Northern Indiana Public Service Co. (NIPSCO)
Port of Indiana
Bethlehem Steel
Chellberg Farm Loop
Burns Harbor
Oak Hill Rd.
Porter
Chesterton
Midwest Steel
Dune Succession Trail
Ogden Dunes
County Ln. Rd.
West Beach Trail
Tolleston Dunes
Oak St.
Grand Blvd.
Marquette Park
Miller Woods Trail
Lake St.
U.S. Steel
Gary

The Pines
500 East Rd.
Tremont Rd.
1400 North Rd.
Calumet Dune Trail
Ly-co-ki-we Trail
Lake Border Moraine
Tremont Rd.
Little Calumet River
Little Calumet River Trail
Former Lake Bottom
Inland Marsh Trail
Portage
Salt Creek
Tinley Moraine
Little Calumet River
Deep River

Zoo
Trail Creek
Lake Border Moraine
600 East Rd.
200 North Rd.
Wozniak Rd.
Pinhook Bog
Heron Rookery
Valparaiso Moraine

35
20
421
94
12
520
20
49
149
94
249
20
6
51
80 90
80 90
80 94
90
65

4

# Miller Woods Trail 👢

**Distance Round-Trip:** 1.1 miles

**Estimated Hiking Time:** 1 hour

**Trail Directions:** Park on the west side of Lake Street by the Paul H. Douglas Center for Environmental Education **[1]**. The hike begins at the west end of the center; go down the wooden stairs that angle north-west and follow the gravel path to the left. You'll pass a hedge on the right and some wooden slat benches on the left.

At .2 mi. **[2]** turn right. The trail enters the marsh via wooden plank bridges. On the right, reeds from four to six feet tall and white water lilies grow around a pond, with still water that reflects the sky. Beyond the water, you'll see a border of scrub, and beyond that a black oak savanna. Miller Woods contains some 280 species of plants. In spring, look for the rare lady's slipper and wild blue phlox along the trail.

By .25 mi. the narrow path enters a wildflower grove. Take the right fork when you encounter a Y. The trail will curve around marshland on the distant right and oak savanna on the left. The hardy oaks and deep-rooted prairie grasses that comprise the savanna have the ability to survive fires.

At .31 mi. a hollow at the base of a black oak tree provides shelter for wildlife; a sandy overlook offers a view of a lovely, small pond covered with lilies. You may already know that the American water lily has pointed, white petals and a yellow center, and the American lotus has pale yellow, rounded petals. If you see something you don't recognize, make a drawing and jot down a description as an aid to memory; then you can identify it later in a wildflower guide. The eastern loop trail curves around and eventually ends with a gravel walkway next to the parking lot at .47 mi.

To walk the western loop, return to the stairs behind the Paul H. Douglas Center and continue hiking west over the gravel trail you've already walked. At **[2]**, rather than take the wooden ramp toward the marsh, continue walking forward onto a little-used path to the west. You'll enter a black oak savanna, a type of plant community that has become rare; you'll pass ferns and sumac on the right, with brambles on your left. Note that oak savanna once covered 35 million acres of land in the Midwest. In late spring, we saw black-eyed Susans and wild strawberries in bloom along this trail.

At .74 mi. the trail curves right **[3]**; then a broad expanse of cattail marsh opens to the left, with the narrow, packed-dirt trail curving right. Notice that the marsh contains an island where black oaks grow high over a tangled understory.

At .85 mi., follow the trail to the right and you'll head uphill into a forest. Throughout Miller Woods you'll find swells (dune ridges) and swales (depressions between these ridges) left by the earlier Lake Chicago when it receded.

At .91 mi., from the top of a sandy knoll, there's a 280-degree view of black oak trees ahead, with a long stretch of marsh **[4]** on the right and more forest beyond it. At 1.0 mi. there's another tiny patch of marsh. Here, look for frogs, snakes, and turtles—three varieties of turtles inhabit Miller Woods. White-tailed deer, opossums, and muskrats have also been seen here.

When you reach 1.11 mi., turn right along a narrow path that leads to the wooden bridges. The hike ends at the bridge, where you'll notice the fledgling oak trees.

1. Paul H. Douglas Center for Environmental Education
2. Wooden plank bridges
3. Curve right
4. Marsh

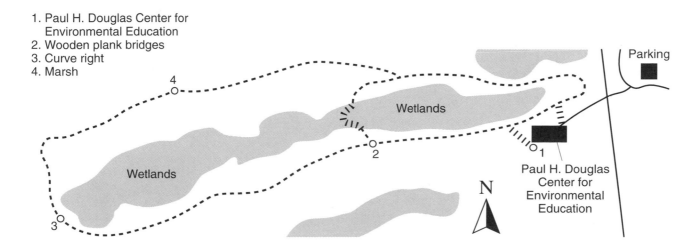

# West Beach—Dune Succession Loop

**Distance Round-Trip:** 1 mile

**Estimated Hiking Time:** 1 hour

**Trail Directions:** Use the parking lot near the Visitor Center **[1]**. East of the lot, look for a sandy path flanked with dune grass and a Dune Succession Loop sign. Begin walking counterclockwise around this loop. We noticed yellow cinquefoil before entering an open area with low, rolling, grassy hillocks that resembled a desert.

At .07 mi., hike uphill toward the wooden steps **[2]**. Note the gulls or other shorebirds overhead. At .14 mi. Long Lake Trail branches to the right. To continue on the Dune Succession Loop, take the wooden steps up to the crest of a forest-topped dune. From here, you can see Lake Michigan, framed by cottonwood trees. At .25 mi. there's a wooden deck with benches; you'll see swooping seabirds in middle distance above foliage-draped sand dunes. West, along the lake's curving, southern shore, rise the smoky, industrial cities of Gary, Hammond, and Whiting.

Stairs descend into a forest dominated by black oak trees. At .35 mi. follow a boardwalk **[3]** that leads out of the forest, turns left to ascend a dune, and passes through a stand of cottonwood trees. Known for its deep roots, this tree helps slow the duneland's shifting sands. At .4 mi., the trail descends into a valley where jack pine trees grow. Here and there, scrubby tufts of grass—marram grass, little bluestem, and others—also help anchor the sand with their extensive root systems.

At .45 mi. there's a wooden bench **[4]** with a view of forest and dunes, and a narrow stripe of the freshwater Lake Michigan behind them. A valley with steep, unanchored sand dunes around it is known as a blowout, a depression where the wind and human use have prevented the growth of plants. At .5 mi. a boardwalk **[5]** begins an arc around a marsh; here, myriad dark and light grasses grow in the water. You can sometimes see rare wildflowers here: horned bladderwort or Kalm's lobelia.

After you've hiked .55 mi., the boardwalk leads to a steep dune to climb; to the north, you'll hear the noise of wind and waves beyond this sheltering foredune. The boardwalk continues left, then ends. Follow the lighter, smoother boards that lead away from the marsh. Look for little bluestem among the grasses on

the lee side (away from the wind) of this foredune. At the Y, continue uphill on the right-hand path through shady, pine forest. Here, you might find bearberries or other plants typical of a cool, northerly climate.

At .85 mi., the trail leaves the forest, and the sandy trail takes you to more wooden stairs. From the crest of the dune **[6]** at .9 mi. you'll see the modern West Beach beachhouse beside the beach and a landscape of ponds and marshland. At the top, you're on the rim of another big blowout, one where the depression often fills with water.

By .95 mi., you'll be standing on the dune ridge with the marsh behind and some low, grassy dunes ahead along the beach. Note the exposed roots of the marram grass, reed grass, and sand cherry. These plants have root systems that help hold the sand. The roots of a single marram grass plant may extend to 20 feet.

Continue walking, and you can take in a wide view of the windswept beach **[7]** and hear the surf rolling in. The trail cuts left, with the low foredune on your left and the swimming beach on your right. At 1.0 mi., the trail ends at the beachhouse **[8]**. From an overlook, you can see a pond; rare toads and cricket frogs live there. We were happy to spot a blue-winged teal. Follow the road from the bathhouse to the visitor center; the parking lot is beyond it.

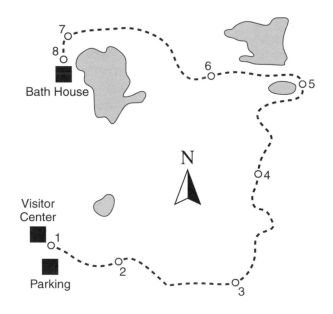

1. Visitor Center
2. Wooden steps
3. Boardwalk
4. Bench
5. Boardwalk
6. Dune crest
7. Beach view
8. Beachhouse

# West Beach Trail Loop 👢👢

**Distance Round-Trip:** 1.65 miles

**Estimated Hiking Time:** 1 hour

**Cautions:** Use caution when you walk the white stripes on the park road.

**Trail Directions:** Park at the Visitor Center **[1]**; the trail begins east of the parking area. Study a sign at the trailhead for additional information about this trail. Begin by entering an opening between sections of wooden fence. You'll see a dune and some cottonwood trees on the right and a black oak savanna on the left. Farther back from Lake Michigan, these dunes and plant communities have succeeded earlier communities and are therefore much older than the foredune communities.

At .1 mi., continue walking forward over a narrow, low path; the appealing, sandy trail to the right—although enticing—is not the right way! At .2 mi., a sign with arrows confirms your direction. At .25 mi., there's a cottonwood savanna that may be wet or marshy. How many different kinds of grasses do you see?

At .4 mi. the Long Lake Trail veers to the right, running south along the base of a dune. You'll see a grassy savanna on the right; continue through a sandy swale (depression) covered with marram grass and brightened in late spring with puccoon.

At .45 mi., some driftwood has a burnt look. Do you know that deep-rooted prairie grasses often survive fire? In summer, look around, and perhaps you'll find a prickly pear cactus among these fields of yellow puccoon, blue bladderwort, and assorted sand grasses. There may also be white water lily flowers and dark green lily pads, with the bright, shimmering pond water between. The trail skirts the edge of Long Lake **[2]**, but you'll be separated from the water by a thicket of low-growing shrubs.

At .75 mi., ignore the narrow path that veers right. Take a left turn instead, and continue walking along the lake. At .9 mi. **[3]**, there's a wooden platform often used for fishing. At .97 mi. **[4]**, use caution when the trail crosses the road via white, diagonal zebra stripes; continue along a sandy path on the other side. You'll cross a grassy prairie that was once the bottom of a large lake.

At 1.2 mi., take a right turn along this prairie—the dunes will be on the left. You're now walking back toward the Visitor Center. When we hiked this trail, we saw dozens of gulls gathering on the roofs of the picnic shelters **[5]** on the right or soaring on the shifting thermal currents.

At 1.25 mi., ignore the side trails leading to the shelters and proceed forward; the correct trail is an unlikely looking narrow path, much less used. On the left, you'll see the sliding slope of a large sand dune; the trail follows along its base.

At 1.3 mi., there's a confirming trail marker, and by 1.4 mi., you'll be heading into a blowout **[6]** guarded by cottonwoods. Although the route across the blowout may not be marked, you might find footprints that lead down into the depression and out the other side. At 1.5 mi., a marker will confirm that you're on the right trail. From it, you can see another blowout, one with a swale, a depression that's filling with water, and green marsh grass. Look ahead and you'll see where the trail curves right, then diagonally left, before ascending the slope— that's where you're headed.

At 1.55 mi., small white rocks have been spread over a sandy mound. From a point just beyond, you can see the parking lot by the Visitor Center. At 1.65 mi., the trail ends at the parking lot's edge.

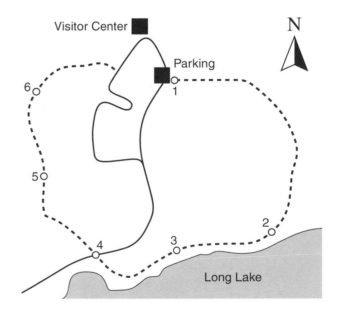

1. Visitor Center
2. Long Lake
3. Wooden platform
4. Road crossing
5. Picnic shelters
6. Blowout

# Cowles Bog to Beach Trail 👢👢👢

**Distance One-Way:** 2 miles

**Estimated Hiking Time:** 1 hour

**Cautions**: The beach has no concessions, bathhouse, rest rooms, or drinking water, so carry what you'll need.

**Trail Directions:** Park .9 mi. north of US 12 on Mineral Springs Road, just south of the entrance to Dune Acres. Walk west across the road to the trailhead [1]. A sign says, "Cowles Bog Trail Foot Traffic Only." You'll walk on a path of leaves matted onto sand and go into a forest. Note that Cowles Bog has been a registered natural landmark since 1965.

By .13 mi., you'll have a good view of cattails rising from this historic pond [2], on the left beyond the trees. Dr. Henry Cowles made early studies of plant ecology here, and modern scientists still use this pond for research. For that reason, visitors are not allowed near it; however, the trail you walk skirts the pond's northern edge.

Notice all the low, leafy green plants—water lilies, arums, and water plantains—along with cattails, ferns, and many grasses and sedges. At .26 mi., on a rainy day in late spring, the water had extended over the trail; we appreciated the boardwalk [3] just beyond. Note the forest floor beside the trail, in season, lavish with ferns.

At .33 mi., a yellow arrow on a post marks the trail, which then skirts the base of a dune. Here, we passed tangled forest, more ferns, and more wetland with big lily leaves on the right. At .55 mi., note the cavities in the trees, where chipmunks, squirrels, and other small mammals find shelter. At .58 mi., a lovely stand of white birch were left of the trail along the main bog.

At .65 mi. [4], we found another swale (a depression between the dunes) filled with water. At .75 mi., we saw ferns three feet tall on the left; the hill on the right was draped with low, leafy, green plants, as if

Nature's Landscaper were using ground cover, instead of lawn.

At .8 mi., ignore the trail ahead, which leads toward the fen. Instead, turn right on a sandy, uphill path and you'll head toward the beach. By .84 mi., you'll be rewarded with a view from a ridge [5]. As this trail leads closer to freshwater Lake Michigan, be aware that Dr. Cowles derived the principles of succession—the reasons behind the gradual, natural, successive shifts in plant communities—right here at the Dunes.

At 1.0 mi., the dune ridge you climb has been here longer than the foredunes ahead; also, this ridge supports an older, more established, and somewhat different community of plants and animals. By 1.07 mi., you've reached the crest of another dune [6]; from here, you'll walk gradually down and through another swale. By 1.29 mi., you'll see a lake on the left and muddy wetlands to the right, beyond the trees.

At 1.33 mi., the sandy path moves uphill and veers away from the lake. Ahead, the forest community has turned into black oak savanna, where slim, young trees reach above the light green carpet of low plants. Note the marram and other grasses, whose roots help anchor the shifting sands. At 1.52 mi., there's a Y ahead; walk right and you'll find a stand of young oak trees. This branch of the trail leads across the foredune ridge [7], down to the beach and the lake. Continue downhill and on the sandy path. At 1.52 mi., note the big smokestack ahead, spouting smoke.

At 1.7 mi., dune grasses have grown over much of the blowout at left. On the right, you'll see cottonwoods and conifers. Unlike the dune ridges you cross on the way to this beach, the shifting foredunes are younger; they were formed by more recent action of wind and waves. By 2.0 mi., you'll have come to the beach [8]. Here, this trail ends; you can either return over the route you came or walk .2 mi. left (west) along the beach. There, in the forested foredune, the Beach to Cowles Bog Trail begins (an alternate route back).

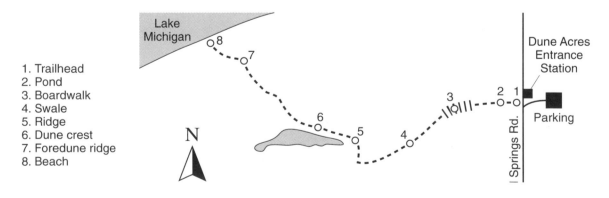

1. Trailhead
2. Pond
3. Boardwalk
4. Swale
5. Ridge
6. Dune crest
7. Foredune ridge
8. Beach

# Beach to Cowles Bog Trail 🥾🥾🥾

**Distance:** 3.0 miles

**Estimated Hiking Time:** 1.5 hours

**Cautions:** Secure belongings out of sight. Carry drinking water and food (there are no rest rooms or concessions at the beach). In summer, consider bringing a swimsuit.

**Trail Directions:** This hike begins at the beach **[1]** where the Cowles Bog to Beach Trail ends. We couldn't find a trail along the beach, although there is another trail leading back into the dunes to the road. To find it, walk west along the beach for about .2 mi.; a wooden post marks the path through grasses into the forest-covered foredunes. You might also find footprints along this route (we followed a man and a dog's footprints, but never saw them). After exploring the lakeshore, head back to the marshland on this trail.

At .2 mi., you'll experience a steep climb **[2]** up the sand dune into a maple-beech forest on the northern slope of the foredune. As you walk, notice how the sandy surface abruptly gives way to dark, soil-covered sand. Be aware that you'll be walking through increasingly older plant communities as you go back from shore. At .4 mi., the trail enters a grassy, sloping savanna covered with black oak trees. Just beyond, there's a red arrow trail marker. Walk farther and you'll soon be gazing at oak forest from a sandy ridge covered with grass and leaves. The leafy trail narrows to a dirt path just one foot wide.

After 1.0 mi., the trail veers left along a ridge. Soon, slim, young oaks rise from the covering of dune grasses. At 1.1 mi., a yellow arrow directs you right, so turn 90 degrees right, rather than continuing forward. In late spring, lovely, yellow cinquefoil blankets the hillside before the path curves left and

downhill. At 1.4 mi., the trail passes the edge of a small lake; there's a border of cattails. At 1.5 mi., climb up wooden steps **[3]**, where the forest opens to a view of the wetland; you'll follow a wide, sandy path to the left. At 1.6 mi., you'll see a pond on the right (notice the milkweed) and a row of pines on the left; at 1.8 mi. there'll be more pines.

The Cowles Bog area harbors the only stand of wild, northern white pines in Indiana; the area became a national natural landmark in 1965. At 1.9 mi. **[4]**, you may return to the north parking lot by walking left for .3 mi. around the fen **[5]**, then heading northeast over a .8 mi. stretch of the Cowles Bog to Beach Trail.

To follow the Beach to Cowles Bog route, continue walking ahead at 1.9 mi. You'll see an open, grassy meadow with power lines on the right. This is a good birding trail; it also leads to the south parking lot for Cowles Bog and the road. At 2.0 mi., there's a long view of the fen on the left, where you can watch for heron. The trail continues along a fence covered with wild grapevines that screen a pond; there's a line of low trees on the left.

You'll probably hear the cries of many birds along this route; this mixture of trees and tangled shrubs, located between two ponds, provides suitable habitat for many species. Depending on the season, you might see brown thrashers, chickadees, or even scarlet tanagers beside the path. Through the trees at left is a long view of fen, nearly covered with cattails.

At 2.5 mi. there's a clear view of a small pond—the trail continues straight ahead. Soon after, you can see a lake and low forest on the right; at 2.6 mi., walk left on the gravel path that runs along the power lines **[6]**. Note that the road is screened by foliage; this path will take you back to the north parking lot for Cowles Bog where the hike ends.

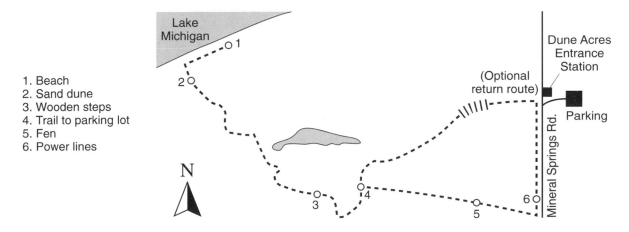

1. Beach
2. Sand dune
3. Wooden steps
4. Trail to parking lot
5. Fen
6. Power lines

# Chellberg Farm Loop 👢👢

**Distance Round-Trip:** 1.2 miles

**Estimated Hiking Time:** 1 hour

**Trail Directions:** Park at the Bailly/Chellberg Visitor Center **[1]**. The trail begins with a bark-strewn path behind the center. Walk north toward Chellberg Farm through a beech-maple forest. There'll be fallen timber along the path and a ravine in the middle distance on the left.

At .1 mi., angle left past the trees; note all the sugar maples. You'll see a building ahead, on down the way, and a sign that explains, "The Chellbergs relied on renewable energy, sun, soil, wind, plants, animals, and people to run their 80-acre farm."

Note that the farm buildings stand on a glacial moraine. At .16 mi. **[2]**, you'll see the sugar shack, a cement block building with a metal roof. This building belongs to a sugar camp where maple syrup was once, and still is, being made by tapping the tree for sap in the spring, then boiling it down. Continue walking on the wide, bark trail toward the wooden buildings ahead.

At .2 mi., there's a building called the Granary. Take a short side loop walk around the cluster of old farm buildings with explanatory signs. You can visit the granary; a windmill and pump house; an herb garden; a brick and shingle house built in 1885; a garden and orchard; a weathered, wooden barn with cows and horses; a chicken house with cackling Rhode Island Reds and Plymouth Rocks; a corn crib; and a pen holding a pair of geese.

The original family, who immigrated from Sweden, spelled their name Kjellberg; three generations of this family lived here and operated the farm until 1972. Since then, it's been a living history site.

At .35 mi., return to the main trail beside the granary. Follow the bark path north, and you'll pass the farm on the west side. You'll next cross a grassy field, with a shed housing old farm equipment on the left. There may also be horses, cows, a pony, or a goat grazing in a fenced pasture. At .43 mi., continue north on a dirt path that goes left of a huge oak tree. Cross a wooden bridge **[3]** and turn left; you'll pass through a forest with many young maple trees and a fat, autographed beech tree.

At .5 mi., take wooden steps down into a ravine lavish with maple trees; notice the new trees sprouting between the brown leaves on the forest floor. Turn right to walk along the bed of a runoff creek. The trail then crosses a creek on a wooden bridge. At .6 mi., take wooden steps up the side of the ravine. Look back after you've reached the hilltop for a lovely view.

At .65 mi., turn left to cross a ravine on a high, wooden bridge. Perhaps you'll hear traffic rumbling along Oak Hill Road **[4]**. At .75 mi., a spur to the right leads to the old Bailly Cemetery. The main trail continues left of the spur, along a gravel and dirt path. At .8 mi., take a sharp left at the sign for Bailly Visitor Center. The narrow, grassy path runs between low shrubs before reentering the forest, and you'll walk a winding, packed earth path. Where the sign says, "Caution ravine ahead," take care walking down—there are no steps.

At 1.14 mi., there was a lavish covering of mayapples on the forest floor. At 1.17 mi., there's a wooden bridge across a (sometimes dry) creek with a gravel bed. The left fork goes back to the Chellberg Farm **[2]**, so take the right fork uphill toward the sugar shack. The trail ends at 1.2 mi. Return to the Visitor Center over the bark mulch path that brought you, or take a shortcut directly to the parking lot. You'll probably see the cars.

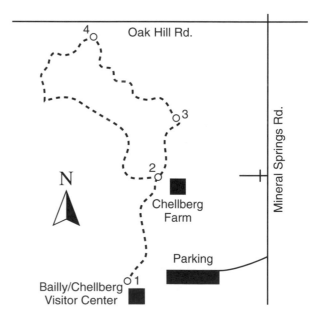

1. Visitor Center
2. Chellberg Farm
3. Wooden bridge
4. Oak Hill Road

# 2. Indiana Dunes State Park

- Climb these shifting sand dunes, anchored by deep-rooted grasses and trees.
- Walk along the beach of freshwater lakeshore and watch the gulls soar.
- Learn about the fragile ecology of the Indiana Dunes; the area has habitats ranging from beach and sand dunes to wetlands and forests.

## Area Information

There were four major glaciations here during the last million years. Working in concert, glaciers, wind, and water created a distinctive and unusual moraine topography near the Lake Michigan shore. The sandy beach and dunes environment was formed by glacial outwash; as recently as 2,000 years ago, what is now the Indiana Dunes State Park was entirely under water. As the larger, glacial Lake Chicago retreated, the moraine ridges remained. Today, near the beach, the highest sand dune reaches 192 feet, and the most distant moraine, a much older one, near Valparaiso, rises 800 feet above sea level.

Thoughtful and informed people recognized the value of this rare environment early in the 20th century; a state park opened here in 1925. Since then, researchers have learned much more about the duneland's fragile ecology. The environment continues to change, as the huge, living dunes shift inland, burying plants as they go. The lakefront is a harsh environment, reaching extreme temperatures in summer and winter; yet, the valleys behind the foredunes are in the lee of the lake winds. Here you can find rare plants from Midwest prairies, northern forests, and scattered wetlands. Today, the park consists of 2,182 acres of land and includes three miles of beach.

You can see an amazing variety of birds in the duneland area; birdwatchers have listed 271 species sighted near the lake between Miller Woods and Michigan City (bounded by US 6 on the south). In season, you can find 22 species of sandpiper and 15 types of gulls, often near the beach. Also, look for owls, red-headed woodpeckers, swallows, eastern bluebirds, nuthatches, meadowlarks, warblers, orioles, and blackbirds.

Wildflowers are another duneland delight. In the spring, you might come across bearberry, bloodroot, rue anemone, or wild geranium while hiking through woodland and see cinquefoil or bearberry while climbing a dune. In summer, you might find jewelweed, fringed gentian, or wintergreen in the woodlands and green- or purple-fringed orchids in the wetlands.

Whether you walk to cover a sweeping expanse of these dunes or only a short distance between two dunes, you're bound to discover something interesting.

**Directions:** Take I-94 to Chesterton. Exit I-94 at SR 49, and go north two miles to reach the gatehouse. You may also access the park by taking the South Shore Railroad from Chicago or Michigan City.

**Hours Open:** The park is open year-round.

**Facilities:** Campgrounds, camp store, nature center, picnic shelters, and a swimming beach are available.

**Permits and Rules:** No alcohol allowed in the park. Do not disturb plants or animals. Swim only in designated areas. Pets must be on a leash and attended at all times. Day hikers should carry out any trash brought in. See park notices and printed materials for additional rules and policies.

**Further Information:** Indiana Dunes State Park, 1600 North 25 East, Chesterton, IN 46304-1142; 219-926-1952.

## Other Areas of Interest

**The Calumet Trail** (also called the Calumet Bike Trail) runs for 9.2 miles along the South Shore Railroad between Dune Acres and Mt. Baldy. This multiuse path along a utility corridor accesses beaches and dunes, forests and wetlands. Bicyclists, joggers, and even cross-country skiers follow this trail.

## Park Trails

**Trail 2** 👢—3 miles—This trail, favored by fern aficionados and wildflower enthusiasts, begins north of the youth camp before passing through climax forest, then crossing the marsh on a boardwalk. The trail does not loop back, but ends where it intersects Trail 10.

**Trail 10** 👢👢👢—5.5 miles—The park's longest trail begins east of the nature center and runs along the marsh and through a white pine forest. The trail passes a tree graveyard in a large blowout before looping back along the beach.

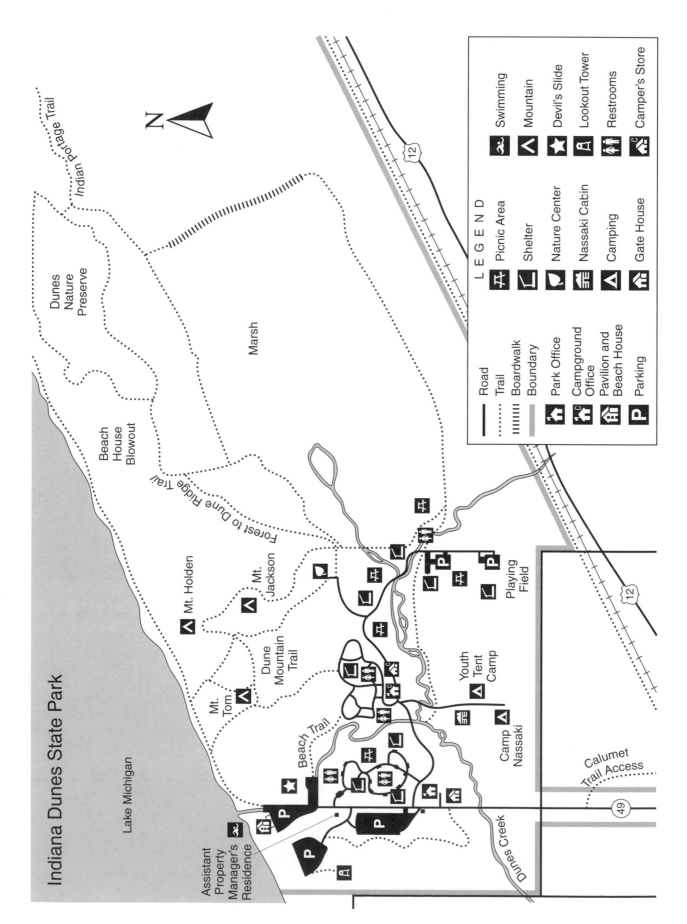

Indiana Dunes State Park

Lake Michigan

Assistant Property Manager's Residence

Dunes Nature Preserve

Beach House Blowout

Marsh

Indian Portage Trail

Forest to Dune Ridge Trail

Mt. Holden

Mt. Jackson

Mt. Tom

Dune Mountain Trail

Beach Trail

Youth Tent Camp

Camp Nassaki

Playing Field

Dunes Creek

Calumet Trail Access

12

49

LEGEND

Road
Trail
Boardwalk
Boundary

Park Office
Campground Office
Pavilion and Beach House
Parking

Picnic Area
Shelter
Nature Center
Nassaki Cabin
Camping
Gate House

Swimming
Mountain
Devil's Slide
Lookout Tower
Restrooms
Camper's Store

# Dune Mountain Trail (Trail 8) 👢👢👢👢

**Distance One-Way:** 1.5 miles

**Estimated Hiking Time:** 1 hour

**Cautions:** It takes strenuous crawling to reach the tops of these dunes where there are no steps. Also, wear shoes to protect your toes when you go skidding down the sand dunes—you could otherwise tear a toe on a hidden root.

**Trail Directions:** Begin walking south of the Nature Center **[1]**. Follow a sandy path beside a wooden fence into the forest.

The trail enters the Dunes Nature Preserve, a 1,530-acre protected area within the state park. At .1 mi., take the left fork of a Y **[2]**. Just beyond, take another left fork, a sandy path that leads uphill. Note the exposed roots of the dune grasses and the Pennsylvania sedge.

At .13 mi., there's a confirming trail sign for No. 8 **[3]**. Nearby, we saw a lovely, dark butterfly, a spicebush swallowtail, the trailing edge of its wings touched with blue. Beyond the hillcrest, note the shifting mixture of plants because of different conditions. At .29 mi. the path veers left and runs slightly downhill. Listen to the birdsong; Canada warblers, eastern bluebirds, or wood thrushes could be making these sounds.

At .36 mi., there's a sign on another hillcrest; ahead lies a black oak savanna. At .4 mi., ignore the downward route to the left, but continue walking ahead on the sandy high ground. Trail 8 veers right, then descends, only to go up, up, up the slope of Mt. Jackson, 176 feet high **[4]**. At .5 mi., look for lovely flowers here, especially in spring. As I sat down to rest, I tallied all the creatures seen on the trail so far: robin, raccoon, chipmunk, butterfly, gray squirrel, and gull.

At .6 mi., note that Trail 8 turns left, heading into a stand of black oak trees. Hiking down these steep, sandy slopes involves skidding and scooping up shoesful of sand. Children love it! In late spring, note the colorful clumps of blue spiderwort and yellow Canadian cinquefoil. The path leads across a sandy moraine; on the right is a swale, the scientists' term for valley, or depression. You step on leaves and fallen logs; milkweed clings to the hill on the left.

By .86 mi., you've reached the crest of another dune, Mt. Holden, 185 feet high **[5]**. From here, there's a teasing glimpse of Lake Michigan, a triangu-

lar view, framed by a V of foliage. Trail 8 signs direct you left, down the west slope of the dune and, again, skidding will get you down. At 1.0 mi. Trail 8 neatly crosses Trail 7 **[6]**; continue walking ahead, uphill, through maple trees. At 1.1 mi., you face several choices; the correct path goes to the right and downhill.

At 1.2 mi., the trail begins to cross a ridge. The sandy trail, now mixed with dirt, slopes downward on either side. Then, wouldn't you know, it heads back uphill! This time wooden steps make the climb easier—you're not slipping backward with every step. At 1.3 mi., a platform overlook shows you the bald, west face of Mt. Tom, elevation 192 feet **[7]**. Continue climbing and you'll have a view of Lake Michigan on the right. On a clear day, you can see the skyline of Chicago. Note the snow fences being used to control the shifting sands.

From the top of Mt. Tom, false trails lead in several directions. Although unmarked, Trail 8 curves right and heads for Lake Michigan **[8]** at a 90-degree angle. At last, you can sing "Climb Every Mountain," for that's what you've just done! Return to the trailhead by retracing your steps or take a shortcut through the campground and follow the road from the campground to the Nature Center.

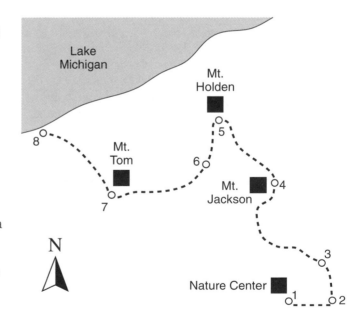

1. Nature Center
2. Y in trail
3. Trail sign
4. Mt. Jackson
5. Mt. Holden
6. Trail crossing
7. Mt. Tom
8. Lake Michigan

# Forest to Dune Ridge (Trail 9) 👢👢👢

**Distance Round-Trip:** 3.75 miles

**Estimated Hiking Time:** 2.5 hours

**Cautions:** Carry drinking water; there is none along the trail.

**Trail Directions:** Begin hiking east of the Nature Center parking lot **[1]** on a wide, sandy path. At .05 mi., take the left branch of the Y leading into the Indiana Dunes Nature Preserve. At .06 mi., Trail 8 heads left uphill; continue on a downhill path for Trail 9, into a black oak forest. You'll see fallen logs and branches, along with ferns and assorted dune grasses.

By .35 mi., you've reached the top of a forested dune and can view a long, curving, sandy slope ahead. Ignore the spur on the right that leads to Trail 10 **[2]**. As we descended a gentle hill, past black oak trees and maple leaf viburnum, we saw the flat, white blooms of anemone. At .45 mi., beyond the maple and sassafras trees, you can see a large dune ahead.

At .62 mi., turn right to begin hiking the loop of Trail 9 that links two major blowouts. You'll be walking through forest on the lee side of the foredunes. By .73 mi., you'll see the scattered, green tufts of sedge and assorted grasses amid the matted brown leaves. At .94 mi., the path has a covering of green moss; it's as if you were walking on carpet. Here, we heard the tapping of a woodpecker.

At 1.04 mi., a connecting path on the right leads to Trail 10, but follow Trail 9 as it curves left. A picnic table and benches **[3]** provide a rest stop. At 1.22 mi., we saw lovely ferns and more sassafras trees, while walking through oak forest. At 1.5 mi., the sandy trail crosses a shallow swale (between the dunes) and heads uphill; on the left, there's a ravine where many vines dangle from the trees. Note the exposed roots **[4]**—the shifting sands have uncovered them—and you'll head toward Lake Michigan.

By 1.6 mi., the narrow, sandy path hugs the foredune ridge, while oaks, pines, and marram grass cling to the slopes of this living hill; on the right you'll see Lake Michigan. At 1.62 mi., turn and look back at the sandy expanse of the Furnessville Blowout **[5]**. This large hollow was formed by forceful winds, burying some plants, while exposing the roots of others.

At 1.7 mi., the trail runs parallel to the shoreline, along the crest of the foredune. From a sandy ridge at 1.96 mi., you'll see several oaks with three feet of their roots exposed; if you view the lake, feel the wind and listen to the breaking waves. You'll be aware of the many forces at work in this environment. Ahead, the trail wiggles back and forth along the dune ridge; there's a shady, forested ravine on the left and the lakeshore on the right.

At 2.0 mi., as the trail drops down, we heard forest birds chirping—possibly warblers or thrushes. At 2.1 mi., a sign confirms Trail 9, as we climb uphill, then down. The trail still follows the crest of the foredunes; notice the way these sand dunes nearest the lake are anchored by dune grasses and cottonwood trees.

By 2.62 mi., we've reached the Beach House Blowout **[6]**. Notice the weathered tree stumps, framed by cottonwood trees. Formed more recently than the backdunes, this foredune ridge has a unique mixture of plants that help stabilize the sand. Yet, with the action of winds from the lake, these dunes keep growing. At 2.82 mi., there's a cliff, rimmed with grass, that drops off on the right of the trail. In late spring, we enjoyed the rustling leaves of the cottonwoods on the left.

At 2.9 mi., continue walking along the rim of the blowout, high above a great expanse of forest. At 2.96 mi., a sign confirms where the trail descends from the rim of the blowout into an oak savanna. At 3.1 mi. **[7]**, turn right at a T junction and follow Trail 9 into the woods; the hike ends where it began, at the Nature Center.

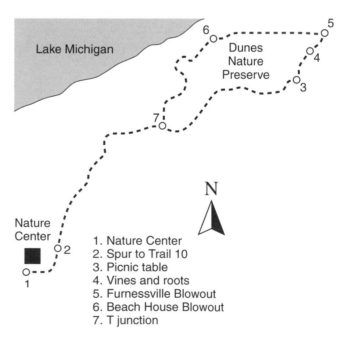

1. Nature Center
2. Spur to Trail 10
3. Picnic table
4. Vines and roots
5. Furnessville Blowout
6. Beach House Blowout
7. T junction

# 3. LaPorte County Parks

- Explore a variety of ecosystems—upland forest, wetland, prairie, and pond—within a limited space.
- Visit the transition zone where Indiana's former forests opened up to prairie land.
- Enjoy lakes and wetlands in a county that has organized parks to preserve them.

## Area Information

Successive waves of advancing and retreating glaciers helped create the lakes and moraines in northern Indiana. In northern LaPorte County, the sandy lake bottom remained after the ancient Lake Chicago receded. In southern LaPorte County, small, freshwater lakes and moraines were formed by glacial action.

After the French explorers first visited this region, they settled here. At that time, much of the region to the east was covered with forest. LaPorte, which means the door or the gate in French, was the place where dense, hardwood forests opened to a mosaic of wetlands and uplands in the west. Although the pioneers were reluctant to farm this treeless terrain, eventually, much of the great marsh was drained, and the grand prairie became farmland. Today, LaPorte county has less than 10 percent of the original wetlands.

Fortunately, LaPorte County has organized samples of distinctive forest, prairie, and wetland communities into city and county parks. Washington Park, on Lake Michigan in Michigan City, occupies the sandy lake bottom and dunes left by the former Lake Chicago. LaPorte's lovely city parks have been developed around natural lakes. Luhr County Park contains a mixture of upland forest, wetlands, prairie, and a pond. Pinhook Bog, a wetland in southwestern LaPorte County, provides increasingly rare habitat for wildlife.

**Directions:** The turnoff for Luhr County Park is located three miles south of LaPorte on Highway 35. Turn west at the sign and drive one and one-half miles on CR 250 South. Then, turn south on CR 150 West and travel one mile. The parking lot is on the right.

**Hours Open:** The park is open year-round from 7:00 A.M. until sunset.

**Facilities:** There are picnic shelters, benches, picnic tables, rest rooms, and a nature center with a wildlife viewing area. A lookout tower overlooks an ecology study area.

**Permits and Rules:** Pets must be on leashes. No hunting or releasing of animals is allowed. Alcoholic beverages are prohibited.

**Further Information:** LaPorte County Parks and Recreation, LaPorte County Courthouse, LaPorte, IN 46350; 219-873-7014, ext. 23 or 219-326-6808, ext. 223.

## Other Areas of Interest

**Pinhook Bog,** a classic sphagnum bog typically found farther north, is located in southeastern LaPorte County. Rare turtles and snakes, several kinds of salamanders, insect-trapping sundew plants, and upright lupines that nourish rare butterflies all inhabit this bog community. You may only visit Pinhook Bog during special tours. For information contact Indiana Dunes National Lakeshore, 1100 North Mineral Springs Road, Porter, IN 46304; 219-926-7561.

## Park Trails

Some sections of the wooded trails are not well defined. In case of doubt, return to the nature center and parking lot via the paved Trail 1.

**Deer Trail Pass—Trail 3** 👢—.36 mile—This shady, wooded trail begins off Trail 2, traverses the park, and ends at the park amphitheater and program area.

**Lumberjack Trail—Trail 4** 👢—.67 mile—Beginning at the picnic shelter on Trail 1, this route goes by the aquatic ecology study area of the pond and passes through forest and seasonal wetlands before skirting the wetland ecology study area.

# LaPorte County Parks

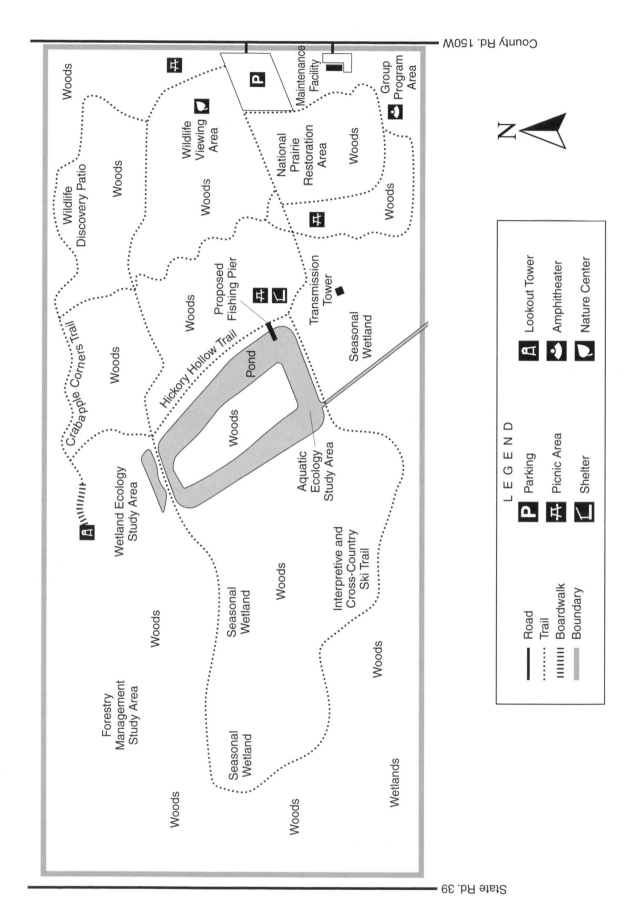

County Rd. 150W

State Rd. 39

**LEGEND**

| | | | |
|---|---|---|---|
| —— Road | P Parking | A Lookout Tower | |
| ···· Trail | A Picnic Area | ◖ Amphitheater | |
| ⊪⊪ Boardwalk | L Shelter | ◗ Nature Center | |
| ▬▬ Boundary | | | |

Woods
Wildlife Discovery Patio
Wildlife Viewing Area
National Prairie Restoration Area
Group Program Area
Maintenance Facility
Crabapple Corners Trail
Hickory Hollow Trail
Proposed Fishing Pier
Transmission Tower
Seasonal Wetland
Pond
Aquatic Ecology Study Area
Wetland Ecology Study Area
Interpretive and Cross-Country Ski Trail
Forestry Management Study Area
Seasonal Wetland
Wetlands

# Hickory Hollow Trail (Trail 1) 👢

**Distance Round-Trip:** .75 mile

**Estimated Hiking Time:** 45 minutes

**Cautions:** In late spring, we found some of the most assertive mosquitoes in the state. Wear long pants and a long-sleeved shirt; use plenty of insect repellent.

**Trail Directions:** This accessible, paved trail begins at the right of the Nature Center **[1]** entrance. Discovery Lane goes to the right; stay on the paved route with the sign for "Autumn Run." You'll walk through a section of mixed hardwood forests where many vines and creepers cling to the trees. The path curves right, and by .1 mi., it has curved left again.

At .2 mi. **[2],** Deer Trail Pass crosses the path; there's also a bench here. Note that the forest floor is thick with plants, rather than leaves. A trail that accesses the Wetlands Boardwalk goes to the right; you'll go there if you hike the Crabapple Corners route (Trail 2). Soon, the forest opens to a fishing pond **[3]**; note the rectangular island in the center. Another small pond on the right has a covering of algae. At .3 mi., turn left and walk past the bench. On the left, the tangle of grasses, flowers, and shrubs that borders the forest provides habitat for wildlife. The trail passes a mowed-grass strip and restful benches along the pond, a popular fishing site. Now, you can see how the pond water goes around the island.

At .45 mi., there is a shelter **[4]** with picnic tables and benches. The trail turns left and reenters the forest, which includes a grove of white pines. At .5 mi., the view becomes more open, for you see a grassy swath where the power lines go through. Note

that a section of this area is being returned to prairie. At .55 mi., there's a row of pines on the left. A sign announces, "Habitat Management Area for Pheasants Forever."

At .65 mi. **[5],** we examined the prairie to find oxeye daisies, black-eyed Susans, and daisy fleabane blooming amid clover and wheat grass. Before there was human habitation, prairies covered 13 percent of what is now Indiana. Big bluestem, Indian grass, stinging nettles, sunflowers, goldenrod, asters, and other plants grew in the tallgrass prairies, providing habitat for a range of ground-nesting birds. Once plowed, the settlers found the tallgrass prairie soils to be surprisingly rich. Notice the variety of grasses and wildflowers in this section of returning prairie.

At .75 mi. the trail ends beside the parking lot.

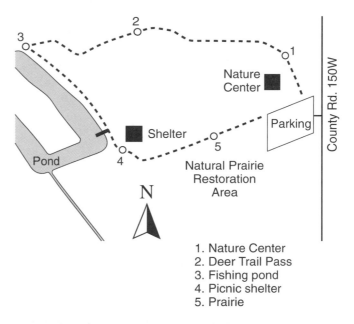

1. Nature Center
2. Deer Trail Pass
3. Fishing pond
4. Picnic shelter
5. Prairie

# Crabapple Corners Trail (Trail 2) 🥾

**Distance Round-Trip:** .80 mile

**Estimated Hiking Time:** 30 minutes

**Cautions:** In season, be prepared for some of Indiana's worst mosquitoes. Although this trail is poorly marked, if you need to, you can return via the easily followed, paved Trail 1.

**Trail Directions:** Trail 2 is accessed via Trail 1, which begins at the Nature Center **[1]**. A sign at the trailhead for No. 2 says, "Discovery Lane"; the trail is also Trail 2. Discovery Lane refers to the richly varied wildlife encountered along this trail. In season, the forest seems to have stereophonic birdsong; in late spring, we saw patches of violets on the right.

At .30 mi. **[2],** continue on the forked path to the right. Here, we saw tiny, white flower petals, strewn on the ground as little circlets from punched paper.

At .4 mi., continue walking through forest toward the boardwalk; ignore the path to the left. Ahead, you'll see a boardwalk **[3]** leading into an open area of marsh grasses surrounded by trees. In season (April and May) you can find marsh marigold blooming. For Indiana's pioneers, this plant had medicinal uses.

By .6 mi., you'll have reached the wooden lookout tower **[4].** In the near distance is a Wetland Ecology Study Area. From the tower, we saw a variety of bright green and blue-green algae, along with assorted mosses and liverworts; stay longer and you might see water mites, spiders, frogs, or water snakes below. Look higher and you might find wood ducks, geese, hawks, blackbirds, or grackles. On the rectangular island in the fishing pond to the southeast, the stand of sumac becomes a palette of artists' reds in autumn.

After you leave the tower via the boardwalk, at .70 mi. ignore the wide, dirt path that goes to the pond; instead, take the little-used spur to the main trail. At .80 mi., this spur joins the paved trail **[5].** Turn left and follow this paved segment of Trail 1, and you'll return to the Nature Center and the parking lot.

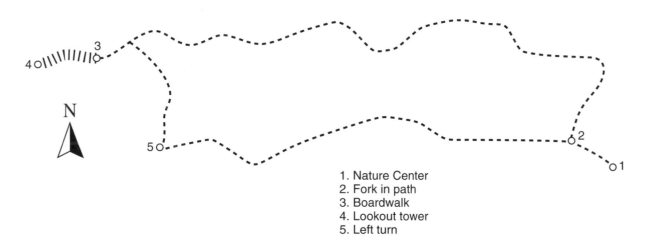

N

1. Nature Center
2. Fork in path
3. Boardwalk
4. Lookout tower
5. Left turn

# 4. Tippecanoe River State Park

- Explore the watershed of a lovely, meandering river with an evocative name.
- Visit nature preserves that protect a fascinating mixture of flora and fauna.
- Picnic on an oxbow island formed by a loop of the river and a newer, more direct channel.

## Area Information

With its most recent course determined mainly by glacial action, the Tippecanoe River provides a special environment for animals and plants. Potawatomi Indians once hunted and fished in this area. Hardy explorers, who had come all the way from Montreal, paddled this river highway and traded along its banks. The early settlers and those who followed cleared forests and drained most of the marshland in the surrounding area. Still, reserves like this park remain.

The site chosen for the park, much of it sandy, is less suited for agriculture than other types of soil. The 2,761-acre park was developed on level land that has scattered sand hills. Long and narrow, the riverine park forms a border along seven miles of the Tippecanoe River and offers various habitats for wildlife: oak and pine forests, marshes, the river with its islands, and abandoned fields. Popular with canoeists, the river park has also developed hiking trails through two nature preserves. Such recreational areas as this park give us a look at the "original America," claims the park's brochure.

**Directions:** Located six miles north of Winamac and south of Bass Lake, you can reach the park via US 35. The park entrance is on the east side of the highway.

**Hours Open:** The park is open from 7:00 A.M. to 11:00 P.M. year-round.

**Facilities:** The area has a campground, including a rent-a-tent option; canoe camp; boat launch; horse camp; picnic areas; and shelters.

**Permits and Rules:** Do not injure or damage plants, animals, or natural features of the park. Keep a dog or cat on a leash. Do not gather wood for fires. Build fires only in approved places. Do not swim in the river. Snowmobiles, ATVs, and golf carts are prohibited.

**Further Information:** Tippecanoe River State Park, Route 4, Box 95A, Winamac, IN 46996; 219-946-3213.

## Other Areas of Interest

The 4,592-acre **Winamac Fish and Wildlife Area** lies west of the park, on the opposite side of US 35. Deer, pheasants, turkeys, and other game are hunted here in season. Call 219-946-4422 for more information.

Farther west, the **Jasper-Pulaski Fish and Wildlife Area** is an excellent site for viewing sandhill cranes during their spring and fall migrations. The impressive cranes roost in the wetlands at night and feed in the area by day, before continuing their journey north or south. For more information, contact 219-843-4841.

# Tippecanoe River State Park

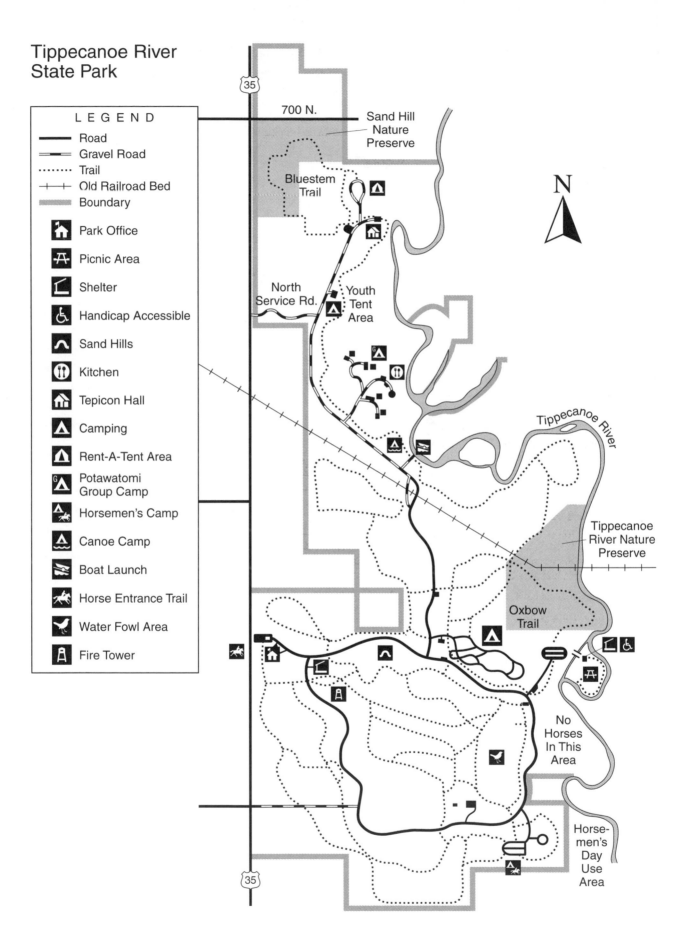

LEGEND
— Road
═ Gravel Road
⋯ Trail
+++ Old Railroad Bed
▓ Boundary
🏠 Park Office
🔱 Picnic Area
⛺ Shelter
♿ Handicap Accessible
⌃ Sand Hills
🍴 Kitchen
🏛 Tepicon Hall
⛺ Camping
⛺ Rent-A-Tent Area
⛺ Potawatomi Group Camp
⛺ Horsemen's Camp
⛺ Canoe Camp
🚤 Boat Launch
🐎 Horse Entrance Trail
🐦 Water Fowl Area
🗼 Fire Tower

N

700 N.

Sand Hill Nature Preserve

Bluestem Trail

North Service Rd.

Youth Tent Area

Tippecanoe River

Tippecanoe River Nature Preserve

Oxbow Trail

No Horses In This Area

Horse-men's Day Use Area

35

35

# Oxbow Trail (Trail 4) 🥾

**Distance Round-Trip:** 1.9 miles

**Estimated Hiking Time:** 1 hour

**Cautions:** This trail winds through habitat for the endangered massasaugua rattlesnake, one of northern Indiana's few poisonous species. Stay on the trail; although they are rare, watch where you step.

**Trail Directions:** Follow park road signs to the Riverside Picnic Area. Trail 4 begins at the far side of the large parking lot [1]. Begin by walking into a grove with large specimens of river birch, pin oak, and black walnut. On the left is stagnant water covering dead trees. On the right is an oxbow channel formed by the river. There is an awesome swamp on the left. A pond is a still, shallow body of water, usually covered with plants. A marsh is a pond dominated by herbaceous plants, and a swamp is a pond dominated by trees. Although a bog is typically acidic, a fen tends to be basic. Thus, I decide it's a swamp, but it could be either a bog or a fen. On both sides of the muddy track there is downed timber, submerged in shallow water. Listen for the birds, but look out for the snakes.

At .15 mi., we can see the channel for the Oxbow Lagoon [2], cut an estimated 1,000 years ago. This is a habitat favored by wood ducks, blue herons, muskrat, beaver, deer, and the massasaugua rattler. At .33 mi. a wooden bridge crosses a barely moving, muddy creek. We could hear woodpeckers and enjoyed watching the water striders form circles on the water's surface. At .36 mi. the trail is a muddy path, four to five feet wide, which passes trees that flourish in Indiana's river floodplains: sycamores, maples, cottonwoods, and willows.

At .56 mi. the path widens as we approach a wooden bridge [3]. Ponds on either side are covered with green algae. We enter a forest, which still sustains damage from a tornado that struck here in 1994. The night before I visited the park, another tornado struck nearby; the park has had damage from flooding, and two of the hiking trails have been closed. At .68 mi. a sign confirms this is Trail 4; an array of dead logs are strewn about this mixed, mesic forest, providing habitat for wildlife.

By .8 mi., the path follows a ridge, with ponds on either side. We heard a deep, twanging sound, like a note played on a stringed instrument. Was that a frog? By .84 mi., the path heads uphill before meeting

Trails 3 and 5 [4], which go toward the campground. Trail 4 enters a pine forest, and the path is strewn with needles. Here and there, young sassafras trees have made their way through a covering of leaves.

At .94 mi., beyond the trees and below on the left is a reedy marsh; towering pine trees, some wrapped with Virginia creeper, stand on the right. At 1.01 mi., the path turns grassy as it enters a mix of shorter, deciduous trees, including lots of the young sassafras. By 1.15 mi., we're walking through pines again, on a spongy, needle-covered trail. At 1.2 mi., there's another pond, this one covered with reedy plants. At 1.25 mi., another trail leads to the campground; Trail 4 goes through pines to the right.

At 1.35 mi., Trail 4 turns left [5], then follows what looks like an old, dirt road, before cutting through more forest to the right of some tents. At 1.51 mi., Trail 4 heads left, skirting the tents, then crosses a campground access road, before turning into a dirt path a mere one foot wide and heading into the trees. At 1.74 mi. [6], you'll cross a dirt access road; walk forward on the path that runs between the campground and the paved road on your right.

At 1.78 mi. you'll no doubt still see the tornado damage [7] from a storm on April 26, 1994. Walk past it on the edge of the road, and you'll return to the parking lot where the trail began.

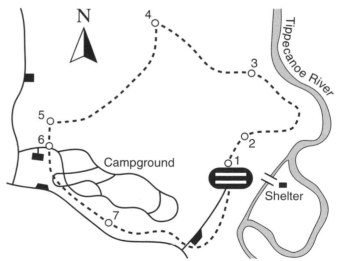

1. Trailhead
2. Oxbow Lagoon channel
3. Wooden bridge
4. Trail intersection
5. Left turn
6. Road crossing
7. Tornado damage

# Bluestem Trail (Trail 8) 🥾

**Distance Round-Trip:** 1.4 miles

**Estimated Hiking Time:** 1 hour

**Cautions:** The mosquitoes along this trail were some of the most bothersome anywhere in the state. Wear long pants and long sleeves. Use lots of insect repellent, even under your clothes. You could also wrap your hair and ears with a scarf, and use a notebook to fan them away.

**Trail Directions:** Park in the lot for the Tepicon Recreation Building **[1]** where the trail begins. Enter a pine and maple forest, where we soon heard the whining of mosquitoes. The trail loops through the Sand Hill Nature Preserve; apparently, mosquitoes receive protection equal to other wildlife. The sand hills in the preserve were created by glacial activity, then shaped and rearranged by wind. At .04 mi., the trail turns right to follow a dirt path bordered by matted leaves. By .07 mi., a three- to five-foot grassy swath cuts straight through the forest. At .17 mi., a cloud of mosquitoes follows as we walk past a stand of young maples.

At .26 mi., there's a bench **[2]** set among pines that are mostly denuded. The trail passes beyond some youthful sassafras trees, before the forest opens to an oak savanna. At .44 mi., we enter forest again, this time a mixture of young maples and white pines. With one swat, I kill four attacking mosquitoes. The pines grow well in sandy soil; the maples do well almost anywhere in the state. At .46 mi., we stopped to look at a wonderful, tiny green plant with a light green, starry center—just before walking past an early drainage ditch.

At .51 mi., look for a long section of open prairie **[3]** on the left. Big bluestem, which may reach six feet tall, has given this trail its name. Here, we also saw wild strawberries blooming and the tall, spiky heads of angelica plant. In this prairie habitat, you might spot gophers or cottontail rabbits. We found another

grove of white pines, not common in Indiana, which also makes this trail special.

At .54 mi., we walk on a path strewn with pine needles and layered with dirt and sand underneath. As you follow the path to the left, note the spikes on these pine trees; at one time, white pines were used for telephone poles. A repairman could easily climb these spikes. Ahead, there's a grove of what looks like Christmas trees below some taller pines. At .66 mi., the sandy path ascends a hill, passing through pines that grow from a bed of oak leaves.

At .69 mi., patches of green moss here and there form a fuzzy carpet along the trail. At .76 mi., the dominant forest mixture shifts to black oak and sassafras. At .89 mi. **[4]**, a spur trail leads to the rent-a-tent campground. Ahead, the trail parallels the road, then turns back to the parking lot. At 1.07 mi., the grassy path through prairie is broken only by occasional, small trees, bordered by forest. By the time we reach 1.1 mi., the sight of oxeye daisies and yellow coneflowers delights us. Trail 8 ends at the parking lot where it began.

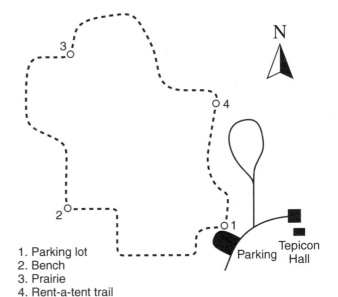

1. Parking lot
2. Bench
3. Prairie
4. Rent-a-tent trail

# 5.  Historic Delphi

- Hike the towpath beside a section of the early Wabash and Erie Canal, which still carries water.
- Stroll through a town rich in history; walk past early Federal, Italianate, Queen Anne, and Gothic Revival style homes.
- Follow a network of trails that cross Deer Creek on suspension bridges, and link nearly everything in town.

## Area Information

Located near the early canal in upper Wabash valley, Delphi was at one time the head of navigation for the Wabash River. The Wabash and Erie Canal, a constructed waterway, was intended to connect Toledo on Lake Erie with Evansville on the Ohio River. Construction took place between 1832 and 1853, but the canal was never completed. Using the flatboats of the time, Delphi merchants could transport produce and other goods downriver, from the upper Wabash all the way to New Orleans.

During the canal era, the town of Delphi was a pork packing center and produced a special kind of lime for use in plaster and a superior paper used in printing. The community also operated several mills, using waterpower from a nearby dam. After the railroads were built, the Wabash and Erie Canal was never completed. Yet, you can still see many 19th-century residences, built when the town was a bustling commercial center. The community has dozens of buildings notable for their period architecture.

**Directions:** Delphi, which is northeast of Lafayette, is located at the intersection of US 421 and SR 25. Several Delphi trails originate at Trailhead Park, one mile southeast of town on SR 25.

**Hours Open:** You can hike the trails year-round during daylight hours.

**Facilities:** You can find picnic shelters, tables, and benches in the town parks; a few trails pass downtown restaurants or roadside fast food places.

**Permits and Rules:** Be considerate of people living in historic, private homes. Place trash in appropriate containers.

**Further Information:** Contact the Delphi Chamber of Commerce, 113 S Washington Street, Delphi, IN 46923; 765-564-3034 or Carroll County Wabash and Erie Canal, Inc.; 765-564-6572.

## Other Areas of Interest

All Delphi's trails along the canal are part of a larger system. Along the Wabash River, 19 counties have developed the **Wabash Heritage Trails**. Between Battle Ground and Lafayette, an eight-mile segment has been completed. A portion of this trail, linking Delphi to Prophetstown State Park (now under development), has been planned, and another segment, in planning, will connect Delphi with France Park and Logansport.

## Area Trails

Each segment of this trail network has a distinctive name, and you can link segments together to make longer hikes. At major junctures, signs will direct you to subsequent named trail. At other junctures, you'll have to guess which way to go.

**Interurban Trail to Delphi City Park** 👟—2 miles— From Trailhead Park, hike the old interurban (electric train) route; then follow historic Main Street until you reach Delphi City Park.

**Downtown Historic Loop Trail** 👟—1.5 miles—This trail is a rectangular route with Franklin and Front Streets as the longest sides of the rectangle. You'll walk past historic residential and commercial buildings, the Carroll County Courthouse, and the historical museum.

# Delphi Towpath Trail 🥾

**Distance One-Way:** 1 mile

**Estimated Hiking Time:** 40 minutes

**Cautions:** Be alert for poison ivy.

**Trail Directions:** Park at Trailhead Park. From the picnic shelter, walk toward Deer Creek. The hike begins at the southeast end of the suspension bridge [1]. Cross the creek on the bridge and turn right at the bench. A sign pointing left says, "Robbins to Old Canals." Note the ragweed garden at the left. At .11 mi., you'll see oak and maple trees (left) and a cornfield (right), farmed by the people for whom the Robbins Trail was named. We also noted patches of meadow, where the wings of a butterfly flashed white, orange, and black.

At .15 mi. [2], the path crosses a ditch—maybe it's the canal! After you cross, turn right to follow the towpath, where a sign says, "Vanscoy Towpath." The towpath, of course, was the packed earth embankment where mules (and often their drivers) walked alongside the loaded barges. The draft animals pulled loads at about two miles an hour. The Vanscoy Towpath follows the old canal (on your right) and leads you through some of the most scenic portions of this waterway.

At .23 mi., the Obear Millrace Trail [3] turns to the left. This route follows the millrace to the site of an early mill. Continue walking along the towpath. At .3 mi., we noticed a hollow in a birch tree, but weren't sure what lived within. Ahead, a bird swooped through the air, black with shiny blue-green on its head—perhaps a tree swallow. At .43 mi., a section of the early canal was clogged with debris. Beyond it, we found a bench, one of several at intervals along the trail.

Berry trees are plentiful along this trail, where we also found bluets (a type of flower). At .68 mi., a wooden bridge [4] crosses the canal on the right. Continue walking straight ahead. At .77 mi., you'll see another path to the left; the towpath continues straight. At .79 mi. an old road runs to the left. Keep walking ahead, and on the right, you'll see where a canal lock [5] formerly operated.

Continue walking along the towpath. At .85 mi., a cable crossed the path—a device to keep out motorized vehicles. Beyond it was Bicycle Bridge Road. We ended the hike here, and walked back the way we had come, to Trailhead Park.

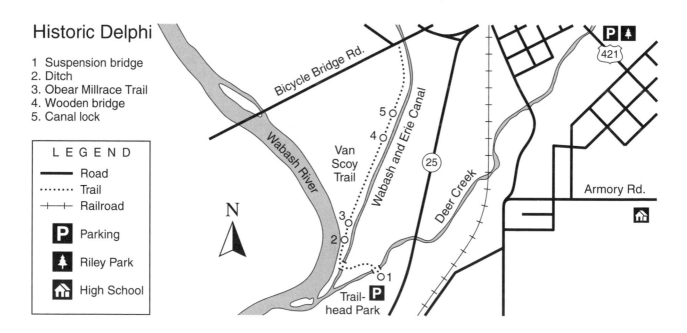

## Historic Delphi

1. Suspension bridge
2. Ditch
3. Obear Millrace Trail
4. Wooden bridge
5. Canal lock

LEGEND

— Road
...... Trail
+-+- Railroad

P  Parking

🌲  Riley Park

🏠  High School

# 6.  South Bend Riverside Parks

- Walk the riverside routes where the area's earliest inhabitants built cabins in the shade of great sycamore trees.
- Hike through riverside parks that provide green oases in a large, metropolitan area.
- Walk along the East Race Waterway, a mecca for kayak enthusiasts, and the first such artificial white-water course in North America.

## Area Information

Like the sandy moraines and depressions nearer Lake Michigan, the river valleys of this region were also shaped by glacial activity. Retreating meltwater from these receding ice masses left the rivers coursing through the channels we know today.

The St. Joseph River watershed, the area's most striking natural feature, flows west through South Bend before turning north. LaSalle and other early explorers paddled this river highway; fur traders followed in their pirogues, bartering trade goods for the valuable beaver pelts, then hauling bundles of furs back through various waterways to company headquarters, as far as Montreal.

The St. Joseph River valley looked appealing to pioneers. Settlers could use timber for their homes; hunt, fish, and gather wild foodstuffs for their families; and transport their goods on the river in flatboats and on barges.

Visitors today find 10 public parks in the metropolitan area that spans this river. The large, 1,250-acre campus of the University of Notre Dame and St. Mary's College also borders the river. Scattered along this segment of the St. Joseph are several islands, many of them still studded with great oaks, sy-

camores, and cottonwood trees. What's more, visitors can explore by using canoe. You can rent these narrow, self-propelled boats in two locations.

**Directions:** From the north or south, drive to downtown South Bend on Business 31; from the east or west, take US 20. Howard Park is a triangular park between Jefferson Boulevard and the St. Joseph River. The East Race Waterway runs north of Jefferson Boulevard along Niles Avenue before turning to rejoin the St. Joseph River.

**Hours Open:** Howard Park is open year-round during daylight hours. The path beside the East Race Waterway is a public sidewalk.

**Facilities:** You can find rest rooms, picnic tables, and benches in the park or near the raceway.

**Permits and Rules:** No swimming in the river. Dispose of trash in proper receptacles. Keep pets on leashes.

**Further Information:** South Bend and Mishawaka Convention and Visitors Bureau, P.O. Box 1677, South Bend, IN 46634-1677; 219-234-0051 or South Bend Parks and Recreation; 219-235-9401.

## Other Areas of Interest

South Bend has several districts that make interesting historic walks. The **Chapin Park National Register District** has the Gothic Revival Horatio Chapin residence, along with other historic homes along curved, brick streets. The **West Washington National Register District** includes the residences of several early entrepreneurs, Studebaker, Oliver, and others, and a 1906 vintage home designed by Frank Lloyd Wright.

## Park Trails

This segment of a longer riverwalk passes beneath downtown streets and pedestrian bridges.

**South Bend Riverwalk** 🥾—2 miles—This riverside route runs west from Ironwood Drive along the north

bank of the St. Joseph River. The route passes through Veterans Memorial Park and goes past the Farmer's Market before entering Howard Park.

# Howard Park to East Race Waterway 🥾

**Distance One-Way:** 1 mile

**Estimated Hiking Time:** 45 minutes

**Cautions:** This trail runs through the heart of a large, urban area. Keep anything valuable out of sight in a locked vehicle. Stay alert while you walk.

**Trail Directions:** Park at the east end of Howard Park **[1]**. The trail runs northeast along the river. You'll pass the sheds used by the South Bend Scullers and Notre Dame Rowing Club, standing in a grassy, tree-studded area on the right. At .05 mi., there's a floating dock where the scullers launch their craft.

The concrete multiuse path hugs the river; a border of trees and a tangle of low, vine-covered shrubs provide cover for wildlife. At .26 mi., you walk under an old metal railroad bridge **[2]**; beyond this, another arched bridge frames South Bend's tallest buildings. By .3 mi., an open, grassy area and a concrete balustrade separate the trail from the river; there's a playground beyond the trees on the right **[3]**.

At .34 mi., an iron gate closes off steps that go below the water. People may be relaxing on the wooden benches **[4]**. Cross a grassy area to the right to find a memorial stone dedicated to American workers who have lost their lives in the workplace. Beyond, at .38 mi., is a monument to St. Joseph County Vietnam Veterans killed in action.

At .5 mi., the paved walkway heads beneath the Jefferson Boulevard bridge **[5]**. On the right is the Emporium, a complex of shops, and the paved trail becomes a boardwalk. Note the new riverfront buildings across the river; the city is known throughout the region for its creative riverfront development.

At .56 mi., the East Race Waterway, a white-water race course created by diverting the river, separates from the main channel; continue hiking along the boardwalk that skirts the right bank of this race-course. At .58 mi., there's an entrance to the ramp people use for launching their small two-person rafts or kayaks **[6]**. Beyond, a wooden bridge leads across the raceway to the James R. Seitz park on the island.

At .66 mi., continue walking by the raceway. On the left, you may see paddlers in kayaks hurtling through the arrangement of chutes and notched blocks that make the currents resemble a powerful mountain stream.

At .77 mi., the footpath runs beneath Colfax Avenue **[7]**; continue walking along the rushing water of the East Race Waterway channel. You'll notice a ramp the paddlers use for takeouts. At .85 mi., the concrete walk goes under the LaSalle Street overpass. Notice that each time the water in the channel drops to a lower level, it creates a noisy backwash. When paddlers run this course, you'll hear their excited yelps and squeals as they cope with the channel's built-in surprises.

At .87 mi., there's a wooden pedestrian bridge; walk under another such bridge at .95 mi. The trail ends where the East Race Waterway rejoins the St. Joseph River **[8]**.

1. Howard Park
2. Railroad bridge
3. Playground
4. Wooden benches
5. Jefferson Boulevard bridge
6. Entrance to ramp
7. Colfax Avenue
8. St. Joseph River

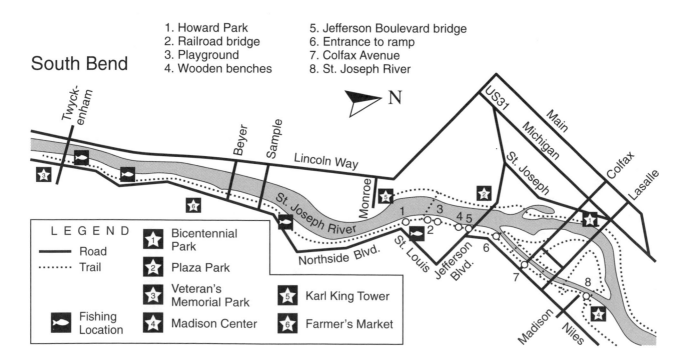

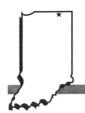

# 7. Elkhart

- Explore meadows, marshes, forests, and open fields along the scenic Elkhart River.
- Visit an early mill; photograph its reflection in a pond; watch grain being ground into flour.
- Hike through lush forests where wildflowers bloom in season.

## Area Information

In the middle of northern Indiana, among the scattered glacial lakes, the lovely Elkhart River meanders northward before joining the larger St. Joseph River. Early explorers, traders, and trappers traveled these water highways. The name Elkhart was conceived by the area's earliest inhabitants, the Indians, who declared that a particular river island resembled the heart of an elk. The Frenchmen who came to the area then called this island Coeur de Cerf.

The fertile land around the city of Elkhart has been farmland for centuries. The first settlers cut timber, pulled out stumps, and plowed under the forests and prairies for agriculture. The Amish, Mennonites, Hutterites, and members of other conservative Christian groups emigrated from Europe to the New World to escape religious persecution. Eventually, many of these people who pushed inland from the East Coast into the Midwest chose this area.

A visit to the countryside will take you to an earlier time, showing you how things were done in the past, when most Hoosiers lived on farms. In rural Elkhart County, you'll see people riding in horse-drawn buggies, pushing garden plows, pulling baby carts, pedaling bicycles, and using many other precursors of machinery.

In Elkhart, an early settlement at a river junction eventually became a sprawling manufacturing community. Despite its growth, Elkhart has preserved many historic buildings, including early commercial buildings, churches, and homes. The downtown has become a showcase for eclectic architectural styles. Elkhart's riverside hiking trails pass many historic sites; for example, out in the county, at Bonneyville Park, you can visit an early waterpowered mill.

**Directions:** Reach Elkhart via US 80/90. Exit at Highway 19, and drive south four miles via SR 19 and Cassopolis Street to Beardsley Avenue. The route for the Elkhart Historic Walk runs through the downtown. There are several urban parks along the St. Joseph River south of Beardsley and east of Main Street. Bonneyville County Park is located two and one-half miles southeast of Bristol on CR 131.

**Hours Open:** You can do the urban hikes year-round during daylight hours. Hours for Elkhart County Parks vary; call 219-535-6458.

**Facilities:** Hikers doing the architecture walk have access to downtown restaurants. The urban parks have rest rooms, benches, picnic tables, playgrounds, and drinking fountains. The county parks have picnic shelters, rest rooms, and playground equipment.

**Permits and Rules:** Urban hikers should obey traffic signs at crosswalks. Put trash in proper receptacles. Be alert for drivers turning right on red. Do not disturb plants or animals.

**Further Information:** Elkhart County Park and Recreation Department, 117 North Second Street, Room 111, Goshen, IN 46526-3231; 219-535-6458.

## Other Areas of Interest

The **Elkhart Environmental Center** combines environmental education with recreation. You may visit a log cabin education center, follow hiking and biking trails, view outdoor exhibits, and watch wildlife. Trails are open from dawn to dusk every day. The location is 1717 East Lusher Avenue, Elkhart, IN 46516; 219-293-5070.

## Park Trails

Many of Elkhart's urban park and county park trails involve multiple, interlocking routes. To follow a particular route, hike according to trail directions in this book.

**The Heart City Bike Tour** 👢👢—10 miles—This tour runs from High Dive Park in the north to the Environmental Center in the south and links several city parks. The Heart City River Walk described in this book is an abbreviated version of this route. For other Heritage Trail routes or more hiking information, ask for a map and brochure at the Elkhart County Convention and Visitors Bureau, Inc., 219 Caravan Drive, Elkhart, IN 46514; 219-262-8161.

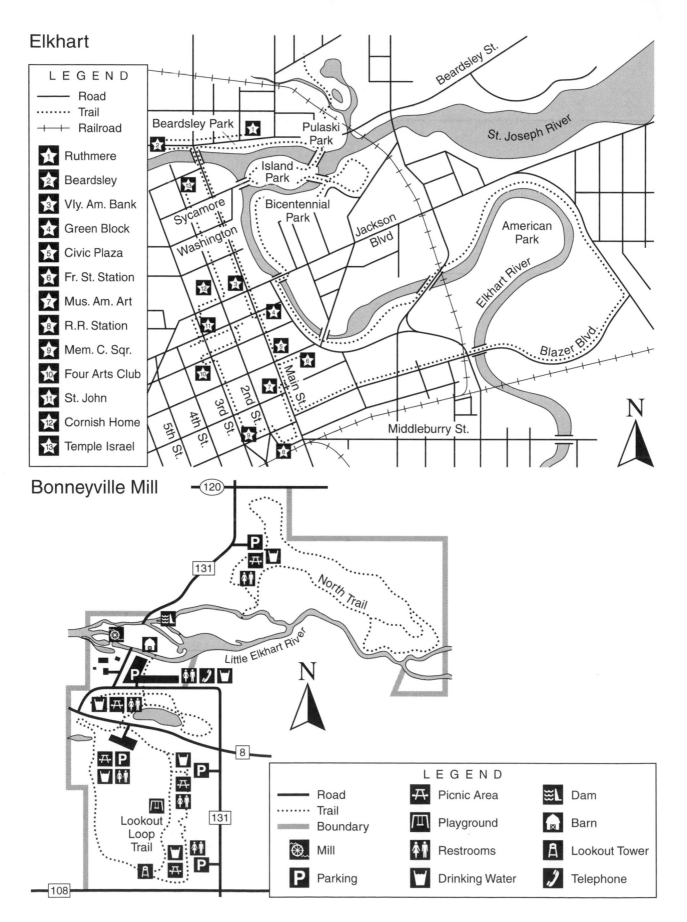

# Elkhart

**LEGEND**
— Road
····· Trail
+++ Railroad

1. Ruthmere
2. Beardsley
3. Vly. Am. Bank
4. Green Block
5. Civic Plaza
6. Fr. St. Station
7. Mus. Am. Art
8. R.R. Station
9. Mem. C. Sqr.
10. Four Arts Club
11. St. John
12. Cornish Home
13. Temple Israel

Beardsley Park
Pulaski Park
Island Park
Bicentennial Park
Sycamore
Washington
Jackson Blvd
American Park
Elkhart River
Blazer Blvd.
2nd St.
3rd St.
4th St.
5th St.
Main St.
Middleburry St.
St. Joseph River
Beardsley St.

N

# Bonneyville Mill

120
131
North Trail
Little Elkhart River
8
131
108
Lookout Loop Trail

N

**LEGEND**
— Road
····· Trail
▬ Boundary
Mill
P Parking
Picnic Area
Playground
Restrooms
Drinking Water
Dam
Barn
Lookout Tower
Telephone

# Elkhart Architecture Walk 🥾

**Distance Round-Trip:** 3.5 miles

**Estimated Hiking Time:** 2 hours

**Cautions:** The route follows public sidewalks in central Elkhart. Watch for traffic when crossing streets; be especially alert for drivers turning right on red.

**Trail Directions:** Park west of the historic Ruthmere Estate [1], built in 1908 and used as a residence by a founder of Miles Laboratories. Begin walking west along the north side of Beardsley Avenue. You'll pass the First Presbyterian Church, cross Main Street, and walk one block through a residential neighborhood.

At .2 mi., you'll see the Havilah Beardsley Monument [2] across the street. Return east to Main Street and you'll pass an appealing residence perched above the St. Joseph River. At .28 mi., turn right and walk south across the Main Street Bridge [3].

At .57 mi., locals gather at the Anderson's Main Street Cafe. Continue walking south until .62 mi., where you'll see the old brick Elkhart Armory Building across the street. As you continue south, you'll pass the Valley American Bank [4] at Main and Jackson. At .8 mi., ignore (if you can) the Underground Boutique across the way. Instead, turn left, cross Main, and follow Lexington east for half a block.

At .85 mi., you can see the Green Block [5] across the street. This early commercial building was built in 1895. Return to Main Street. At .88 mi., turn left and walk two blocks south on Main Street to Franklin. At 1.02 mi., the appealing Civic Plaza [6] has benches, planters, picnic tables, and shade. Continue south; at 1.1 mi., turn left and walk east to the Franklin Street Station [7].

At 1.19 mi., return west to Main Street and turn left at 1.28 mi. You'll pass the old Elco Theater, a 1920s movie palace built in formal English style. Continue south and you'll reach Marion Street at 1.36 mi. Here, cross Main Street to visit the Midwest Museum of American Art [8]. Continue walking south, and at 1.48 mi., note the old brick alley on the left. At 1.67 mi., follow Tyler Street, also paved with brick, west to the Elkhart Railroad Station [9]. Turn right and head north on 2nd Street.

At 1.81 mi., you'll see the Winchester Mansion at 529 South 2nd Street. At the corner, turn left, walk along Harrison, and you'll reach the Memorial Central Square [10] at 2.0 mi. Turn right and walk north on 3rd Street. At 2.22 mi., you'll see the early Elkhart High School building. At 2.32 mi., turn left and walk one-half block to the Four Arts Club [11], a charming, small building of pale brick with white columns in front.

Return to 2nd Street, and you'll note the Municipal Building at the corner of High Street and 2nd. Head north on 2nd Street to Lexington. At 2.55 mi., walk east on Lexington for one-half block to the old YWCA. Return to 2nd Street, and at 2.62 mi. you'll see the GTE Building. Cross 2nd Street and walk west on Lexington for one block. At 2.72 mi., you'll find the gothic St. John the Evangelist Episcopal Church [12]. Across from the church, at 326 West Lexington, note the Samuel Strong building, done in Romanesque style.

Return to 3rd Street and turn left. At 3.16 mi., the Cornish Home [13], at 129 South 2nd Street, designed by Turnock in an Italianate style, now houses an architectural firm. At 3.2 mi., Peg's Beauty Shop, formerly a residence, has been graciously restored.

At 3.47 mi., the corner of Potawatomi and 2nd Streets, is the Temple Israel [14], a vine-draped stone building on the right at 430 North 3rd Street. Your walk ends; you can return to Ruthmere via the Main Street Bridge and Beardsley Avenue.

1. Ruthmere Estate
2. Beardsley Monument
3. Main Street bridge
4. Valley American Bank
5. Green Block
6. Civic Plaza
7. Franklin Street Station
8. Museum of American Art
9. Elkhart Railroad Station
10. Memorial Central Square
11. Four Arts Club
12. St. John the Evangelist
    Episcopal Church
13. Cornish Home
14. Temple Israel

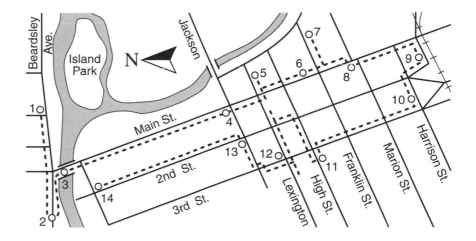

# Elkhart Riverside Parks 🥾

**Distance Round-Trip:** 3.7 miles

**Estimated Hiking Time:** 2.5 hours

**Cautions:** This is a city environment. Store belongings out of sight in a locked vehicle. Be alert to your surroundings, and look carefully before crossing streets.

**Trail Directions:** Park in the public lot [1] for High Dive Park across from the Coachmen offices. Begin walking on a paved trail west of the parking lot. Walk south across Beardsley through Pulaski Park toward the river. You'll pass the site of the early Pulaski Post Office. At .06 mi., cross the St. Joseph River on the Centennial Footbridge [2].

When you reach Island Park at .13 mi., follow a loop trail around the island. From this loop, you'll see two channels of the St. Joe and where the Elkhart River joins them. At .2 mi., a pavilion [3] on the left shelters picnic tables. At .28 mi., ignore the sidewalk to the right, and continue on a blacktop path.

At .32 mi., there's a pedestrian bridge to the right, but don't take it. You'll pass a memorial to Comrade Irish as you head left over a red brick path. At .42 mi., there's another riverside pavilion [4]. At .46 mi., turn right onto a pedestrian bridge [5].

At .52 mi., turn left for a loop walk around this park; the path follows the river. At .62 mi., a bench has a view of Beardsley Island Park. Continue until you've completed this loop. Note the rest rooms [6] at .79 mi.

At .82 mi., leave this loop by walking west into a wooded area; the path skirts the south channel of the river. At .92 mi., the paved path curves left toward a school [7]; you walk through mowed, grassy bottomland with large trees.

At 1.0 mi., there are three sycamore trees that branch from the same trunk. At 1.15 mi., turn right, cross the automobile bridge [8], and cross Jackson Boulevard. At 1.22 mi., take a brick path left across the river into Burton Upon Trent park. Continue walking southeast along Waterfall Boulevard.

At 1.25 mi., the path splits into upper and lower levels; take the lower one. At 1.35 mi., walk under a green pedestrian bridge [9], then up concrete steps. Follow the sidewalk along Waterfall Drive southeast to Franklin Street.

At 1.43 mi., you can hear the waterfall [10] before you see it. Continue to the waterfall, and at 1.55 mi., leave the sidewalk, walking left onto the wide, paved path through a grassy lawn. On the right is an office building [11]. At 1.64 mi., cross a wooden bridge [12]. Follow a gray, paved path along the river; when it divides, take either branch—they'll come back together.

At 1.73 mi., we walked left along Prairie Street on a narrow sidewalk toward the bridge. At 1.8 mi., we crossed railroad tracks, then crossed Prairie Street, before entering American Park; we could see the river on the right, with apartment buildings [13], a lawn, and tennis courts on the left. At 1.9 mi., there's a sitting area for viewing ducks. Continue walking past the apartments through a tranquil, riverside setting.

At 1.98 mi., you'll find benches. At 2.0 mi., ignore the pedestrian bridge on the right, and keep walking forward. At Jackson Boulevard, take a path that runs right between the street and the river.

At 2.31 mi., you'll walk along Goshen Avenue. At 2.37 mi., cross the road at the back of the high school [14], and continue along Goshen Avenue. At 2.53 mi., we passed Elkhart Central High School on the right.

At 2.52 mi., turn right at Blazer Boulevard and follow a curving, downhill concrete walk. At 2.83 mi., cross a service road, then take the bridge across the river. At 3.02 mi., follow the white, painted ladder pattern at the edge of the road as it curves across the railroad tracks; use it to reach with the sidewalk along Waterfall Drive. At 3.1 mi., cross Prairie Street; you'll see downtown buildings toward the west.

The trail ends here; walk north another .6 mi. along Main Street, cross the bridge, and walk east to find the parking lot.

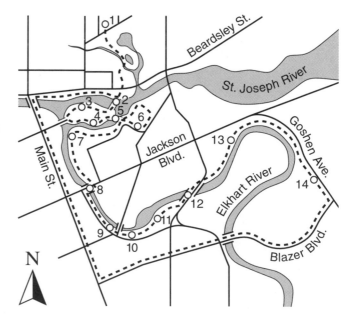

| | |
|---|---|
| 1. Parking lot | 8. Bridge |
| 2. Centennial Footbridge | 9. Pedestrian bridge |
| 3. Pavilion | 10. Waterfall |
| 4. Pavilion | 11. Office building |
| 5. Pedestrian bridge | 12. Wooden bridge |
| 6. Rest rooms | 13. Apartments |
| 7. School | 14. High school |

# Bonneyville Mill—North Loop Trail 🥾🥾

**Distance Round-Trip:** 1 mile

**Estimated Hiking Time:** 45 minutes

**Cautions:** The various, unmarked mowed-grass paths made it difficult to follow the entire North Loop Trail. This trail description takes hikers for one mile only, from the mill to the river.

**Trail Directions:** Begin hiking north of the main parking lot **[1]**. Cross a wooden bridge, and follow the sidewalk past a picnic shelter. Continue north, across a grassy area and another wooden bridge. You'll see a waterfall **[2]** and hear the rushing of falling water on your right.

At .08 mi., a nearby bridge offers a great view of water as it rushes over a stone dam in a stream fringed with grasses and overhung with willows. At the third bridge, take a left turn on a bark mulch path that leads to Kum Mol Rie **[3]**. The trail passes through maple-beech forest, studded with sassafras and sycamores. At .12 mi., take a sharp right turn, and stay on the bark trail. At .14 mi., there's a newer wooden bridge **[4]**. The bed of this stream has deposits of gravel and sand brought here by glacial action. On the other side of the stream, follow the bark mulch trail to the right.

At .23 mi., the well-mulched trail follows the creek; we heard a frog croaking before it plunged into the water. The meandering path crosses a muddy runoff channel, where a seasonal stream enters the creek at the right; stay on the bark path. Note the Virginia creeper draped on the trees. At .28 mi., turn left at the sign for Kum Mol Rie, following a trail that

turns into gravel; you may hear the croaking of frogs from a pond on the right.

At .45 mi., you'll find Kum Mol Rie **[5]**, a picnic shelter with satellite tables. Follow a mown, grassy path into the forest beyond; soon, a wide expanse of meadow **[6]** will open on the right. In mid-June, we found patches of oxeye daisies and wild strawberries and heard the chirping of hidden birds. At .58 mi., the trail entered an oak savanna, where yellow coneflowers and other blooms looked as if someone had spilled a seed packet. At .67 mi., the trail entered the woods again; we passed black walnut trees and a green bush with red berries.

At .76 mi., the bark mulch path gave way to mowed grass; there was a fledgling savanna on the left. At .77 mi., another mowed-grass path angles across the trail; this spot could be called the butterfly crossing **[7]**. After looking at photos later, we thought the lovely, orange butterfly with delicate brown markings might be some type of fritillary. Lavender clover and tall angelica plants bloomed here, and crows cawed in the distance.

We took the trail right, toward the river. To the left, the meadow grasses resembled a wheat farm; to the right was dense forest. The wide crescent of mowed grass—the trail—curved left at the river, but then petered out; unable to continue, we stood a while, watching some ducks negotiate the surging river **[8]**, before retracing our steps to the mill.

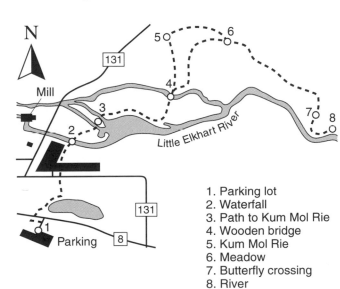

1. Parking lot
2. Waterfall
3. Path to Kum Mol Rie
4. Wooden bridge
5. Kum Mol Rie
6. Meadow
7. Butterfly crossing
8. River

# Bonneyville Mill—Lookout Loop Trail 👢👢

**Distance Round-Trip:** .83 mile

**Estimated Hiking Time:** 30 minutes

**Cautions:** Route is not well marked, but, in general, forms a narrow loop along the road that runs N and S.

**Trail Directions:** Find the trailhead beside the lookout parking lot south of Bonneyville on CR 8; begin walking on a grassy path in front of lookout tower **[1]**. There's savanna on the left and a clump of fat conifers on the right. The aroma of real trees is better than any purchased pine air freshener spray. Beyond a group of tall, pink flowers, we saw the moving blur of a white-tailed deer.

At .19 mi., there was mowed grass on the right; we walked close to pines on the left and discovered a long view that opened ahead. At .22 mi., we passed savanna on the left, with a clipped meadow on the right. By .25 mi., there was another distant view, a grassy, downhill slope framed by evergreens.

By .28 mi., we had reached the Meadow Shelter **[2]** on the right. From here, we had a lovely view west, with pines and a grassy slope nearby, savanna in the middle distance, and dense forest beyond. Continue walking forward, but stay on the left side of the grassy clearing. At .32 mi., take the right fork of a trail that enters an oak forest. By .37 mi., you'll be standing before a large berry patch **[3]**; turn right onto a grassy path that runs up a slope.

At .4 mi., pass through an opening in a fence, cross a gravel road, enter an opening in another fence, and continue on a grassy swath. At .46 mi., turn left at the berry bushes (you'll see large wooden pegs in the grass on the right). The wide, grassy path has oak trees and sumac on the left, with pines framing a broad expanse of meadow on the right. At .52 mi., take the fork on the left, and follow the bark-covered slope down and left.

At .57 mi. the trail becomes grass again; you hike through a cool forest of oaks; pines; and tangled, wild grapevines with pine needles littering your path. The picnic tables ahead are those of the Meadow Shelter. From here, a spur leads west to a playground **[4]**. Walk across the grass and uphill; there are rest rooms. The trail continues at the left, where it enters an oak-hickory forest with many sassafras trees. At .78 mi., some small boulders **[5]** are on the right. Walk uphill and at .83 mi., you've reached the end of the trail. Here, if you haven't yet done so, climb the lookout tower for a great view.

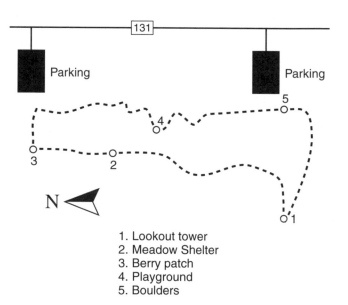

1. Lookout tower
2. Meadow Shelter
3. Berry patch
4. Playground
5. Boulders

# 8.  Potato Creek State Park

- Hike through the rolling terrain between the lake country to the east and the great marsh to the west.
- Visit a park where one avid birdwatcher has noted 294 species.
- Discover surprising variety within a 1,250-acre park: a large lake, streams, marshes, upland forests, and fields of prairie grasses.

## Area Information

The low, rolling terrain of Potato Creek State Park lies in a geological transition zone. About 13,000 to 14,000 years ago, this region was covered with ice. Receding glaciers and accompanying meltwaters formed glacial lakes and moraines to the east and created the Great Kankakee Marsh to the west. Glacial forces also scoured the channel for Potato Creek and left behind deposits of gravel, sand, and other loose materials.

The area's earliest inhabitants gathered duck potatoes that grow along this creek and used them for food. Today, the plain in the park's northwest corner is nearly flat, yet elsewhere low hills rise to more than 800 feet. The 327-acre lake was formed by stopping the waters of Potato Creek with an earthen dam. Potato Creek continues to run, flowing into the lake from the southeast and out toward the northwest.

Worster Lake, named for the man who first proposed this reservoir during the 1930s, is the major body of water in the park. In 1997, the park's wetland acreage was estimated at 650 acres of the 3,840 total area. The park also has expanses of prairie, and about one-third of it is covered with forest.

Park management is trying to return natural areas to their former condition, before settlement began in the early 19th century. Several wetlands that had earlier been drained—marshes, swamps, and beaver ponds—

are being restored. Native prairie grasses have been planted and sections of prairie maintained by controlled burning. Other parts of the park are being allowed to return to the original hardwood forest.

The Swamp Rose Nature Preserve, a rectangular area in the park's northeast corner, encloses a lake that has slowly turned into wetland. You can find several rare plants in the preserve, and beaver also favor the habitat.

**Directions:** Located southwest of South Bend in St. Joseph County, you can reach the park via US 31. Just north of Lakeville, turn west on SR 4 and drive four miles to the entrance.

**Hours Open:** The park is open from 7:00 A.M. to 11:00 P.M. year-round.

**Facilities:** Family cabins, campground, camp store, nature center, picnic shelters and tables, swimming beach, and boat rental (including handicapped accessible) are available.

**Permits and Rules:** Do not injure plants or animals in the park. Stay with any pet dog or cat; keep it leashed. Carry out any trash you bring in; if camping, put trash in the proper receptacle. Swim only in designated areas. Observe speed limits. No snowmobiles are allowed.

**Further Information:** Potato Creek State Park, 25601 State Road 4, P.O. Box 908, North Liberty, IN 46554; 219-656-8186.

## Other Areas of Interest

**Lake Maxinkuckee,** southwest of Plymouth, is a large, natural lake with many options. You can walk across the lovely grounds of Culver Military Academy on the north shore or stroll through the quaint, small town of Culver. Call Plymouth Chamber of Commerce for more information; 219-936-2323.

## Park Trails

Park trails are well marked, with trail numbers on posts along each route. Note that the Swamp Rose Nature Preserve has no park trail.

**Bicycle Trail** 👢👢👢—3.3 miles—Follow this route for a walk around the west end of the lake. The path crosses Potato Creek, goes up and down wooded hills, through valleys, more forests, and wetlands.

**Trail 2** 👢👢👢—2.0 miles—This is the nearest trail to the nature preserve. You'll pass through wetlands, a beech-maple forest, and a creek; climb Steamboat Hill; and enjoy a view from the highest point in the park.

**Peppermint Road Self-Guiding Trail** 👢—.9 mile—Pick up a leaflet for this walk at the nature center; the walk takes you along an old roadbed where 10 markers are keyed to this printed information.

# Potato Creek State Park

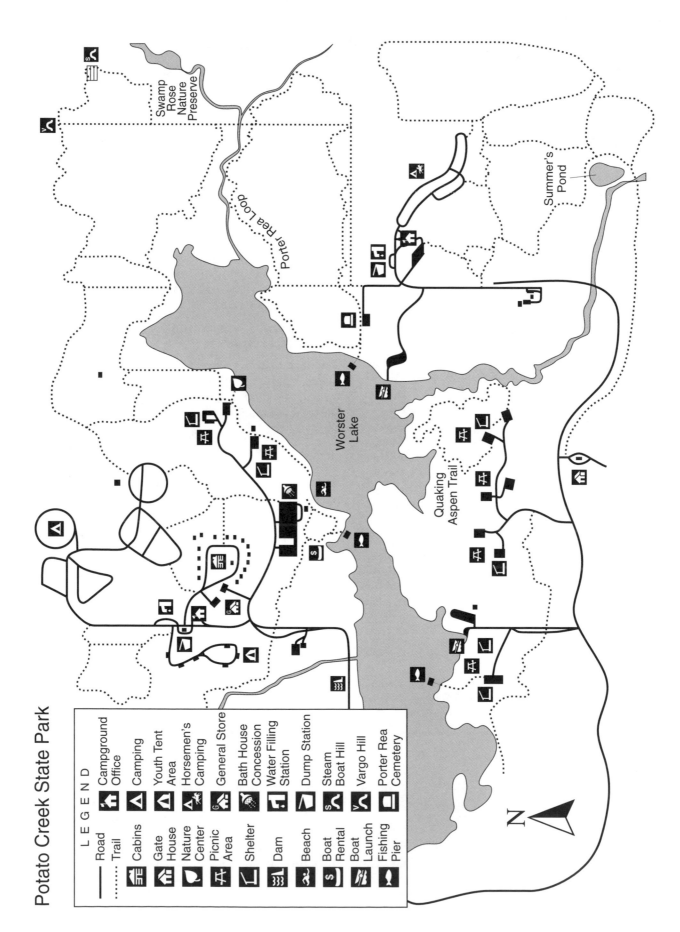

Swamp Rose Nature Preserve

Porter Rea Loop

Worster Lake

Summer's Pond

Quaking Aspen Trail

Porter Rea

LEGEND

| | | | |
|---|---|---|---|
| — | Road | | Campground Office |
| ⋯ | Trail | | Camping |
| | Cabins | | Youth Tent Area |
| | Gate House | | Horsemen's Camping |
| | Nature Center | | General Store |
| | Picnic Area | | Bath House Concession |
| | Shelter | | Water Filling Station |
| | Dam | | Dump Station |
| | Beach | | Steam Boat Hill |
| | Boat Rental | | Vargo Hill |
| | Boat Launch | | Porter Rea Cemetery |
| | Fishing Pier | | |

N

# Quaking Aspen Loop 👢👢

**Distance Round-Trip:** 1 mile

**Estimated Hiking Time:** 40 minutes

**Trail Directions:** Park at the Quaking Aspen Shelter [1]. Find the sign for the trailhead at the edge of the grassy picnic grounds. The wide, gravel path enters a maple-beech forest; although such trees dominate this forest community, look also for hawthorn, black cherry, and sassafras. Potato Creek [2], which you see on the right, was a source of important wild foods for the area's earliest settlers. The creek flows in and out of Worster Lake before it joins the Kankakee River.

Walk left along a fenced overlook [3]; at .1 mi., you'll see the water below. You may notice a fat, much-carved beech tree before walking into a shallow ravine. At .2 mi., in late spring, we found a natural garden with mayapples on the left. An L-shaped boardwalk makes it easier to cross the ravine without damaging any plants. If you'd like a rest, the bench of hewn, weathered logs makes a great viewing spot for this woodland scene. One park leaflet lists 40 kinds of wood warblers; how many do you hear?

At .35 mi. take the well-marked path uphill and turn left; ignore the narrow cross path. Continue walking and you'll see a fenced enclosure [4] designed to keep out deer. The enclosure helps university researchers study the eating patterns of white-tailed deer and their effect on park flora. Bear and wolves once kept deer populations in check in Indiana, but not any more. The trail ahead has gentle ups and downs, and at .5 mi., you'll see Worster Lake on the right, screened by forest. Around you, there's a disorderly display of fallen timber—nature's own artistic chaos.

By .7 mi., you'll have come to another boardwalk. There's an observation deck [5] for watching heron, geese, ducks, and other waterfowl. You can still see sunken trees in the dammed creek, and you might also see frogs, turtles, or snakes near the shore. Green algae had spread over the surface; we noted an awful smell, but couldn't say what it was from.

At .8 mi., we saw a round, metal cover on the trail. Here and there in the park, there is other evidence of earlier human use. Nearby, wild grape and other vines wrapped around many trees. Did you know that vines sometimes kill the tree that supports them by shutting off sunlight?

At .95 mi., the forest floor was littered with uprooted, broken trees: beech, maple, and other varieties lying every which way. By 1.0 mi., you're back at the picnic shelter.

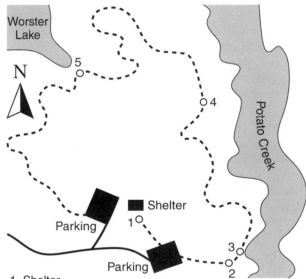

1. Shelter
2. Potato Creek
3. Fenced overlook
4. Fenced enclosure
5. Observation deck

# Porter Rea Loop 👢👢

**Distance Round-Trip:** 2.5 miles

**Estimated Hiking Time:** 1 hour 50 minutes

**Trail Directions:** Follow signs to Porter Rea Cemetery **[1]**. The trailhead for Trail 4 begins south of the graveyard. You'll hike on a paved path five feet wide, with low shrubs on the left. Note that the cemetery to the right, dating from 1884, has many interesting stones. We also saw an old hand pump, formerly used to bring up well water. Between the trees ahead, you see a bit of Worster Lake, but don't take the curved, white walk to it. Instead, follow Trail 4, a grassy swath to the right.

At 1.0 mi., the forest on the right gives way to prairie; the lake **[2]** is on the left. Listen for the meadowlarks. At .13 mi. a wooden bridge takes you from the meadow into low forest. At .2 mi. the trail turns right; ignore the narrow, lakeside path ahead. At .23 mi., take a left. At .27 mi., you can see the lake between the trees. On the right, there are oaks, amid a profusion of forest debris.

At .3 mi., a pile of rounded rocks resembles a garden, but could well be glacial erratics. Here, the trail is bark mulch and packed earth; you follow a low ridge along the edge of the lake. At .48 mi., the trail returns to the lake. Look carefully at what remains of the water-logged tree trunks **[3]**—we saw a blue heron perched there before he flew away. Next, the trail leaves the lake again, to cut across a corner of the forest.

At .5 mi., there is a gravel path through marshland; here, watch for a baby redear turtle sunning itself on a log or a dragonfly flitting among the broken stalks. At .55 mi., ignore the path ahead, and turn left where the sign says 4. From the wooden observation deck **[4]** at .6 mi., you can take in the great, curving border of tall cattails along the lakeshore. We also saw striking, greenish, ball-shaped angelica flowers on giant purple stalks; these plants, increasingly rare, grow up to six feet tall.

At .65 mi., some old steps lead up a rock wall; at the top, take a rock and dirt path to the left. In summer, this path has a border of daisies. At .8 mi., the path passes through a savanna with many young trees, then enters forest again. At .9 mi., ignore a path into the ravine at left. Continue ahead, and you'll soon see the reassuring sign for Trail 4. This grassy track is the trail! The path has more turns, ups, and downs as you follow it through forest and ravine.

Note the Virginia creeper and clinging vines before you come to the picturesque creek. Ahead, at 1.0 mi., is a wooden observation platform **[5]** above a still-water pond formed by a creek that originates in the nature preserve. After leaving the observation platform, turn left (there's a sign). The path will be strewn with red needles from the pine trees once planted here in an attempt to establish a plantation. Note the small boulders on the left. At 1.1 mi. the path veers right, away from the stream, and enters more forest. At 1.2 mi., we saw a giant oak tree across Trail 2 on the left; here, continue walking straight ahead for Trail 4.

At 1.3 mi., the trail enters a beech-maple frost community where we noticed many tiny maple trees struggling to grow beside a meandering stream. At 1.4 mi., we saw lovely, large water plantains before reaching the wooden ramp. After crossing the tiny stream, continue walking up a gentle slope. At 1.45 mi. the ravine at the left contains many giant, uprooted trees. Here, we were intrigued by a huge black walnut tree with multiple trunks. At 1.55 mi. **[6]**, the path turns right to follow an old road. At 1.63 mi., the road becomes a gravel path that soon turns into grass.

At 1.7 mi., you'll walk on a mowed-grass path with trees on the left, a meadow on the right. At 1.8 mi., the path enters forest again. Soon after, we noticed a grove of young, shagbark hickory. At 2.1 mi., the path was a wide swath of mowed grasses; we walked through open savanna with a scattered mixture of trees. At 2.2 mi., we encountered an old, overgrown crossroad **[7]**, but did not take it. Trail 4 continues straight ahead. At 2.4 mi. the trail ends at a park road. To the right, we could see the parking lot near the cemetery, where this hike started.

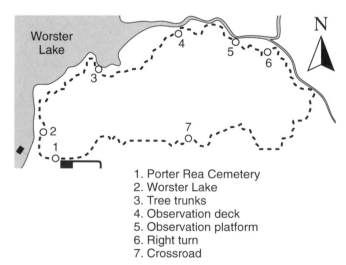

1. Porter Rea Cemetery
2. Worster Lake
3. Tree trunks
4. Observation deck
5. Observation platform
6. Right turn
7. Crossroad

# 9. Chain O'Lakes State Park

- Hike along seven miles of shoreline formed by a series of connected lakes.
- Follow paths where Miami Indians used to walk, near their wigwam homes at Bowen Lake.
- Stand on the bridges that cross narrow channels, and you can watch people paddle canoes below you from one lake to the next.

## Area Information

The most recent glaciers, which left their mark on this area about 10,000 years ago, generated rivers of melting water. As conditions changed and the Ice Age ended, the series of circular lakes in the park formed. Called kettle lakes by geologists, they formed when an ice block, surrounded by glacial till, melted and filled the depression with water.

The glacial meltwater, filled with debris, also carved the channels between eight of the lakes in the park. Several more lakes in the park are not connected.

Before settlement by Europeans, Miami Indians occupied a small village on the north shore of Bowen Lake; at one time, there were 30 or so wigwams, fashioned of tree bark, standing on the lakeshore. Later, newcomers named the lake for William Bowen, one of the earliest settlers.

Today, the park offers experiences unlike other Hoosier parks. Canoeists can put in at Miller Lake; paddle east through channels connecting three small lakes; and cross Sand Lake, Bowen Lake, and Dock Lake before arriving at Long Lake, which is the end of the chain. Hikers find trails around these lakes and use bridges to cross the narrow channels. In this park, the lack of motorboats on the water greatly enhances a wildlife-watching experience. On other lakes, the motorized buzz of speedboats and the shrieks of water-skiers frighten wild creatures away.

**Directions:** The park is located four miles south of Albion on SR 9. From Fort Wayne, drive northwest on US 33 for 20 miles, then north on SR 9 for 4.5 miles to reach the park entrance.

**Hours Open:** The park is open year-round from 7:00 A.M. to 11:00 P.M.

**Facilities:** The park has a campground, small grocery store, family cabins, boat and canoe rental, nature center, picnic shelters, swimming beach, and a refreshment stand.

**Permits and Rules:** Do not injure or damage wildlife or any natural feature of the park. Do not gather wood for fires. Keep dogs and cats on leashes. Camp or build fires only in designated places. Swim only at the beach. Observe rules posted on signs. Carry out any trash you bring in; overnight campers can use receptacles.

**Further Information:** Chain O'Lakes State Park, 2355 East 75 S., Albion, IN 46701; 219-636-2654.

## Other Areas of Interest

Northwest of Chain O'Lakes State Park a wide band of small, natural lakes stretches northeast across several counties. These lakes are especially numerous between Warsaw and Angola, with each lake having a unique character. **Lake Wawasee** is the largest of this group; **Lake Webster** is beautiful. Author Gene Stratton Porter once had a home on **Sylvan Lake,** where she wrote best-selling novels. For more information about these lakes, call Chain O'Lakes State Park at 219-636-2654.

## Park Trails

Hiking trails are marked with numbered signs. Please stay on the trail.

**Trail 4** 👢👢—1 mile—This route takes you from Sand Lake through woodland, along two connected lakes, Mud Lake and River Lake, and ends at Norman Lake. Wildlife habitats include forests, lakes, swamps, and open fields.

**Trail 7** 👢—1.8 miles—From the Sand Lake fishing pier, you walk in a loop past Bowen Lake and Weber Lake before returning to the pier. The route passes along the narrow, glacial channels and crosses lowlands and upland forests.

# Chain O'Lakes State Park

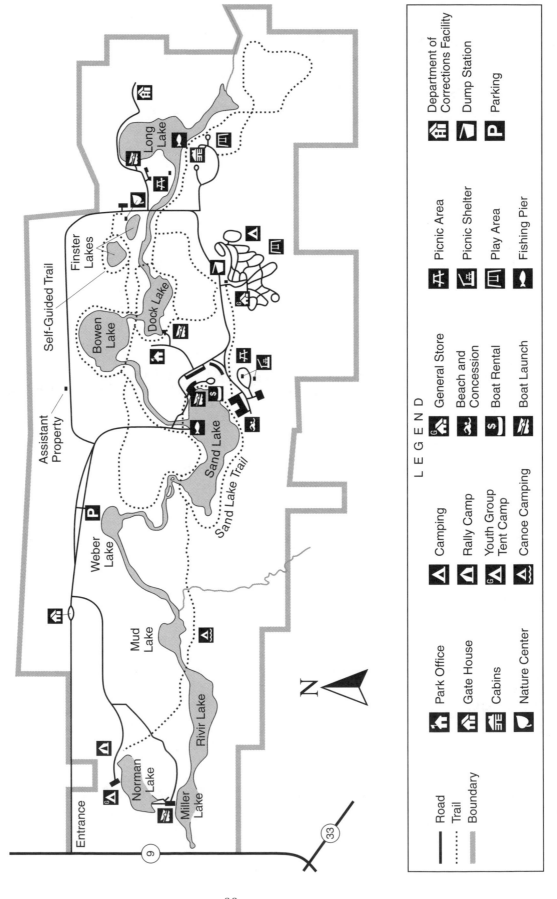

## LEGEND

| | | | | |
|---|---|---|---|---|
| —— | Road | | | |
| ···· | Trail | | | |
| ▬▬ | Boundary | | | |

| | Park Office | | General Store |
| | Gate House | | Beach and Concession |
| | Cabins | | Boat Rental |
| | Nature Center | | Boat Launch |

| | Camping | | Picnic Area |
| | Rally Camp | | Picnic Shelter |
| | Youth Group Tent Camp | | Play Area |
| | Canoe Camping | | Fishing Pier |

| | Department of Corrections Facility |
| | Dump Station |
| P | Parking |

# Self-Guided Nature Trail— Trails 8 and 9 👢👢

**Distance Round-Trip:** .5 mile

**Estimated Hiking Time:** 45 minutes

**Cautions:** Watch for roots and stones.

**Trail Directions:** Follow park signs to the Nature Center **[1]**, and park across the road. Before your walk, visit the old, brick schoolhouse that contains the Nature Center. Ask for their leaflet that keys information to the markers on this trail. Then, begin hiking on Trail 8, to the right. Note the Virginia creeper growing by the marker. You'll walk through thick, upland forest with black walnut trees, a berry patch on the left, and a pond on the right.

At .8 mi., Trail 8 goes to the left **[2]**. Here, take Trail 9 (it may be unmarked) to the right for a counterclockwise loop around the larger of the two lovely Finster lakes. As you walk through this upland forest, you'll seldom see the deep lake because of the trees. At the next marker, you may see poison ivy; study the arrangement of the three leaves, and note how the leaf on the end extends farther than the others. Now that you recognize the plant, avoid it.

At .1 mi., there's an ancient bench **[3]** resting on a kame, a hill formed by glacial deposits. Big Finster Lake **[4]** is about 12,000 years old. Although it covers only a few acres, the water is more than 40 feet deep. One appealing feature of the lake is the variety of emergents, the plants growing in shallow water near the shore. The emergents' roots reach into the water and their leaves extend above the surface. While you walk, notice the sand below the dirt surface of the trail.

At .2 mi., there's a narrow spur to a bog **[5]** where cattails grow. Interestingly, the male flowers and the female flowers occupy the same stalk; the thick, brown female flower occupies the lower part of the stalk and the thinner, male flower occupies the upper part. At the bog, you might see painted turtles sunning themselves. At .23 mi., take the right fork **[6]** of a Y (it's number 8). Here, young maples surround some ancient trees. At .3 mi., you'll see red oaks, which are common in this park. Notice the pointed, bristly lobes of their leaves.

Beyond the oaks are wild grapevines, an important food source for birds and mammals. During late summer, fall, or even winter, you may see the fruit. The dead trees have been left to provide animal habitat. You could see owls, bluebirds, or raccoons near such trees. In this park, about 85 species of birds and 49 different kinds of mammals depend on such dead or dying trees for food or shelter.

At .37 mi., note the shagbark hickory with its light, loose strips of bark and distinctive arrangement of leaves. Squirrels and other animals use the nuts of this hickory for food. At .4 mi., there's a large bramble patch **[7]** that also helps sustain wildlife. Dozens of different birds or mammals use these thickets for cover or depend on the plants as a food source.

At .45 mi., you'll see a black cherry tree, with its dark, scaly bark. In early summer, the tree blooms with clusters of white flowers; in late summer, the small, red cherries will appear. Beyond it, you'll walk through second-growth forest, woodland that has returned to its natural state after being used for orchards. Thus, apple, crab apple, or hawthorn trees may be mixed with the native hardwoods that are growing back in the process called succession.

By .5 mi., you'll have completed a loop trail that returns to the Nature Center.

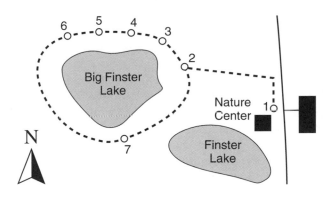

1. Nature Center
2. Trail 9
3. Bench
4. Big Finster Lake
5. Spur to bog
6. Y in trail
7. Bramble patch

# Sand Lake Trail (Trail 5) 👢👢

**Distance Round-Trip:** 1.3 miles

**Estimated Hiking Time:** 1 hour

**Cautions:** The trail can be marshy. Avoid stepping on the droppings of waterfowl, but look for their nests in spring.

**Trail Directions:** Follow park signs to the Sand Lake boat launch **[1]**. Park between the boat rental and the beach, and begin walking south of the rental office on a wide gravel path. In summer, you may see rental canoes at the edge of the lake.

This route will take you clockwise around the lake. At .1 mi. there's a swimming beach on the right and a bathhouse **[2]** on the left. Cross a grassy area with picnic tables; then at .15 mi., follow the trail into the woods.

The trail curves uphill and at .2 mi. takes a right turn. At .3 mi., the gravel surface of the trail becomes mowed grass.

On the right, note the emergents (plants with roots in the water) that border the lake. Here, listen for birds and frogs and, in summer, watch for butterflies feeding around the flowers.

At .4 mi., you walk closer to the water. There's a maple forest on the right, dark and shadowy, compared with the glints of sunlight on the lake **[3]**. At .5 mi., there's a tall, shagbark hickory tree on the left; farther along, the view is more open. At .7 mi., the trail may be drier, even though it's still skirting the marsh.

At .8 mi., take a right turn and continue following the lakeshore. Just beyond the turn, two fallen tree trunks form an overhead gate. At .83 mi., a wooden bridge **[4]** spans the narrow channel that connects Sand Lake and Weber Lake. Just beyond, Trail 7 comes in from the left to join Trail 5; the two routes follow Sand Lake's north shore, with a wide path having a surface of bark mulch.

Several ancient maple trees with multiple trunks add interest to this walk. At .9 mi., an elderly beech tree on the left has so much writing on its bark, it resembles a chalkboard. At .95 mi., notice the glacial erratics here and there on the trail (they're buried partly below the surface).

At 1.0 mi. **[5]**, the trail opens into a gravel parking area near some mowed grass and a wooden fishing pier **[6]**.

Take a minute to walk onto the pier and look at the plants below in the tea-colored water. One green plant, shaped like a branch of coral, we later identified as riccia, a type of liverwort. At 1.1 mi., a wooden bridge **[7]** over the channel to Bowen Lake allows canoes to pass underneath it. A canoe was slowly going under the bridge as we approached.

At 1.2 mi., the path runs close to the road on the left, with tall reeds on the right. Occasionally, this common reed, a type of grass, grows between 8 and 10 feet tall. At 1.3 mi., Trail 5 ends at the parking lot.

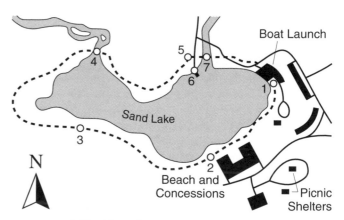

1. Boat launch
2. Bathhouse
3. Sand Lake
4. Wooden bridge
5. Trail to parking area
6. Fishing pier
7. Wooden bridge

# 10.  Pokagon State Park

- Hike through lovely areas that feature a variety of ecotypes: lakes, streams, forests, wetlands, and prairies.
- Treat yourself to a stay at the park's fine inn, and dine at the terrace restaurant, while birds chirp high in the trees.
- Choose from among 10 miles of trails, perhaps the most interesting hikes in the northeast.

## Area Information

Millions of years of the Ice Age has left its mark on the terrain in northeastern Indiana. When the Saginaw Lobe of the vast Wisconsin Glacier retreated at last, it created in this area kettle lakes of assorted sizes, bounded by kames (isolated hills formed of glacial debris), and left links between Snow Lake, the three basins that comprise Lake James, and Lake Lonidaw.

As a result, these lakes form a water boundary around the land, creating a peninsula. Before European settlers came, this area was favored by Potawatomi Indians. In fact, Pokagon State Park is named for two Potawatomi leaders, a father and son who transferred title to three million acres to the federal government for about three cents an acre. After the sale, Chief Leopold Pokagon retired to live beside a lake in Michigan. His son, Simon, educated at both Notre Dame University and Oberlin College, lectured and traveled widely; he became known as a spokesman for the First People's cause.

Because of the area's fascinating geology, the hiking trails in the park are varied. One trail leads to a glacial kame known as Hell's Point, the highest point in the park. Another trail circles a large marsh where you might see the endangered Blanding's turtle. Near the lakes are smaller ponds where rare flowers, tiny orchids, for example, bloom in season.

Along another trail, there is a free-flowing artesian well.

**Directions:** The park is located south of I-80/90, west of I-69, and five miles north of Angola. When arriving via I-69, turn west on SR 727 and follow signs to the gatehouse.

**Hours Open:** The park is open from 7:00 A.M. to 11:00 P.M. year-round, except Thanksgiving, Christmas, New Year's Day, and Martin Luther King Day.

**Facilities:** The area includes a hotel, restaurant, cabins, campgrounds, nature center, swimming beach, boat docks and rental, toboggan slide and rental, and cross-country ski rental.

**Permits and Rules:** Please do not injure or damage any living or inanimate feature of the park. Keep dogs and cats on leashes. Camp or build fires only in designated places. Observe speed limits and other posted regulations. Drive motorized vehicles only on paved roads. The park office has a complete list of rules.

**Further Information:** Pokagon State Park, 450 Lane 100, Lake James, Angola, IN 46703; 219-833-2012.

## Other Areas of Interest

The **Pigeon River Fish and Wildlife Area,** near Mongo in neighboring Lagrange County, also attracts wildlife viewers. The reserve runs east and west along a moraine that flanks the Pigeon River. Bird watchers can easily make new checks on their species lists, because there are wading birds and waterfowl in abundance. Within this Fish and Wildlife Area is the Tamarack Bog Nature Preserve, which features the largest remaining tamarack swamp in the state. The tamarack tree, with its rough bark and clusters of blue-green needles, drops its needles after the growing season. Call 317-232-4052 for information about the nature preserve.

## Park Trails

Trails are well marked with numbers on posts keyed to trail numbers on the map.

**Trail 1** 👢👢—1.5 miles—This trail runs along Lake James and passes the Nature Center, before ending at the Apple Orchard picnic area. Follow it and you're

likely to hear woodland birds and see waterfowl along the lake; in spring, you can enjoy the many wildflowers in bloom.

**Trail 6** 👢👢—1 mile—This trail runs through a swampy, primitive area, passing near a lake just outside the park on private land. You can see marsh plants and animals in this habitat.

# Pokagon State Park

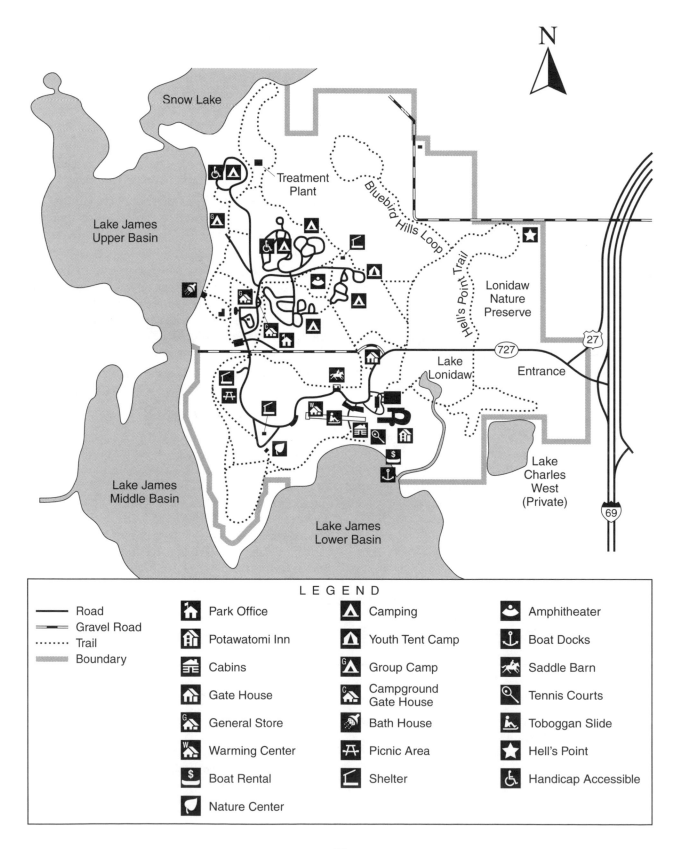

Snow Lake

Lake James Upper Basin

Lake James Middle Basin

Lake James Lower Basin

Treatment Plant

Bluebird Hills Loop

Hell's Point Trail

Lonidaw Nature Preserve

Lake Lonidaw

Entrance

Lake Charles West (Private)

727

27

69

N

## LEGEND

| | | | | | |
|---|---|---|---|---|---|
| — | Road | Park Office | Camping | Amphitheater |
| ═ | Gravel Road | Potawatomi Inn | Youth Tent Camp | Boat Docks |
| ⋯ | Trail | Cabins | Group Camp | Saddle Barn |
| | Boundary | Gate House | Campground Gate House | Tennis Courts |
| | | General Store | Bath House | Toboggan Slide |
| | | Warming Center | Picnic Area | Hell's Point |
| | | Boat Rental | Shelter | Handicap Accessible |
| | | Nature Center | | |

# Hell's Point Trail (Trail 3) 👢👢👢

**Distance Round-trip:** 2.5 miles

**Estimated Hiking Time:** 1.5 hours

**Trail Directions:** Begin hiking at the southwest corner of the large parking lot behind the Potawatomi Inn **[1]**. You'll hike onto a wide, bark mulch path, passing a brown building. At the sign for the Potawatomi Nature Preserve, turn right onto a gravel track and enter a maple-beech forest. Notice the green, leafy water plantain and other emergents at the edge of the pond on your right.

At .1 mi., a spur to Lake Lonidaw **[2]** runs to the left; Trail 3 continues to the right. At .17 mi., there's a wooden bridge across a wetland; through the process of succession, the pond water is now nearly covered with grasses and low trees. In season, you can see rare orchids and lots of blazing stars. At .23 mi., another bridge with wooden benches **[3]** allows you to sit while listening to stereophonic birdsong and gazing at the open, reedy marshland framed by forest. You can see beaver, muskrat, and mink near the lake.

At .27 mi., Trail 6 goes to the right; to continue to Trail 3, head up a low hill, actually a glacial ridge. At .34 mi., there are more marsh-loving plants on the forest floor. Here, we also noticed a large, flared, yellow fungus, but could not later identify it. At .44 mi., a loop of Trail 6 returns; to stay on Trail 3, take a left turn where a sign points toward Hell's Point.

By .56 mi., the trail has become grassy and passes through marshland before entering an oak forest. At .61 mi., you cross a road **[4]**; the trail continues on the other side beyond a rock. At .7 mi., a wooden bridge crosses a strip of wetland within the forest. You walk upward as you head toward Hell's Point, a glacial kame that is the highest point in the park. A wooden bridge spans a tiny streamlet. Notice the height of the trees; some of the sugar maples here are 90 or more feet tall.

At 1.13 mi., a gravel path leads through forest debris left there for wildlife habitat. By 1.17 mi., you've reached Hell's Point **[5]**, a glacial kame that stands 1,100 feet above sea level; the hill was formed about 14,000 years ago when the Wisconsin Glacier receded. At the crest, there's a great, open view of meadow and forest, framed by a pair of oak trees.

From here, the trail descends via a series of wooden steps and landings and becomes a gravel path, passing berry bushes before entering a forest of oak, black walnut, and tulip trees. By 1.4 mi., you walk through low, silky grass. Then, at 1.45 mi. **[6]**, Trail 7, a lasso-shaped route that circles a marsh, leads to the right. For Trail 3, continue walking forward, back toward the inn. A gravel path leads through a forest with a mixture of tulip trees, maples, and giant oaks. Tiny plants on the forest floor compete for light and space.

At 1.9 mi. **[7]**, a trail to the right leads to the Spring Shelter, where an artesian well provides good drinking water. For Trail 3, continue walking ahead over gravel and leaf mulch. At 2.0 mi., there's a marshy pond on the right. Also, a short segment of this trail is shared with the horseback riders on Trail 2, so watch where you step!

You'll walk with marshland on both sides and enter a forest of tall pines. At 2.1 mi., take Trail 3 left across the road **[8]**, and keep going straight. You'll see more conifers and some small boulders, probably glacial erratics; the path is strewn with needles.

By 2.3 mi., you'll be hiking downhill through forest. Soon, the path jogs right, then left, and becomes bark mulch again. By 2.5 mi., you'll be back at the parking lot.

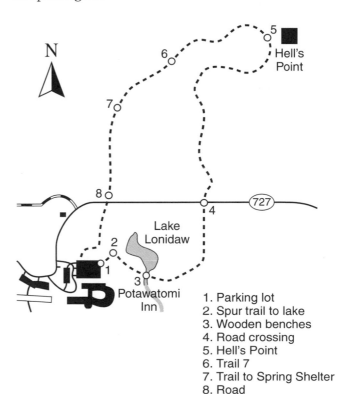

1. Parking lot
2. Spur trail to lake
3. Wooden benches
4. Road crossing
5. Hell's Point
6. Trail 7
7. Trail to Spring Shelter
8. Road

# Bluebird Hills Loop 👢👢

**Distance Round-Trip:** 2 miles

**Estimated Hiking Time:** 1 hour

**Cautions:** Use lots of insect repellent. Consider wearing long pants and a long-sleeved shirt.

**Trail Directions:** This trail is accessed by Trail 3. To shorten the distance, start along Trail 3 from the northwest end of the parking lot **[1].**

Turn left on Trail 7 and as you leave Trail 3, you'll enter hardwood forest **[2],** with a scattering of pines. At .22 mi., there's a boardwalk across marshland, where you can notice the water plantains. During a rainy summer, we found the insects (i.e., mosquitoes) especially aggressive here. At .25 mi., a confirming marker for Trail 7 stands on a low hill. Note the sandy surface of the trail, as the dirt has washed away.

At .36 mi., the dirt path narrows; take a grassy path upward to the right over these rolling hills. At .42 mi. **[3],** turn right to begin the loop that will return to this point. You'll walk on a mowed, grassy track through an upland meadow where big bluestem and iron-wood grow, along with occasional trees. At .49 mi. **[4],** there's a bench on high ground, with a splendid view of wildflowers in season. Watch for bluebirds and tree swallows. Here and there, in the distant landscape, are savanna-covered hills.

At .53 mi., follow Trail 7 straight ahead—ignore the grassy path to the right. You'll pass what looks like a nursery for small trees and shrubs; then at .63 mi., you'll discover a sudden, great view of a marshy lake. In summer, reflected sunlight on the floating, green algae made it look like snow. Early in the 20th century, this lake was drained for farming; park officials have allowed it to return to wetland. The stark, dead trees and dead shrubs nearby give it an eerie look.

On the Trail 7 loop, through a remote part of the park, you may not see other hikers; yet, I guarantee you'll see wildlife. We saw common birds—sparrows, cardinals, red-winged blackbirds—without even trying. At .71 mi., it's a good place to stop, look, and listen for bird calls. The trail then enters a grove of black walnut trees; here, in tall grass that the park maintenance crew had neglected to mow, we encountered a thick, black snake, about two feet long; it quickly slithered away into the tall grasses.

At 1.0 mi., there's a special bench **[5],** a memorial to a man who loved nature, donated by his family. Behind the bench, the trail descends into a lower section of meadow. At 1.5 mi., the trail enters oak-hickory forest; after watching the wind ripple the leaves of the trees on the left, we decided they were quaking aspens.

At 1.27 mi., we came upon the remnants of an old fence. The grassy path ran between meadow (left) and forest (right). At 1.3 mi., we were walking in clover, through a lovely and hilly savanna. By 1.54 mi., we had returned to Trail 3 again and could follow it back to the inn.

1. Parking lot
2. Hardwood forest
3. Right turn
4. Bench
5. Memorial bench

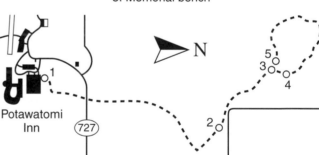

# 11. Fort Wayne

- Hike back through history; visit a place where promises were made and broken, battles were lost and won.
- Follow early Indian riverside trails where three rivers come together: the St. Joseph, St. Mary's, and Maumee.
- Walk in the shade of giant sycamores, cottonwoods, and walnut trees, while songbirds warble, hidden in the vine-covered shrubs.

## Area Information

It's hard to believe that this level region of sprawling suburbs and productive farmland was once covered by ice masses and glacial Lake Maumee. The area's earliest inhabitants settled near the junction of three rivers 10,000 years ago. Before the Europeans arrived, Miamis and other early inhabitants fished in the rivers, hunted in the forests, and gathered food along the streams.

Where the city of Fort Wayne now stands, the St. Joseph River and the St. Mary's River flow together into the Maumee. Unlike other Indiana rivers, the Maumee River flows toward Lake Erie, rather than toward the Ohio River.

Even though the Great Black Swamp extended east of Fort Wayne, early settlers read their future in the confluence of three rivers. The French built forts here, and British soldiers were massacred here. For a time, the Miami Indians were tough to displace.

Today, Fort Wayne has grown into the second largest city in Indiana. Yet, visitors can still walk through history along Heritage Trails that connect historic sites and vintage buildings. They can also follow the ancient routes along the river; Fort Wayne's several riverside parks are now linked by a River Greenway.

**Directions:** You can reach downtown Fort Wayne via I-69 from the south; exit US 24, Jefferson Boulevard, drive northeast, then turn east onto Main Street. From the north, exit Coldwater Road south, drive south on Clinton Street, and continue across the river to reach Main Street.

**Hours Open:** The Fort Wayne Heritage Trails follow city sidewalks; the River Greenway system links public parks, using narrow, riverside public right-of-ways. It is best to complete these hikes during daylight hours.

**Facilities:** Downtown has several pay parking lots. Hikers will note occasional restaurants along various routes. Two hotels are located downtown; you will find several dozen additional hotels and motels at intersections along I-69. City parks have drinking fountains, rest rooms, picnic tables, benches, and parking areas.

**Permits and Rules:** For the Heritage Trails, secure valuables out of sight in a locked vehicle. Be aware of your surroundings at all times. Do not litter. Use caution and follow walk lights when crossing downtown streets. For the River Greenway, no alcoholic beverages are allowed. Use caution and follow traffic signals. Motorized vehicles are not allowed.

**Further Information:** Fort Wayne and Allen County Convention and Visitors Bureau, 1021 South Calhoun Street, Fort Wayne, IN 46802; 219-424-3700 or 800-767-7752. Fort Wayne Parks and Recreation Department, 705 East State Boulevard, Fort Wayne, IN 46805; call 219-427-1253 to report problems in the parks.

## Other Areas of Interest

The **Crooked Lake Nature Preserve,** located northwest of Fort Wayne beside one of the state's deepest lakes, offers trails through forest and wetland habitats. Contact Division of Nature Preserves, Indiana Department of Natural Resources, 402 West Washington Street, Room W267, Indianapolis, IN 46204; 317-232-4052.

## City Trails

The Heritage Trails are marked infrequently with a logo sign. The River Greenway trail is also marked infrequently, using a different logo.

**West Central Heritage Trail** 👢—3.2 miles—The route runs through a largely residential neighborhood and links 14 historic buildings or sites. One residence, now a bed-and-breakfast, was the childhood home of film star Carole Lombard.

**Swinney Park** 👢—1 mile—This riverside park, which spans the St. Mary's River, has a hiking trail on either side of the river; the River Greenway also runs through it. A swimming pool, skateboard center, and the Jaenicke Gardens are major features.

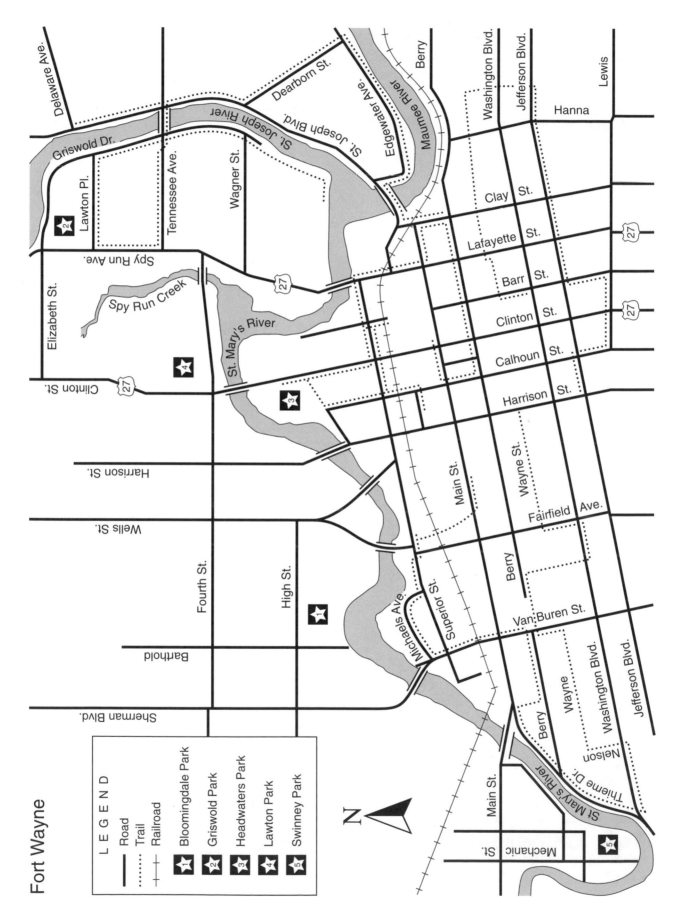

Fort Wayne

LEGEND
- Road
- Trail
- Railroad
- Bloomingdale Park
- 2 Griswold Park
- 3 Headwaters Park
- 4 Lawton Park
- 5 Swinney Park

# Central Downtown Heritage Trail 🥾

**Distance Round-Trip:** 1.5 miles

**Estimated Hiking Time:** 1.5 hours

**Cautions:** When you cross busy downtown streets, be alert for drivers turning right on a red light.

**Trail Directions:** Begin at the northeast corner of Main and Clinton Streets at the statue of Anthony Wayne on horseback [1]. Major General Wayne led the forces that defeated the Miami Confederacy, then built the fort that inspired the city's name.

Walk west along the Main Street sidewalk. You'll notice the old brick Journal Gazette building on the corner. Continue walking west along Main Street. The intersection of Calhoun and Main was formerly a transportation center. Walk south along the east side of Calhoun.

At .15 mi., the Allen County Courthouse [2], the fourth built in this county, occupies nearly an entire block. At .19 mi., at the corner of Calhoun and Berry, look left and you'll see the tower of the Lincoln National Bank and Trust Company [3], touched with gold.

Turn left and walk east along the north side of Berry Street. Notice several mottoes on the courthouse. At .3 mi., you'll see the new, modern building of the Lincoln National Corporation [4] across the street; this block-long complex houses the Lincoln Museum, a repository for important Lincoln material. Continue walking east, and you'll see the Elektron Building, formerly used for the county library, which now houses law offices. Continue walking east, and you'll pass attractive plantings of locust trees.

At .41 mi., a modern brick building houses the GTE Telephone Museum. Across the street, the City Building [5], once a city hall and jail, has become a historical museum. Continue walking east, and you'll pass a plaque that commemorates the work of Mother George—a noted Civil War nurse.

Continue walking along Berry Street to the corner of Clay, and turn left. There's an arts building [6] now at .57 mi., the location of a fort (Fort Wayne) erected by Major General Anthony Wayne's men in 1794. Walk farther north along Clay Street. At .63 mi., the corner of Main and Clay, look across Main Street to see a grove of trees [7]. Here, two other early forts were built.

Turn left and walk along the south side of Main Street. At .72 mi., the corner of Main and Lafayette Streets, turn right and go two blocks. Walk underneath a railroad overpass to the St. Mary's River. Across the river, near the Spy Run Bridge, you can imagine the activity when the landing [8] was used by early pirogue traders. The French Canadian pirogues carried people and supplies to trade for valuable fur pelts. Walk west along the sidewalk on the north side of Superior Avenue.

Pass the Old Gashouse Saloon, and continue walking west. Cross Barr Street, continue to Clinton Street, and at 1.08 mi., turn right on Clinton.

By 1.21 mi., you'll have reached Headwaters Park [9], now a popular festival location. Across the street is the site of once-popular League Park, the home field for baseball games for 50 years. At 1.33 mi., return to Superior Street, cross Clinton, and walk west along Clinton Street. On the left, you'll notice the new Fort Wayne Public Transportation Corporation station. Beside it, there's a quaint, stone Canal House [10], Fort Wayne's only remaining building from the canal era.

At 1.41 mi., turn south and walk along Calhoun Street. At 1.49 mi., turn right, cross Calhoun Street, and enter the block-long Columbia Street, planted with sycamores. This is the location of the Landing [11]. During the canal era, the Landing was the heart of a thriving canal warehousing district. Now, some buildings are empty; others have become night clubs—one features jazz and blues. Continue south on Calhoun Street until Main Street. Head east and you're back at the start of your hike.

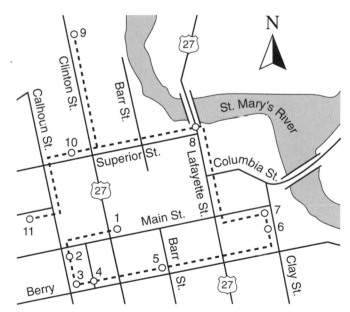

1. Anthony Wayne statue
2. Allen County Courthouse
3. Lincoln National Bank and Trust Company
4. Lincoln National Corporation
5. City Building
6. Anthony Wayne's fort
7. Site of early forts
8. Landing area
9. Headwaters Park
10. Canal House
11. The Landing

# Kekionga Heritage Trail 🥾

**Distance Round-Trip:** 2.5 miles

**Estimated Hiking Time:** 2 hours

**Cautions:** Be alert to your surroundings. Use care when crossing city streets.

**Trail Directions:** Begin hiking in downtown Fort Wayne at the northeast corner of Clay and Berry Streets [1]. Walking north along Clay, you'll see a brick arts center on the corner across the street. At Main Street, .06 mi., the trail angles right under a railroad overpass; follow it across the bridge [2]. From the center, look upstream and you'll see the St. Mary's River (left) and the St. Joseph River (right) as they join the Maumee (behind you), which flows toward the Great Lakes.

At .2 mi., turn onto Edgewater, which follows the left bank of the Maumee River. Cross Edgewater and follow the sidewalk northeast. Ignore signs for the River Greenway trail. This area, now known as Lakeside, has been inhabited for about 10,000 years. People of the Miami Nation called the neighborhood Kekionga, the blackberry patch. As you walk, look for these arched, thorny bushes along the way.

In the vicinity of .25 mi., according to legend, was the ancient apple tree under which the Miami woman, Tacumwah, was born. An outstanding businesswoman, Tacumwah became the mother of a leader known as Chief Richardville. Follow Edgewater, staying on the sidewalk as it curves left to Dearborn Street in a neighborhood of modest homes shaded by maple trees.

At .5 mi., cross Loree Street, and go one more block along Edgewater. At .58 mi., at the corner of Dearborn, you'll see a stone monument across the street [3]. This marker commemorates the Battle of Kekionga, during which Chief Little Turtle and Miami warriors courageously defended Kekionga from attacks by the U.S. Army.

Turn left on Dearborn, and go four blocks to St. Joseph Boulevard. At .8 mi., note the round, blue sign for the Heritage Trail. Cross Dearborn and use the sidewalk on the opposite side. Continue walking toward the St. Joseph River; you'll see a white stone wall that separates the boulevard from the greenway. At .86 mi., make a right turn onto St. Joseph Boulevard. Walk along the sidewalk, cross Tennessee Avenue at the bridge [4], and continue to Delaware Avenue. At a site near the river once stood the second fort [5] built by the French, erected in 1750. The worst of several battles between the Miamis and General Harmar's troops also took place here in 1790.

Return along St. Joseph Boulevard to Tennessee Avenue. Turn right, walk across the bridge, and turn right onto Griswold Drive. Walk two blocks, then turn left. Walk west on the sidewalk along Lawton Place. At 1.71 mi. is the Chief Little Turtle Memorial and Grave [6]. Follow the memorial walkway south among the plantings, almost to the alley. You'll see a council ring formed of rocks under the shade of large maple trees.

Continue walking west along Lawton Place to Spy Run; the name alludes to the work of William Wells. At 1.88 mi., turn south. At 2.0 mi., you'll see a park with a Civil War monument [7] across the street. Continue south, cross Tennessee Street, and turn left, back toward the St. Joseph River. You'll walk a tree-lined street, with the Williamsburg Apartments on the left and small homes on the right. At 2.2 mi., turn right and head south on the river pathway.

At 2.5 mi., gates across the pathway leading to the Confluence of Rivers [8] were closed and locked, so we ended the hike there. At this river junction, the French-Canadian Voyageurs sometimes began the portage overland (i.e., they walked and carried the boats and their contents) to reach the Wabash River to the southwest.

Walk west on Wagner Street, turn south on Spy Run, and you'll return to the downtown area.

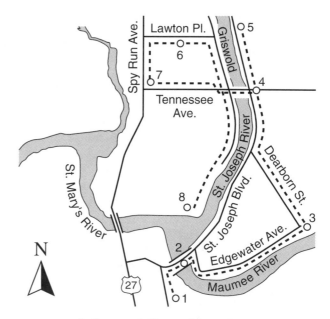

1. Corner of Clay and Berry Streets
2. Bridge
3. Monument to Battle of Kekionga
4. Bridge
5. Site of second fort
6. Grave of Chief Little Turtle
7. Civil War monument
8. Confluence of Rivers

# Lawton Park to Main Street Bridge 🥾

**Distance One-Way:** 1.45 miles

**Estimated Hiking Time:** 40 minutes

**Cautions:** Secure belongings out of sight in your locked vehicle. Stay alert for bicycles using this path, especially on weekends. Be careful when crossing the streets.

**Trail Directions:** You may use the Lawton Park parking lot. The hike begins at the River Greenway logo sign **[1]**, across Clinton Street from the park's southwest corner. Follow the boardwalk along abandoned railroad tracks; at .01 mi., turn right onto a wooden bridge. Watch for ducks and geese in the silty water of the St. Mary's River to the left. At .09 mi., there's a wooden deck **[2]** with a peaceful view. By .13 mi., you've arrived at Traders Point Plaza **[3]**; beyond, the concrete path curves around an old brick pump house. There's a grove of cottonwood trees on the right.

To the left, the river is screened by trees and shrubs; wild grapevines and blackberry brambles provide wildlife cover. At .23 mi., take the left fork of a concrete path that descends under the Fourth Street Bridge **[4]**. At .37 mi., the paved trail skirts another old building; then the path returns to the river. At .5 mi., walk beneath the Harrison Street Bridge, painted a creamy white, then through a grassy, open area. At .56 mi., a quaint, restored railroad station **[5]** on the right breaks a line of trees and shrubs. The appealing, renovated Cass Street Depot now houses the Fibers With Folkart shop.

At .63 mi., an elaborate iron gate frames a view of the river. Shad, carp, sunfish, bass, and bluegill have been pulled from these waters. At .76 mi., walk under the wide overpass for Wells Street **[6]**; note that erosion below has been held in check by rocks. The paved trail continues through a grassy, parklike area separated from the river by a line of trees. Note the variety of plants here and the trees: sycamore, ash, willow, locust, and elm. Not surprisingly, surviving wildlife has adapted to this habitat in an urban

setting. You might see chipmunks, raccoons, squirrels, or muskrats, and listen to all the songbirds!

At .94 mi., the paved path runs beside railroad tracks (on your right). Beyond, also on the right, is a small playground. Across the way you'll find Bloomingdale Park **[7]**. At 1.14 mi., take the left fork, heading toward the river, where you'll find marvelous, ancient sycamore trees. At 1.18 mi., you'll walk under another overpass; the supports have been decorated with artful graffiti. Ahead, on the left, there may be mudflats left by receding, high river water; look for a border of violets. By 1.32 mi., there's another boardwalk; you'll walk under an old railroad bridge. At 1.45 mi., the hike has ended at the Main Street Bridge **[8]**. Retrace your steps to return to Lawton Park.

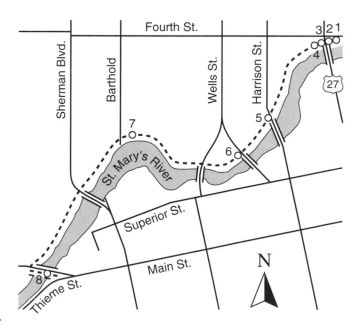

1. River Greenway sign
2. Wooden deck
3. Traders Point Plaza
4. Fourth Street Bridge
5. Restored railroad station
6. Wells Street overpass
7. Bloomingdale Park
8. Main Street Bridge

# Foster Park Loop 🥾

**Distance Round-Trip:** 1.93 miles

**Estimated Hiking Time:** 45 minutes

**Cautions:** Be alert for skateboarders and bicyclists on this paved, multiuse trail.

**Trail Directions:** Enter at the north entrance (the end of Rudisell). There's a parking lot **[1]** beyond the playground and tennis courts. This route runs counterclockwise around the perimeter of the park. Begin walking west of the parking lot, where you see a paved section of the River Greenway. From the river overlook, you can appreciate the rocky waterfall **[2]** in the St. Mary's River.

At .04 mi., the path goes uphill and toward the golf course. Notice the World Trail signs **[3]** at .07 mi.; they offer instructions for fitness exercises to do along this segment of the trail. You don't have to do them. Notice that the paved path now resembles a road between the golf course **[4]** and a line of trees.

At .27 mi., there's a marvelous, spreading oak tree on the right. Here, the fitness course offers metal devices: steps, rings, beds, and bars to go with the exercises you're told to do. On the left, the golf course, with its scattered specimen trees, looks like a bent grass savanna. On the right, you'll find areas of mowed grass beside a band of riverside trees.

By .5 mi., the fitness trail has ended **[5]**, and the forest comes close to the trail. Note the fruit-bearing blackberry branches. At .72 mi., you'll have a long, open view of the golf course as you walk past, and the trees are still close to the trail on the right. In summer, you can walk in the shade of overhanging branches; continue along this old park road.

At .93 mi., turn left onto an auxiliary trail. You'll see a golf course on the left; a row of low, wooden stakes on the right; and a baseball diamond **[6]** across the road. Keep walking on the paved path. At 1.01 mi., you'll notice well-kept homes on the right, across Hartman Road. Your path heads uphill, but, in summer, there's shade. At 1.5 mi., the Old Mill Road merges with Hartman on the right.

At 1.52 mi., continue walking, and veer slightly left, following the sidewalk along Old Mill Road. At 1.6 mi., you'll see the formal entrance **[7]** to the park, lavish with floral plantings, west of Foster Parkway. Turn left, at 1.63 mi., where a brick walk leads toward a lattice arbor, a garden **[8]**, and benches. Ahead, note the River Greenway logo across the road. Take this paved path toward the river. On the left is a small log cabin **[9]**, a reproduction of the one Abraham Lincoln was born in.

At 1.67 mi., there's a view of the river on the right. Here's where you turn left; go toward the tennis courts and playground. By 1.82 mi., you'll be walking beneath wondrous, ancient trees; there's a fat, old sycamore with a split trunk and a mighty black oak. By 1.93 mi., you'll be back at the overlook, where you first saw that tumbling, frothy waterfall.

So, the trail ends where it began. You'll see the parking lot on the left.

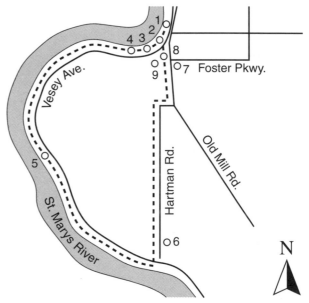

1. Parking lot
2. Waterfall
3. World Trail signs
4. Golf course
5. End of fitness trail
6. Baseball diamond
7. Park entrance
8. Garden
9. Log cabin

# 12. Bluffton

- Walk a paved, riverside trail that follows the upper Wabash River.
- Listen to birdsong coming from the trees and shrubs along the riverbank.
- Enjoy the small town, former home of naturalist Charles Deam.

## Area Information

The upper Wabash valley has a rich history rooted in the Ice Age. As one of the last lobes of the Wisconsin glacier retreated, the Bluffton area acquired moraines that characterize the Bluffton Till Plain. A phenomenon known as the Miami Torrent released gushing meltwaters and glacial debris that swept through the Wabash valley. Later, Miami Indians inhabited this region, long before the first European settler built a cabin here in 1829. Unlike the rivers at Fort Wayne, which flow into the Great Lakes watershed, the Wabash River at Bluffton curves across the state, then turns southward, eventually merging into the Ohio River watershed.

Follow the highways into the town of Bluffton and you'll pass tidy, squared-off farms, set among patchwork fields and scattered woodlands; notice that the land has been carved by rivers and streams. Thus, these plains are not entirely flat, for the glacial moraines and subtle swales create a terrain that's gently rolling. Along the Wabash River valley and its tributary streams, the high branches of sycamores, maples, and oaks frame river views. Hiking through those forests that remain, you will see branches from beech, hickory, ash, maple, or tulip trees form shady arches across the trail.

The growing Bluffton community features the distinctive Wells County Courthouse, a bustling medical center, and a vital downtown core. Savvy local officials have developed a River Greenway along River Road, then extended this paved trail to the gatehouse of Ouabache State Park. Thus, hikers (as well as bicycle riders) can cover the distance from downtown to the park on a riverside trail. What's more, locals have enriched the habitat for wildlife—especially birds—resulting in a diminished mosquito population. This helps make the area a delight for hikers.

**Directions:** The original section of the Bluffton River Greenway runs between the Wabash River and River Road and ends at CR 450 East. The newer portion of the trail begins north of White's Bridge and goes to the state park gatehouse.

**Hours Open:** The Bluffton River Greenway has no posted hours; daylight hikes are recommended!

**Facilities:** Bluffton has cafes and rest rooms downtown. The trail has benches, but no rest rooms. Ouabache State Park has boat rental, campgrounds, a rustic pavilion, picnic shelters and tables, a swimming pool, and a fire tower.

**Permits and Rules:** Do not litter. Keep a pet dog or cat on a leash. Follow rules on posted signs.

**Further Information:** Bluffton and Wells County Chamber of Commerce, 202 South Main Street, Bluffton, IN 46714; 219-824-0510.

## Other Points of Interest

While in Bluffton, you might enjoy a stroll in the riverside **Kehoe Park,** located downtown. Call Bluffton Parks and Recreation; 219-824-2200.

Bluffton was once the hometown of Hoosier naturalist **Charles L. Deam,** who lived on Wayne Street, just across the road from the River Greenway trail. Remembered mainly for his classic books on Hoosier flora, Deam also discovered many new plant species.

Three miles northwest of Bluffton, on the northeast side of Highway 116, you can visit the **Deam Oak Memorial;** here, you'll see a hybrid white and chinquapin oak that Deam discovered in 1904.

## Area Trails

The paved path of the River Greenway is easy to follow; the original segment is handicapped accessible. Note, however, that the trail at White's Bridge and the state park gatehouse runs through meadow and forest on the opposite side of the river. Hikers must cross the bridge on the road.

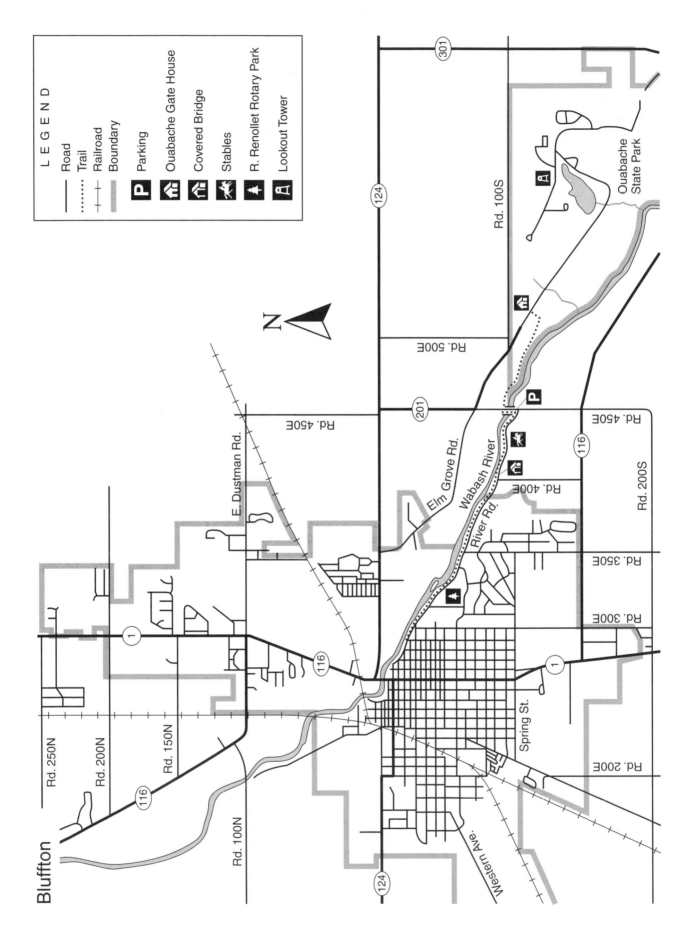

Bluffton

# River Greenway—White's Bridge to Downtown 👢

**Distance One-Way:** 1.42 miles

**Estimated Hiking Time:** 40 minutes

**Cautions:** You share this paved trail with wandering waterfowl; watch out for their droppings!

**Trail Directions:** Park south of the river and just southwest of White's Bridge **[1]**, which is on CR 450 E, north of the intersection with River Road. There are picnic tables in a pine grove beside the parking lot **[2]**, but no rest rooms or drinking water. Begin hiking northwest of the parking lot along a paved, riverside trail 10 feet wide.

Sycamores and maples flank the Wabash River, swollen with water in spring. The waters of this river flow unchecked into the Ohio River. Over the months and years, the water level rises and falls; savvy builders have learned—the hard way—not to locate their homes in the floodplain. Along the trail, listen for mourning doves; you might even see them. In season, you might find red-orange trumpet flowers tangled around a tree. Note the bird feeders hung on branches beside the walkway. At .2 mi., note the sign for Blue Moon riding stables **[3]** across the road.

At .29 mi., notice that high water has cut an oxbow channel into the opposite bank of the river; a long, narrow island has formed, populated mainly with maple trees. At .34 mi., you'll see Rivercrest stables **[4]** across the road on the left; we also saw day lilies near us on the right, along with jewelweed and lovely willow trees by the river. Blackberry bushes add to the food available to wildlife (and humans); along this path we heard many hidden birds.

At .44 mi., a red, covered bridge **[5]** over the walkway crosses a small, tributary stream. Note the sign, "Walk your horses while on this bridge or ten dollars fine." At .49 mi., there's more paved parking and a shady fishing spot. You'll pass cornfields on the left. If the corn grows knee-high by the fourth of July, Hoosier farmers say that's a good sign. At .57 mi., you'll see spacious homes on grassy embankments on the left and find a restful bench along the trail.

At .67 mi., enter the Bluffton town limits **[6]**. Note the yellow alert sign for drivers; at times, the road becomes a waterfowl crossing! At .76 mi., someone has placed a memorial white cross and wreath here for Melinda Gerber. You'll still see upscale homes on high ground at the left and find a red-brown fence on the right. Note that someone keeps these broad lawns mowed all the way to the road.

At .84 mi., there's more fencing and a wrought iron bench near large cottonwood trees. At .9 mi., an open space on the right allows good views of the river, both upstream and down. Perhaps you'll take time for a photography moment!

At 1.0 mi., there's another bench; beyond it, another duck crossing sign. By 1.13 mi., you'll have entered the Ray Renollet Rotary Park **[7]**. Note the rough, gray bark and deeply furrowed trunk of the young, memorial cottonwood trees.

At 1.14 mi., the trail runs close to the river. You'll pass the Liberty Tree memorial; the planting was inspired by an elm tree in Boston, Massachusetts, which became a symbol of liberty in 1765. At 1.21 mi., we enjoyed watching a group of mallards paddling around the water. By 1.33 mi., we had reached the foot of Wayne Street **[8]**; ahead, we could see more houses, closer together. At 1.39 mi., there was an unmarked stone (perhaps this will be another monument) at the foot of Liberty Street. At 1.42 mi. the trail curves onto River Road, so we ended the walk here.

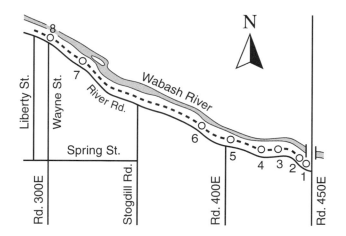

1. White's Bridge
2. Parking lot
3. Blue Moon stables
4. Rivercrest stables
5. Covered bridge
6. Bluffton town limits
7. Ray Renollet Rotary Park
8. Wayne Street

# White's Bridge to Ouabache State Park 🥾

**Distance One-Way:** 1 mile

**Estimated Hiking Time:** 30 minutes

**Cautions:** Be alert for bicyclists, who share this trail.

**Trail Directions:** If you've walked the River Greenway from downtown Bluffton, you'll need to cross White's Bridge to continue. The trailhead **[1]** for this segment begins north of White's Bridge on the east side of CR 450 E. You'll walk on a blacktop path where a wooden gate keeps out motorized vehicles. There's an open meadow **[2]** on the left; on the right, we heard the calls of birds hidden in the trees screening the Wabash River.

At .07 mi., a small stream empties into the river. Although the Wabash is laden with silt farther down, here the water looked green. Ahead on the trail was a cornfield, and beyond it, some farm homes. To the left were violet thistles, with wildflowers on the right. Beyond them, wild grapes wrapped the ancient maple, beech, and walnut trees screening the river; below them, various low, green plants flourished on the mudflats.

As you walk, look for different kinds of grasses in the meadow: big and little bluestem, wheat grass, light green foxtail grass, and others. In summer, some thistles were six feet tall. At .42 mi., there was a river overlook **[3]**, a place where water flows over white rocks into the river. As you pass a clay cliff, notice that the exposed roots of sedges reach down to hold

the soil. At .5 mi., the path curves left, and you'll walk with meadow on both sides.

At .64 mi., the trail curves left around a wooded area **[4]**; on the right, the view opens, and you'll see more meadow. Among the grasses, we saw tall, white flowers on purplish stalks; later, we thought they looked like a photograph of false Solomon's seal. By .72 mi., you'll be hiking through forest on both sides, on a smooth, curvy paved path that resembles a road. Wild strawberries were in bloom when we passed; green, leafy shrubs were hung with bright red berries.

At 1.0 mi., we had reached the gatehouse **[5]** for Ouabache (they pronounce it oh-bah-chee) State Park. Here, the trail ends.

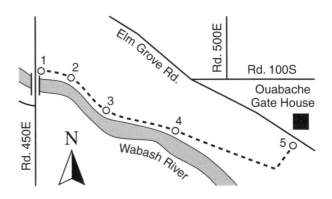

1. Trailhead
2. Meadow
3. River overlook
4. Wooded area
5. Ouabache gatehouse

# 13.  Ouabache State Park

- Observe a herd of American bison grazing on a grassy savanna.
- Encounter a cluster of butterflies with bright, mosaic patterns on their luminous wings.
- Circle a lake where quacking waterfowl make nests in the spring.

## Park Information

Originally, Ouabache was operated as the Wells County State Forest and Game Preserve. During this time, most of its timber stands were cleared and erosion set in. Through the efforts of the Civilian Conservation Corps (CCC) and Works Progress Administration (WPA), the area began returning to its natural state. In 1983 Ouabache became a state park.

This park features many modern amenities, such as an Olympic-size swimming pool, tennis and basketball courts, and a three-mile asphalt bike trail. A wildlife exhibit that features American bison is located north of the fire tower.

The Wabash River provides the park's southern boundary. Throughout the park you can see many types of wildlife—deer, fox, squirrels, and others.

**Directions:** You can reach Ouabache State Park via I-69, Highway 201, and CR 100 South.

**Hours Open:** Ouabache State Park is open year-round. The gatehouse is attended 24 hours a day in summer.

**Facilities:** The park has boat rental, fishing, camping, an interpretive naturalist service, picnicking, swimming, and a fire tower.

**Permits and Rules:** Do not litter, injure wildlife, or damage natural features of the park. Keep a pet dog or cat on a leash. Set up camp, go swimming, or build fires only in designated areas. Drive only on park roads. Follow rules on posted signs.

**Further Information:** Ouabache State Park, 4930 East SR 201, Bluffton, IN 46714; 219-824-0926.

## Other Areas of Interest

Southeast of Ouabache State Park, the community of Berne lies in the heart of Amish farmland. South of Berne on SR 27 you'll find **Amishville, U.S.A.,** the village of Ceylon, and a covered bridge known as the Ceylon Bridge across the Wabash River. The area's lakes include Rainbow Lake, which has a road around it. Just south of Geneva is the **Limberlost State Historic Site;** this was formerly the log cabin home of novelist Gene Stratton Porter, who studied the flora and fauna near her home.

## Park Trails

Park trails are infrequently marked with numbers on stakes. When a trail crosses a parking lot or passes through a grassy picnic area, there may be no markers at all, so look for an opening or a worn path.

**The Ouabache Trail** 👢👢—6 miles—Labeled Trail 5 on park maps, this long loop runs around the park's perimeter. Follow a particular segment, or walk the entire distance. If you do, you'll walk through various habitats within the park, including pine plantations, hardwood forests, meadows, and wetlands.

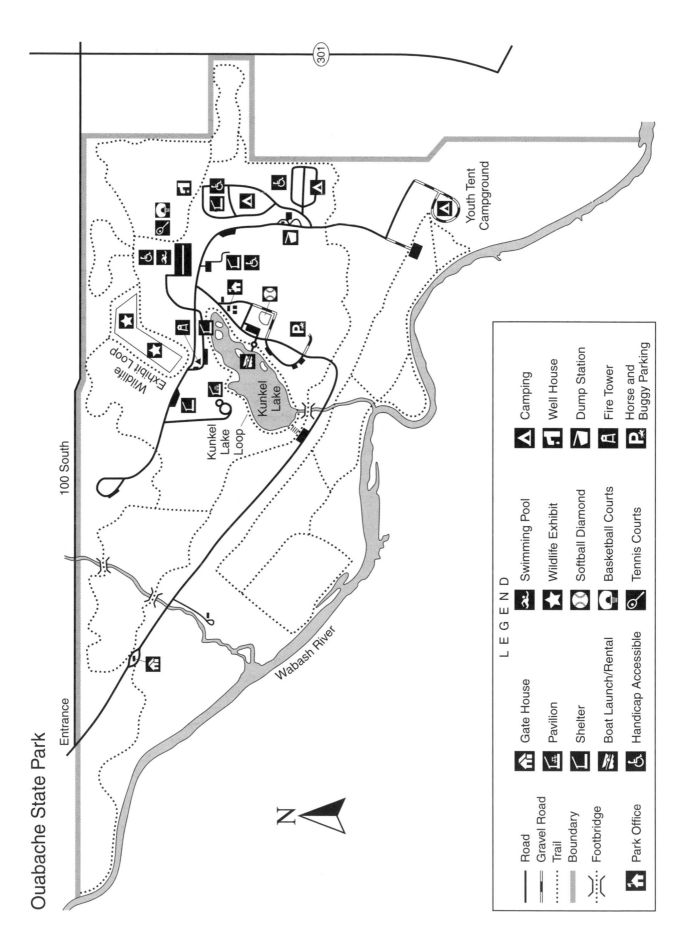

Ouabache State Park

Entrance

100 South

Wildlife Exhibit Loop

Kunkel Lake Loop

Kunkel Lake

Wabash River

Youth Tent Campground

301

N

LEGEND

Gate House
Pavilion
Shelter
Boat Launch/Rental
Handicap Accessible
Park Office

Swimming Pool
Wildlife Exhibit
Softball Diamond
Basketball Courts
Tennis Courts

Camping
Well House
Dump Station
Fire Tower
Horse and Buggy Parking

Road
Gravel Road
Trail
Boundary
Footbridge

56

# Wildlife Exhibit Loop 🥾

**Distance Round-Trip:** 1 mile

**Estimated Hiking Time:** 30 minutes

**Trail Directions:** Follow the park road to the Wildlife Exhibit **[1]**. You'll find it beyond a gravel parking lot across the road from the fire tower. Behind picnic tables, shaded by pine trees, a wire fence encloses the 20-acre Wildlife Exhibit. Trail 1 circles this exhibit just outside the fence. Begin hiking to the left of the enclosure, walking clockwise. We can't promise you'll see northern white-tailed deer, but you'll surely see American bison, grazing on the grassy savanna behind the fence.

At .15 mi., we saw a huge, horned bison resting in the corner **[2]** as we walked around the enclosure. Only about 30,000 of these animals remain in North America, even though there were an estimated 63 million before the Europeans arrived. One researcher claims, however, that Indiana never had large numbers of them. Continue following the narrow, grassy track straight along the northwestern perimeter of the fence. On the left are low shrubs, good habitat for birds; on the right, within the enclosure, clover dominates the mixture of grasses. At .16 mi., on a hot summer day, we came upon another bison, resting in the shade, near a pile of fallen logs.

Did you know that a bison image decorates the Indiana state seal? Continue walking ahead on a narrow, gravel path. At .26 mi., we found the central herd of bison; one was a youngster with red-brown fur. At .28 mi., Trails 4 and 5 go to the left **[3]**. Keep walking along the perimeter; from the trail we could see ponds behind a locked gate. At .39 mi., the path turned right around another corner **[4]** and became a wider swath of mowed grass. At left, the meadow blooms with wildflowers throughout the season.

At .42 mi., we noticed quaking aspen trees, with prairie on the left and more clover behind the fence. At .5 mi., the trail veers to the right **[5]**. Soon there's a strip of forest, and the view opens up to a meadow beyond the trees. On the right, some useful board gates—locked when we were there—provide access to the enclosure for caretakers. At .6 mi., where the path becomes a double-track gravel road, we saw the whir and flash of a cardinal in flight.

Also at .6 mi., we noticed a weathered, red building **[6]** inside the fence on the right; at .68 mi., there's another.

Continue walking along the fence. At .81 mi., there's savanna **[7]** on the right and more trees on the left. Turn the corner to complete the loop, and you'll recognize the picnic grounds.

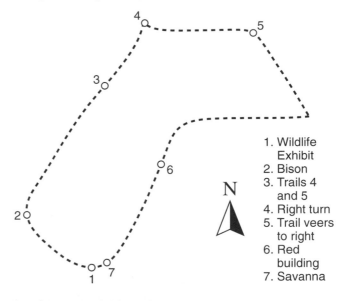

1. Wildlife Exhibit
2. Bison
3. Trails 4 and 5
4. Right turn
5. Trail veers to right
6. Red building
7. Savanna

N

# Kunkel Lake Loop 👢👢

**Distance Round-Trip:** 1 mile

**Estimated Hiking Time:** 50 minutes

**Cautions:** Watch where you step; many waterfowl also use this trail.

**Trail Directions:** Park at the boat launch **[1]**; then cross the park access road. The trail begins on a dirt path that angles left from this road toward the lake. You'll soon walk through a tunnel formed by low tree limbs and a tangle of vines. Occasional, narrow paths on the right (not the main path) lead to the lakeshore, about 20 feet to the right. Continue walking ahead. You'll see oak forest on the left. At .04 mi., there's a picnic table. The trail, which has become gravel, ascends a grassy ridge that divides the forest and the lake.

At .11 mi., there's a stand of tall, white pines at the left; the path curves right. You'll probably hear crickets and water running. There's an overflow drain **[2]** behind a cement block wall. At .19 mi., steps lead up from a parking lot **[3];** there'll be trees to the left. Keep walking ahead and look around: we found wild roses blooming among the blackberries. At .26 mi., you'll enter the woods again, where we noticed redbud trees among maple and beech trees. Alas, too late in the season to see redbud trees in bloom.

At .38 mi., the trail passes between sections of a wooden fence. Next, walk across a parking lot and behind a wooden lodge **[4].** Look in the woods about 50 feet to the left of the water's edge; you'll see an opening—that's the trail. At .5 mi., there's a stake marker for Trail 4. Here also, we saw the first blue-bird nesting area, part of a park project to provide them habitat.

At .57 mi., the trail turns left toward some rest rooms; nearby, a row of picnic tables stands in the shade. At .65 mi., go around the rest rooms **[5]**, and walk between the parking lot (on the left) and the

forest (on the right). You may see more picnic tables; the lake is on the right.

At .68 mi., there is wooden playground equipment on the right. Keep walking ahead on the grassy swath, which is the trail. We saw geese, tending their young, half hidden in the grasses. The trail here is a faint, narrow, grassy path that curves around the marshy end of the lake. At .87 mi., cross a wooden bridge that spans a stagnant creek; beyond, there seemed to be no path—just follow the lakeshore. Soon, you may see geese, ducks, and other waterbirds that inhabit the lakeside picnic area. Perhaps another photo moment?

By 1 mi., you've circled the lake, and the Kunkel Lake Loop has ended.

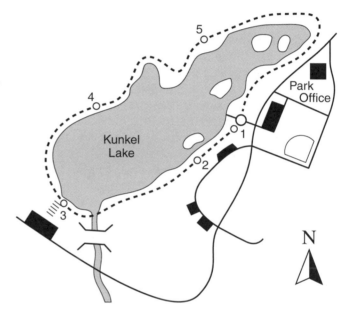

1. Boat launch
2. Overflow drain
3. Steps
4. Lodge
5. Rest rooms

# Central

A block of 29 counties between the Illinois state line and the Ohio border makes up the central region.

## Topography

Smoothed by glacial action, the central region consists mainly of gently rolling plains. Drive across this region and you'll see that land once covered with forest is now used for agriculture. The is one part of the state that prompts visitors to say, "I drove through Indiana once, and it looked really flat—all those cornfields!"

The Tipton Till Plain does blanket most of this region; yet, the landscape is not featureless. A network of waterways flows through channels formerly used by glacial meltwater. Here and there, rivers and streams have cut through the rolling plains and low, rounded hills to expose layers of soil and the underlying bedrock. In the west, rivers have cut through the glacial drift to form narrow canyons, creating appealing scenery. In the northeast, several concentric moraines mark the boundaries of the earlier glacial Lake Maumee.

The area has seven major types of soil; most common are a gray-brown silt and a yellow-brown clay, soils that color the region's silt-laden rivers.

## Major Rivers and Lakes

The rivers and streams that drain central Indiana were formed over the centuries by advancing and retreating glaciers, ancient storms, and periodic floods. The Wabash River, which flows through the central region's fertile plains, turns southward to form the boundary with Illinois before merging with the Ohio.

In the central region, the watersheds of the Wabash and its tributaries—Sugar Creek, the Raccoon, the White and Blue Rivers, the Mississinewa, and others—provide habitats favored by certain plants and animals. Various state, county, and city parks; picnic areas; and nature preserves in these riparian corridors make appealing settings for hiking trails. In Indiana, the central region lacks the natural, glacial lakes of the north. In the west, Raccoon and Cagles Mill Lakes, reservoirs developed mainly for flood control, are also used for recreation. In and around Indianapolis, the Eagle Creek, Morse, and Geist Reservoirs also offer lake-related recreational opportunities. In the east, Prairie Creek, Summit, and Brookville Lakes (also reservoirs) offer challenges for hikers as well.

## Common Plant Life

An early description of Turkey Run states, "Along Sugar Creek . . . black walnut, ash, sycamore, and hackberry trees reach enormous proportions. Some walnut trees are four feet in diameter, with clear lengths of 30 to 40 feet." Early accounts mention the dense forests that once covered most of this region; here and there were tallgrass prairies. The deep roots of great oak trees and the intricate root systems of prairie grasses meant that such species survived wildfires. You can sometimes see these survivors as savannas in this region.

Forest communities still exist in certain protected areas and private land in the central region. Maple and beech trees or oak-hickory groups often dominate forest communities. In the central region, sycamores, cottonwoods, tulip trees, red and white pines, locust, walnut, cedar, and ash trees are also part of the mixture.

The smaller redbud and dogwood trees, known for their lovely spring blossoms, grow well in the central region. In the shrub layer, you might find spicebush, pawpaw, various berry bushes, greenbrier, leatherwood, trumpet creeper, wild grapes, and poison ivy. In prairie communities, look for big and little bluestem, aster, goldenrod, bluegrass, rosinweed, ragweed, panic grass, and poverty grass.

It's fairly common to find trillium, violets, dandelions, mayapples, daisies, coneflowers, honeysuckle, Queen Anne's lace, burdock, yarrow, cattails, Indian paintbrush, trumpet vines, goldenrod, or asters—depending on the season. Less often seen, purple orchis, Dutchman's breeches, or lady's slippers become a special treat for the eyes.

## Common Birds and Mammals

Although much of the area's original forest and prairie habitat has been replaced by farmland, a surprising number of bird species still thrive. Hawks, owls, and woodpeckers—including downy, hairy, red-headed, and pileated—still inhabit the shadowy woodlands. You can see herons, kingfishers, cormorants, goshawks, teal, and egrets along the rivers. Ducks, geese, and cranes find habitat near undisturbed ponds.

Of the bison, elk, deer, and wolves once common to the central region, only white-tailed deer remain. At dawn or near dusk, you may still see deer, leaping over the fences that run along woodland or bounding across farmers' stubbled fields. The chipmunks, squirrels, and raccoons that once roamed the forests of the central region have found new homes near suburban backyards. Rabbits bound across city lawns. Coyotes, red foxes, opossums, badgers, beaver, and skunks live in wilder places. Frogs, turtles, salamanders, and water snakes live near quiet ponds or streams. Colorfully patterned butterflies often flit among the wildflowers in nature preserves or beside country roads. Look for the spicebush swallowtail, meadow fritillary, red admiral, or the monarch butterfly in the central region.

## Climate

The climate of this region has been described as temperate, continental, and humid. The mean temperature ranges from an average January low of 22 degrees Fahrenheit to an average high of 86 in July.

Measurable precipitation may occur for several days during any month of the year. Although snow is more likely during December, January, or February, it may also fall unexpectedly during November, March, or even April.

Occasionally, tornadoes may strike, especially in spring; thunderstorms may also occur in spring or summer, particularly in late afternoon. In Indiana, expect—and be prepared for—variations in temperature from one day to the next, and even from one hour to the next.

## Best Natural Features

- The richly textured mosses, lichens, and ferns in the rock hollows along Sugar Creek
- The gorgeous spring wildflowers, especially near woodland streams
- Great sycamore trees, ancient oaks, and impressive black walnut trees along the rivers
- Sandstone canyons that shelter hemlock, wintergreen, and other plant species typical of cooler climates
- Butterflies in stained-glass colors, sipping nectar from summer flowers

# 14.  Parke County

- Walk down Main Street past the old Mansfield Roller Mill, an early covered bridge, and weathered shop buildings.
- Take photos of the Mansfield Covered Bridge and the lovely waterfall nearby.
- Hike a seldom-used gravel road that passes through forest reserves and crosses scenic creeks.

## Area Information

Bedrock of the Pennsylvanian period underlies much of the rolling hill country in scenic Parke County. Amazingly, researchers have found nearly complete fossils of sharks buried in the layered material of this period. Apparently, the sharks swam in a lagoon, once part of an inland sea, that covered this area.

Built during the 19th and early 20th centuries, the wooden structures that cross the area's rivers and creeks were originally designed for travel by horse and buggy. An enclosed bridge helped minimize the horses' fear when crossing an open, high bridge over water. Some of the best bridge builders of the era constructed these bridges; they were built to last. Thus, Parke County now has 32 covered bridges, perhaps the greatest concentration in the country.

Parke County has organized five color-coded driving routes over roads that pass or go through these charming bridges. Although these routes are crowded on weekends at peak fall foliage time (early October), there are times when these roads are little used (spring and summer weekdays during work

hours). Early in the century, local residents often walked these roads to get from one village to another.

**Directions:** Mansfield, with its historic mill, covered bridge, and buildings, is located southeast of Rockville, the county seat. Coming from the north or south, follow Highway 59 to the Mansfield exit.

**Hours Open:** This public road is best hiked in daylight during hours of minimal use.

**Facilities:** Snacks and rest rooms are available in the village of Mansfield.

**Permits and Rules:** Walk facing traffic on the left side of this two-way gravel road. Stay alert for motor vehicles. Do not damage or harm any plants or animals. Plan to complete the hike before dark. The Parke County Convention and Visitors Bureau does not recommend walking this or any other of the five routes during heavy traffic of the annual Covered Bridge Festival.

**Further Information:** Parke County Convention and Visitors Bureau, P.O. Box 165, Rockville, IN 47872; 765-569-5226.

## Other Areas of Interest

Although not known for its hiking trails, the large **Raccoon Lake State Recreation Area** north of Ferndale also has walkable roads, most with lovely scenic views of the large lake. The park is well maintained; the picnic grounds are especially appealing. For more information contact Indiana Department of Natural Resources; 317-232-4200.

## Area Trails

**Ferndale to Mansfield** 🥾—7 miles—For a long hike continue walking through Ferndale on CR 1000E, go around Rocky Fork Lake, and complete the loop tour by walking back into Mansfield. This route, which includes the Big Rocky Fork Bridge, follows the back roads. Use caution and stay alert for traffic. Do not hike during the annual Covered Bridge Festival.

**Rockville to Bridgeton** 🥾—12 miles—For a longer hike, walk from the 1883 vintage depot (now the Visitor Information Center) in Rockville along another segment of the Black Loop to Bridgeton. You'll see several covered bridges and end the hike at the historic Bridgeton Mill. Again, walk this route when there is little traffic.

# Mansfield to Ferndale 🥾

**Distance One-Way:** 4.8 miles

**Estimated Hiking Time:** 2 hours

**Cautions:** Stay alert for traffic; leave the road if you hear a motor vehicle coming

**Trail Directions:** Park at the Mansfield Roller Mill Historic Site. Begin walking at the Mansfield Covered Bridge **[1]**, a red, double-span wooden structure built in 1867 by Joseph Daniels. Walk north along Main Street past low, ramshackle shops and concession stands, which spring to life during Parke County festivals.

At .25 mi., pass shops with a western look, including one called the Now and Then Company Store. At left, the Hilltop Craft House **[2]** opens only on weekends. The Mansfield Roller Mill, the dominant building in this back-road village, has been featured on scenic calendars and postcards. Continue walking north up a hill, past the overlook **[3]**, where you'll enjoy a view of the river.

At .65 mi., ignore a downhill gravel drive on the right; continue walking ahead on CR 830E. You'll enter a forest of sugar maples. At .8 mi., continue uphill past a dam. We noticed daisies in bloom, tangled Virginia creeper, and tulip trees. At 1.0 mi., there's a Quonset building **[4]** with an unusual limestone facade and an assortment of road-grading vehicles.

The road curves right, then dips suddenly into picture-postcard forest. At 1.5 mi., a rustic fence runs along a meadow where butterflies hovered over tall, violet flowers when we passed. At 1.6 mi., you'll see a rock outcropping **[5]** on the left and pass fertile bottomland on the right. At 1.7 mi., both sides of the road are screened by foliage and fences.

Continue walking north. The expanse of forest at left is on private property involved in a Division of Forestry program. Note the scars on the trunk of a beech tree from wrapping with barbed wire fencing. At 1.9 mi., a short stretch of blacktop surface soon gives way to gravel again. At 2.0 mi., an ancient cottonwood tree on the right is entwined with vines. A tan butterfly with a dark, dotted pattern on the trailing edge of its wings was—possibly—a regal fritillary.

The road curves right, then crosses a bridge. At 2.6 mi., there's a sandstone outcropping at left; near the forest of mixed hardwoods we saw yellow coneflowers. At 2.7 mi., the forest canopy arches above the road.

At 3.0 mi., you'll see farm fields on the right **[6]**, beyond the unmowed wildlife cover. Just beyond stands the Chartwell Farms Guest House **[7]**. Then, the view opens up, and at 3.6 mi., the river runs along at the right. At 3.7 mi., you cross a bridge **[8]**; the long stretch of forest on the left has become a cornfield. At 3.9 mi., turn right onto a paved road, CR 325 South **[9]**; you'll walk between a creek valley on the right and the Cecil M. Harden Lake Flood Control Project on the left **[10]**.

At 4.0 mi., the cornfield at left, with its border of sunflowers, is framed by big trees. You'll hike past a parking lot. Note the warning: Be alert for flooding.

At 4.7 mi. there's an open view of the creek at the right, and by 4.8 mi., you've arrived at Ferndale **[11]**. In this minuscule village, where the hike ends, we found two houses and one grocery and gas station!

## Parke County

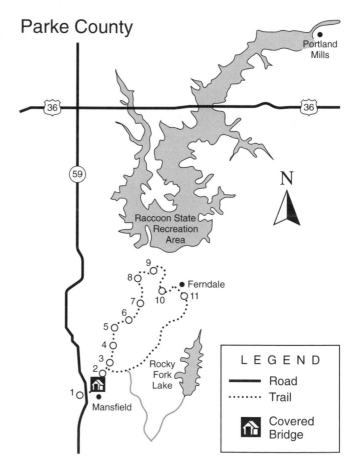

1. Mansfield Covered Bridge
2. Hilltop Craft House
3. Overlook
4. Quonset building
5. Rock outcropping
6. Farm fields
7. Chartwell Farms Guest House
8. Bridge
9. 325 South
10. Flood control project
11. Ferndale

# 15.  Turkey Run State Park

- Trails wind through some of Indiana's most challenging hiking country: up hills, along sandy paths, through forests, along cliffs, through canyons, and into caves.

- Hike through the state's scenic backcountry; enjoy leafy forests with myriad shades of green; a red, covered bridge and old, log buildings; and a sweeping view of bright canoes on Sugar Creek.

- Several trails provide access to Rocky Hollow Falls Canyon Nature Preserve, which still has the virgin forest used by Miami Indians as a hunting ground.

## Area Information

During the last Ice Age, glacial debris was carried by meltwater as glaciers receded. This action formed unusual geologic features while scouring the soft sandstone cliffs along area rivers. Forceful erosion and less violent weathering formed caves, cliffs, canyons, ravines, and rocky hollows. The brown, silty waters of Sugar Creek drain a forest that was the setting for an early grist mill and settlers' homes. Waterfalls trickle down walls of Mansfield sandstone; you can still find the rounded stones, glacial till, and glacial erratics along Sugar Creek.

You'll see giant sycamores and black walnut trees near the water. Although the wolves and bears are gone, red-tailed hawks, deer, and squirrels still thrive in the forests of maple, beech, hickory, and oak. Ferns, mosses, and lichen flourish in the cool, damp canyons. Raccoons play on the roof of the park lodge. This popular park is a year-round favorite, with each season bringing to it fresh beauty.

**Directions:** Reach the park via US 41; turn east and follow SR 47. You'll see a sign to turn left into the park.

**Hours Open:** The park is open all year. Park visitors may arrive and depart between 7:00 A.M. and 11:00 P.M.

**Facilities:** The Turkey Run Inn (park lodge) and restaurant are open all year. For lodge reservations call 765-597-2211. The park also has cabins, campgrounds, a nature center, picnic shelters and tables, a saddle barn, a covered bridge, and historic buildings.

**Permits and Rules:** Carry out any trash you bring in. Do not injure or damage any of the park's plants, animals, or geologic features. Swimming is prohibited. Camp or build fires only in designated areas.

**Further Information:** Contact Turkey Run State Park, Marshall, IN 47859; 765-597-2635.

## Other Areas of Interest

The **Portland Arch Nature Preserve** south of Attica is a National Natural Landmark. A tributary to Bear Creek flows through this preserve, where a natural, arched bridge has formed in Mansfield sandstone. The forest contains white pine, hemlock, wild cherry, and pawpaw trees, along with the more common maple and beech. There are two trails; both are self-guided nature walks, with numbers along the trails keyed to information in leaflets available at the trailheads. Explore a canyon where ferns, mosses, and lichen form decorative patterns on the walls of the cliffs. Call 317-232-4052 for more information.

## Park Trails

Trails are well maintained and well marked in this popular park. Each trail is numbered; the number is painted on wooden stakes at intervals along the trail. Be aware that on some segments, two trails may share the same route.

**Trail 9** 👢👢👢—1 mile—This trail through rare, virgin forest and two scenic canyons could also double as a fitness course. Located on the north side of Sugar Creek, you can reach it via Trail 5.

**Trail 1** 👢—3 miles—This route follows Sugar Creek, passes giant sycamores and black walnut trees, and leads to a historic covered bridge and the early Lusk home. The return route loops through forest.

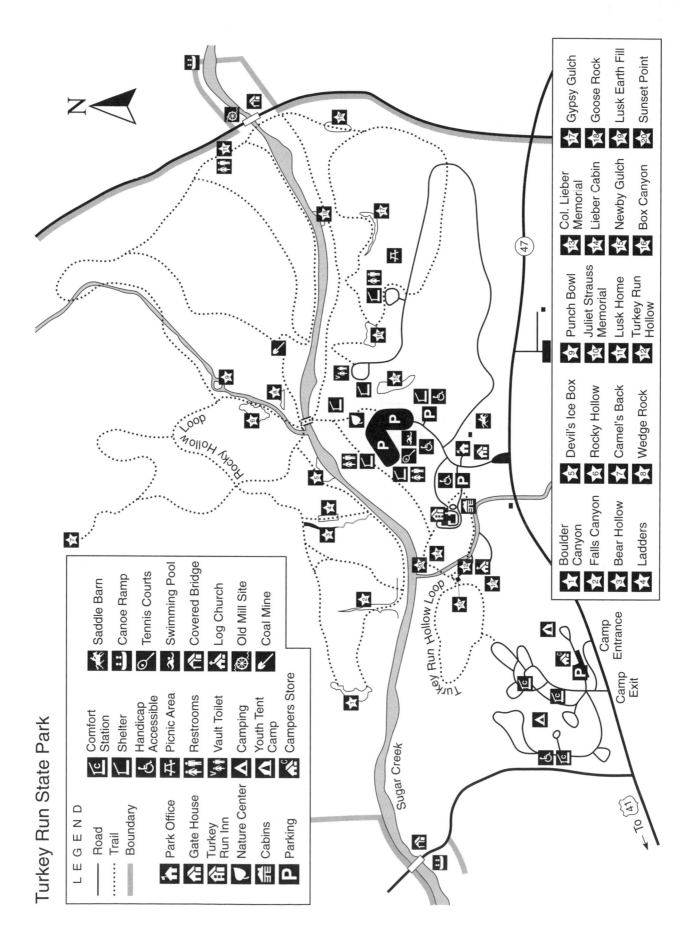

# Turkey Run State Park

**L E G E N D**

| | |
|---|---|
| —— | Road |
| ......... | Trail |
| —— | Boundary |

| | | | |
|---|---|---|---|
| | Park Office | | Comfort Station |
| | Gate House | | Shelter |
| | Turkey Run Inn | | Handicap Accessible |
| | Nature Center | | Picnic Area |
| | Cabins | | Restrooms |
| P | Parking | | Vault Toilet |
| | | | Camping |
| | | | Youth Tent Camp |
| | | | Campers Store |

| | | | |
|---|---|---|---|
| | Saddle Barn | | Canoe Ramp |
| | Tennis Courts | | Swimming Pool |
| | Covered Bridge | | Log Church |
| | Vault Toilet | | Old Mill Site |
| | | | Coal Mine |

| | | | | | | |
|---|---|---|---|---|---|---|
| ★1 | Boulder Canyon | ★5 | Devil's Ice Box | ★9 | Punch Bowl | ★13 | Col. Lieber Memorial | ★17 | Gypsy Gulch |
| ★2 | Falls Canyon | ★6 | Rocky Hollow | ★10 | Juliet Strauss Memorial | ★14 | Lieber Cabin | ★18 | Goose Rock |
| ★3 | Bear Hollow | ★7 | Camel's Back | ★11 | Lusk Home | ★15 | Newby Gulch | ★19 | Lusk Earth Fill |
| ★4 | Ladders | ★8 | Wedge Rock | ★12 | Turkey Run Hollow | ★16 | Box Canyon | ★20 | Sunset Point |

Sugar Creek

Rocky Hollow Loop

Turkey Run Hollow Loop

Camp Entrance

Camp Exit

To 41

47

# Rocky Hollow Loop (Trail 3) 👢👢👢👢

**Distance Round-Trip:** 1.7 miles

**Estimated Hiking Time:** 1.45 hours

**Cautions:** The trail has wooden stairways and ladders that lean against canyon walls. Take care to avoid slipping on slick steps or mud, or skidding on loose rocks in the canyon.

**Trail Directions:** Park by the Nature Center; then follow the path behind it to the Suspension Bridge. Cross Sugar Creek. Trail 3 begins as a left-hand route off Trail 10 **[1]**. A wooden staircase takes you to a platform with a view of the creek. A gravel path then leads through a maple grove, high above the valley, where birds chirp and ferns thrive.

At .2 mi. **[2]**, the Devil's Ice Box below the trail is a rock enclosure, open on the creek side, where water dripping in rivulets creates a cooling effect.

The trail continues past a large beech tree; notice the smooth, gray bark, which has, unfortunately, inspired lovers to carve their initials. On the left, a group of massive boulders range from 4 to 15 feet high. Stairs and a wooden bridge form an overlook **[3]** for a scenic view of the creek. Note the gravel island, formed of rocks deposited there by a receding glacier.

Next, the trail enters the often muddy, slippery streambed of a ravine called Bear Hollow at .4 mi. **[4]**. Note the lavish mixture of ferns, grasses, wildflowers, mosses, lichen, and vines that drape these striated rocks. Close your eyes, and feel the damp air cooling your skin. Listen to the water trickle, drip, drip onto fallen timber and sandstone rock. At .5 mi. **[5]**, Trail 5 goes left; instead, turn right, use a tall, skinny ladder beside a waterfall, and climb out of Bear Hollow.

The smooth path you walk on and the gentle way it curves through a maple-beech forest invite relaxation—but not for long. This forest path through the Rocky Hollow Falls Canyon Nature Preserve, likely used by the area's earliest inhabitants, also runs uphill and down. As you hike, note the variety of trees: American beech, with smooth, gray bark and oval leaves; black walnut, with deeply furrowed bark and groups of leaflets; American sycamore, with lighter bark that loosens and curls; and even eastern hemlock, an evergreen with small, flat leaves. Some trees here are an estimated 300 to 400 years old.

At 1.0 mi., Trail 10 **[6]** veers to the left. While hiking you might see wild turkeys or turkey vultures, along with the more common chipmunks, squirrels, and toads. By 1.4 mi., you'll have descended the steps into Rocky Hollow **[7]**, one of the park's most

fascinating features. The park's Mansfield sandstone cliffs and canyons were formed about 260 million years ago. Much later, surging meltwater that moved through this area carried glacial debris; the harder rocky material ground the softer stone walls of Rocky Hollow and deposited the boulders and gravel on parts of the trail.

The trail follows the creek bed, as you walk upstream, scrambling over boulders, skidding on gravel, or skirting a foot-wide ledge on the canyon walls. Note the small cavities—not quite caves—that might once have been used for shelter. Mosses, ferns, and lichen, including rare species, climb the canyon walls or grow between the rock formations. Note the unusual Wedge Rock at 1.5 mi. **[8]**. Given the park's popularity and the heavy use of these trails, wildlife may be elusive. Yet, painted turtles, leopard frogs, and snakes, including ring-necked and copperhead, inhabit this area. For your sake and theirs, whatever you encounter, be still, let the creature be, and walk away.

The climb (or crawl) out of this canyon may reward you with a great feeling of accomplishment. By 1.6 mi. **[9]**, you'll be walking on the upper level again, along a forested path, and by 1.7 mi., this hike ends at the suspension bridge. Use it to cross Sugar Creek; then follow a segment of Trail 1 to return to the inn and the parking lot.

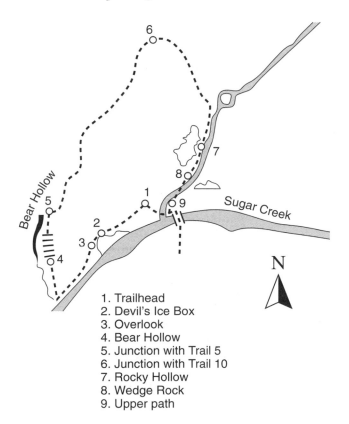

1. Trailhead
2. Devil's Ice Box
3. Overlook
4. Bear Hollow
5. Junction with Trail 5
6. Junction with Trail 10
7. Rocky Hollow
8. Wedge Rock
9. Upper path

# Turkey Run Hollow Loop

**Distance Round-Trip:** 1.74 miles

**Estimated Hiking Time:** 45 minutes

**Cautions:** Use insect repellent liberally, especially before doing the Trail 7 loop.

**Trail Directions:** Park near Turkey Run Inn **[1]**. Find the sign "To Trail 6" on the south side of the loop drive at the inn entrance. Walk south past a group of cabins. This hike, which makes a figure-eight loop via Trails 6 and 7, begins on a gravel path at .04 mi. to the right. At .08 mi., follow a boardwalk **[2]** and wooden staircase that lead into a ravine. Note the horizontal, striated fissures on the rock cliff on the left.

There's a giant white oak here, among other trees, on a peninsula formed by an oxbow creek. Despite the rainy spring, we saw only a trickle of water. At .13 mi. **[3]**, a path to the right is an optional walk via a spur to the streambed; you walk a less-traveled route straight ahead. At .11 mi., note the ferns, mosses, lichen, roots, and vines on a cliff above the water.

At .21 mi., a sandy path along a creek runs through crevasses between the rock formations. Cross the stream using the rocks submerged in water. At .26 mi., notice the ferns and eastern hemlocks clinging precariously to the edge of the cliff. Follow a mud path past another sign for Trail 6. Note the cool, moist environment, favored by the hemlock, a tree more typically found farther north. At .32 mi., use a wooden bridge to cross the stream; then continue along the path downstream. You can see rock formations on the left. At .41 mi., Trail 6 joins Trail 7 **[4]**, a self-guiding nature trail. Continue walking ahead on Trail 7.

Wild turkeys once roosted in the trees within these canyons. After their population was greatly reduced, the birds were reintroduced in 1980. Note the fat, fallen logs. These sandstone canyons were cut by glacial meltwaters an estimated 12,000 years ago. Follow Trail 7 across a wooden bridge that leads to steps up the cliff.

By .55 mi., you'll be standing on a promontory **[5]** with a wooden railing. Here, lovely mosses decorate the cliff, and a grove of hemlock grows near the edge. Depending on the season, the light green of new growth may contrast with the dark, mature branches of the hemlock. Behind, you can see the stream that empties into Sugar Creek at Sunset Point. At .59 mi., there's an overlook. Continue on this loop along Sugar Creek. You'll climb wooden risers and pass dead, rotting trees. A sign for Trail 7 confirms that this path of tamped earth and twigs is the correct one.

At .65 mi., you'll learn about sugar maples, pass piles of timber, and see more hemlock. Here, we saw a woodpecker at work on a white oak tree. At .68 mi., the trail turns back to follow the creek **[6]**. Nearest the creek, you'll most likely see sycamores; beyond them, hemlocks, beech, maple, then oaks. Notice the exposed tree roots along the trail—erosion continues.

At .74 mi., the trail moves inland, and you pass a tiny waterfall. By .85 mi., you've reached the top of some steps; turn right and walk uphill to the wooden overlook and benches. Here, you see a rock bowl called Glacial Gulch **[7]**, formed by meltwater. The trail then cuts through upland hardwood forest. We saw giant mayapple plants on the forest floor and heard many birds high in the canopy.

At .94 mi., a spur **[8]** leads to the campground. Instead, take Trail 7, which veers left and downhill through a maple-beech forest. Here, we noticed a gray squirrel, sitting on a branch, munching on beech nuts. Vines—wild grape, poison ivy, and Virginia creeper—clung to most trees. At 1.07 mi., wooden steps lead into a hollow. Then, more wooden steps lead into a gulch. At 1.12 mi., walk left along the streambed; you'll pass boulders, some with moss, and notice hemlocks, maples, ferns, and lichen growing on the cliff.

At 1.17 mi., note the deposits of iron oxide $(Fe_2O_3)$ that make the orange color above on the cliff face. At 1.33 mi., your figure-eight loop hike ends **[9]**. Return to the inn and parking over the same segment of Trail 6.

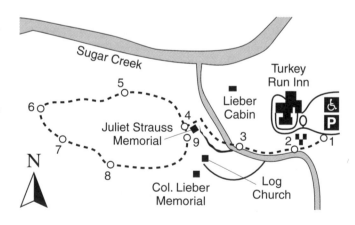

1. Trailhead
2. Boardwalk
3. Spur to streambed
4. Junction with Trail 7
5. Promontory
6. Turn in trail
7. Glacial Gulch
8. Spur to campground
9. End of Trail 7

# 16.  Shades State Park

- Hike through a rugged, moody forest much like the dense woodlands settlers found in this region early in the 19th century.
- Explore deep ravines and high, sandstone cliffs above scenic Sugar Creek.
- Observe native white pine trees, stands of hemlock, and the Canada yew more often found in forests farther north.

## Area Information

At the western edge of the Tipton Till Plain, the glacial meltwaters that formed Sugar Creek have also created deep ravines, rugged bluffs, and sandstone canyons as the waters surged west into the Wabash River. The exposed Mansfield sandstone and siltstone bedrock left by this glacial action has formed an area of special scenic beauty.

Many legends about the park have been told over the years. One describes a large Piankeshaw (American Indian) village that once thrived on what is now parkland. Another story tells of a decisive tribal battle held here. Yet another describes a pair of ill-fated lovers for whom Lover's Leap was named.

Less developed than neighboring Turkey Run State Park, the 3,082-acre Shades State Park appeals because of deliberate, minimal development in a splendid setting. Prospect Point, which is 210 feet above the water level, Lover's Leap, Inspiration Point, and Steamboat Rock have impressive views of the Sugar Creek valley. Most hiking trails lead through ravines with unique rock formations and distinctive mixtures of wildflowers, ferns, mosses, and lichen.

**Directions:** Drive eight miles west of Crawfordsville on SR 47, turn north on SR 234, then take CR 800 South left to the park entrance.

**Hours Open:** The park is open year-round; summer hours are 8:00 A.M. to 11:00 P.M. Only registered campers may stay overnight.

**Facilities:** The park has a campground, including an area for backpackers; a flight strip for small planes; and picnic areas. Deer's Mill covered bridge and a public access ramp for canoes are located northeast of the hiking trails.

**Permits and Rules:** Do not injure or damage anything within the park. Do not collect loose branches for firewood. Carry out any cans, bottles, or packaging you brought in.

**Further Information:** Shades State Park, Route 1, Box 72, Waveland, IN 47989; 765-435-2810.

## Other Areas of Interest

Stroll through the historic, central core of **Crawfordsville** on sidewalks shaded by ancient trees. Visit several historic buildings. The Ben Hur Museum, former home of author Lew Wallace, and the Henry Lane Mansion, residence of an early businessman, have appealing expanses of manicured lawn. Although the famous beech tree, under which Lew Wallace sat to write his novels, has been taken down, there's a marker where it once stood. Call 765-362-5200 for tourism information.

## Park Trails

Although trails are marked with numbers on stakes, some twists and turns of the route do not have this information. If a trail enters a canyon, you may need to hike along a stream, or even on the streambed, until a marker directs you to the path at the end.

**Trail 7** 👢👢👢👢—.875 mile—This route, which begins north of the Hemlock picnic area, loops through Kickapoo Ravine. Hike through mature forest, up and down hills, and walk along a rocky streambed.

**Trail 10** 👢👢—1.5 miles—This hike, which begins at Dell Shelter and winds through second-growth forest, leads to Pine Hills Nature Preserve.

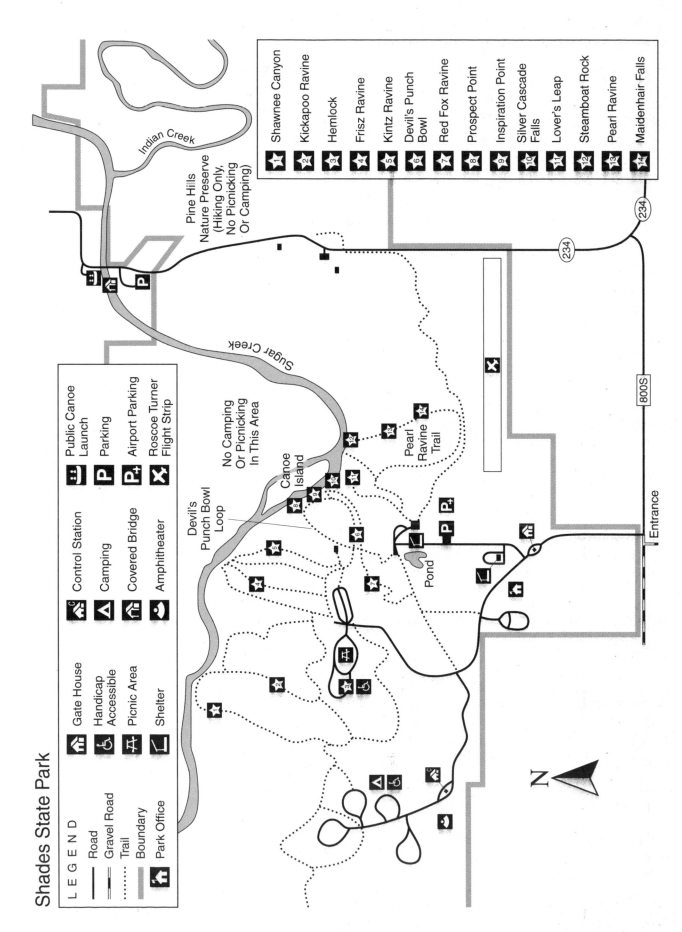

# Shades State Park

## LEGEND

- Road
- = Gravel Road
- ⋯ Trail
- Boundary
- 🏠 Park Office
- 🏠 Gate House
- ♿ Handicap Accessible
- ⛺ Picnic Area
- 🏕 Shelter
- 🏠 Control Station
- ▲ Camping
- 🏠 Covered Bridge
- 🔊 Amphitheater
- 🏕 Public Canoe Launch
- P Parking
- P＋ Airport Parking
- ✈ Roscoe Turner Flight Strip

Indian Creek

Pine Hills Nature Preserve (Hiking Only, No Picnicking Or Camping)

Sugar Creek

No Camping Or Picnicking In This Area

Canoe Island

Devil's Punch Bowl Loop

Pearl Ravine Trail

Pond

Entrance

234

800S

N

| | |
|---|---|
| ★1 | Shawnee Canyon |
| ★2 | Kickapoo Ravine |
| ★3 | Hemlock |
| ★4 | Frisz Ravine |
| ★5 | Kintz Ravine |
| ★6 | Devil's Punch Bowl |
| ★7 | Red Fox Ravine |
| ★8 | Prospect Point |
| ★9 | Inspiration Point |
| ★10 | Silver Cascade Falls |
| ★11 | Lover's Leap |
| ★12 | Steamboat Rock |
| ★13 | Pearl Ravine |
| ★14 | Maidenhair Falls |

# Devil's Punch Bowl Loop (Trail 1) 🥾🥾

**Distance Round-Trip:** .75 mile

**Estimated Hiking Time:** 1 hour

**Cautions:** The descent into Devil's Punch Bowl involves climbing down steep, wooden stairs. Hold onto the railings, and proceed with care.

**Trail Directions:** Use the parking lot across from Hickory Grove shelter **[1]**. Walk right along a gravel path past picnic tables for about .01 mi. The trail enters the forest on the right. At .05 mi., a spur trail to the right uses steps **[2]** to descend into a large, circular grotto called the Devil's Punch Bowl—well worth the effort. The official trail continues ahead.

If you go into the punch bowl, you'll find lovely views of a curving creek that tumbles over a shale streambed, meandering through woodland. Notice the pothole at the left, formed by a melting ice chunk. Continue walking down; at .26 mi. on the spur trail, there's an explanatory sign. Cut by two streams, the memorable Devil's Punch Bowl **[3]** was given this name by early settlers, who referred to the area as the Shades of Death. At .35 mi. on the spur, wooden steps lead farther down into the creek bed. Notice the crooked branches of eastern hemlock that cling to the upper edge; here on the cliff, you'll find mosses, lichen, and ferns, along with a patchy area stained orange by iron oxide.

If you continue along this creek bed in the direction of Sugar Creek, you can see Silver Cascade Falls **[4]**. Retrace your steps back through the canyon, and climb the wooden stairs to the upper level. Walk right and you'll be back on the main trail.

At .1 mi. on the main trail, take the right fork of a Y into beech-maple forest. Note the distinctive, somber mood of the place. The trail runs along a wooden rail fence; there's a grove of hemlocks on the right and an impressive view of the layered, rock canyon wall.

At .24 mi., continue walking forward on the hilltop. By .34 mi., you'll have reached Inspiration Point **[5]** and have a lovely view of Sugar Creek. In season, canoes often pass below, paddling the way the Miami Indians did when they lived in this area. From the point, walk along the fence toward the creek. You'll see more hemlock and beech trees and also find inspiration (at least we think so) at Prospect Point **[6]**.

Below, Sugar Creek flows around a rough, uninhabited island, sand bars, and deposits of gravel. On the island you'll see an untamed tangle of sycamores and maples, uprooted trees, and dangling vines. Called Canoe Island, this is a sometime stopping place for paddlers doing day trips downstream. When you leave Prospect Point, take a gravel path that angles left, away from the valley. You'll walk past ancient beech trees, some with miniature caves formed by their roots. Continue walking this loop on high ground and you'll soon be back at the trailhead.

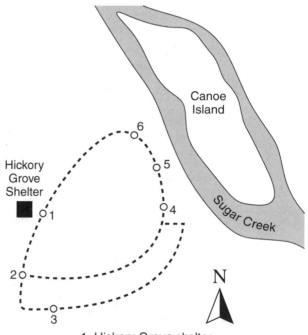

1. Hickory Grove shelter
2. Steps down to spur trail
3. Devil's Punch Bowl
4. Silver Cascade Falls
5. Inspiration Point
6. Prospect Point

# Pearl Ravine Loop (Trail 2)

**Distance Round-Trip:** 2.0 miles

**Estimated Hiking Time:** 1 hour

**Cautions:** Steep steps and a rocky climb up a stream-bed create some of the most challenging hiking in the area.

**Trail Directions:** Park east of Dell Shelter; take a gravel path to a sign, "Lover's Leap Trail 2" **[1]**. At .02 mi., take a fork to the right **[2]**; you'll walk on a narrow, packed earth trail that winds downhill into maple-beech forest. Pass decaying, fallen timber, before coming to wooden bridges and steps at .21 mi. The steps lead down into a sometimes dry ravine, filled with mossy logs and dark, green hemlock trees. At .26 mi., the trail veers right **[3]**; you walk past exposed tree roots toward more wooden stairs.

Did you come for a workout? At .31 mi., head left along a wooden fence into a grove of hemlock trees. Soon you'll be able to hear the hushed rumbling of Sugar Creek. At .35 mi., the trail turns right, onto a narrow wooden bridge; follow a series of steps and levels downward—yet, you'll still be high above Sugar Creek.

At .47 mi., **[4]** there's a dramatic view of the Sugar Creek valley. Notice the way hillside trees on the opposite bank of the creek have followed a pattern of succession, from the sycamores near the water's edge to the ancient oaks on the hilltop. At .53 mi., a wooden platform overlooks Pearl Ravine **[5]**, which empties into Sugar Creek.

At .61 mi., the trail turns into the creek bed and you walk upstream; there are ferns, mossy logs, and scattered boulders ahead of you and on both sides. At .85 mi., you'll see Maidenhair Falls **[6]**, a thin trickle of water that spills from a rock shelf. Take the steps on the left; then walk along the narrow clay embankment toward wondrous moss-covered rock slabs. Jagged cliffs and bent hemlock trees cast shade from above. We found no trail markers, so we followed human footprints in the mud and continued walking upstream.

At .95 mi., turn left, walk toward a fallen log that crosses a streamlet, and walk under it. At 1.1 mi., you seem to leave what the park calls "very rugged." After that, it's only "rugged." At 1.41 mi., there's a wooden stairway going up (no elevators anywhere) **[7]**. At the top, the trail enters a forest where tall, straight trees reach for the sky; the forest floor is covered with low, green plants and twigs.

At 1.29 mi., the trail forks; here, go right toward a wooden bridge. At 1.37 mi., a longer, stepped wooden bridge **[8]** takes you through a forested ravine with maple and tulip trees. At 1.43 mi., ignore the wider path to the left, and go right on the narrower gravel track. By 1.77 mi., the scene might seem familiar—this is the beginning of the Pearl Ravine Loop. So, if you choose, you can do it all again!

Otherwise, go left over a wooden bridge and down the steps. At 2.0 mi., you'll end this hike at the trailhead. Look left and you'll see the parking lot.

1. Trailhead
2. Right fork in trail
3. Right turn
4. View of Sugar Creek Valley
5. Overlook
6. Maidenhair Falls
7. Stairway
8. Bridge

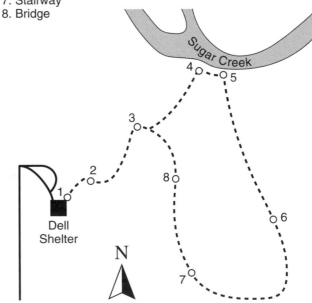

# 17. Pine Hills Nature Preserve

- Cross unusual backbone ridges where the land slopes sharply away on either side of the narrow trail.
- Study a tall, sandstone cliff face that's naturally pocketed with holes, scoured out by balls of a harder material.
- Leap, climb, or crawl to reach the top of a narrow ridge called the Devil's Backbone.
- Explore the beds of two streams that converge, then flow into Sugar Creek.
- Appreciate the rare plants and animals in the first nature preserve in Indiana.

## Area Information

Over the ages, erosion from Clifty and Indian Creeks has carved several distinctive, narrow rock formations, known as backbones, into the hills south of Sugar Creek. In some places, steep slopes drop off on both sides of the trails along these rock ridges. The largest backbone is six feet wide, 100 feet high, and decorated with images of the native but now extinct passenger pigeon.

Long before it became a nature preserve, settlers built a dam across Clifty Creek and used the resulting waterpower to operate a wooden mill. Later, other entrepreneurs started a pine plantation, and some of these pines remain. For a time, there was a vacation resort in another part of this unusual, scenic area.

This 470-acre park was dedicated as Indiana's first nature preserve in 1969. Since that time, a total of 20,000 acres of land with unique geological features has been set aside in the state to protect plants and animals—some of them increasingly rare. Some preserves are within larger state parks; others exist alone. A few sites have been designated as national natural landmarks as well.

**Directions:** Located east of Shades State Park, you can reach Pine Hills by driving eight miles southwest of Crawfordsville and turning north onto SR 234. If coming from Shades State Park, exit the park, drive east, and take the next two left turns.

**Hours Open:** The park is open year-round.

**Facilities:** The preserve has a small parking lot.

**Permits and Rules:** Carry out any trash you bring in. Do not disturb any plants or animals; do not damage any of the park's unusual natural features. No camping or fires are allowed. Motorized vehicles are prohibited. Children should be closely supervised.

**Further Information:** Division of Nature Preserves, Indiana Department of Natural Resources, 402 West Washington Street, Room W267, Indianapolis, IN 46204; 317-232-4052.

## Other Areas of Interest

Many of the paddlers you see navigating the silty water of Sugar Creek have had help from outfitters upstream in Crawfordsville. In season, **Clements Canoes** and other companies send flotillas of canoes or rafts downriver, then truck these boats back to town after clients have finished their trips. Call Clements Canoes at 765-362-2781 or 765-362-9864.

## Park Trails

You can recognize paths through the forest, but trails are not well marked. The trails cross high, narrow backbone ridges that drop off on one or both sides. Pay attention to the route you take, so you can return the same way, if necessary. In some places, the clear path you're walking might suddenly disappear— creek overflow has washed it away.

Pine Hills Nature Preserve has only the two loop trails; however, they are often combined to total 1.3 miles. Within the preserve, you can see several spurs that link loop trails with other parts of the park. Please hike on existing trails.

# Pine Hills Nature Preserve

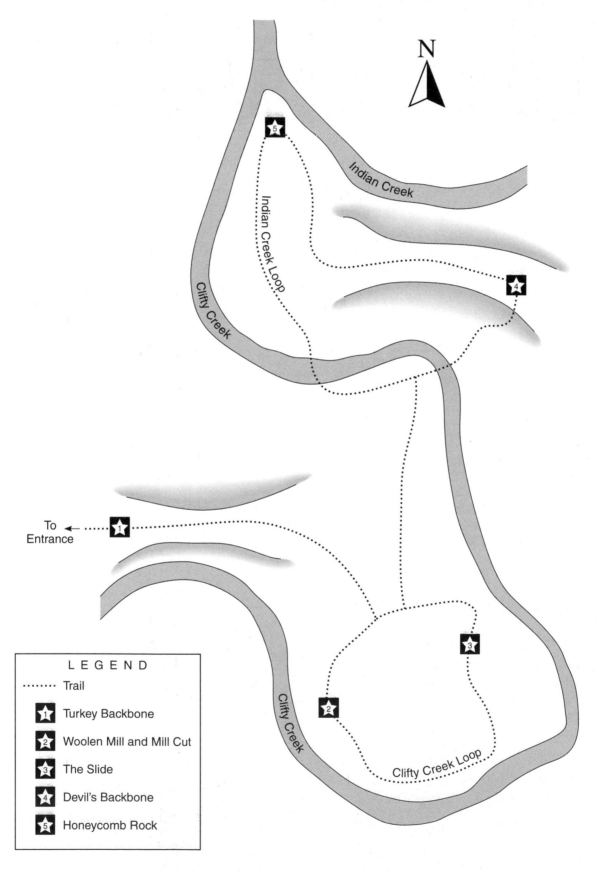

**Indian Creek**

**Indian Creek Loop**

**Clifty Creek**

☆5

☆4

To
Entrance ←

☆1

☆3

☆2

**Clifty Creek**

**Clifty Creek Loop**

**N**

LEGEND

⋯⋯ Trail

☆1 Turkey Backbone

☆2 Woolen Mill and Mill Cut

☆3 The Slide

☆4 Devil's Backbone

☆5 Honeycomb Rock

# Clifty Creek Loop 🥾🥾

**Distance Round-Trip:** 1.77 miles

**Estimated Hiking Time:** 50 minutes

**Cautions:** The Turkey Backbone (ridge) has steep slopes on either side. Supervise children; do not hike at night. Note that there are no rest rooms.

**Trail Directions:** Park across from the entrance to Pine Hills Nature Preserve. Climb steps over the fence. Begin hiking east on a wide path **[1]** into a maple-beech forest with scattered pine trees. Vines grow around many trees. You'll descend a gentle slope on a mixture of gravel and leaves over dirt.

At .64 mi., you'll see wooden stairs that lead to an overlook and the Turkey Backbone sign. The trail follows the backbone **[2],** where you'll notice a spectacular falling away, for the forested slopes drop sharply on both sides of the trail. This and other backbones in the preserve are perhaps the finest examples of incised meanders east of the Mississippi River. They were formed by receding glaciers.

From the overlook **[3]** at .66 mi., there's a great view of the Clifty Creek valley; huge slabs of rock flank the curving stream. These rocks, chunks of Bordon sandstone formed during the Mississippian period, have been exposed and eroded over the centuries.

Continue following the path to the east as the trail descends. At .71 mi., there's a stand of pines on the slope at the left. This area was once planted heavily with white pines, scotch pines, jack pines, and Norway spruce, which were raised and harvested on a plantation **[4].** More recently, deciduous hardwoods, which require less light, have been crowding out the planted trees.

At .86 mi., turn right at the sign, and walk toward the Mill Cut Backbone and The Slide on the Clifty Creek Loop. By .89 mi., you'll be walking past the forested site **[5]** of the early Pine Hill Woolen Mill, a waterpowered operation that spun yarn from raw wool.

At .91 mi., a sign marks the location of the Mill Cut Backbone. You can still see a notch cut in the backbone. When the mill was operating, water flowing through the cut ran down a flume and powered the mill equipment. The narrow, dirt trail curves left, through a mixed forest of maple, beech, sycamore, elm, walnut, and tulip trees. You'll soon see the layered rock formation known as The Slide **[6]** across the creek. Probably formed by alternate freezing and thawing, the surface of The Slide has been too unstable for most plants to take root.

At 1.07 mi., an access trail **[7]** to the north loop goes right. You can take this trail to the Indian Creek Loop (see Trail Directions). To return to the entrance, walk forward on the Clifty Creek Loop for another .1 mi. where you complete the loop **[8].** You'll return over the Turkey Backbone, the way you came.

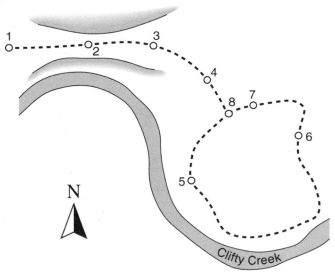

1. Trailhead
2. Turkey Backbone
3. Overlook
4. Tree plantation
5. Pine Hill Woolen Mill site
6. View of The Slide
7. Trail to north loop
8. End of loop

# Indian Creek Loop

**Distance Round-Trip:** .98 mile

**Estimated Hiking Time:** 1 hour

**Cautions:** One segment of the trail follows a narrow ridge, known as the Devil's Backbone, which is 100 feet above ground level. The ridge has steep drop-offs on both sides. Getting onto the backbone requires scrambling up a steep, rocky slope, then climbing onto the top. Once you're up there, you can stand upright and walk across it. Be aware that these backbones are hazardous, especially for young children. Also, time your hike so you're not on these backbones or finishing this hike after dark.

**Trail Directions:** This hike begins on the northern curve of the Clifty Creek Loop **[1]**. Begin walking north on the forested trail that links both loops. Soon, you are making your way over rocks in a creek; the trail is not marked. It helps to follow human footprints—if any—in mud until the path turns left to run along Clifty Creek. At .21 mi., a sign confirms that the ridged and pockmarked rock cliff above is the Devil's Backbone **[2]**. At .37 mi., there's a splendid view of this craggy rock formation rising above the creek. Note the carvings along the backbone, which is flat on the top and about six feet wide. To walk across, climb up the rocks to the east end of it. Attach anything you're carrying to your body so you'll have free use of your arms and legs. In some ways, it's like climbing out of water onto a boat deck. Good luck!

At .38 mi., a layered rock outcropping marks the end of the Devil's Backbone. Here, begin the descent over loose clay, somewhat organized into steps. By .54 mi., you'll be standing on the lower level, a flat promontory **[3]** above the two creeks, as they merge

and flow into Sugar Creek. From this point, you can gaze at Honeycomb Rock, a wall of Upper Mississippian sandstone with unusual, rounded openings on the surface.

At .65 mi., the trail, such as it is, crosses Clifty Creek; use the best set of stepping stones **[4]** you can find. Follow a narrow, earthen path toward the south loop. At .72 mi., a sign points to the entrance of the preserve. Usually, this return path runs along Clifty Creek, but when we were there, high water had washed away the entire trail. If this should happen, walk upstream in the creek for about 30 feet, and you'll pick up the trail again on the right.

By .93 mi., you'll be walking along a sandy path. At .98 mi., the trail splits **[1]**; take the path on the right, for it leads back to the entrance.

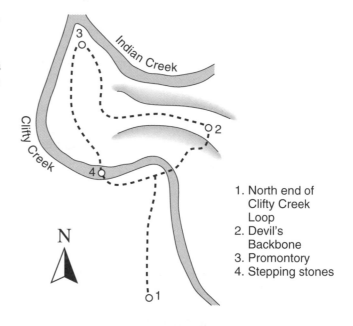

1. North end of Clifty Creek Loop
2. Devil's Backbone
3. Promontory
4. Stepping stones

# 18.  Lafayette/West Lafayette

- Walk through more than two centuries of history on a trail from historic Battle Ground into the city of Lafayette.
- Follow a shady, creek-side trail, hike along the forested riverbank, and complete the river route through city parks.
- See 99 different trees on three trails in under four hours.

## Area Information

About 8,000 to 10,000 years ago, when the vast Wisconsin ice sheet retreated, it scoured new channels for rivers, lakes, and streams. Receding glacial meltwaters left flat, upland plateaus, gravel riverine terraces, and low-water sandbars. A dense oak-hickory forest once covered the eastern two-thirds of what's now Tippecanoe country; the western third was prairie. West of the Wabash River is the tableland where Purdue University now stands. By 1869, when Purdue was founded, acres of grassland had been plowed for farms, although the first campus buildings stood in a flower-strewn meadow. As Purdue's campus expanded over time, greenery gave way to parking lots. Then landscapers took over, enhancing the 144 buildings and flat, 647-acre site with terraces, parks, fountains, and, especially, with trees.

East of the Wabash River, the Wabash Heritage Trail runs through a riverside ribbon of the early forest. The trail crosses the Wabash River on a vintage iron bridge that replaced an earlier ferryboat operation. Downstream, a narrow channel of the river separates the trail from Heron Island, now a wildlife sanctuary. You can access the island only by boat; Davis Ferry Park has a boat ramp.

**Directions:** *Wabash Heritage Trail:* To reach the trailhead, exit I-65 at SR 43 North. Drive two miles, turn right at 225, and go two more miles to Battle Ground. Follow signs to the Tippecanoe Battlefield Memorial. Use the parking lot between the museum and the monument. The trail begins south of the Wah-ba-shik-a Nature Center, in sight of the parking lot. *Purdue University Trails:* From I-65, exit Route 43 South and turn right at State Street (SR 26), or exit Route 26 West and follow SR 26 to State Street. Turn north at Grant, go right three blocks, then left onto Northwestern to the parking garage beside the Purdue University Visitor Center.

**Hours Open:** The trails are open year-round.

**Facilities:** For the *Wabash Heritage Trail,* the Trading Post in Battle Ground has food supplies. There are rest rooms and picnic tables at the Tippecanoe Battlefield complex. Several benches and a few picnic tables have been placed beside the trail. Toward the end of the hike, the Lafayette Municipal Golf Course has rest rooms, as does Riehle Plaza. The *Purdue Visitor Center* adjoins the Northwestern parking garage. The 200-room Union Club Hotel, at the corner of Grant and Northwestern, phone 765-494-8913, is on the Gold Trail. Find benches and picnic tables along these trails, rest rooms inside buildings, and cafeterias inside Stone Hall (Blue Trail) and the Union Building (Gold Trail).

**Permits and Rules:** *Wabash Heritage Trail:* Horses, bikes, or motorbikes are not allowed; rule breakers are fined. Littering is prohibited; carry trash out with you and dispose of it properly. *Purdue University Trails:* Park only in designated areas. Bicycles and in-line skates are prohibited on some walkways.

**Further Information:** *Lafayette:* Greater Lafayette Visitors Bureau, 765-447-9999; Tippecanoe County Parks and Recreation, 4449 State Road 43 North, West Lafayette, IN 47906; 765-463-2306. *West Lafayette:* Purdue University Visitor Center, 504 Northwestern Avenue, West Lafayette, IN 47906; 765-494-4636.

## Other Areas of Interest

The 96-acre **Tippecanoe Battlefield Park** with its striking limestone monument, developed at the site where General William Henry Harrison's men camped, is a national historic landmark. The park has an interpretive center with museum and gift shop. Call 765-567-2147.

Plans have also been made to extend the Wabash Heritage Trail south along the river's right bank to **Fort Ouiatenon** county park, located four miles south of West Lafayette on South River Road. Call 765-743-3921.

The new **Prophetstown State Park,** expected to open by the year 2000, will be developed on a 2,700-acre site southeast of Battle Ground. The park will feature three museums, two living historical villages, and an intertribal burial ground.

Set amid 81 acres of grassy fields and forested hillsides, West Lafayette's **Happy Hollow Park,** accessed off Happy Hollow Road, has picnic shelters, cookout facilities, and over two miles of hiking trails; 765-775-5110.

# Lafayette/West Lafayette

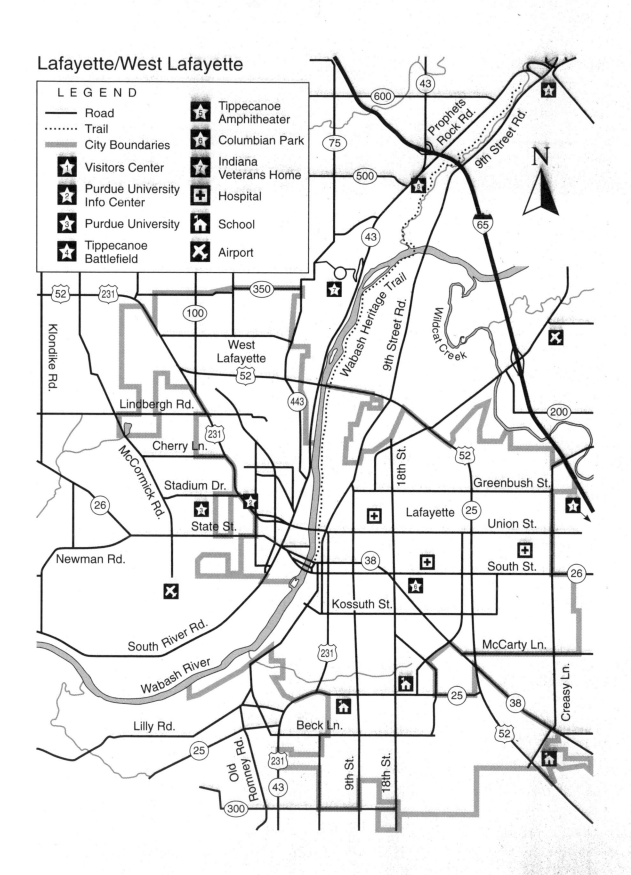

# Wabash Heritage Trail 🥾🥾

**Distance One-Way:** 8 miles

**Estimated Hiking Time:** 4 hours

**Cautions:** South of the trailhead, this linear trail has no water, rest rooms, or telephones until you reach the Lafayette Municipal Golf Course six miles south. Also, be aware of your energy level; if you reach the Wabash River and begin to feel tired, it's still closer to go back to the trailhead than to continue into Lafayette.

**Trail Directions:** Begin walking south of the Wah-ba-shik-a Nature Center **[1]**. Turn right at the trail sign, and descend concrete steps. Climb steps to the bridge across Burnett Creek. Turn left. At .2 mi., a loop trail to the right leads to historic Prophet's Rock.

Continue left along the sandy path. Turn right at the arrow on a stake. Pass between wooden barriers that keep vehicles off the trail. Cross a streamlet on a wooden bridge. Climb log steps and you've completed .5 mi. Beyond a log walkway and a wooden footbridge, the path returns to the creek. Cross another footbridge.

At 1.4 mi., the trail passes to the right of pylons **[2]** supporting highway I-65. Climb a staircase made of slim logs and root stairs. After another bridge, turn right at the arrow. At 1.8 mi., Burnett's Road **[3]**, cross the creek on steps made of concrete cylinders **[4]**. At 3.0 mi., you can see the Wabash River ahead. A .5 mi. a spur **[5]** leads to picnic tables. The main trail

divides, and you can either walk straight ahead or turn right at an arrow to walk south along the creek bank. Both routes come together again where an arrow points left to the main trail.

Climb over a rusty railing, and turn right at the road. Walk toward the old iron bridge **[6]**—you've come 3.6 mi.

Some hikers turn back here, returning to their vehicles in Battle Ground. Others have a second vehicle waiting at Davis Ferry Park or in downtown Lafayette.

Continue south. At 4.0 mi. the Wabash River flows in two channels around Heron Island **[7]**. At 5.0 mi. you'll find two picnic tables **[8]**. The trail curves left, through tall grasses, returns to the river, leaves it again, and crosses a meadow.

At about 6.0 mi., you'll see the Lafayette Municipal Golf Course **[9]**. The trail ends at Riehle Plaza. You'll reach it if you continue walking south, with the river on your right. The next park south is McAllister **[10]**.

You may see and hear small radio-controlled planes in the air above Lyboult Field **[11]**. At 7.0 mi., you'll pass Riverfront Park **[12]**, then continue south past Digby Park **[13]**. At about 7.5 mi., the Harrison Bridge spans the river on your right. Continue south on the trail along Canal Road to staircases leading to the Amtrak station, the restored Big Four Depot, and Riehle Plaza **[14]**. The trail ends about three blocks east of Lafayette's downtown.

## Wabash Heritage Trail

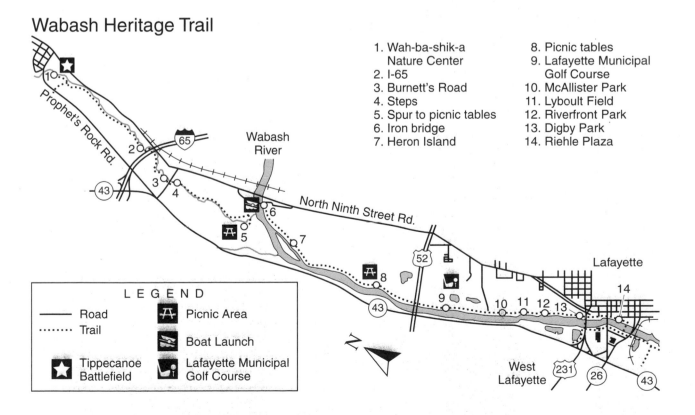

1. Wah-ba-shik-a Nature Center
2. I-65
3. Burnett's Road
4. Steps
5. Spur to picnic tables
6. Iron bridge
7. Heron Island
8. Picnic tables
9. Lafayette Municipal Golf Course
10. McAllister Park
11. Lyboult Field
12. Riverfront Park
13. Digby Park
14. Riehle Plaza

LEGEND
— Road
······· Trail
★ Tippecanoe Battlefield
🅰 Picnic Area
🚤 Boat Launch
Lafayette Municipal Golf Course

# Celery Bog Nature Area

**Distance One-Way:** 1 mile

**Estimated Hiking Time:** 45 minutes

**Cautions:** Waterproof boots are a must in this wetland nature area. Protect the wildlife habitat by keeping pets on a leash. Motorized vehicles and bicycles are not allowed on the trail.

**Trail Directions:** Drive from Lindberg Road down a curving gravel drive, past bluebird houses in a cornfield on the left and a woodsy area on the right, and park in the gravel lot **[1]**. The lot has two van-accessible parking spots, but the trails themselves are not handicapped accessible.

Walk along the woodchip path at the north end of the small parking lot. This path parallels a service road with corn stubble (in late February) on the left, brush and woods to the right. Turn right at the trailhead sign **[2]**. A section of fence, one log wide with a little rusty baling wire on it, was to the right of the path.

Continue .04 mi. to an area where the trail divides **[3]**. Turn right and follow the path, keeping right at the Y. The path slopes down toward the water past two small boulders on the left.

At .12 mi. **[4]**, a wetland information sign explains that Celery Bog is a valuable wetland that helps clean the water and stop floods. Continue along the path up a slope to a large boulder **[5]**, then turn left.

At .30 mi., another information sign **[6]** gives a history of the area, once a glacial lake, and explains the difference between a marsh (water flows through it), a bog (acidic, no water flow), and a swamp (a wetland with woody species). Celery Bog is technically a marsh, though historically called a bog. We detoured from the main trail here to take a short, narrow path between two watery areas. Watch for low branches here that may try to capture your hat.

Return to the boulder and keep going straight ahead (west). You will arrive at the spot in a more open area where the loop began. Walk to the right along the service road, and follow it toward the woods. At the entrance to the forest **[7]** at .53 mi., a sign identifies the Scifres-Maier Woods Nature Preserve. We entered the woods and walked to a Y intersection **[8]**, there keeping to the right.

At .65 mi., a boardwalk or bridge **[9]** enabled us to cross the very marshy area. A sign in the middle of the bridge explains that this was once called a "man-eating swamp," thought then to be a bottomless sinkhole, but really a shrinking wetland.

The boardwalk ends **[10]** at relatively dry land, and the path curves around to the next sign, which gives helpful information about "reading the forest." An undisturbed forest has several layers, but the sign notes that these trees are either large or small; there are no medium-sized trees here. This missing layer shows that the area was grazed at one time, so the large trees were left and the smaller plants eaten. Now the mid-sized trees are growing back.

Shortly before the path returns to the Scifres-Maier Woods sign, we saw that a large tree had fallen across the way and had been sawed into logs to clear the path. The big root end lay on one side, looking as if possibly lightning had struck, and the top lay on the left side of the path. When trees die, they are left to make homes for birds and animals. At 1 mi., we were back at the sign. Retracing our way back along the service road, dodging mud puddles, we passed the park trailhead and arrived at the parking lot.

This park is located in an urban area bordered by a new housing development, a farm, businesses, an electric substation, and streets, but Celery Bog Nature Area is a small, protected jewel for wildlife and education.

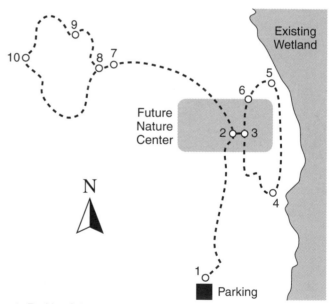

1. Parking lot
2. Trailhead sign
3. Trail divides
4. Wetland information sign
5. Large boulder
6. Wetland history sign
7. Scifres-Maier Woods entrance
8. Y intersection
9. Boardwalk begins
10. Boardwalk ends

# Purdue Blue Trail 👟

**Distance Round-Trip:** 1.75 miles

**Estimated Hiking Time:** 1.25 hours

**Cautions:** Stay alert for bicycles along Northwestern Avenue; if startled, avoid leaping in front of them!

**Trail Directions:** *Note:* The "Trees of Purdue University" trail guide provides a detailed map of the trees found along this trail. You should pick up a copy of that guide to lead you through your hike.

Begin the Blue Trail in front of the Purdue Visitor Center at the stand of river birch; see No. 1 in the leaflet. Cross Northwestern Avenue, turn right, and walk along the street. At .1 mi. American yellow-woods guard the entrance to the Physics Building. In spring, they bear white flowers; in autumn, they display coppery orange leaves. Continue along Northwestern, turn left at .2 mi., and walk along Stadium Street. At .25 mi., notice the minipark across the street; relax here while squirrels entertain you.

Return to the trail, and walk west to Stadium Mall Drive. On the opposite corner, at .3 mi., you'll see a tulip tree, the official state tree. Continue south along University Street. Pass two buildings, and you'll come to a golden-rain tree; expect yellow flowers in midsummer and bronze seed pods in the fall.

Walk farther south on University to a Siberian elm at the armory's southwest corner. Notice the tree's rough, corrugated bark and tiny leaves. Continue south to Third Street where a shingle oak shelters squirrels. Cross an access road and turn left. Walk east along the fence about 20 feet to a Kentucky coffee tree. Beyond the fence, follow a curving sidewalk south and southeast. Ahead, east of Computer Science, you'll see a tall hedge maple. Continue along the paved walk southeast, past Amur maples with slim, pointed leaves and tiny, half-wing seeds. Walk south past two buildings on the left; you'll hear the splashing of Founder's Park fountain before you see it.

Founder's Park, at .75 mi., lies in the heart of the original campus. Workers who lunch at concrete chess tables watch chipmunks skittering amid pines.

Walk southwest for the specimen hican tree, a hybrid of pecan and shellbark hickory. Return to the Founder's Park fountain, and pass a sweet gum with leaves like five-pointed stars. Walk southeast across grass to the pin oak. Take the sidewalk left, beside Stone Hall, and turn left at the sidewalk. Follow the sidewalk and drive to the corner of Stone, then cross Oval Drive to the grassy, open Memorial Mall. At 1.0 mi. walk left at an angle to the oval Katsura tree; then look right across the grass to see a memorable horse chestnut tree. *Caution:* The nuts of this tree are poisonous.

Now, look north across the open mall, and walk northwest toward a clump of trees left of the flagpole. On your left, floral plantings frame the distant Founder's Park fountain. Beneath the trees are brick paving, restful benches, and John Purdue's grave. Listen for the chatter of birds.

Continue north across the mall. A European beech tree marks the entrance to Stanley Coulter Hall. Turn right, past benches, then turn left before the wall. Walk toward the Bell Tower, but turn left at the corner, then walk west to 1.25 mi. Turn right, walk past the Psychology Building, and turn that corner. Cross a service road to find the black locust trees and the Peirce pines, planted in 1874. Continue west, noticing the basswood stands by the Psychology Building.

Now, follow the curving walk northwest and north, past the parking meters. The trail becomes a gray, surfaced path after the armory. On the right, a black walnut tree is nature's feeding station. At 1.5 mi., note the red oak across the grass. Cross the road and walk toward Schleman Hall (SCHL) to locate the sergeant cherry and the tall, slim red pines.

Next, round the corner, walk to Creative Arts 3, then turn northeast between two buildings. Cross the road, turn right at the Physics Building, and walk to the corner. On the right is Purdue Mall, where Loeb Fountain spouts like a geyser over modern sculpture. The ash trees are left of the kiosk. Walk northeast under the skywalk to the parking garage across the street at 1.75 mi.

# Purdue Gold Trail 👢

**Distance Round-Trip:** 1.5 miles

**Estimated Hiking Time:** 1 hour

**Cautions:** Be alert for bicycles. Use caution when crossing the streets.

**Trail Directions:** *Note:* The "Trees of Purdue University" trail guide provides a detailed map of the trees found along this trail. You should pick up a copy of that guide to lead you through your hike.

Cross Northwestern Avenue to the Materials and Electrical Engineering (MSEE) building. Turn left, walk southeast, then turn right at the corner; watch for chipmunks as you walk beneath the skywalk. Turn left around the corner of the Electrical Engineering building (EE); the trail begins with a bitternut hickory at the left of EE's entrance.

Cross a service road, and walk toward Knoy Hall of Technology (KNOY). You'll follow a curving sidewalk past a fat pine tree. Cross a terrace with concrete benches and urns of flowers. At .1 mi. No. 2, north of KNOY, marks a windbreak of Canadian hemlock. Continue toward Northwestern Avenue, but turn right at the rock. At the corner of KNOY, discover a pair of Serbian spruce trees.

Continue south along KNOY; the walkway becomes a Y. After observing No. 4, an American beech tree, take the right fork of the walk beside the Nuclear Engineering (NUCL) building. At the southeast corner of NUCL, walk left around a hedge to No. 5, a sycamore maple set in a grassy lawn with a metal fence. Follow the walkway south, cross a service road at .25 mi., and stay on the walkway near the street; you'll find a persimmon tree at the southeast corner of Grissom Hall (GRIS).

Continue southwest, across the drive. Walk south along busy Grant Street to find No. 7 east of the Purdue Memorial Union Club (PMUC). At .5 mi. at the corner of Purdue Memorial Union (PMU) stands a splendid, white pine. At the corner of Grant and State, a clump of redbud trees bloom every spring.

Walk toward the reflecting pool to find No. 10, a hedge maple. At the southwest corner of PMU, a large, silver linden with many branches shades a main floor terrace. Cross the walkway to Stewart Center (STEW), where a Swiss stone pine (No. 12) guards the southeast corner.

Return to the walkway between STEW and the Purdue Union Building (PUB); turn right and walk between the concrete benches toward State Street, but do not go to it. Instead, turn right at the lamppost, and follow a walkway with plantings on both sides. You'll pass No. 13, a cut-leaf beech with fine leaves. Cross the sidewalk at the end of the Hicks Undergraduate

Library (HIKS) and look right to see No. 14 beside the entrance to STEW. Walk west toward the southeast corner of STEW. Notice No. 15, an Allegheny serviceberry, on the right. Turn north, along the end of STEW; beyond the building's northwest corner is a honey locust. Turn right, going east along the north wall of STEW, and you'll have walked .75 mi.

You'll find the next five tree specimens scattered along the south side of Academy Park. No. 17, a chestnut oak, has a tannin used in treating leather. East, across the sidewalk, examine a trident maple. Continue east along the north wall of STEW and cross the walkway to PMU. Left of the entrance, discover a trio of American holly trees.

Walk northwest across the paved brick circle to find a pair of pear trees, one chanticleer, the other redspire, rising from the grassy mound. Walk northwest to find trees No. 22 through 24 sheltered between three campus buildings. At the southeast corner of Wetherill (WTHR) is a pyramidal English oak. Walk north between WTHR and Heavilon Hall (HEAV). On the left, beyond concrete benches, look for a tree with a twisted shape and scaly bark. This is an ironwood tree, known for its strength.

Walk east, between Brown (BRWN) and HEAV. On the right, a decorative oak-leaf mountain ash produces white flowers in spring, red fruit in the fall. Continue east between BRWN and HEAV, 1.0 mi. Just past the buildings, turn left, then take the walkway northeast.

You'll find the next six trees in a straggly line north of GRIS and BRWN. Cross a parking lot to reach the rugged hackberry tree at the corner of GRIS. The trail heads west along BRWN; you'll pass a Chinese dogwood, a white fringe tree, and a red buckeye. Continue on the walkway as it curves north. On the left is a shagbark hickory (No. 29).

Cross the service road diagonally to find a pair of osage orange trees at the northwest corner of BRWN. Cross the service road again, and to the right of a yellow fire hydrant, note No. 31, a planting of blue beeches. Continue west; turn right just before the bicycle racks, and follow the walkway north. On the right, there's a cluster of ornamental Washington hawthorns. At 1.25 mi. continue north along the west side of Potter Engineering Center (POTR); you'll come to No. 33, a dogwood known for its lavish spring display.

Walk west. On the right, at the Loeb Fountain plaza, the walkway has been enhanced by crabapple trees. Return to the walkway. Turn left and walk toward the skywalk, past an interesting metal sculpture. The south side of Materials and Electrical Engineering (MSEE) has been planted with groves of snowdrift crabapple (No. 36). That's the last marker; cross Northwestern to the parking garage, at 1.5 mi.

# 19.  McCormick's Creek State Park

- Follow trails through scenic canyons and forested ravines that were once a hunting ground for Miami Indians.
- Choose from nine trails that range in difficulty from easy to rugged.
- Explore historic Wolf Cave, the focus of many legends.
- Hike past bubbling creeks where water flows over exposed bedrock.
- Learn about ferns, such as maidenhair, silvery spleenwort, blunt-lobed woodsia, and many others that grow along the trail.

## Area Information

McCormick's Creek, named after the first settler in the area, flows through a rugged canyon before it joins the broader White River. Washed by streams, eroded by water and wind, this flat and rolling land, with its deep indentations, was created by massive, glacial action. Miami Indians, who once camped along the White River, used the rugged creek and canyon as a hunting ground; here, they found a plentiful supply of deer, turkeys, grouse, squirrels, and other game.

In 1816, John McCormick established a 100-acre homestead near the canyon and waterfalls. McCormick and other settlers cut sections of forest for farming and grazed livestock on the flatter uplands. Residents of the area enjoyed picnics and hikes at McCormick's Creek throughout the 19th century. Eventually, the creek's rugged setting and scenic beauty prompted a physician to buy land here in 1888. Dr. Denkewalter built a sanitarium on the site of what's now the Canyon Inn.

McCormick's Creek was Indiana's first state park, dedicated in 1916. Originally just 350 acres, the park now covers 1,853 acres. A small cave, two natural stone bridges, and distinctive formations of exposed bedrock, along with the cliffs and waterfalls, make this park special. What's more, 115 species of spring wildflowers have been sighted in the park; here, spring flowers bloom during March, April, and May. You can see snow trillium, hepatica, bloodroot, Dutchman's breeches, trout lily, shooting star, violets, bluets, and other species. The peak time for seeing diverse blooms is the last week of April.

**Directions:** The entrance to the park is two miles southeast of Spencer on SR 46.

**Hours Open:** The park is open year-round.

**Facilities:** The Canyon Inn has guest rooms and a dining room open to the public. You can also find camping, cabins, a nature center, picnic areas, a saddle barn, a swimming pool, tennis courts, and a large recreation center.

**Permits and Rules:** Do not injure or damage wildlife or any of the park's natural features or built structures. Keep dogs and cats on leashes. Set up camp, build fires, and swim only in designated places. Motorists should observe speed limits and drive only on park roads. Snowmobiles are prohibited.

**Further Information:** Canyon Inn, P.O. Box 71, Spencer, IN 47460; 812-829-4881. McCormick's Creek State Park, Route 5, Box 282, Spencer, IN 47460; 812-829-2235.

## Other Areas of Interest

**Morgan-Monroe State Forest,** a scenic forest reserve near Martinsville, has small lakes, a nature preserve, campsites, picnic shelters, and hiking trails; 765-342-4026.

---

## Park Trails

Trails are marked with posts keyed to trail numbers. However, you will find such posts only now and then.

**Trail 3** 👢👢👢👢—2 miles—Begin hiking at the falls, and follow the creek bed downstream.

Wildflowers are plentiful in the spring. The trail ends near the old quarry.

**Trail 9** 👢—1.5 miles—This loop route that circles an old water tower begins at Deer Run Picnic Area, passes fields, and goes through forests.

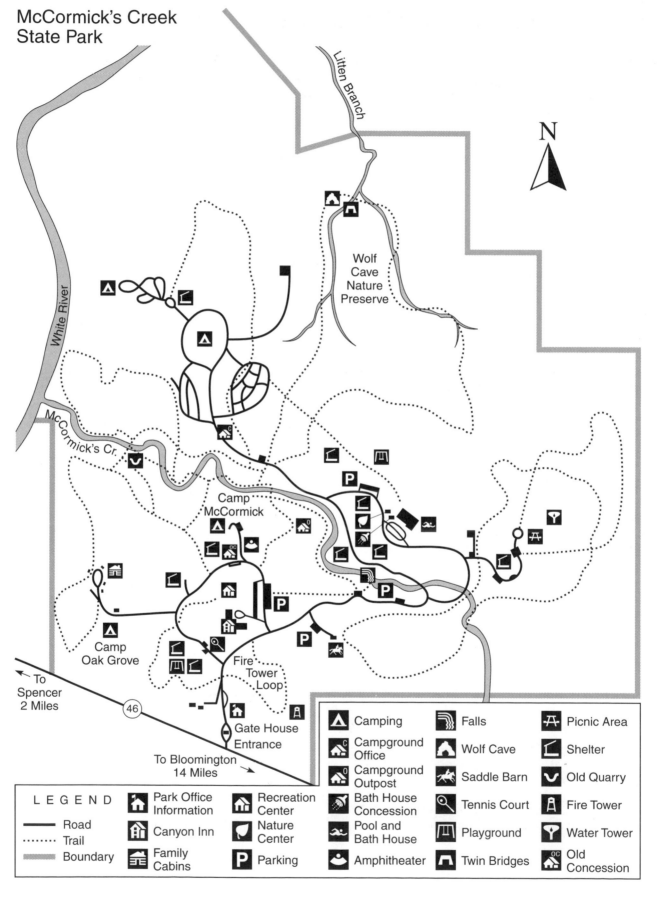

# McCormick's Creek State Park

**Litten Branch**

**White River**

**McCormick's Cr.**

Wolf Cave Nature Preserve

Camp McCormick

Camp Oak Grove

Fire Tower Loop

Gate House Entrance

46

← To Spencer 2 Miles

To Bloomington 14 Miles →

| | | |
|---|---|---|
| Camping | Falls | Picnic Area |
| Campground Office | Wolf Cave | Shelter |
| Campground Outpost | Saddle Barn | Old Quarry |
| Bath House Concession | Tennis Court | Fire Tower |
| Pool and Bath House | Playground | Water Tower |
| Amphitheater | Twin Bridges | Old Concession |

**LEGEND**

— Road
···· Trail
▬ Boundary

Park Office Information
Canyon Inn
Family Cabins

Recreation Center
Nature Center
Parking

# Fire Tower Loop (Trail 4) 🥾🥾🥾

**Distance One-Way:** 1.9 miles

**Estimated Hiking Time:** 1.5 hours

**Cautions:** Parts of the trail are not well marked. To follow one unmarked segment, walk forward along the creek bed. Also, the trail was much rougher and the mosquitoes especially pesky during the last 1.2 miles.

**Trail Directions:** Find the trailhead [1] about 30 yards southeast of Canyon Inn, across the road. Although unmarked, you'll recognize the wide, clay path that turns to gravel and enters a beech-maple forest. The trail veers right as it descends into a ravine. The path crosses a creek bed then climbs the hill; as you walk, enjoy a look at the picturesque ravine on the left. Ahead, the path becomes pine needles, then turns left.

At .2 mi., walk right onto a wide, gravel area [2] that looks like a road. This packed, gravel path veers left, past young elm and tulip trees at the forest edge; there's a forested ravine and low ridge on the right. Continue up a slight hill; we saw splendid ferns on a shady slope on the right. Notice the way these leaves divide, and you might identify them. There are three types. Once-cut ferns divide into leaflets. Twice-cut ferns have leaflets and subleaflets, and thrice-cut ferns further divide into lobes. Can you find any once-cut ferns? They might be one of these three: the once-cut Christmas tree fern, an evergreen that has an ear at its base; the once-cut ebony spleenwort, which has a dark brown, shiny, smooth stalk; or the once-cut sensitive fern, with wavy-edged leaflets, cut deeply in toward the stem.

At .3 mi. [3], cross an old, narrow, unused road; beyond it, a fire tower rises from a clearing. The tower has 106 steps, claims a 10-year-old girl who's just come down them. The trail, still gravel, curves right. At .35 mi., there's a sign for Trail 4 [4], directing you left. The forests are wonderful, with many feathery black walnut trees; the trail meanders along the top of a ridge.

At .5 mi., take a wooden bridge [5] across a streamlet. At .7 mi., the trail crosses the park entrance road [6] north of the gatehouse. Continue walking straight to stay on the trail; you'll cross a grassy clearing and reenter the woods. Beyond, a wooden railing helps buttress the packed dirt path. Note that the trail will get much rougher from now on; you'll encounter roots, sand, stones, and other natural debris on a path that follows a tiny tributary creek downstream.

At .8 mi., you may still hear traffic on a park road. Then, the path leaves the creek and widens; here it has been topped with gravel. Follow this route as it turns back upstream through another creek valley. At 1.0 mi. [7], note the huge chunks of broken bedrock beside the water. Limestone quarries once operated in the area, but were not successful; it was difficult to get the huge chunks out. The trail crosses the creek; walk across on logs, sticks, rocks—whatever looks steady. Ahead is a wooden bridge.

The trail leads uphill again; here, railroad tie steps aid hikers to follow another ridge. At 1.45 mi., you cross a park road [8]. There's a grassy area with picnic shelters on the right. Continue walking forward, across the grass; then look along the edge of the forest. You'll see a Trail 4 sign. At 1.7 mi., continue through the forest. The trail ends at the Recreation Center [9].

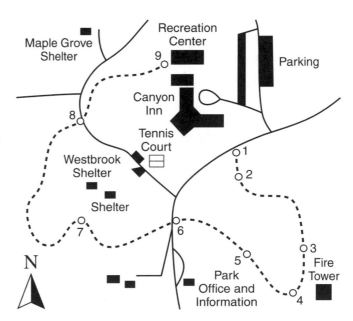

1. Trailhead
2. Gravel area
3. Old road
4. Trail 4 sign
5. Wooden bridge
6. Park road
7. Bedrock
8. Park road
9. Recreation Center

# Wolf Cave Trail (Trail 5) 👢👢👢

**Distance Round-Trip:** 2.5 miles

**Estimated Hiking Time:** 1.75 hours

**Cautions:** Take a flashlight to use when exploring the cave. Wear long pants to prevent scraped knees when crawling through the cave.

**Trail Directions:** Use the parking lot **[1]** for Wolf Cave Nature Preserve. Walk north into an old maple-beech forest. You'll soon pass large, funnel-shaped depressions called sinkholes, the surface covered with ferns and other greenery. At .1 mi. **[2]**, the trail will take you down into and up out of one of these sinkholes. As you walk, notice the cracked limestone bedrock that juts out here and there in the streambed.

At .23 mi. **[3]**, Trail 8 crosses the one you follow (Trail 5). Continue walking straight ahead over a gravel and pressed-earth path. Note the large, impressive beech trees, their smooth gray bark marred by the carvings of initials. While we walked we heard a bird call "whi-whi-weep," but could not identify it.

The trail dips into a ravine, heads across a wooden bridge, passes a bench, and goes down embedded rock steps before curving to the left. At .5 mi. **[4]**, you'll cross one of the streambeds that feed Litton Branch. When we crossed, the streambed was dry, making it easy to see how gravel and weakly acidic groundwater widened the cracks in the bedrock.

At .9 mi. **[5]**, you'll see Wolf Cave to the right. The low, wide opening, set in a half circle of rocks, is deceptive, because the long, narrow cave passageway extends southwest of the entrance for about 100 feet. In some places, the roof of the passageway is only 2.9, 3.6, or 1.7 feet above the cave floor. From the far end of it you can see the Twin Bridges **[6]**, a pair of natural arches that were once part of a more elaborate cave system. After exiting the cave, walk around it and return to the entrance; then walk right on the main trail.

The trail curves right, and there's a confirming sign for Trail 5 at 1.0 mi. **[7]**. You'll cross another small stream via a wooden bridge. The water splashes and gurgles over a rocky streambed as it flows toward Litton Branch. In one place, it forms a tiny waterfall as it spills over bedrock slabs.

At 1.27 mi. **[8]**, the trail crosses the stream again. In fact, the creek is only one of a network of streambeds in this wide and lovely ravine. You'll pass giant sinkholes with restful benches here and there. The trail meanders across the creek twice more, following it upstream.

At 1.5 mi. you'll continue walking through forest. We enjoyed seeing the black locust trees in bloom and saw many mayapples, but blossom time was over.

At 1.8 mi. **[9]**, the trail makes a sharp right turn. These hiking trails, you may recall, were used by Miami Indians, as well as the wealthy residents of a sanitarium that once stood on the site of the present Canyon Inn. At 2.0 mi. continue walking on the curving trail. At 2.3 mi. **[10]**, the trail crosses Trail 8 again. Keep walking straight ahead to eventually reach the park road that leads to the campground. Walk left along this road, and you'll be back at the parking lot. The hike ends here at 2.5 mi.

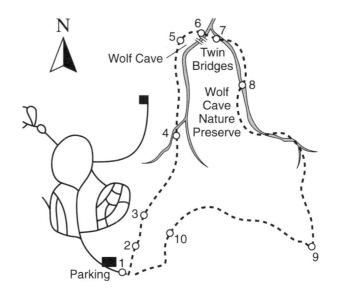

| | |
|---|---|
| 1. Parking lot | 6. Twin Bridges |
| 2. Sinkhole | 7. Sign for Trail 5 |
| 3. Trail 8 | 8. Stream crossing |
| 4. Streambed | 9. Right turn |
| 5. Wolf Cave | 10. Trail 8 |

# 20.  Indianapolis Parks and Recreation

- Circle a lake that's now a bird sanctuary, located within one of the nation's largest urban parks.
- Walk wooded park trails that explore the former estates and gardens of the city's wealthy families.
- Follow a self-guided trail that features native wildflowers, as well as hummingbird, butterfly, and aquatic gardens.
- Hike past a segment of the early canal in the Broad Ripple neighborhood.
- Follow long, urban trails over former railroad beds that link city neighborhoods.

## Area Information

Located at the confluence of the White River and its several tributaries, the capital city of Indiana now sprawls over the surrounding Central Till Plain. This web of scenic rivers, banked by low hills and transformed over the centuries by erosion, enhances the appeal of this commercial hub city.

Miami Indians and people of the Delaware and other tribes once hunted along these rivers. In fact, the name Indianapolis means peopled by Indians. The Delaware lived along the White River in bark houses and grew maize, beans, and squash. The first white settler in the area, a Frenchman known as LaSalle, arrived by canoe in 1681. Game was still abundant and fish still plentiful in the waterways used as travel routes through dense, hardwood forests. By 1845, a substantial number of settlers— many from Scotland, Ireland, and Germany—had displaced these tribes.

**Directions:** Drive to Eagle Creek Park via I-65 and exit at 71st Street; follow signs to the park's north entrance. To reach Holliday Park, follow US 31 (Meridian Street) to the intersection of 64th Street (west) and Arden Drive (east). Note that the Holliday Park trails described are on both sides of Meridian Street.

**Hours Open:** Eagle Creek Park is open year-round from dawn to dusk. Holliday Park is also open year-round.

**Facilities:** Eagle Creek has a marina, swimming beach, nature center complex, amphitheater, ice skating pond, lodge, and retreat house. Holliday Park has a visitor center, rock garden, wedding circle, some ruins, flower gardens, and several overlooks.

**Permits and Rules:** All plants, animals, and structures within the park are protected by city ordinance. Please do not litter. Gathering firewood and building ground fires are prohibited. Dogs must be on leashes. No snowmobiles, saddle horses, or ice fishing are allowed. Please keep valuables locked in the car trunk.

**Further Information:** Eagle Creek Park Office, 7840 West 56th Street, Indianapolis, IN 46254; 317-327-7110. For Holliday Park and other parks call Indianapolis Parks and Recreation; 317-327-7275.

## Other Areas of Interest

**Fitness trails** have been developed at the following parks: Bellamy, Broad Ripple, Brookside, Christian, Douglass, Eagle Creek, Garfield, Riverside, Sahm, and Southeastway. Be aware that the city limits of Indianapolis are at the Marion County line. Call Indianapolis Parks and Recreation; 317-327-7275.

## Park Trails

For the Eagle Creek Bird Sanctuary Loop, walk around the lake; this trail is not marked, so orient yourself to the lake. The Eagle Creek Nature Walk, the short loop, although not marked, is well defined. Holliday Park has an interlocking network of paths; minor junctions may not be marked at all. Here, orient yourself to the parking lots (on the upper level) and the river (down below).

The 3,100-acre Eagle Creek Park has 10 miles of hiking trails. Special trails include a Fitness Trail and a permanent Volksmarch route. Trails link Lilly Lake, the marina, amphitheater, and the water sports center; 317-327-7110.

Holliday Park features several short trails on wooded hills that slope down toward the White River; 317-327-7275.

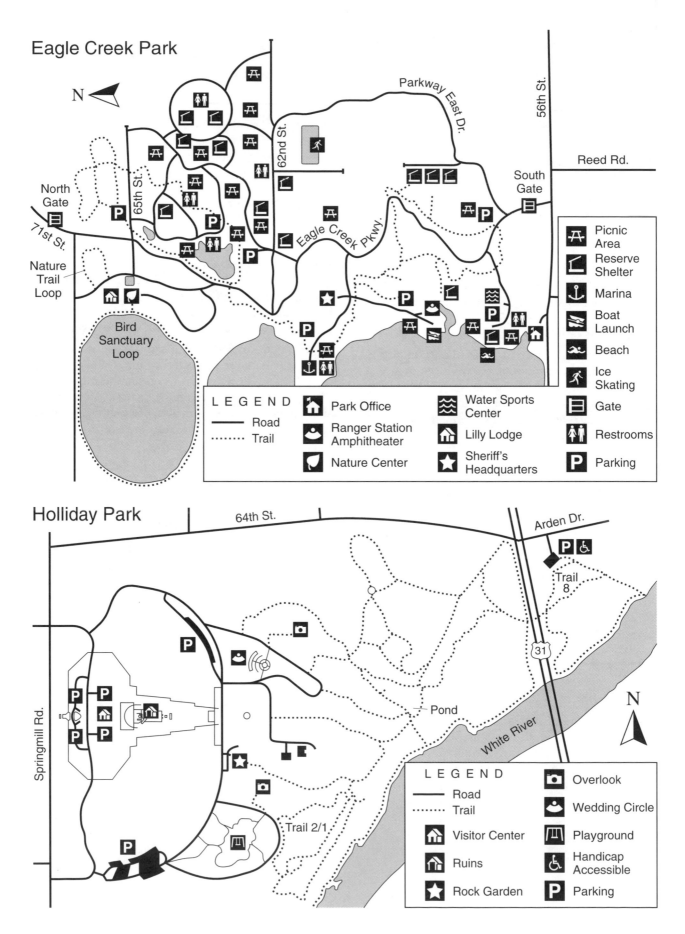

# Eagle Creek Park

N

Parkway East Dr.

56th St.

Reed Rd.

62nd St.

65th St.

North Gate

71st St.

Nature Trail Loop

Bird Sanctuary Loop

Eagle Creek Pkwy.

South Gate

## LEGEND

—— Road

· · · · · Trail

🏠 Park Office

👤 Ranger Station Amphitheater

🍃 Nature Center

〰️ Water Sports Center

🏠 Lilly Lodge

⭐ Sheriff's Headquarters

🏕️ Picnic Area

⛺ Reserve Shelter

⚓ Marina

🚤 Boat Launch

🏊 Beach

⛸️ Ice Skating

🚪 Gate

🚻 Restrooms

🅿️ Parking

# Holliday Park

64th St.

Arden Dr.

🅿️ ♿

Trail 8

31

Springmill Rd.

Pond

White River

Trail 2/1

N

## LEGEND

—— Road

· · · · · Trail

🏠 Visitor Center

🏠 Ruins

⭐ Rock Garden

📷 Overlook

👤 Wedding Circle

🎠 Playground

♿ Handicap Accessible

🅿️ Parking

# Eagle Creek Bird Sanctuary Loop 👢👢👢

**Distance Round-Trip:** 1.24 miles

**Estimated Hiking Time:** 1 hour

**Cautions:** We had to walk across a logjam under water between segments of the unmarked trail that circles the lake.

**Trail Directions:** Drive to the Nature Center. The trail begins on the south side of the building **[1]**. You'll walk on a bark trail between wooden fences. We passed a red-tailed hawk perched on a limb inside its cage. Just past a series of cages, the trail turns slightly left and follows a fence into a maple-beech forest.

At .06 mi. **[2]**, the trail merges with a paved road, then continues right, entering the forest again as it begins a loop around the lake. You'll walk clockwise—just stay left of the round lake. Ignore a narrow path to the left; then at .16 mi. **[3]** walk through an opening in a chain-link fence.

The trail curves left around some trees, before coming to an observation point at .23 mi. **[4]**. After enjoying a view of the lake, ignore a path at the left, and take a path to the right, downhill. The trail then becomes a gravel path, which follows a ridge before it curves right. As we walked out on this peninsula, we heard meadowlarks and other songbirds in the prairie grasses on the left. At .5 mi. **[5]**, stay on the gravel path as it curves around the lake. Here, we saw the first of many spicebushes, with round, bright red berries and pointed, dark green leaves.

At .65 mi. **[6]**, the path turns to cross an earthen embankment that divides the bird sanctuary lake from the larger reservoir to the left. Unfortunately, the chilly drizzle the day we were there kept us from seeing any birds. At .82 mi. **[7]** where there's a chain across the path, walk right. Ahead, the path widens until it could almost be a road; there are gravel mounds on the left. We noticed cottonwood trees growing beside the lake, with their scalloped, heart-shaped leaves, and some large sycamores, their pale, patchy bark wrapped with wild grapevines.

At 1.0 mi. **[8]**, the path turns to a dark gray, hard surface; here, we encountered another chain across the path—this one was rusty, probably meant to deter motor vehicles. Crawl under (or climb over) the chain, and you'll walk on a wide, roadlike course past a ravine filled with weathered logs on the left. At 1.1 mi. **[9]**, a wooden deck provides an overlook, a lovely view of the lake, here framed by oak trees. By 1.2 mi. **[10]**, we've arrived at Lilly Lodge. This building, along with a similar one housing the Nature Center, was constructed in the mid-20th century. These woodland lodges were intended as retreats; now the Lilly Lodge is used for meetings.

Continue walking south, and at 1.24 mi., you'll be back at the Nature Center. Note that the center has a wildlife viewing area inside—a great place to watch wildlife on a drizzly day.

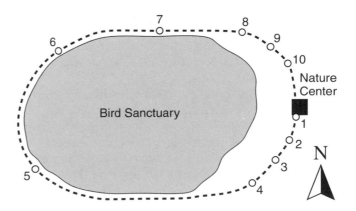

1. Nature Center
2. Trail merge
3. Fence opening
4. Observation point
5. Gravel path curves
6. Earthen embankment
7. Chain
8. Surface changes
9. Wooden deck
10. Lilly Lodge

# Nature Trail Loop 🥾

**Distance Round-Trip:** .3 mile

**Estimated Hiking Time:** 30 minutes

**Cautions:** The trail has a surface of natural debris. Wear closed shoes, not sandals, to protect your feet.

**Trail Directions:** Park at the Nature Center. Walk north, following signs to Lilly Lodge. The building, now used for small conferences, was once a woodland retreat for the Eli Lilly family. The trail begins [1] across the road.

You'll walk on a bark mulch path into a mature forest where large beech and maple trees grow. You'll also find yellow poplar (tulip trees), white ash, and black cherry trees. In fact, Eagle Creek Park, which includes open meadows and wooded terrain, as well as the lake, has more than 100 varieties of trees.

At .04 mi., there's a giant beech tree [2] broken off at the top of its trunk. Turkey vultures have built a nest there. We saw delicate shell fungus growing on a fallen log and several distinctive, small trees with surprisingly large leaves. These trees are pawpaws, says my companion. And the high, even notes coming from that hidden bird? That's the song of a wood thrush, she claims.

Amazing how much more we see when a naturalist walks with us! It's remarkable how what's most vital in a forest often remains hidden from view. High in the branches of another large beech tree, the naturalist says, there's a nest made by great horned owls. At .05 mi., we take the left branch [3] of the forked trail—the other branch leads to the road.

White-tailed deer often wander through this preserve. We looked for footprints, but didn't see any. At .07 mi., we encountered a large beech tree on the left, near other giant, fallen beech trees that look as if they were ripped from the earth. Some of the beeches still living here, it is said, have been here for centuries; one particular Douglas fir log is reportedly 600 years old.

At .11 mi., the trail ends at the pavement in front of Lilly Lodge. Walk south, along the edge of the forest and back toward the Nature Center. On the way, look for a bear print [4] on one of the beech trees, said to have been etched there by Daniel Boone. Although this may or may not be true, Boone did travel through Eagle Creek valley, during a trip he made while working as a surveyor for the U.S. government. This hike ends at the Nature Center.

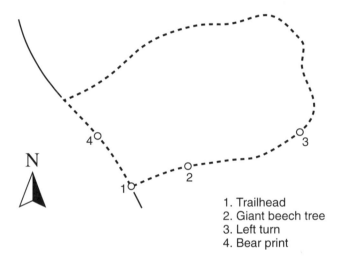

N

1. Trailhead
2. Giant beech tree
3. Left turn
4. Bear print

# Holliday Park—Trail 8 🥾

**Distance Round-Trip:** .4 mile

**Estimated Hiking Time:** 30 minutes

**Cautions:** Be careful when crossing Meridian Street after the hike ends. Walk on the designated trail. Also, note that the .1-mile path to the river is paved for wheelchairs and strollers.

**Trail Directions:** Drive to the intersection of US 31 (Meridian Street) and Arden Drive. Turn east on Arden Drive, and park in the paved lot southeast of the intersection. Walk on a paved trail that starts downhill from the corner of the parking lot **[1]**. Continue walking through shadowy woodland; there are dark rocks left of the trail. You'll see hawthorn and sycamore trees, with violets in bloom if you come in the spring.

At .05 mi. **[2]**, one branch of the trail leads down to the White River, a distance of another .05 mi. At the river is a small, wooden pier **[3]**, often used by fishermen.

Also at .05 mi., another branch of Trail 8 goes right. Follow it and you'll soon cross a long, wooden bridge **[4]**. The forest has a landscaped look, with white stones placed here and there in the ground cover. The smooth, dirt path, with its border of timber, resembles a woodland path in a country estate. Yet, this is a city park.

At .15 mi., you'll walk under large arches that support Meridian Street **[5]**, and you can hear the traffic overhead. Ahead are giant elms and feathery-leaved black walnut trees, many draped with wild grapevines. Among them, a few tangled, dead vines

look like twisted ropes. At .21 mi., Trail 7 goes left **[6]**, while Trail 8 curves right, where marshy plants border the trail. You'll cross another long, wooden bridge over a tiny creek as you walk through a picturesque ravine. Notice the streambed of sand and gravel.

At .32 mi., Trail 6 goes left **[7]**; turn right to complete Trail 8, which follows a gravel path, bordered with wood, and use the gravel steps **[8]** to climb up 64th Street. To return to the parking lot, cross busy Meridian Street (there is no walk light). Use caution. Or, walk back down the gravel steps, and return over the trail that brought you.

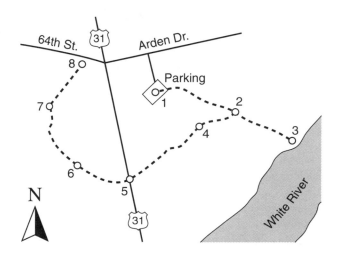

| | |
|---|---|
| 1. Trailhead | 5. Meridian Street |
| 2. Trail branch | 6. Trail intersection |
| 3. Pier | 7. Right turn |
| 4. Bridge | 8. Gravel steps |

# Holliday Park—Trails 2 and 1 👢👢

**Distance Round-Trip:** .5 mile

**Estimated Hiking Time:** 30 minutes

**Cautions:** The park trails are a series of interlocking loop trails; they are quite short and not well marked. To return to the parking lot, go away from the river and back up the hill.

**Trail Directions:** Trail 2 begins southeast of the playground, beyond the loop drive. It's marked by the number 2 and an arrow on a rock **[1]**. The gravel path crosses a grassy area before it enters the cool, shadowy forest. At .05 mi., you come to a T junction **[2]**. Either way is correct—you'll walk around either side of a loop.

At .09 mi., the path turns right, with steps going down; use this route (which is not marked) as a spur trail to the river **[3]**. You can hear the gurgling of a creek and see the broad White River through the trees. At .14 mi., return to the gravel and wooden steps. Climb the steps, turn left, and continue walking on the gravel path. This is probably Trail 1, but there were no signs. Below, on the left, there's a leafy glade and a network of tiny creeks that flow into the river.

You'll walk a narrow (two- to three-foot) gravel path with a wooden border. The hillside on the right has low ground cover, assorted shrubs, and slim, young trees. At .22 mi., continue along this gravel path that skirts the hillside. A long, silty pond now fills the low area at your left. Beyond it, there's the river. At .24 mi., wooden steps at your left provide another spur trail to the river. Continue walking straight, and cross the wooden bridge, the route to the remainder of the trail.

At .27 mi., a wooden bench, surrounded by forest, stands beside a trickling stream. If you continue forward, you'll see a wooden deck with an overlook **[4]**, which has a view of marvelous black walnut and redbud trees and little wildflowers with petals that resemble four-leafed clovers. At .3 mi., turn left and climb the wooden staircase. In early summer, we saw forget-me-nots in bloom here. At .35 mi., the low spiderwort makes a lovely ground cover with its dark, waxy leaves. By .4 mi., you've reached another wooden overlook **[5]**. Beyond it, up the hill, there's a wildflower garden; we especially enjoyed the coneflowers.

Short, but sweet, this hike ends here.

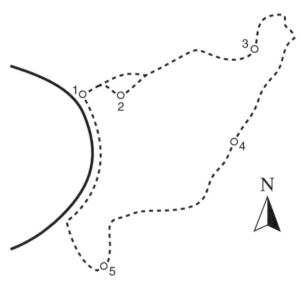

1. Arrow on a rock
2. T junction
3. Spur to river
4. Overlook
5. Overlook

# 21. White River State Park

- Take a nature break, yet still see the skyline of bustling downtown Indianapolis.
- Follow a canal between museum plazas, office parks, and apartment complexes.
- See a historic canal that flows into a modern channel, then spills into the White River.
- Enjoy watching ducks that make this canal their home.

## Area Information

Known as the Crossroads of America, Indianapolis has been a transportation center since its earliest inhabitants traded from bark canoes. Early residents shipped timber downstream by flatboat; during the steamboat era, the community became a trading center for the region.

An early 19th-century transportation plan called for canals, a network of waterways linked to navigable rivers. Authorized in 1836, the Central Canal project intended to link the Wabash and Erie Canal with the Ohio River. By 1839, however, the Indiana government lacked the necessary funds. Eventually, completed sections of the canal were used for hydraulic power, fresh water, and recreation.

Today, you can stroll beside a section of this early waterway in the Canal Walk District, where it flows into a modern canal in the 250-acre White River State Park.

**Directions:** From I-65 or I-70 take a downtown exit and drive to Monument Circle. Two blocks south of the circle, turn west and proceed to 801 West Washington Street. Here, follow signs and a trail of arborvitae in concrete tubs around the old brick Beveridge Paper Company building to find the Pumphouse Visitor Center.

**Hours Open:** The Riverwalk Promenade and the Canal Walk are open year-round. Gates at the Riverwalk Promenade open during daylight hours.

**Facilities:** The Pumphouse Visitor Center, with its rest rooms, drinking water, and picnic tables, opens daily year-round except state holidays. Call 317-634-4567 for hours.

**Permits and Rules:** Bicycles, motorcycles, and other vehicles are prohibited on the Riverwalk Promenade; climbing on the boulders is not allowed. Use trailside containers for trash. Swimming in the canal is prohibited.

**Further Information:** White River State Park, 801 West Washington Street, Indianapolis, IN 46204; 317-634-4567.

## Other Areas of Interest

Within White River State Park, the **Indianapolis Zoo,** 1200 West Washington Street, abuts the Riverwalk Promenade. Set in a 164-acre complex and open from 9:00 A.M. daily, year-round, the zoo has nearly 4,000 animals, many in simulated natural habitats; the state's largest aquarium; and daily dolphin shows. Call 317-630-2001.

**Broad Ripple Park,** one of 140 public parks in Indianapolis, flanks the White River between Broad Ripple Avenue and 64th Street. Known for its restaurants, the Broad Ripple neighborhood also has a section of early canal. Call Indianapolis Department of Parks and Recreation; 317-327-7428.

Stroll across the 152-acre grounds of the **Indianapolis Museum of Art,** 1200 West 38th Street. Admire the architecture of five art pavilions while walking past extensive gardens with lovely White River valley views; 317-923-1331.

## Park Trails

White River State Park has only two trails.

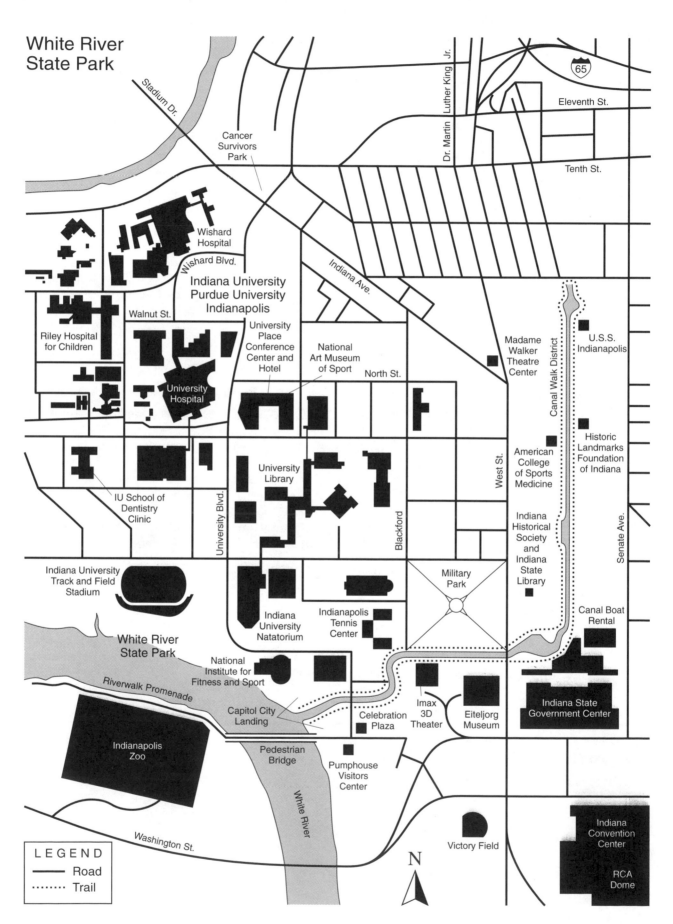

## White River State Park

Stadium Dr.

Dr. Martin Luther King Jr.

65

Eleventh St.

Tenth St.

Cancer Survivors Park

Wishard Hospital

Wishard Blvd.

Indiana Ave.

Indiana University Purdue University Indianapolis

Walnut St.

Riley Hospital for Children

University Place Conference Center and Hotel

National Art Museum of Sport

North St.

Madame Walker Theatre Center

Canal Walk District

U.S.S. Indianapolis

University Hospital

West St.

American College of Sports Medicine

Historic Landmarks Foundation of Indiana

University Library

Senate Ave.

IU School of Dentistry Clinic

University Blvd.

Blackford

Indiana Historical Society and Indiana State Library

Indiana University Track and Field Stadium

Military Park

Canal Boat Rental

White River State Park

Indiana University Natatorium

Indianapolis Tennis Center

Riverwalk Promenade

National Institute for Fitness and Sport

Capitol City Landing

Celebration Plaza

Imax 3D Theater

Eiteljorg Museum

Indiana State Government Center

Indianapolis Zoo

Pedestrian Bridge

Pumphouse Visitors Center

White River

Washington St.

Victory Field

Indiana Convention Center

RCA Dome

### LEGEND
—— Road
········ Trail

N

# Riverwalk Promenade 🥾

**Distance Round-Trip:** 1.7 miles

**Estimated Hiking Time:** 55 minutes

**Cautions:** The park staff locks heavy, swinging gates at posted times (after dark) each day; complete this hike in daylight.

**Trail Directions:** Turn left in front of the Pumphouse Visitor Center [1], and cross the Pedestrian Bridge [2]. The trail appears on the right, flanked by pines and limestone boulders, and veers toward the White River. Designed by architects and walled by 1,272 giant limestone boulders, the trail has been lined with trees that bloom in the spring or bear edible fruit. You can also reach the trailhead via a path around the south side of the zoo.

The walk begins down a straightaway; here and there, blocks and plantings [3] frame the skyline of downtown Indianapolis beyond White River State Park. On the right, the modern white globes and black posts add distinction to the Pedestrian Bridge, once used for traffic on the old National Road. Below, you may see ducks standing on rocks in the river, shaking water from their wings.

At .8 mi. the trail turns [4] to follow the river. Here, you'll find carved information about Indiana limestone, used in the Empire State Building in New York and the Washington, D.C. National Cathedral.

Notice the white pine plantings used along the trail as windbreaks. In the spring, trailside magnolia and dogwood trees bloom in a profusion of red, white, and pink. Notice the serviceberry trees, favored by birds and by runners, who stop to nibble the fruit.

At .9 mi. the Rose Window [5], a stone and steel wheel, seven feet, six inches in diameter, stands among evergreens. In some places, triple-stacked limestone blocks form walls 15 feet high. In other locations, these blocks form benches, tables, or even windows framing river views.

Indiana limestone was formed after a vast sea covered the Midwest more than 300 million years ago. The exoskeletons of marine creatures furnished calcium for this Indiana bedrock, which was exposed after the melting glaciers moved north.

On this trail, joggers may run past, huffing and puffing, or schoolchildren sometimes walk home. At 1.0 mi. [6] a concrete embankment appears below the trail, and you can see the Indiana University and Purdue University at Indianapolis (IUPUI) campus across the river. Below, to the right, debris that floated ashore clutters the grassy bank, a reminder to put trash in the park receptacles.

On the left at 1.1 mi. [7] an amphitheater furnished with limestone slabs would be perfect for a performance by the Flintstones. As the path approaches the street, you'll hear the buzz of motor traffic and the squeals of children at play.

Return over the same route, and you'll have walked 1.7 mi.

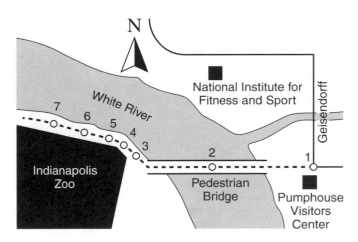

1. Pumphouse Visitor Center
2. Pedestrian Bridge
3. White River
4. Trail turns
5. Rose Window
6. Concrete embankment
7. Amphitheater

# Canal Walk Trail 🥾

**Distance Round-Trip:** 2.6 miles

**Estimated Hiking Time:** 1 hour

**Cautions:** This is icy in winter. Be careful on wet patches and the steps.

**Trail Directions:** Inside the Pumphouse Visitor Center, graphic exhibits show the IMAX 3D Theater, the Indianapolis Zoo, Eiteljorg Museum of American Indians and Western Art, Victory Field, the National Institute for Fitness and Sport, Central Canal, Military Park, River Promenade, and Pumphouse Visitor Center—all included in the White River State Park, Indiana's only urban state park.

Outside, head toward the Pedestrian Bridge, where water from the new section of canal spills into the White River, forming waterfalls **[1]**. Begin the hike on either side of the canal, crossing back on a pedestrian bridge whenever you choose. Walk upstream along a paved walk that flanks formal pools. At .15 mi. study Totem, a modern design by sculptor Rinaldo Paluzzi in Celebration Plaza **[2]**. The path of concrete rectangles leads around a splashing fountain. At .3 mi., beside the Blackford Bridge **[3]**, ramps and stairs behind it lead to the grounds of the IMAX 3D Theater.

Continue walking past benches decked with flowers and lattices draped with tangled ivy. Across the canal, the Military Park, a marshaling center during the Civil War, was Indianapolis' first city park. Walk beneath the West Street Bridge, where the canal becomes a lagoon. You can rent canal boats here **[4]** in summer. After you leave the state park, continue through the Canal Walk District, operated by the city.

The walk takes you past the site of the Central Canal, authorized in 1836, intended to link the Wabash and Erie Canal with the Ohio River. Although the entire network of canals was never completed, the Central Canal became a source of hydraulic power, fresh water, and recreation.

The modern, paved walkways continue on both sides of the canal, taking you under Ohio Street and past bright, painted Indianapolis Art Center murals. At .6 mi. **[5]**, New York Street crosses overhead and

the Marriott Residence Inn appears on the right. Across the water, notice the Canal Square complex; north of it is the Bethel African Methodist Episcopal Church, and beyond it, the American College of Sports Medicine. At .8 mi., notice the rumble of trucks above on Michigan Street. Now and then, you can see ground-floor office workers with Canal Walk views behind slatted blinds, shuffling papers in glass-walled cubicles.

Continue beneath a sea-green pedestrian bridge; in a plaza on the right stands a polished, granite memorial to the U.S.S. Indianapolis **[6]**. Known as President Franklin D. Roosevelt's personal ship, the vessel earned 10 battle stars during World War II and transported the first operational atomic bomb. Ultimately, she was sunk by a Japanese submarine; the names of her crew members have been carved on the side. Of the 900 aboard, only 317 survived five days in the water—including attacks by sharks.

Beyond this brick plaza, the canal ends in a keyhole-shaped lagoon. Complete the walk on the opposite side for a total distance of 2.6 mi.

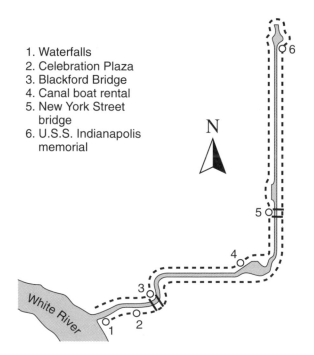

1. Waterfalls
2. Celebration Plaza
3. Blackford Bridge
4. Canal boat rental
5. New York Street bridge
6. U.S.S. Indianapolis memorial

# 22.  Fort Harrison State Park

- Hike wide trails through one of the largest tracts of hardwood forest in central Indiana.
- During the spring, enjoy a riot of wildflowers along the trail.
- Look for beaver at work building dams on scenic Fall Creek.
- During the fall, admire the rich, changing colors of maple, beech, and oak trees.

## Area Information

Receding glaciers left this area of rounded hills and flowing creeks. When meltwaters drained, deposits of sand and shale remained in the streambeds. The area's earliest inhabitants found great hunting south of the receding ice mass. Woodland Indians hunted game in these forests and fished in the streams.

Deciduous forests of maple-beech and oak-hickory still thrive in this environment. Early settlers cut timber and cleared the land for farming. Yet, the park's hardwood forests resemble the woodlands that once covered much of Indiana.

Founded in 1903, the early buildings of Fort Benjamin Harrison stood on a 2,500-acre property. By 1991, after the government had closed Fort Harrison, the state of Indiana got permission for a state park and nature preserve in a 1,700-acre area. Many park trails follow routes formerly used for map reading and other military training courses.

Within the park, Lawrence Creek and its tributaries drain into a 3.5-mile section of larger Fall Creek. Forests cover much of the rounded hills. Deer, beaver, squirrels, turtles, and frogs inhabit the woodlands and streams. Visitors can watch waterfowl gliding across Delaware Lake and Duck Pond. Although a heron rookery in the park is off limits to visitors, you can sometimes see the birds and their nests from a distance.

The wide, packed trails with their gentle slopes offer access to woods and ravines, lovely with wildflowers in spring. Shelters and picnic tables near the ponds allow visitors to watch geese and ducks while enjoying a meal. In summer, a tram provides transportation over Harrison Trace, which links Delaware Lake with the Duck Pond.

**Directions:** Located in northeastern Indianapolis, you can reach the park via I-465. Exit at 56th Street East, drive 2.2 miles to Post Road, turn left, and drive .7 mile to the park entrance.

**Hours Open:** The park is open year-round. From Memorial Day weekend to Labor Day hours are 7:00 A.M. to 9:00 P.M. During spring and fall, the park is open from 8:00 A.M. to 7:00 P.M. Winter hours are shorter. Call for dates when seasonal hours change.

**Facilities:** The park, although still being developed, has an interpretive center and a naturalist (317-591-0122), picnic shelters, playgrounds, a bicycle trail, a saddle barn, and horse trail rides. East of the gatehouse, the Fort Harrison Golf Resort and Conference Center offers meals and lodging; 317-543-9592.

**Permits and Rules:** Motorized vehicles are not permitted on hiking or multiuse trails. Metal detectors are prohibited. Dogs and cats must be attended and kept on a leash. Firearms and weapons must be either carried unloaded and unstrung or locked inside a vehicle, except when using them in an activity authorized by written permit.

**Further Information:** Park Office, Fort Harrison State Park, 5753 Glenn Road, Indianapolis, IN 46216; 317-591-0904.

## Other Areas of Interest

The 7.5-mile **Monon Trail** follows the early Monon Railroad route from Carmel at 96th Street through Nora and Broad Ripple to Fall Creek near 30th Street. North of Broad Ripple, the trail passes through wooded areas or open fields; to the south, where it runs through city neighborhoods, it's popular with joggers and skaters. For more information call Indianapolis Parks Department; 317-327-PARK.

## Park Trails

Wooden signs with yellow lettering and directional **V** indicate the route to take at each turn or junction.

**Harrison Trace Trail** 🥾—2.5 miles—This paved, multiuse trail within Fort Harrison State Park loops around both Delaware Lake and the Duck Pond, linking distant picnic sites with the parking area west of Delaware Lake. The route is wheelchair and stroller accessible, with a tram serving as a shuttle in the summer.

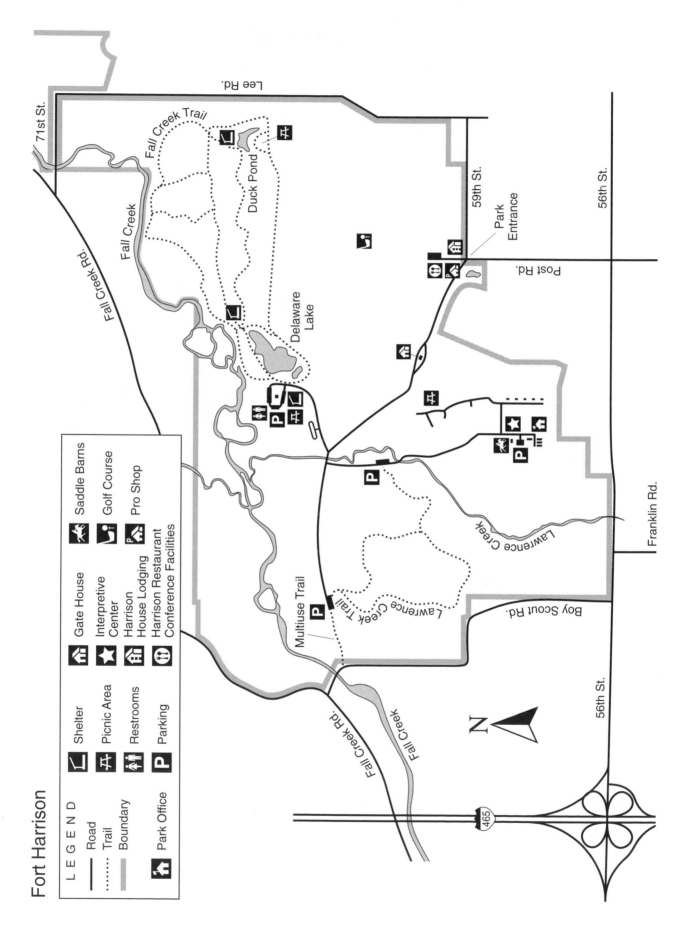

Fort Harrison

LEGEND

| | | | |
|---|---|---|---|
| Road | | | |
| Trail | | | |
| Boundary | | | |

Park Office

Shelter
Picnic Area
Restrooms
Parking

Gate House
Interpretive Center
Harrison House Lodging
Harrison Restaurant Conference Facilities

Saddle Barns
Golf Course
Pro Shop

Lee Rd.

71st St.

Fall Creek Trail

Fall Creek

Fall Creek Rd.

Duck Pond

Delaware Lake

59th St.

Park Entrance

Post Rd.

56th St.

Lawrence Creek

Lawrence Creek Trail

Multiuse Trail

Boy Scout Rd.

Franklin Rd.

56th St.

Fall Creek Rd.

Fall Creek

N

465

# Lawrence Creek Trail 👢👢

**Distance Round-Trip:** 2 miles

**Estimated Hiking Time:** 1 hour

**Cautions:** Sections of the trail become slippery when muddy and wet.

**Trail Directions:** Begin at the eastern trailhead [1] across from the parking lot. The access trail leads up a gravel path through a forest thick with maple trees; mosses thrive on the fallen timber or small branches that rest on the forest floor. Dogwood trees bloom in spring along the wide, twig-strewn path. At .34 mi. [2] a sign marks the junction with the Lawrence Creek Trail loop. Turn left and walk toward stacked logs that resemble a fence. At .36 mi. [3] avoid the path blocked by logs and turn right at the sign.

Because the Lawrence Creek Trail gets less use, you can often hear birds: a chee-ear, chee-ear or the caw, caw of a crow. Tall, spindly trees reach up for sunlight that at times breaks into cathedral-like rays. The trail winds above the creek, past swampy ponds where foot-high mayapples raise tiny umbrellas. Walk downhill, across a creeklet, and uphill again, where patches of violets and other wildflowers bloom profusely in spring.

At .71 mi. [4] ignore the left path; follow the Lawrence Creek sign to the right. If you see rusty-red needles on the trail, they may have fallen from a solitary pine. At .82 mi. [5] veer right onto a graveled section, and ignore the ruts on the left. Here and there, tan snails on the trail look like tiny tubas. At 1.05 mi. [6] veer right where a trail sign marks a curve.

At 1.12 mi. [7] ignore the narrow, gravel path at left that comes in from the Walnut Plantation trailhead.

Continue forward to 1.14 mi. [8] and ignore the ruts ahead. Instead, turn where a sign, which may be hidden by greenery, marks a sharp, angled turn to the right. Occasional numbered signs on trees date from the period this trail was used as a military training ground. At 1.43 mi. [9] a trail sign marks a right curve through another stretch of forest. At 1.59 mi. a trail sign marks a left turn off the loop and onto the now-familiar path to the eastern trailhead.

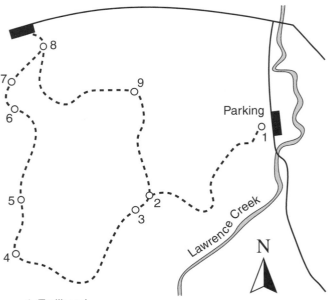

1. Trailhead
2. Trail junction
3. Right turn
4. Sign
5. Gravel section
6. Curve
7. Path to Walnut Plantation
8. Sharp right turn
9. Curve

# Fall Creek Trail 👢👢

**Distance Round-Trip:** 2.12 miles

**Estimated Hiking Time:** 1.75 hours

**Cautions:** Muddy sections of the trail near the creek can be slippery. Spur trails leading from the main trail to the creek encourage children to wander off. Be alert for poison ivy and poison sumac.

**Trail Directions:** Park at the Delaware Lake Picnic Area. The trail begins **[1]** in a grassy area east of the northernmost parking lot. At .1 mi. continue on the gravel path, avoiding the paved, multiuse trail on the right. You will see bushes that look like honeysuckle blossoming on the left and redbud trees curving along the right, which are lovely in spring.

After .1 mi. **[2]** the gravel surface becomes packed earth, and the trail skirts Fall Creek. Occasional narrow spurs link the main trail with the sandy riverbank, with its views of muddy water and tiny islands. Along the main trail, flowers bloom profusely in spring: purple and white violets; buttercups; trillium; a delicate white blossom with five petals and yellow center; another like a candle, its tall, white center spiked with orange. At the junction with Harrison Trace (.2 mi.) **[3]** stay on the Fall Creek Trail; a sign directs you to the path on the left.

As you hike, look for a rough, conical cut on a slim tree stump—quite likely a beaver has felled this tree. Turn left at any of the several spur trails (roughly from .1 to .25 mi.) **[4],** and you'll see beaver dams made of forest debris. From the riverbank, you may also see turtles basking on waterlogged branches. Although we didn't see beaver at work, you might see one navigating the swift water, holding a branch with its teeth.

Return to the main trail, which veers away from the creek at .35 mi. **[5]**. Beside the path, you might spot toadstools, mayapples, and violet coneflowers, the red blur of a cardinal in flight, the fresh tracks of deer. Longer spurs (20 to 30 feet) on the left lead back to the creek, where there are more sandy overlooks.

At .6 mi. **[6]** a side trail to the right connects with Harrison Trace. Follow the Vs on the Fall Creek sign, and continue forward. After climbing over fallen trees, ascend the first of two hills. On the second slope, exposed tree roots form a stairway, as the trail continues through lovely hills and valleys.

Near 1.0 mi. **[7]** you can use concrete slabs as chairs or tables. Another small, white flower with lots of points looked like the white baneberry in a reference book. At a fork in the trail, a marker in the center blocks the wrong route.

Truly, this is the scenic route, a winding path past mayapples in a forest thick with maples, past an occasional rock, over tiny streams, and up tree root stairs. At .75 mi. **[8]** a right-hand trail leads to Harrison Trace. Ahead, a dirt path takes you through more forest. Do not take turnoffs. At 1.0 mi., go left around an abandoned building in camouflage paint, then take a gravel path right.

At 1.1 mi. **[9]** the trail crosses Harrison Trace; continue forward on the gravel, where you will see yellow branchy flowers with green centers. The vista opens, with a meadow on the left and lots of Queen Anne's lace in summer. Ahead, that pretty little lake with the tiny island is known as the Duck Pond. When we first saw it, the silvery water was framed with arching redbud trees, but there was only one duck!

At the shelter house, 1.2 mi. **[10],** the Fall Creek Trail turns right, leaving the grassy picnic grounds. The gravel path passes marshland on the right, where white dogwood grows, then travels left and down, forming an **S** curve. At the next sign, ignore a side trail blocked by a brush pile. At 1.8 mi. **[11]** cross Harrison Trace, the paved, multiuse trail, one more time, and continue straight. Then turn left onto the first segment of the trail, a walk along Lawrence Creek, which takes you back to the parking lot.

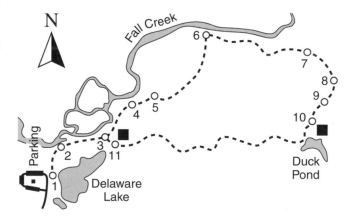

1. Trailhead
2. Gravel ends
3. Trail junction
4. Spur trails
5. Move away from creek
6. Side trail
7. Concrete slabs
8. Trail to Harrison Trace
9. Trail crossing
10. Shelter house
11. Trail crossing

# 23. Mounds State Park

- Walk past earthen mounds once used for ceremonial purposes by the Adena and Hopewell people.
- Hike scenic trails that pass through forested ravines where bubbling creeks lead to the White River.
- Visit a Nature Center to learn about artifacts uncovered when archaeologists opened the Great Mound.

## Area Information

When Europeans discovered the interior of North America, it had been inhabited for thousands of years. During the waning of the Ice Age, the area's earliest inhabitants used fluted projectile points to hunt mammoth, bison, and smaller game. Subsequent cultures consumed large amounts of mussels and left mounds of their shells. People in the Woodland tradition built increasingly complex mounds for burial and for ceremonies between 1000 B.C. and A.D. 400. At one time there were more than a dozen prehistoric mounds within the boundaries of what is now Mounds State Park.

Excavation of the Great Mound, which you see covered again with grass, revealed that it was built in two stages. Heavily burned clay floors covered the original surface. The second section, built later, contained a log tomb used for human burial. Shards of pottery, projectile points, and bear teeth carved from bone have been found in the area excavations. The pottery, etched with chevron and diamond designs, featured motifs typical of the middle Woodland period.

Mounds State Park, established in 1930, contains some of the earliest prehistoric mounds and earthworks in Indiana. The structures were built during the late Archaic and early and middle Woodland periods. The Great Mound and five others in the park are circular. Other mounds have rectangular, figure eight, and fiddle shapes.

**Directions:** Exit I-69 at SR 32 west. Go 2 miles to Chesterfield, and turn southwest on SR 232 for 1.5 miles to the park entrance.

**Hours Open:** Park is open daily, year-round from 7:00 A.M. to 11:00 P.M.

**Facilities:** Camping facilities, outdoor swimming pool, Nature Center, picnic tables, and shelters.

**Permits and Rules:** Do not injure or damage any plant, animal, or structure within the park. Camp or build fires only in designated places. Drive only on park roads and park in designated places. Keep pet cats or dogs on leashes at all times. Do not feed wild animals.

**Further Information:** Mounds State Park, 4306 Mounds Road, Anderson, IN 46017; 317-642-6627.

## Other Areas of Interest

**Summit Lake State Park,** a 2,680-acre Department of Natural Resources property developed around a man-made lake, has facilities for hiking, fishing, boating, and camping.

## Park Trails

**Trail 3** 👢👢👢—1.75 miles—Follow this meandering loop from the Pavilion through ancient forests and past early earthworks before crossing a marshy area on a boardwalk. Then turn back to hike through a bottomland along the White River.

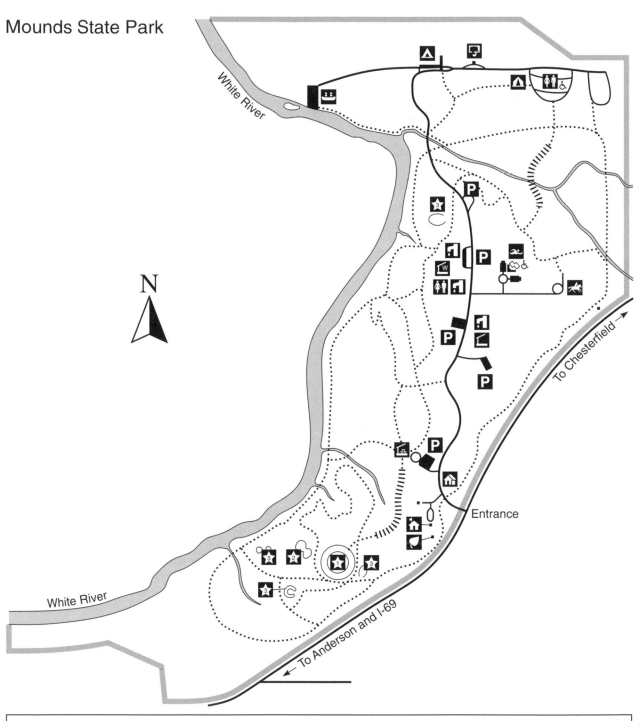

# Mounds State Park

White River

N

To Chesterfield →

Entrance

White River

To Anderson and I-69 ←

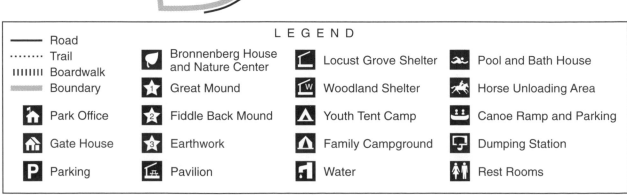

L E G E N D

— Road
···· Trail
|||||||| Boardwalk
▬▬ Boundary

🏠 Park Office

🏠 Gate House

**P** Parking

🏛 Pavilion

🍃 Bronnenberg House and Nature Center

⭐ Great Mound

⭐2 Fiddle Back Mound

⭐3 Earthwork

◩ Locust Grove Shelter

◩W Woodland Shelter

⛺ Youth Tent Camp

⛺ Family Campground

◪ Water

〰 Pool and Bath House

🐎 Horse Unloading Area

🛶 Canoe Ramp and Parking

🖥 Dumping Station

🚻 Rest Rooms

100

# Scenic Mounds and Earthworks Trail 👢👢

**Distance Round-Trip:** 1.5 miles

**Estimated Hiking Time:** 1 hour

**Cautions:** This route was poorly marked and maintained, but well worth the effort to follow.

**Trail Directions:** From the park entrance take the road to the right and park at the Pavilion **[1]**. The trail begins west of the Pavilion. Look for a series of gravel steps that curve dramatically downhill into upland maple-beech forest. Note the sandy bed of a tiny stream as you cross on a boardwalk.

At .13 mi. **[2]**, turn left on a wide gravel path that follows the river. You'll see ravines cut by rain and runoffs on the left and soon get an open view of the White River **[3]**, framed by arching branches, on the right.

At .23 mi. there's a small cave on the left. Next, you'll see a rough, wooden fence on the right. At .35 mi. **[4]**, there's an old millstone beside the trail and shallow rapids on the right. Continue upward along the river and past a small, gravel clearing with a log bench, ignoring other paths. By .45 mi. you will have reached the trunk of a huge, broken beech tree.

At .53 mi. the gravel path heads gently up a slope. There's a ravine on your left. Follow this trail as it curves left and passes a section of fence. At .64 mi. take a packed-earth trail to the left **[5]**; then at .78 mi. ignore a fork to the left.

You'll follow the trail through a grove of giant trees, including some black oaks and shagbark hickories. Beyond the trees at .85 mi., there's the sound of motor vehicles on a road.

At .91 mi. **[6]**, turn left onto a gravel path that leads to the Great Mound **[7]**. Constructed more than 1,500 years ago, this mound has a circumference of 1,200 feet, a height of 9 feet, and a base 60 feet wide. Note the moatlike depression around it, except the earthen ramp that provides access to the center.

Excavated during the 1960s, it was built in two stages: the Adena people built the earlier structure and the Hopewells added to it later. Used for religious ceremonies, it has the appearance of an amphitheater with a grass ring around the outside that might have been for seating.

At 1.0 mi., walk away from the Great Mound and return to the trail. Turn left and walk east, away from the river. The gravel path heads toward Mounds Road **[8]**, then turns left to run alongside the road. You'll walk in the shade of evergreen trees.

At 1.24 mi. **[9]**, a brick walk leads left to the New England-style Bronnenberg House, now on the National Register of Historic Places. Currently in use as a Nature Center and museum, the center has an interesting collection of Adena artifacts: pottery, beads, and effigies of wolves, ducks, and human beings.

After visiting the center, walk left (north) along the herb garden **[10]**. In summer, you might see assorted coneflowers, yarrow, and summer savory. Continue walking north along park roads past the park office and you'll eventually return to the Pavilion at 1.5 mi.

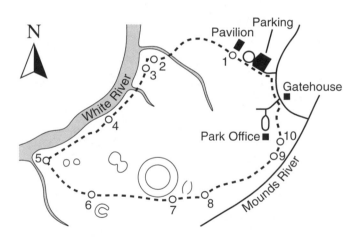

1. Pavilion parking lot
2. Wide gravel path
3. White River
4. Old millstone
5. Left turn
6. Path to Great Mound
7. Great Mound
8. Mounds Road
9. Brick walk to Bronnenberg House
10. Herb garden

# Great Mound to Pavilion 🥾🥾

**Distance One-Way:** .32 mile

**Estimated Hiking Time:** 30 minutes

**Cautions:** Use mosquito repellant liberally. If you lose the trail, head **away** from the river and toward high ground (where the parking lots are).

**Trail Directions:** The trail begins at the Great Mound **[1].** Look for a grassed-over gravel path that curves right (and goes north), running along the fence enclosing the mound. This path looks less used than the gravel path along the south side of the Great Mound. You'll walk through forest, where we saw many red squirrels bounding here and there.

At .07 mi., the path veers right and moves deeper into the forest. At .1 mi. **[2],** turn right at the sign for Trail 1. You'll soon see a bench. During a rainy summer, we found the path to be muddy.

At .19 mi. **[3],** continue ahead over a boardwalk through a lovely ravine, where a mossy stone dam has created waterfalls that splash onto rocks and nourish a pond. In season, white-petaled arrowhead flowers bloom here. There is also a bench where we sat for a while to contemplate the place of mosquitoes in the infinite scheme of nature.

At .25 mi. another dam creates a waterfall when the water is high. Continue on the boardwalk **[4].** The trail climbs through the tree-covered hillside. Here we saw a martin house without any martins. At the top of the hill, at .32 mi. **[5],** the trail ends. You'll see the Pavilion, with the parking lot to the right.

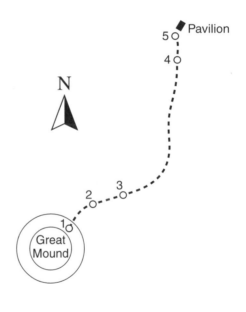

1. Great Mound
2. Sign for Trail 1
3. Boardwalk
4. Boardwalk ends
5. Trail ends

# 24. Muncie

- Follow a segment of an east-west trail designed to cross several of America's major north-south trails.
- Hike a rails-to-trails corridor once used by the Cardinal, a passenger train named for Indiana's state bird.
- Walk a paved path that runs from an old brick depot into the countryside.

## Area Information

The National Trails System Act in 1968 opened the way for developing the American Discovery Trail, a cross-country route designed to be the backbone of a trail system that includes major nationally known trails and less known regional and local routes. The American Discovery Trail, in its entirety, covers more than 6,356 miles and passes through 15 states, including Indiana.

When completed, the Cardinal Greenway, a segment of the ADT, will extend over 60 miles of former railroad corridor between Marion and Richmond. Groundbreaking for construction of phase I from the Wysor Street Depot in Muncie to CR 534 East, southeast of Prairie Creek Reservoir, took place in August 1998.

**Directions:** Whether coming from the west or the east, follow SR 32 into downtown Muncie, until you reach Madison Street. Turn north at Madison and go four blocks to Wysor Street. Turn east and proceed two blocks to Wysor Depot. You can park in the public lot beside it. The trail, which heads southeast, begins at the depot.

**Hours Open:** The completed section of the Cardinal Greenway is open from dawn to dusk year-round.

**Facilities:** There are benches along the trail where you can rest. Restrooms can be found at the depot and periodically along the trail. A water fountain at the depot is the only source of water along the trail.

**Permits and Rules:** Do not litter; carry out trash or place in proper receptacles. Respect the privacy of property owners along the trail.

**Further Information:** Cardinal Greenway, 614 East Wysor Street, Muncie, IN 47305-1945; 765-287-0399.

## Other Areas of Interest

The **Minnetrista Cultural Center** and **Oakhurst Gardens** in Muncie occupy a splendid setting on property formerly owned by the Ball family. The Minnetrista Cultural Center complex offers exhibits, events, and programs. The Discovery Cabin in Oakhurst Gardens functions as a Nature Center. Stroll southwest along Minnetrista Boulevard and see the restored homes of former members of the Ball family on landscaped sites overlooking the river. Call 765-282-4848 for more information.

# Cardinal Greenway—Wysor Depot to Ball Community Park 🥾

**Distance Round-Trip:** 3 miles

**Estimated Hiking Time:** 1 hour

**Cautions:** Use caution crossing the streets. Be alert for bicyclists, especially on weekends.

**Trail Directions:** The paved trail, which blocks motor vehicles, begins east of the Wysor Depot **[1]** in front of Ed's Warehouse. On the left, you'll see new railroad tracks and on the right there's a thicket of trees and shrubs.

The blacktop surface you walk on—12 feet wide—resembles a road. Soon, sycamore and sumac screen the railroad tracks at left. By .37 mi. **[2]**, you can see modest homes behind the greenery.

At .51 mi. **[3]**, there's a long, low warehouse on the left. At .56 mi. there's a miniplaza with benches and trash bins. Continue walking southeast and you'll pass a fence on the left overgrown with a tangle of greenery and wildflowers. In midsummer, you might see giant sunflowers growing in neighboring backyards and hear trains rumbling in the distance.

At .81 mi. **[4]**, you'll walk under a railroad overpass before crossing another street. The trail then passes under a second railroad. The wall ahead at the left is decorated with colorful urban graffiti, like an art project gone awry.

Here and there, stone markers identify this trail as the Cardinal Greenway. There's a marker at 1.18 mi. **[5]**. The foliage beside the trail becomes more interesting, with young locust trees, wild grapevines, and pretty blue asters.

At 1.51 mi. **[6]**, you'll cross Willard Street as you keep walking through a neighborhood of small homes. At the time we hiked, phlox was blooming amid the large, old sycamore and black walnut trees. By 1.84 mi. we had crossed another road. Beyond, the trail was enhanced with red-orange trumpet flowers and Queen Anne's lace. Some wild thistles had grown to 10 feet tall.

At 2.12 mi. **[7]**, we crossed Memorial Drive. At 2.16 mi. the main trail continues forward, but take a spur to the right toward the Ball Corporation Park. At 2.36 mi. **[8]**, cross another street; the straight path continues beyond it. For an urban trail, we marveled at the number of birds chattering in trees that grow between the trail and backyards.

At 2.57 mi. **[9]**, the spur trail ends. Cross Macedonia Street and take a jog to the left. You'll soon be in Ball Community Park (the locals identify it with both names) **[10]**. Here there are picnic tables, grass, and a few trees, but alas, no rest rooms. To get back to the depot (and the trailhead), walk north along Macedonia, west on Willard, then north again on Hackley Street. You'll have walked about 3 miles.

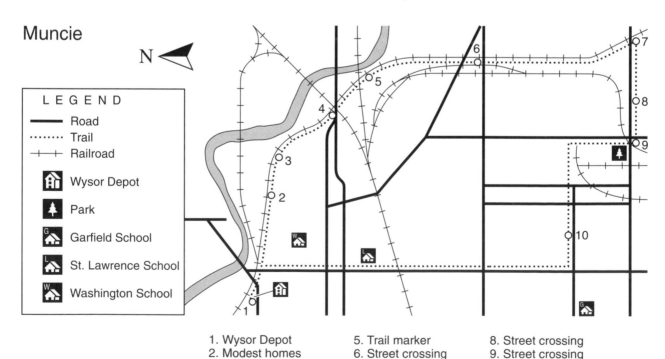

Muncie

N

LEGEND
- Road
- Trail
- Railroad
- 🏠 Wysor Depot
- 🌲 Park
- 🏫 Garfield School
- 🏫 St. Lawrence School
- 🏫 Washington School

1. Wysor Depot
2. Modest homes
3. Warehouse
4. Railroad overpass
5. Trail marker
6. Street crossing
7. Memorial Drive
8. Street crossing
9. Street crossing
10. Ball Community Park

# 25. Richmond

- Hike past a waterfall, a remnant of a much earlier falls that helped form Whitewater Gorge by migrating upstream.
- Explore vertical cliffs that contain fossil records of the primitive animals that once lived here.
- Walk through a bird sanctuary that provides favorable conditions for about 50 species of native birds.

## Area Information

When the Wisconsin glaciers were receding, a giant lobe of glacial ice lingered in the east fork of the White River Valley. As the ice lobe melted each summer—before freezing again each winter—the powerful floodwaters cut a channel in ancient bedrock, forming the Whitewater Gorge. River water brought layers of sand, gravel, and silt into the gorge; forests grew on this land, which was inhabited by Woodland Indians.

Early in the 19th century, Quaker immigrants from North Carolina and German immigrants who had come through Cincinnati began building a community east of the river. The water supplied power for several early mills. There were also many quarries here.

Today, the Whitewater Gorge, which bisects the Richmond community, is used mainly for recreation. Paleontologists and geologists visit the gorge to study the rock formations and abundant fossil remains. The trail that runs along the gorge, part of the American Discovery Trail System, provides a rare look at several historic sites in a distinctive natural setting.

**Directions:** Take I-70 to exit 151. Turn south onto US 27 and drive two miles to Waterfall Road. Turn right and go one mile. Park on the left beside the trailhead for Whitewater River Gorge. To reach Springwood Lake Park, cross Waterfall Road and you'll see the lake.

**Hours Open:** Richmond Parks and Recreation trails are open during daylight hours. Hayes Arboretum trails are open 9:00 A.M. to 5:00 P.M. Tuesday through Saturday, 1:00 P.M. to 5:00 P.M. Sunday, and are closed on Monday.

**Facilities:** Springwood Lake Park has picnic tables, rest rooms, and a Nature Center. The Whitewater River Gorge has benches and tables.

**Permits and Rules:** Do not damage any natural or constructed features in these parks. Carry out all trash or place in proper receptacles. Mountain biking, horseback riding, and off-road vehicles are prohibited.

**Further Information:** Richmond Parks and Recreation Department, 765-983-7275; Richmond and Wayne County Convention and Tourism Bureau, 800-828-8414.

## Other Areas of Interest

**Glen Miller Park,** located east of US 27, north of US 40, and west of the Hayes Arboretum, is a grassy public park enhanced by shade trees. Known for its rose gardens, the park also has picnic tables, shelters, and rest rooms.

## Park Trails

**Whitewater River Gorge Trail** 👢👢👢—3.5 miles—Walk the length of the trail to access an estimated 450 million years of geological history, overlaid with thousands of years of human history.

Check with park officials, however, to determine trail conditions before proceeding. Call 765-983-7275 for more information.

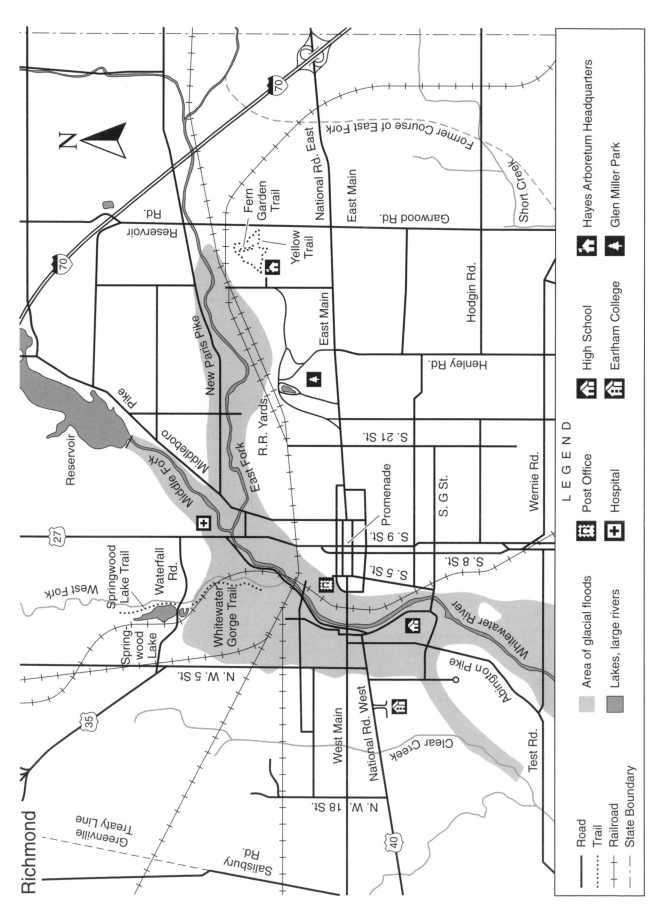

Richmond

N

LEGEND

Road
Trail
Railroad
State Boundary

Area of glacial floods
Lakes, large rivers

Post Office
Hospital

High School
Earlham College

Hayes Arboretum Headquarters
Glen Miller Park

106

# Whitewater River Gorge Trail 👢👢👢

**Distance One-Way:** 1 mile

**Estimated Hiking Time:** 1 hour

**Cautions:** After a stormy spring, the trail was a mess of debris—a real challenge, yet a fascinating place to be. Unmarked paths went off in many directions and parts of the trail had been washed away.

**Trail Directions:** Look for a sign that says "Gorge Trail Entrance" at the trailhead **[1]**. Here is a view of Thistlethwaite Falls **[2]**, an ancient waterfall that helped form the gorge as it slowly migrated upstream. Walk right between the fence and a bush, and take concrete steps down the hillside. From a small overlook, you'll see a wide, clay peninsula below, with water gushing over striated rock layers. Note that both sides of the north-south gorge are covered with forest.

At .1 mi. **[3]**, we could see layers of rock in the creek bed below the clear, flowing water. The gorge, formed by floodwater, reaches down through glacial till and shaley limestone for several hundred feet. Note the powerful, natural forces at work here. We saw a tiny island made of natural debris that had formed beneath an ancient sycamore tree.

Walk through forest downstream on a dirt path four feet wide, following a creek that forms low, ripply rapids. At .2 mi. **[4]**, there's a lovely view framed by overhanging tree limbs. A few Potawatomi Indians were living here in tepees when the first settlers arrived. Continue following the creek as the trail becomes sandy. Virginia creeper and other vines dangle from trees along the trail.

At .31 mi., we climbed across a fallen tree trunk before the trail veered right, away from the creek. At .39 mi. **[5]**, we could see an old railroad bridge above us; the path goes right. Wooden bridges helped with crossing a sometimes dry creek. Then, at .49 mi., the trail turns left to go up and across a wooden suspension bridge about two feet wide. The trail then goes right and follows the creek again. At the next junction, ignore the vehicle ruts and go right.

At .64 mi. **[6]**, another narrow, wooden suspension bridge takes you back across the creek. After crossing the bridge, turn left at the trail marker. You'll walk left of a green chain-link fence at the edge of mowed grass. The path becomes rockier as it returns to the stream. You are passing through a bird sanctuary owned by Friends United Meeting, a Quaker group, so look and listen for birds. The Quakers were among the area's earliest settlers.

At .75 mi. **[7]**, the trail goes right and passes close to someone's backyard. A marker calls attention to the vertical cliffs in the gorge. About 450 million years ago, an ancient inland sea covered this region. Many fossils of primitive animals from that period have been found in the gorge's exposed rock strata. Continue walking forward through grass. You'll hear traffic from the road above and see pylons that support it.

At .86 mi., we found the trail had been washed away on both sides of the creek. When we checked farther downstream, below the Bridge Avenue crossing **[8]**, we could find no sign of a trail. In this case, climb the slope up to Bridge Avenue (on the west side of the gorge). Then use city sidewalks to return to Waterfall Road, or end the hike by returning to Thistlethwaite Falls over the route you came.

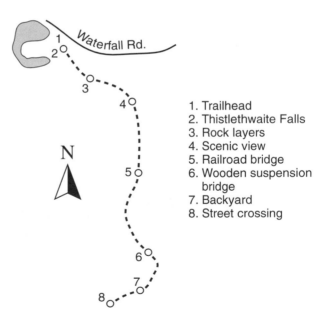

1. Trailhead
2. Thistlethwaite Falls
3. Rock layers
4. Scenic view
5. Railroad bridge
6. Wooden suspension bridge
7. Backyard
8. Street crossing

# Springwood Lake Trail

**Distance One-Way:** .54 mile

**Estimated Hiking Time:** 30 minutes

**Cautions:** Watch where you step—there are marshy sections and the droppings of waterfowl.

**Trail Directions:** Begin walking at the gate to Springwood Lake **[1]**. You'll follow a gravel path beside the lake—it's on the left. Trees have been planted here and there on this reservoir lake where people come to fish for redear sunfish, largemouth bass, and channel catfish. In summer, you'll see geese and other waterfowl swimming in the distance.

At .08 mi. near a wooden overlook **[2]**, you can see small islands in the lake covered with scrub. Then, at .15 mi., the path curves around a maple tree with several trunks. On the right, scattered trees rise from the mowed-grass surface. On the left, a line of trees and shrubs hugs the shore.

At .17 mi. **[3]**, there are chin-up bars for walkers who use this as a *parcours* trail. Just after that, we saw a small blue heron in a stagnant section of the pond. Beyond it the water was covered with lime-green algae. A sign said the water was undergoing treatment.

At .22 mi. **[4]**, there's a playground to the right. At times, you'll notice that water overflows onto the gravel path and forms marshland on the left. You'll next hike past a stone wall on the left before coming to a wooden bridge. Cross the creek here where children like to slide down a small dam into the water.

At .3 mi. **[5]**, turn left, pass between sections of fence, then cross a mowed, grassy area. On the right you'll see an enclosed picnic shelter; on the left there are shrubs and trees that screen the creek. Here, great sycamores rise above the west fork of the Whitewater River. Continue walking left along the perimeter of a grassy field.

By .41 mi. **[6]**, you'll come to a hard surface gravel road, closed to vehicles when we were there. Follow this road as it curves left. At .49 mi. you'll see a gate (which was open) and a path leading to the Nature Center. Continue walking ahead toward a gray building with a blue door at the edge of the forest. At .54 mi. **[7]**, you arrive at the Nature Center, where the hike ends. Retrace your steps to return to the parking lot.

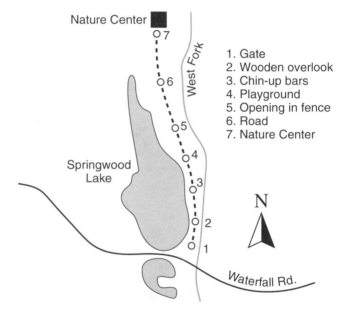

Nature Center

West Fork

Springwood
Lake

1. Gate
2. Wooden overlook
3. Chin-up bars
4. Playground
5. Opening in fence
6. Road
7. Nature Center

N

Waterfall Rd.

# Yellow Trail—Hayes Regional Arboretum 👢👢

**Distance Round-Trip:** 1.03 mile

**Estimated Hiking Time:** 45 minutes

**Cautions:** This trail was poorly marked.

**Trail Directions:** Park south of the Nature Center [1] and walk around it. The trail begins northeast of the center. Look for a yellow marker. Follow a bark mulch path into a thick beech-maple forest. Note that the arboretum—in its entirety—features 172 woody plants native to this region. In summer, we saw a beautiful spicebush swallowtail butterfly soon after starting this trail

Cross a gravel road and keep walking ahead on the bark mulch trail. At a fork, take the trail to the right, cross another gravel road, and walk ahead on the bark mulch trail. You'll pass through a forest with splendid oaks and pretty tulip trees. You might also see and hear woodpeckers or even an indigo bunting.

At .24 mi. [2], take steps down to a wooden ramp; then go left over a wider bark mulch path past several beech trees. At .33 mi. [3], there's an amphitheater—also called Woodland Chapel—set among maple and beech trees. At .42 mi [4], avoid a second wider trail to the amphitheater. Instead, go right on a narrower, dirt track. You'll soon walk on a ridge above a splendid ravine, where a stream flows over a brown, rocky bed and through the lush forest. Deer, groundhogs, raccoons, and other creatures drink from this stream.

At .46 mi. you'll cross a wooden bridge and pass through forest with many beech trees. Look for dogwood trees that blossom in the spring. At .5 mi.

[5], the yellow trail goes left and uphill. Soon you'll see a welcome wooden bench; in summer you can rest here in the dappled shade. The path crosses a road; continue walking ahead. At .63 mi., the trail crosses another wooden bridge and another road; continue on bark mulch.

People doing the arboretum's auto-drive tour of the forest use the curving road through the forest. You'll cross a road at .84 mi. [6], pass another bench, and follow the path uphill. At .98 mi., after you cross another road [7], continue along the path where there is a yellow marker. At 1.03 mi. [8], you'll see the ruts of an older road no longer used. Cross it and keep walking ahead. At 1.06 mi. you'll find that the trail ends near a bench just east of the trailhead where you began walking. Walk around the Nature Center and you'll return to the parking lot.

1. Nature Center
2. Wooden ramp
3. Amphitheater
4. Right turn
5. Wooden bench
6. Road
7. Road
8. Older road

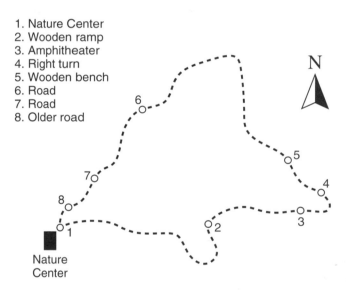

# Fern Garden Trail—Hayes Regional Arboretum 🥾

**Distance Round-Trip:** .2 mile

**Estimated Hiking Time:** 30 minutes

**Trail Directions:** Starting at the end of the Yellow Trail **[1]**, walk east along the fire break road for 75 feet to reach the trailhead for the Fern Garden Trail **[2]**. Turn left and cross the Salamander Stream on a bridge **[3]**. You may recognize the feathery maidenhair ferns on your left as you begin walking. The trail turns right and follows the stream. The trail features some 20 species of ferns or related plants that are native to the Whitewater River basin.

Look for bulblet ferns on the left about 25 feet along the trail; you'll see a sign every 25 feet. Ahead on the right you might recognize the sensitive fern, once displayed prominently in my grandmother's parlor. Beyond it, you'll find a patch of ostrich ferns—look carefully on the right. You may also see silvery spleenwort on the left before the trail crosses the creek on a bridge at .06 mi. **[4]**. Once across the creek, look for common woodsia. The trail then crosses back over another bridge where there is Christmas fern on the right.

The trail loops east and north, and the Springhouse Trail goes to the right at .08 mi. **[5]**. Continue walking to see New York fern on the left at about .1 mi. and lady ferns ahead on the right. You've probably noticed by now that ferns are nonflowering plants that grow well in shade. They reproduce by spores or underground runners.

At .14 mi. **[6]**, a spur path returns to the trailhead. Continue walking straight ahead. You may see field horsetail, broad beech fern, or purple-stemmed cliff brake along the path. Notice how varied they are. Also, some ferns are deciduous and others are evergreens.

This fern garden, established in 1964, honors Mabelle Hayes, the wife of the arboretum founder. The hillside setting also has a wonderful display of wildflowers in spring. Continue walking to the end and pass rattlesnake fern on the right. The trail ends at .2 mi. **[7]**, where it turns south to cross Salamander Stream.

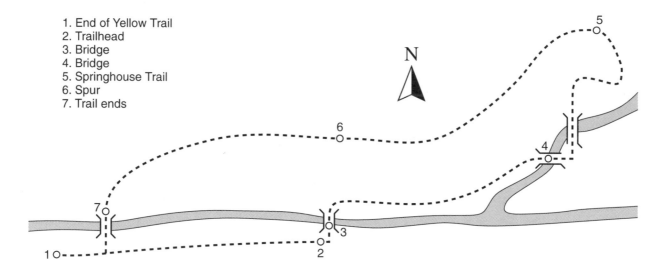

1. End of Yellow Trail
2. Trailhead
3. Bridge
4. Bridge
5. Springhouse Trail
6. Spur
7. Trail ends

# 26.  Whitewater Memorial State Park

- Wander through a nature preserve that has an unusual number of hornbeam trees.
- Follow trails that lead along steep ridges, over the crest of rolling hills, down into scenic ravines, and across open fields.
- Watch beaver at work along the creek that feeds beautiful Whitewater Lake.

## Area Information

Whitewater Memorial State Park, established in 1949 as a memorial to the men and women who served in World War II, is one section of a larger reserve that includes the Brookville Reservoir.

The east fork of the Whitewater River flows south of Richmond, past farmers' fields and patches of woodland, before being retained by a dam north of Brookville. Northeast of the Brookville Reservoir, another dam holds back the waters of Whitewater Lake, creating a smaller scenic lake amid the gently rolling terrain of southeastern Indiana.

Beside Whitewater Lake, the Hornbeam Nature Preserve contains fine examples of hornbeam trees (also known as blue beeches) and hop hornbeam trees (also called ironwoods). You can find pileated woodpeckers here, along with the nocturnal owl, whose call is "who wi who wooh!" The nature preserve has also become known for its spring wildflowers.

The 1,514-acre park was developed initially by community members from four counties: Wayne, Fayette, Franklin, and Union. Two years after Whitewater Memorial became the 16th park in Indiana's state park system, the dam across Silver Creek was completed to form Whitewater Lake. The 37-acre Hornbeam Nature Preserve was dedicated in 1974. Then, in 1980, Whitewater Memorial State Park acquired an additional 196 acres from the federal government, increasing the park size to 1,710 acres.

**Directions:** Drive south of Richmond on Hwy. 27, or east of Connersville on SR 44 to the town of Liberty. Continue south of Liberty for two miles; follow the signs west to the park.

**Hours Open:** The park is open daily between 7:00 A.M. and 11:00 P.M. Boat, bicycle, and family cabin rentals take place in the summer.

**Facilities:** The park has a campground, boat rentals and ramps, cabins for rent, a swimming beach, saddle barn, picnic areas, and more than 11 miles of hiking trails.

**Permits and Rules:** Do not damage any plant, animal, or natural or man-made structure in the park. Store any firearm or other weapon unloaded; keep it in a case or inside a locked vehicle. Dogs or cats must be leashed. Camp, build a fire, or swim only in designated areas. Drive only on roads and park in parking lots. Metal detectors may be used with written permission. Snowmobiles are prohibited. Carry out any trash you bring in.

**Further Information:** Whitewater Memorial State Park, 1418 South State Road 101, Liberty, IN 47353; 765-458-5565.

## Other Areas of Interest

**Brookville Lake** is a 5,260-acre reservoir formed by damming the east fork of the Whitewater River. It has created a boating community in what was once farmland and forest. Fishermen angle for striped bass, bluegill, and perch from their vantage points in the water, and hunters—in season—hope to bag deer, rabbits, raccoons, wild turkeys, and other game in the surrounding forests.

## Park Trails

**Trail 4** 👢👢👢—3.25 miles—Rugged, yet rewarding, this trail will take you into the heart of Hornbeam Nature Preserve and allow you to explore Whitewater Lake's northwest shoreline with its scenic lake vistas. Follow the park road across the dam that forms the lake; then cross the spillway. You can park at the trailhead. For a shorter walk, hike from the spillway to the parking lot for the nature preserve. For a long (7.75 miles) hike around the lake, follow Trail 4 along the northwest shore, then return via Trails 3 and 2 to complete the loop.

# Silver Creek Shelter Loop (Trail 6) 👢👢👢👢

**Distance One-Way:** .78 mile

**Estimated Hiking Time:** 1 hour

**Cautions:** Although I had hoped to do more hiking here, the trail was so poorly maintained I walked north on the trail but walked back on the road.

**Trail Directions:** Follow park signs to Silver Creek Shelter. Begin hiking on Trail 6 **[1]** east of the parking lot. You'll find the trailhead north of the rest rooms.

You'll pass a sheltered picnic table, then find that the trail forks at .05 mi.; walk left, for the path on the right is Trail 5. At .1 mi., there's a ravine at the left.

You'll see a marker confirming Trail 6. Continue walking forward along a ridge. On the left is a cleft in the earth; on the right is a meadow screened by saplings. By .15 mi. **[2]**, the trail curves left, then crosses the streambed using a wooden ramp.

At .2 mi., you walk a narrow earthen path upstream; there's another cleft in the earth on the left. Park maintenance people have cut through logs that have fallen across the trail—allowing hikers a way through—then left the remaining trunks, branches, and leaves for wildlife cover.

At .23 mi., the path curves to follow the same creek downstream, before it moves back uphill. At .27 mi. **[3]**, there's a ramp, and oak is increasingly part of the forest mixture. The trail passes another

sign for Trail 6, then heads uphill and veers slightly right. On the right is a meadow.

The view opens as you reach the top of the hill. Here, the meadow has become savanna, for the expanse of prairie grasses is now broken by scattered young trees.

At .4 mi., we noticed an area of mashed grasses (perhaps 30 feet wide) on both sides of the trail, suggesting that deer had recently used this as a rest area. By .45 mi. **[4]**, we were walking through black oak savanna on a mowed-grass trail past many thistles and berry bushes. Soon we could see a bit of the park road at left. At .47 mi. the trail crossed it, then continued on the other side, the path framed by the arching branches of a black walnut tree.

Although the meadow was lovely with more butterflies, thistles, and purple wildflowers, the trail (which was grass) had not been mowed and seemed too poorly defined to follow. At .55 mi., we went back to the road **[5]** and followed it downhill to the family campground. On the way, we noticed the purple blooms of crown vetch on the hill to the left and a distinctive osage orange tree, hung with green balls. At .78 mi. **[6]**, we tried to pick up Trail 6 again where it headed left into the woods and down to Brookville Lake.

However, the narrow earth path petered out among muddy patches of dirt and stacks of dead trees so we ended the hike at .78 mi. and walked back by the road to the Silver Creek Shelter. Do save energy for this—it's up a steep hill—then the hike ends.

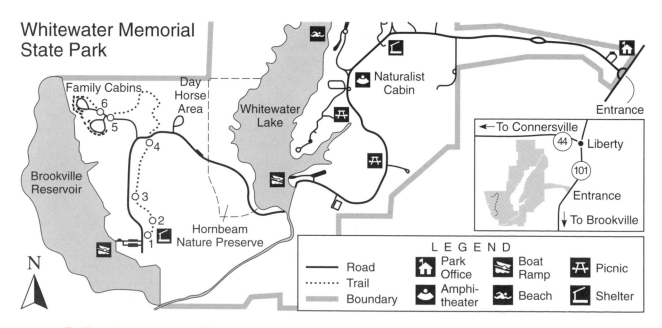

1. Trailhead
2. Trail curves left
3. Ramp
4. Black oak savanna
5. Park road
6. Road intersection

# South

The southern region, bounded by the central region to the north, the Wabash River to the west, and the Ohio River to the east and south, consists of the remaining 32 counties.

## Topography

The southern region of Indiana has the most varied terrain in the state. The moving ice masses that scoured the hills and plains of the north and central regions didn't extend to parts of the south. During the lengthy Pleistocene Age, the complex glacial shifts modified the east and west regions, but left the middle of southern Indiana unglaciated. Thus, this region consists of varying physiographic bands that reach from the central region into the Ohio River valley. From west to east, these bands of lowland, upland, and plains form the most distinctive hills, valleys, and rock formations in the state.

The Knobstone Escarpment, rising about 300 feet above the surface and extending north to south for 100 miles, is the region's most prominent geologic feature. The Mitchell Plain, extending south of Bloomington to the Ohio valley, has a variety of karst formations and sinkholes that funnel surface water into the Lost River and other underground streams. Southern Indiana also has more than 700 caves; the Wyandotte Cave, which is fairly dry, is the state's largest cave.

## Major Rivers and Lakes

The Wabash River flows southward, forming the western boundary of the southern region before joining the Ohio River. As the Ohio River's second-largest tributary, this water route through once-dense forests was heavily traveled by the state's early settlers. The Patoka, White, Blue, Muscatatuck, and Whitewater Rivers, as well as their tributaries, help drain this complex watershed.

Turtle Creek, Cagles Mill, Lake Monroe, Patoka Lake, and the Whitewater Reservoir have been formed by damming rivers in this region. In contrast to the Wabash River, which is undammed, the Ohio River flows south and west through a system of dams and locks.

## Common Plant Life

The southern region's earliest settlers were so impressed with the trees that they named entire communities for them: Oaktown, Cypress, Sassafras, Magnolia, and Laurel.

In the Lower Wabash valley, bald cypress, swamp chestnut oak, pecan hickory, swamp privet, and other species more typical of the Mississippi valley exist in the floodplains. Although not a native plant, the golden rain tree adds distinction to small towns in the state's southwest corner. Pin oak, beech, sweet gum, and soft maple grow in areas of poor drainage.

The unglaciated, central areas of the southern region have forests of mixed hardwoods; beech-maple or oak-hickory often dominate. In rare canyons in the southern uplands, you can find hemlock and mountain laurel; these and other cool-climate plants are more often found farther north.

The vast Hoosier National Forest, which has about 220 miles of hiking trails, includes forestland in nine southern counties. State parks, forests, and recreation areas and several large, forested county parks are scattered through the region. The Charles C. Deam Wilderness, southeast of Bloomington, is Indiana's only nationally recognized wilderness area. Donaldson Woods, a nature preserve within Spring Mill State Park, has important stands of virgin timber: the regal white oak, sugar maple, and beech trees have been here for centuries.

The city of Bloomington takes its name from the fields of wildflowers once found here. With less land in the southern region devoted to agriculture, there is more wildlife habitat. Wildflowers in this region include spider lilies and feather foil flowers that live in the Wabash River floodplains. Rose gentian, trailing arbutus, and fire pink favor the central hill country. Deam's foxglove, named for the Hoosier naturalist, grows only in a few locations. Running buffalo clover, found only in tiny Ohio County, is on the federally endangered list.

## Common Birds and Mammals

White-tailed deer, their populations no longer held in check by bears, bobcats, or wolves, still wander about southern forests and meadows. In season, hunters reduce their growing numbers. The opossum, a marsupial, has a pouch for carrying the young. Cottontail rabbits; red, gray, and fox squirrels; chipmunks; woodchucks; muskrats; and skunks also inhabit the region. Smoky and pigmy shrews inhabit the south's unglaciated regions, and the loose dirt of mole tunnels often crosses the trails.

Indiana claims a dozen species of bats; many of them winter in the caves of this region. Wood rats frequent the south's rocky escarpments or caves. Over time, hunting and encroachment of habitat have reduced southern wildlife populations; yet, many species have adapted. In the tourist town of Nashville, residents can hear raccoons, just after dark, foraging in their metal garbage cans.

In southern Indiana, you may see the sparrows, cardinals, blue jays, robins, Canada geese, and wood ducks. More difficult to sight—and perhaps more rewarding—are Canada geese flying overhead in formation, bald eagles bringing food to their young, a lone osprey nest built high in a dead tree, or a flock of wild turkeys scratching about in a meadow.

## Climate

The southern region has a climate described as warm, temperate, continental, and humid. An average low of 27 degrees Fahrenheit in January rises to an average high of 89 degrees in July. The average annual precipitation ranges from 41 to 45 inches a year in the south—the highest in the state. Expect rainfall on seven or more days of the month during April, May, June, or July. Note that precipitation in late winter is more likely to be rain than snow.

## Best Natural Features

- Uplands, lowlands, ridges, and escarpments created long ago by massive geologic forces
- Forest-clad hills and deep ravines—among the most scenic in the state
- Cool-climate canyons that shelter hemlock and wintergreen
- Forest trails where Abraham Lincoln hiked during his Hoosier boyhood
- Karst formations, sinkholes, caves, and underground rivers
- The bald knobs that give the Knobstone Escarpment its name

# 27.  Harmonie State Park

- Enjoy wide, mowed trails through the bottomland of the Wabash River and its border of low hills.
- Share forest glades with white-tailed deer, squirrels, and other wildlife.
- Walk among the pecan, shellbark hickory, sycamore, and silver maple trees that thrive in the river bottomland.

## Area Information

The park is located 25 miles northwest of Evansville and 4 miles south of New Harmony, a historic village where two different communal living experiments were conducted over the years. Settled first by German, then later by Scottish immigrants, this is an area of Wabash River floodplains where meandering streams cut through forested hills.

New Harmony's earliest settlers, the followers of Father George Rapp, came to this remote area to escape religious persecution. These Rappites worked hard and chose a simple lifestyle as preparation for the second coming of Christ.

In 1824, Robert Owen, an industrialist and social reformer from Scotland, bought the town from Father Rapp. By encouraging the development of reason, Owen and his followers opened an early free, public school; a kindergarten; and a public library. They also provided equal learning opportunities for girls and boys.

At Harmonie State Park, the picnic shelters near the gatehouse are separated by Rush Creek from the campground, but linked by a paved bicycle trail. The picnic shelters located farther south have been set on scenic ridges. The park's hiking trails, a total of 7.5 miles of them, are wide enough for park maintenance vehicles to pass through; thus, the maintenance crew can access remote, hidden areas and do their work efficiently.

**Directions:** Drive four miles south of New Harmony. Turn west at park signs, and enter at the gatehouse.

**Hours Open:** The park is open year-round. Visitors, unless they are staying at the campground, may enter the park after 7:00 A.M. and must leave before 11:00 P.M.

**Facilities:** Harmonie has modern campsites, a family cabin, picnic shelters and tables, a swimming pool, a horse trail, and a boat launch ramp for the Wabash River.

**Permits and Rules:** Do not injure or damage any plant, animal, or structure in the park. Dogs or cats must be on leashes. Camp only in the campground; build a fire or park only in designated areas. Keep motorized vehicles on park roads; snowmobiles are prohibited.

**Further Information:** Harmonie State Park, Route 1, Box 5A, New Harmony, IN 47631; 812-682-4821.

## Other Areas of Interest

**Wesselman Woods Nature Preserve** in Evansville consists of 197 acres of old-growth forest. There's a Nature Center at the entrance to this fenced area; however, the enclosure makes the preserve inaccessible after hours and on Mondays, when the park is closed. For more information, call the Department of Natural Resources, Division of Nature Preserves, 317-232-4052.

The **Hovey Lake Fish and Wildlife Area** near Mt. Vernon contains 4,400 acres of habitat favored by birds, amphibians, and reptiles; the best way to view this wildlife is by nonmotorized boat.

## Park Trails

**Trail 3** 👢👢👢—1 mile—Starting at the Poplar Grove picnic area, hike past the water tower, walk through the valley of a small stream, and climb a hill above the Wabash River.

**Trail 4** 👢👢👢—2.5 miles—For even more challenges, climb steep, forest-covered hills, and descend into ravines in a loop route that links several picnic areas.

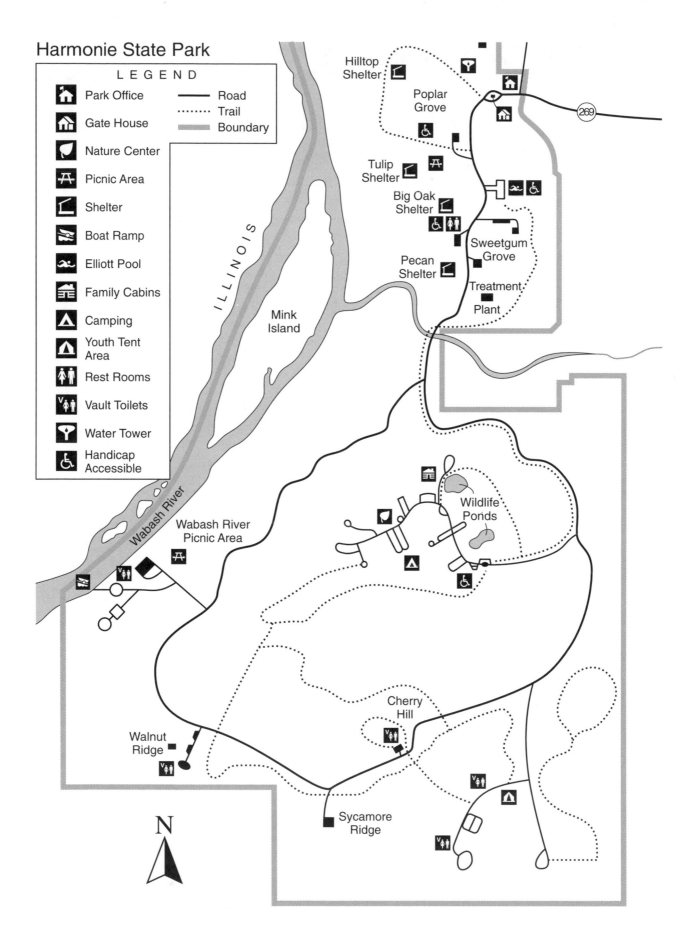

# Harmonie State Park

**LEGEND**

| | |
|---|---|
| Park Office | Road |
| Gate House | Trail |
| Nature Center | Boundary |
| Picnic Area | |
| Shelter | |
| Boat Ramp | |
| Elliott Pool | |
| Family Cabins | |
| Camping | |
| Youth Tent Area | |
| Rest Rooms | |
| Vault Toilets | |
| Water Tower | |
| Handicap Accessible | |

ILLINOIS

Wabash River

Mink Island

Hilltop Shelter

Poplar Grove

269

Tulip Shelter

Big Oak Shelter

Pecan Shelter

Sweetgum Grove

Treatment Plant

Wildlife Ponds

Wabash River Picnic Area

Cherry Hill

Walnut Ridge

Sycamore Ridge

N

# Wildlife Ponds Walk (Trail 5) 👢👢

**Distance:** 1.4 miles

**Estimated Hiking Time:** 45 minutes

**Trail Directions:** Follow park signs to the camp-ground. Park at the control station at the camp-ground entrance. Walk back along the park road for .1 mi.; the trailhead for Trail 5 is on the north side **[1]**. You'll walk on a wide, grassy strip and enter a savanna with scattered sycamore and black walnut trees beneath an open sky. At .28 mi. **[2]**, continue walking on a closely mowed grass swath about 10 to 12 feet wide.

We noticed sweet gum and sassafras trees and the familiar Queen Anne's lace blooming among the grasses. A tree-filled ravine slopes to the left; listen for the birds. At .42 mi., the trail enters the forest again, following a ridge. There's a pond below, at right **[3]**; we heard a woodpecker among the broken trees and decaying logs.

Continue walking forward on the wide path, now a mixture of grass and dirt, almost a road, that passes oak trees, sweet gum, and beech. At .53 mi., the path curves right, then heads downhill. From a wooden overlook **[4]**, we could see a hillside covered with maple, sassafras, and beech. Return to the path.

At .65 mi., turn right **[5]** and walk downhill on mowed grass toward the pond, covered with algae. The trail continues uphill using wooden steps. Turn right at the next marker for Trail 5, and walk farther uphill.

By .9 mi., you've reached a road **[6]**. Turn right and follow the pavement back to the control station. We especially enjoyed the native coneflowers and daisies blooming near the campground entrance. Dozens of butterflies hovered above them; visitors with cameras seemed happy to get this on film. The hike ends here beside the parking area.

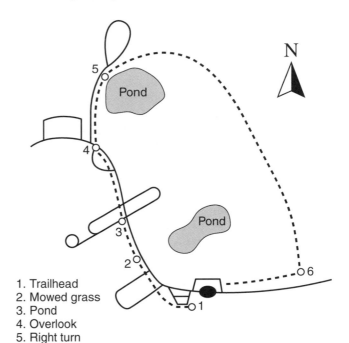

1. Trailhead
2. Mowed grass
3. Pond
4. Overlook
5. Right turn
6. Road

# Campground Loop (Trail 2) 👢👢

**Distance Round-Trip:** 1.9 miles

**Estimated Hiking Time:** 1 hour

**Trail Directions:** Near the control station, on the south side of the campground entrance road, begin walking on a white gravel path that soon becomes grass **[1]**. Note the unmowed habitat area on the left, a marvel of hollow stumps and logs, surrounded by grasses and sedges. The trail veers right, and at .06 mi. **[2]**, there's a gate to stop motorized vehicles. As we walked through the gate, we could hear mourning doves.

The trail enters a forest with a narrow ditch at the left and tangled vines and debris on the right. Beyond the shade of a shagbark hickory tree, the path moves into an open area, with tall grasses on the left. At .23 mi. **[3]**, we found a pair of beech trees with shared trunks. At .3 mi., we saw mounds of earth from small animal excavations on the right. We walked on gravel with arching branches overhead, then observed the way logs, grasses, and low, green plants had anchored the bank of earth on the right. Virginia creeper and other vines wrapped many trees. At .63 mi., a sign confirms Trail 2 **[4]**. The path, still wide, having a covering of gravel, curves left and goes downhill. Continue to walk through flatland; we saw bouncing bet blooming on the right.

At .65 mi. **[5]**, the trail crosses a bridge above a silty creek; a fence protects plants on the left—perhaps a research project. The roadlike path follows the creek, running past mossy, rotten logs. Ferns had grown up through matted leaves; red trumpet flowers bloomed. We passed a forested hill on the left and an exposed, clay bank on the right. At .86 mi. **[6]**, we passed a spur connecting to Trail 4 on the left, but kept walking ahead. The trail uses a fallen log for a bridge over a clear water creek with a gravel bottom, then turns right at 1.03 mi. You'll cross a wooden bridge; then the path curves right, and uphill, out of the valley.

At 1.19 mi. **[7]**, turn right onto the ridge top; there's a fat maple tree on the left, with many thick branches. As you walk along the crest of the ridge, the forest becomes more open to the sky. Ahead, at 1.48 mi., the canopy closes above you, and the wide path curves to the right. We walked past ancient, gnarled maples on the left, wrapped with twisted vines; on the right is a meadow. By 1.66 mi. **[8]**, we'd returned to the campground.

The hike has ended; to return to the parking area, follow the curving campground road past the Nature Center to the control station.

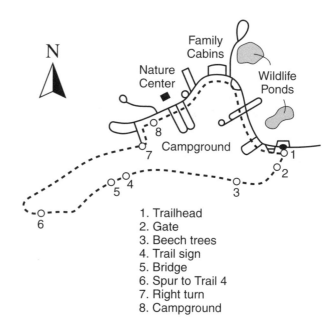

1. Trailhead
2. Gate
3. Beech trees
4. Trail sign
5. Bridge
6. Spur to Trail 4
7. Right turn
8. Campground

# 28.  Historic Vincennes

- Walk through the extensive landscaped grounds of the George Rogers Clark National Historical Park, a monument to the leader who captured an early British fort at this location with the aid of 170 men.

- Pass Grouseland, the stately home of William Henry Harrison and his family while he was governor of the Indiana Territory. Harrison eventually became the ninth president of the United States.

- Enjoy Ouabache Trails Park, where hiking trails rise more than 100 feet, extending from the Wabash River floodplain into the rolling, forested uplands to the east.

## Area Information

Although much of the American struggle for independence took place in the eastern colonies along the Atlantic seaboard, critical shifts of power also occurred in the interior of North America. West of the Appalachian mountains, in the vast Indiana Territory, frontiersmen banded together for protection against Indians. At scattered fortresses throughout the territory, the power shifted from French to British, while early settlers valiantly fought cold, hunger, and disease, plus sporadic attacks by indigenous people, whose ancestors had lived in the region for 10,000 years.

Although the British, who encouraged Indian attack on pioneer settlements, controlled outposts at Kaskaskia and Cahokia in what is now Illinois, at what is now Vincennes, Colonel George Rogers Clark successfully organized armies of a few dozen volunteers dedicated to Americans controlling the region. In early 1779, while the British forces at Vincennes were depleted, Clark led his force over 180 miles of wilderness toward the end of winter before mounting a successful attack on the British garrison.

Success at subsequent battles—north of what is now Lafayette and near Fort Wayne—prevented scattered Indian tribes from forming what might have become a confederation of tribes. As a result of Clark's success, more Indians decided to become neutral.

In 1787, the Continental Congress established the Territory Northwest of the River Ohio, from which several Midwestern states evolved, including Indiana.

**Directions:** Reach Vincennes via US 41; take the Willow Street exit to reach the historic heart of town along 2nd and 3rd Streets at the foot of Main Street. Ouabache Trails Park is on Fort Knox Road, two miles north of Vincennes.

**Hours Open:** The Vincennes Historic Walk takes place over public sidewalks. You can hike the Ouabache Trails Park trails year-round.

**Facilities:** Vincennes has restaurants, lodging, and public benches along the sidewalks. Ouabache Trails Park has a campground, picnic areas, playgrounds, and sports playing fields.

**Permits and Rules:** Do not litter; place trash in appropriate containers. Alcohol is prohibited in Ouabache Trails Park.

**Further Information:** Vincennes and Knox County Convention and Visitors Bureau, P.O. Box 602, Vincennes, IN 47591. George Rogers Clark National Historical Park, 401 South Second Street, Vincennes, IN; 812-882-1776. Ouabache Trails Park, Knox County Parks and Recreation Department; 812-882-4316.

## Other Areas of Interest

Between 6th and 15th Streets along Willow are three cemeteries, with a mixture of grassy lawns, scattered shade trees, and fascinating carved headstones. **Memorial Park** overlooks a lake.

**Rainbow Beach,** in Vincennes, at 2204 Washington Avenue, is a 40-acre city park with tennis and volleyball courts, picnic shelters, a band shell, and a large, public swimming pool. Call Rainbow Beach at 812-886-3424.

**Sugar Loaf Indian Mound,** located behind the YMCA building on Wabash Avenue, is a natural landform built by wind deposits at the end of the glacial age. Late Woodland Indians used it as a burial ground; early settlers knew it as Prospect Hill. A spiral staircase leads to the top for a panoramic view.

## Park Trails

**Ouabache Trails Park** 👢👢👢—4 miles—The park has a network of looping trails on a site east of Fort Knox II, an early military post that became a staging area for the Battle of Tippecanoe.

# Vincennes Historic Walk 🥾

**Distance Round-Trip:** 1.3 miles (plus .3-mile return)

**Estimated Hiking Time:** 2 hours

**Trail Directions:** Begin walking on the sidewalk behind the Visitor Center for the George Rogers Clark National Historical Park **[1].** Walk toward the Wabash River, passing left of the memorial **[2].** You'll go clockwise around the memorial for a closer look at the classic, Greek-inspired structure built of granite and Indiana limestone. Fittingly, the site chosen for the memorial was the former location of Fort Sackville. At .1 mi., you'll have a view of the river **[3];** note the statue of Francis Vigo, an Italian merchant who helped finance Clark's campaign.

Continue around the memorial on the wide expanse of terrazzo that forms a plaza. At .25 mi., walk southeast between rows of redbud trees and sweet gums. At .3 mi., you'll reach the Old Cathedral **[4]** and two other earlier churches. Turn right, then right again to walk toward the cemetery. Buried here were Joseph Dubois, other soldiers, and early residents of Vincennes. Return to the sidewalk and walk past the front of the church.

After leaving the church, walk left toward the Lincoln Memorial Bridge **[5].** At .48 mi., begin crossing the bridge. Just .1 mi. upstream (on the right) was the Buffalo Trace Ford, where these large,

migrating mammals forded the Wabash River. At the other end of the bridge, cross the two-lane road to the Lincoln Trail Historic Site **[6];** the monument marks the place where 21-year-old Abraham Lincoln and his family entered Illinois. Return over the bridge; then take the sidewalk that angles through a town park, Patrick Henry Square **[7].** Continue walking toward 2nd Street, and at .83 mi., turn left, crossing Patrick Henry Drive.

Walk three blocks east on 2nd Street to the Old Bank; then turn left onto Broadway to 1st Street and turn right. You'll pass the Market Street Station **[8],** now a popular restaurant. Continue right along a brick walk that parallels 1st Street. At .93 mi., you'll pass a historic site where the State Bank of Indiana was chartered in 1834. Next, continue walking east for five blocks along 1st Street. At 1.01 mi., you'll see an old brick warehouse **[9],** formerly used as a wholesale grocery. Cross Seminary Street, and you'll come to the Old French House **[10],** a cottage that was home to fur trader Michel Brouillet in the early 19th century. At 1.2 mi., cross 1st Street, and walk past a row of historic buildings on the left. At 1.25 mi., you'll see Grouseland on the left **[11].** Grouseland was the residence of territorial governor William Henry Harrison, who later became president of the United States. Here, this historic walk ends. Walk back to the George Rogers Clark memorial using 2nd Street, and cross the memorial grounds to return to parking.

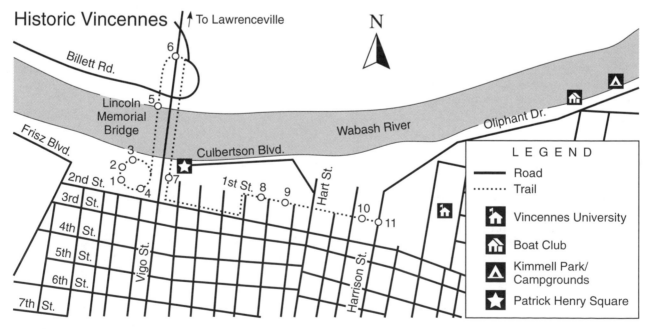

**Historic Vincennes**

To Lawrenceville

N

Billett Rd.

Lincoln Memorial Bridge

Frisz Blvd.

Wabash River

Oliphant Dr.

Culbertson Blvd.

2nd St.

3rd St.

1st St.

Hart St.

Vigo St.

4th St.

5th St.

6th St.

7th St.

Harrison St.

**L E G E N D**

—— Road
······ Trail
🏠 Vincennes University
🏠 Boat Club
🔺 Kimmell Park/ Campgrounds
⭐ Patrick Henry Square

1. Visitor Center
2. Memorial
3. View of river
4. Old Cathedral
5. Lincoln Memorial Bridge
6. Lincoln Trail Historic Site
7. Patrick Henry Square
8. Market Street Station
9. Brick warehouse
10. Historic buildings
11. Grouseland

# 29.  Shakamak State Park

- Follow trails that skirt the shore of picturesque lakes set in woodland.
- Explore marshy lands where water lilies bloom in profusion.
- Walk in the footsteps of the Kickapoo Indians, who gave the name *Shakamak* (river of long fish) to the nearby Eel River.

## Area Information

The land where the park developed was once a hunting ground favored by Kickapoo Indians, who supported the efforts of the leader Tecumseh to form an alliance of tribes. However, the defeat of Tecumseh's forces at the Battle of Tippecanoe in 1811 (while their leader was away) helped open this region for settlement.

Pioneers in the area became involved in mining coal, farming, operating mills, and making bricks. The abundant wildlife—white-tailed deer, raccoons, squirrels, and other small mammals—that once made great hunting creates great wildlife watching as well. Also, in the park's oak and pine forests, you might see cardinals, nut hatches, blue jays, or red-headed woodpeckers, and you can see various waterfowl along the shores.

Established in 1929, the park was developed largely by Civilian Conservation Corps workers during the early 1930s. There are three lakes within the park boundaries, each formed by a dam: Lake Shakamak, Lake Kickapoo, and Lake Lenape.

In all, the park has 6.5 miles of hiking trails. Two trails form loops around Lake Shakamak and Lake Lenape, and a park road provides a route around Lake Kickapoo.

**Directions:** Located southwest of Indianapolis, Shakamak can be reached via US 41. Turn east onto SR 48 at Shelburn and go five miles to the gatehouse.

**Hours Open:** The park is open between 7:00 A.M. and 11:00 P.M.

**Facilities:** Each of the three lakes has rental boats and a launch ramp. Family housekeeping cabins have been set in the woods along Lake Shakamak. A campground, saddle barn, tennis courts, swimming pool, and picnic shelters are among the other facilities.

**Permits and Rules:** Do not injure or damage any living or inanimate thing within the park. Camp, build fires, or swim only in designated areas. Drive only on roads. Snowmobiles and metal detectors are prohibited.

**Further Information:** Shakamak State Park, 6265 West State Road 48, Jasonville, IN 47438; 812-665-2158.

## Other Areas of Interest

The **Minnehaha Fish and Wildlife Area** near Sullivan is an 11,500-acre reserve. Hiking trails provide access to a variety of waterfowl, including shorebirds and birds of prey. For more information call the Department of Natural Resources at 317-232-4052.

## Park Trails

**Trail 1** 👢👢—3.25 miles—Follow this route across the dam and around Lake Shakamak. Enjoy many types of waterfowl along the way.

**Trail 3** 👢👢—1 mile—This route through oak-hickory forest along Lake Lenape's north shore loops through the territory of white-tailed deer.

# Lake Lenape Loop (Trail 4) 👢👢👢

**Distance Round-Trip:** 3.11 miles

**Estimated Hiking Time:** 2.5 hours

**Trail Directions:** Park at the Lake Lenape Shelter and boat ramp. The trail leads into the forest from the southeast corner of the parking lot **[1]**. A boardwalk goes across a shallow ravine. You'll walk on a white gravel path three feet wide that leads across two wooden bridges. The trail follows a ridge and passes a wooden bench.

At .16 mi. **[2]**, steps lead down to a small covered bridge. You'll encounter more steps. Then at .22 mi., Trail 3 **[3]** goes to the left. Continue on Trail 4 to the right and round the east end of the lake, walking clockwise. By .25 mi., the path has become packed earth. The trail curves left at a sign, then enters a ravine.

At .32 mi. **[4]**, turn right at the sign and follow the two-foot-wide dirt path around the lake. At .42 mi. **[5]**, there's a wooden bridge. At .48 mi., there's another bridge; then the trail curves back and forth on the ridge tops.

In the pine grove at .56 mi. **[6]**, we found some interesting chanterelles. Then there's another marker before a wooden platform with wide steps leading downhill at .65 mi. **[7]**. You'll pass a picnic table, and the trail next turns left to cross a bridge over a nearly dry in July creek.

At .8 mi. **[8]**, you can see a creek below with clear water and a sandy bottom. At .3 mi., we found a narrow one-foot-wide bypass around a fallen tree. Beyond, another mound of fallen branches. After following the trail left, then right, through briars, we were rewarded by a wider, packed-earth path—at least two feet wide!

At 1.0 mi. **[9]**, a wooden ramp crosses a streamlet; beyond we must thank the park maintenance crew for clearing the way by cutting through logs. At 1.17 mi., we walked along a lengthy, zigzag wooden ramp.

At 1.23 mi. **[10]**, another ramp crosses a creek enhanced by ferns. Climb upward, then from the top of the hill, look back to see a lovely woodland scene. Ahead, the path goes right; a sign confirms Trail 4 before the trail leads to another wooden ramp at 1.43 mi. **[11]**, a great viewing platform for wildflowers. The trail leads under another fallen tree, then goes right at the fork, past clover, Queen Anne's lace, and brickhorn.

By 1.6 mi., the path becomes straight as it approaches the campground at 1.7 mi. **[12]**. At the campground, follow the access road to the left, past the parking lot to the park road. Take the road to the right, through the forest to the dam for Lake Lenape. Hike along the road and across the dam. Turn right at the next T in the road and you'll be back at Lake Lenape shelter and boat ramp, a hike of 3.11 mi.

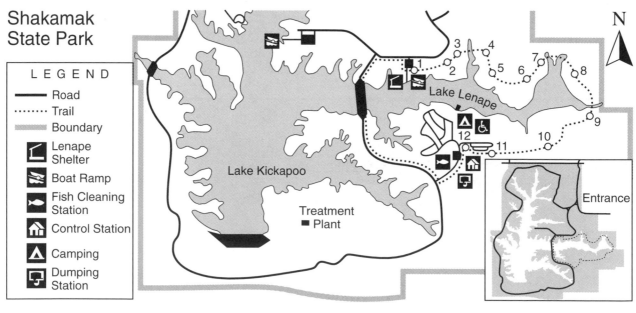

## Shakamak State Park

LEGEND
— Road
...... Trail
▬ Boundary
⬛ Lenape Shelter
⬛ Boat Ramp
⬛ Fish Cleaning Station
⬛ Control Station
⬛ Camping
⬛ Dumping Station

Lake Kickapoo

Treatment ▪ Plant

Lake Lenape

Entrance

N

1. Parking lot
2. Steps
3. Trail intersection
4. Right turn
5. Wooden bridge
6. Pine grove
7. Wooden platform
8. Creek
9. Wooden ramp
10. Ramp
11. Wooden ramp
12. Campground

# 30.  Jasper/Dubois County

- Hike a wooded trail—teeming with wildlife—that winds through a golf course.
- Enjoy a region where spring and fall temperatures hover around 70 degrees Fahrenheit.
- Take a walk past Jasper's historic churches, lovely gardens, and parks.

## Area Information

Dubois County lies at the heart of scenic southwestern Indiana, a region of forests and wildlife, rolling hills, and meandering creeks. Scenic backroads entice you to explore the shorelines of lakes or head into dense forests.

The county (pronounced "dew boys") was named for Toussaint duBois, a soldier who served under General William Henry Harrison before buying land near Portersville. Reverend Joseph Kundek encouraged more German-speaking Catholics to migrate to the area, laying a cultural foundation that includes respect for high-quality craftsmanship and a strong work ethic. Jasper, taking its name from a precious stone mentioned in the Bible, became the county seat in 1830. Known for its many woodworking industries, the town of 10,800 celebrates its German heritage with a yearly Strassenfest (street festival).

The smaller Huntingburg, platted in 1837, has a population of 5,300. Many of the buildings are of brick; the Uhl Pottery Company is located here. Many renovated buildings give the town a special character, occasionally recognized by the film industry. *A League of Their Own; Soul of the Game;* and *Hard Rain* were all filmed here.

Even smaller, the community of Ferdinand in the southeast corner of the county was named for the emperor of Austria in 1840. St. Ferdinand Church and the Monastery of the Immaculate Conception are located here. Today, the county is known for its low unemployment rate.

Dubois County has several important buildings listed on the National Register of Historic Places: the Shiloh Meeting House and Cemetery in Madison Township, Lemmon's Cumberland Presbyterian Church in Boone Township, and St. Joseph Catholic Church in Jasper.

**Directions:** Jasper and Huntingburg can be reached via State Highway 231 and by SRs 162, 164, and 356. Sultan's Run—the golf course and the nature trail—is at 1490 N. Meridian Road, north of SR 164 (east of Jasper).

**Hours Open:** The historic walks and nature trail are open all year.

**Facilities:** In Huntingburg, the large, friendly Dutchman Inn has a restaurant, pool, and many services. There are also several other good motels in Jasper. There are both modern and primitive campsites at Patoka Lake (in eastern Dubois County and neighboring counties) and campsites at Ferdinand State Forest and Dubois County Park. Jasper and Huntingburg have good restaurants and supermarkets. There are convenience stores along the highways. Parks and camping areas have picnic tables.

**Permits and Rules:** Respect the privacy of residents when walking past renovated, historic homes. Dispose of trash in proper receptacles.

**Further Information:** Dubois County Tourism Commission, P.O. Box 404, Jasper, IN 47547-0404; 812-482-9115. You can also visit Web site **www.duboiscounty.org**. You'll find the Jasper Chamber of Commerce, P.O. Box 307, at 302 West 6th Street, Jasper, IN 47547-0307; 812-482-6866.

## Other Areas of Interest

Stroll along **Huntingburg's 4th Street** (between Geiger and Van Buren Streets) to appreciate this antique alley, or dine with the locals at the Fourth Street Deli, the Gaslight Restaurant, or the Overtime. Yesterdays Antiques & Collectibles and other shops have a detailed map and information about the antique shops.

Also, call ahead (Dubois County Tourism), and you can arrange for a tour of the **Huntingburg League Stadium.** Many of the volunteer tour leaders acted as extras during the filming of the movie *A League of Their Own.* The stadium, located on the south side of town at 1st and Cherry Streets, has a century-old grandstand, large trees, and the original light towers.

Located near the village of Shoals, **Jug Rock Nature Preserve** is a small but very scenic area with tall sandstone cliffs, an unusual jug-shaped rock 50 feet high, and lovely views of the East Fork of the White River. **Dubois County Park,** on SR 162, one mile north of SR 64, has campsites and a handicapped-accessible lakefront. There are also a playground, volleyball and basketball courts, tennis courts, and horseshoe pits. Jasper/Dubois County also makes a good base from which to explore the **Hoosier National Forest** (see park #33) to the east, or the **Lincoln Parks** (see park #31) farther south.

# Sultan's Run Nature Trail 👢👢

**Distance One-Way:** 1.25 miles

**Estimated Hiking Time:** 45 minutes

**Cautions:** Listen for golfers and watch for golf balls when the trail crosses the fairways. Also, take precautions against ticks.

**Trail Directions:** Park near the clubhouse. Walk from the clubhouse to the overlook for the 18th hole. The trail enters the forest **[1]** to the right of this overlook on a dirt and grass path. At .08 mi. **[2]**, there's another overlook for the 18th fairway. Just beyond, you'll see a maintenance road—but continue walking straight.

At .23 mi. **[3]**, turn right; here, enjoy a scenic view of the green for the 2nd hole. You'll encounter a brush pile on the left, placed there to create wildlife habitat.

Continue along the path, and you'll walk in and around the greens and fairways . . . and up and down the wooded ravines. From the vantage point at .32 mi. **[4]**, you can see the tee for the 3rd hole on the right, and the pond known as Lake Splashdown. Continue walking left of the 3rd tee and the trail enters the woods.

At .47 mi. **[5]**, a sign marks the Wild Turkey Watch; the best time to see turkeys in the meadow is early morning. The trail enters a meadow, then ascends a steep hill. At .53 mi. **[6]**, there's a paved path for golf carts—watch for traffic!

At .56 mi., we noticed big bluestem, a native Hoosier grass, over six feet tall.

At .61 mi., the trail enters a wooded area. The trail then passes a small lake. At .70 mi. **[7]**, look for large wood duck boxes that have been placed beside the water. At .75 mi. **[8]**, there's a squirrel crossing; at .77 mi., turn right.

After turning left into a meadow, the trail enters a protected area, where no golfers can enter, even to look for lost balls. In this area, big bluestem and other tall prairie grasses flourish on both sides of the trail. This is a favorite bedding place for deer.

At .93 mi. **[9]**, the trail crosses the tee area for the 13th hole. Use caution; watch for golfers teeing off here. Before there was a golf course here, this was a famous horse farm. The legendary champion Supreme Sultan used to run across these hills. Many noted horses were sired here; each hole on the golf course has been named for one of these champions.

At .93 mi., the trail enters another patch of woods. At 1.04 mi. **[10]**, watch for traffic on the golf cart path. Just beyond, watch for snakes. The one we saw was about four feet long; its dull, light brown skin and darker markings made excellent camouflage. At 1.15 mi., we saw a wood duck box on the left and heard ducks on the pond. A family of beavers also lives here as their marks on a nearby tree indicate. A beaver watch sign marks the area for hikers.

The trail ends at 1.25 mi.; admire the waterfall at the 18th hole when you return to the clubhouse.

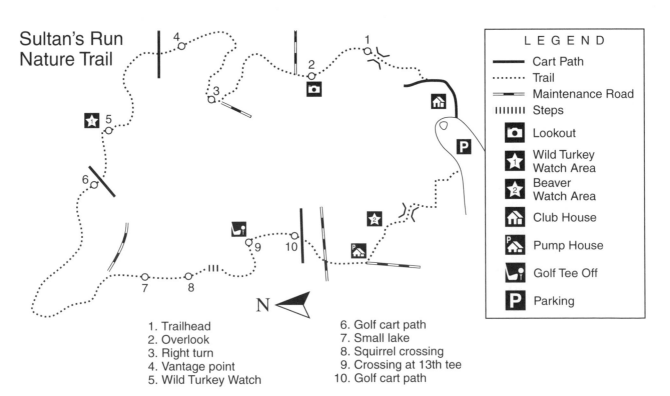

Sultan's Run Nature Trail

**LEGEND**

—— Cart Path
········ Trail
=■= Maintenance Road
||||||| Steps
📷 Lookout
⭐ Wild Turkey Watch Area
⭐2 Beaver Watch Area
🏠 Club House
P🏠 Pump House
🏌 Golf Tee Off
P Parking

1. Trailhead
2. Overlook
3. Right turn
4. Vantage point
5. Wild Turkey Watch
6. Golf cart path
7. Small lake
8. Squirrel crossing
9. Crossing at 13th tee
10. Golf cart path

N

# 31.  The Lincoln Parks

- Walk through the shadowy forests where Abraham Lincoln spent his boyhood.
- Visit a memorial dedicated to Lincoln's mother, Nancy Hanks Lincoln, who died when Abraham was nine years old.
- Wander around the log buildings and animal pens typically used on rural Indiana farms during the Lincoln era.

## Area Information

Thomas Lincoln, a carpenter and farmer, and his young family made their way across the Ohio River to southern Indiana in 1816. Attempts at farming farther south had ended in disputes over the title to the land; thus the elder Lincoln was pleased to find land in southern Indiana's hardwood forests, in a tiny community where fresh water was plentiful and the hunting was good.

Thomas Lincoln was able to purchase land south of Pigeon Creek; after traveling on horseback for 60 miles, he made payments at the land office in Vincennes. Young Abraham helped his father build a rude cabin before the first winter. Two years later, Nancy Hanks Lincoln died of an illness caused by ingesting milk from cattle that had eaten the white snakeroot plant.

A cousin, Dennis Hanks, whose mother had died in a similar way, then came to live with Thomas Lincoln, young Abe, and his older sister, Sarah, who took charge of the household tasks despite her youth. Eventually, Thomas returned to Kentucky in search of a wife; a widow with three children of her own all returned with him to Pigeon Creek, where, under their parents' wise leadership, the two families merged.

Today, two parks commemorate this American president's boyhood years. The Lincoln Boyhood National Memorial, north of SR 162, is operated by the National Park Service. Here, you'll find the living,

historical farm, complete with clucking and bleating animals, as well as a nature preserve called Sarah Lincoln's Woods, and the grave site memorial to Abraham's mother. On the south side of the highway, you'll find the sites of early mills that Abraham Lincoln visited, along with the grave of his sister, Sarah Lincoln Grigsby.

**Directions:** Drive south of Dale on SR 62; turn east on SR 162. You'll see a sign for the Lincoln Boyhood National Memorial on the left and another sign for the Lincoln State Park on the right.

**Hours Open:** Lincoln State Park is open daily between 7:00 A.M. and 11:00 P.M. The Lincoln Boyhood National Memorial is open daily between 8:00 A.M. and 5:00 P.M. except Christmas and New Year's Day.

**Facilities:** The Boyhood Memorial has a large Visitor Center, a cabin site memorial, a living historical farm, a nature preserve, and hiking trails. The state park has an amphitheater, campgrounds, cabins, picnic shelters, a Nature Center, historic sites, hiking trails, and a lake with boat rental and a swimming beach.

**Permits and Rules:** Do not injure or damage any plant, animal, or structure in either park. Swim, camp, and build fires only in designated areas. Carry out any trash you bring in, or place it in the proper receptacle. Motorized vehicles are not allowed on park trails.

**Further Information:** Lincoln Boyhood National Memorial, National Park Service, Lincoln City, IN 47552; 812-937-4541. Lincoln State Park, Box 216, Lincoln City, IN 47552; 812-937-4710.

## Other Areas of Interest

The **Colonel William Jones State Historical Site,** Gentryville, was once the residence of a civil war leader. Some researchers believe that Abe Lincoln did odd jobs for the family.

## Park Trails

**Lincoln State Park Trail** 👢👢—3.7 miles—Also known as James Gentry Trail or Trail 4, this long loop from the historic residence, once owned by Gentry (who owned a general store where Abraham Lincoln clerked), circles Weber Lake.

**Lincoln Parks Connecting Trail** 👢👢—1.75 miles—This unnamed path, which parallels the main state park road on the east side in Lincoln State Park, connects the state park with the Lincoln Boyhood National Memorial property to the north.

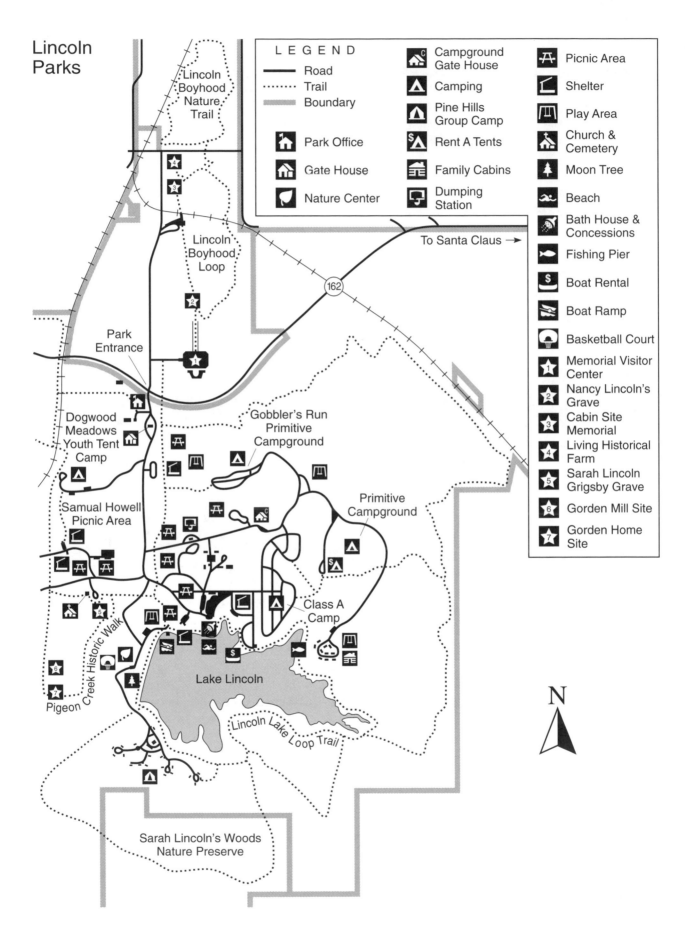

# Lincoln Parks

**LEGEND**

— Road
····· Trail
▬▬ Boundary

🏠 Park Office
🏠 Gate House
🍃 Nature Center

⛺ᶜ Campground Gate House
⛺ Camping
⛺ Pine Hills Group Camp
$ Rent A Tents
🏚 Family Cabins
🚮 Dumping Station

🎪 Picnic Area
🏕 Shelter
🎠 Play Area
⛪ Church & Cemetery
🌲 Moon Tree
🏊 Beach
🚿 Bath House & Concessions
🎣 Fishing Pier
$ Boat Rental
🚣 Boat Ramp
🏀 Basketball Court
⭐1 Memorial Visitor Center
⭐2 Nancy Lincoln's Grave
⭐3 Cabin Site Memorial
⭐4 Living Historical Farm
⭐5 Sarah Lincoln Grigsby Grave
⭐6 Gorden Mill Site
⭐7 Gorden Home Site

Lincoln Boyhood Nature Trail

Lincoln Boyhood Loop

To Santa Claus →

162

Park Entrance

Dogwood Meadows Youth Tent Camp

Samual Howell Picnic Area

Gobbler's Run Primitive Campground

Primitive Campground

Class A Camp

Pigeon Creek Historic Walk

Lake Lincoln

Lincoln Lake Loop Trail

Sarah Lincoln's Woods Nature Preserve

N

# Lincoln Boyhood Loop Trail

**Distance Round-Trip:** 1 mile

**Estimated Hiking Time:** 45 minutes

**Trail Directions:** Begin walking on one of the two brown stone allees [1] that heads north of the Visitor Center toward the flagpoles [2]. Pass the flagpoles and continue walking straight. The trail enters the cemetery [3] where Nancy Hanks Lincoln, mother of the president, and other pioneers lie buried. You'll see her gravestone at .06 mi.

Walk beyond the iron fence and take the path to Lincoln Farm. The wide, stately path of clay-colored gravel passes benches shaded by ancient trees. At .29 mi., you'll cross the southern boundary of what was once Thomas Lincoln's 100-acre farm. Here, Abraham Lincoln spent 14 important years. Continue walking; pass a shelter house [4] and tables, then a railroad crossing [5].

At .35 mi., walk between sections of a split-rail fence [6]; you'll see the garden plots and cornfield of the living history farm ahead of you [7]. We heard a rooster crow and saw a lovely bluebird. At .42 mi., follow the trail left for a look at the cabin site memorial. At .46 mi., you'll pass a spur trail that leads 100 yards west to the Lincoln Spring. Sheep, lambs, cattle, chickens, and other livestock wander about a farm much like the one where Lincoln lived.

In addition to farming, Thomas Lincoln also worked at carpentry. Notice the variety of hides on display at the carpenter shop: coyote, red fox, raccoon, opossum, muskrat, groundhog, and beaver. After visiting the farm, return to the maple tree on the main trail, at .58 mi.

Turn left at the signs for the Trail of 12 Stones [8]. This segment of the Lincoln Boyhood Loop route features important dates in Lincoln's life and circles back to the Visitor Center. At .64 mi., the first stone commemorates Lincoln's birthplace in Hodgenville, Kentucky. On the left, at .67 mi., a link trail [9] leads to the Lincoln Boyhood Nature Preserve.

Continue walking ahead on the gravel path to complete the Lincoln Boyhood Loop. You'll pass several stones, some with rather tenuous connections to Lincoln's life. The fourth stone, for example, at .78 mi., was brought here from the Berry-Lincoln store in New Salem, Illinois.

The woodland path is lovely, much finer than the rude paths Lincoln walked as a boy. At another stone marker, you'll find bricks from the Lexington, Kentucky, home of Abraham Lincoln's stepmother. Beyond it, at .84 mi. [10], you'll come upon a stone brought from the White House where President and Mrs. Lincoln lived in Washington, D.C. Continue walking and you'll find a stone transported from the site of Lincoln's Gettysburg Address [11].

Note the maple, oak, and shagbark hickory in the forest as you pass. Just before the end of the Trail of 12 Stones, you'll see a pillar brought from Lincoln's 10th Street home [12]. Continue walking back toward the Visitor Center, and you will pass a monument to Nancy Hanks Lincoln, contributed by the community of Springfield, Illinois.

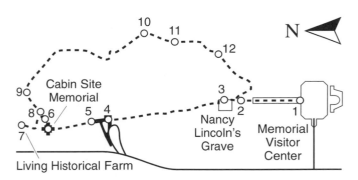

1. Trailhead
2. Flagpoles
3. Cemetery
4. Shelter house
5. Railroad crossing
6. Split-rail fence
7. Living historical farm
8. Trail of 12 Stones
9. Spur to nature preserve
10. Stone from White House
11. Stone from site of Gettysburg Address
12. Stone from Lincoln's home

# Lincoln Boyhood Nature Trail 👢

**Distance Round-Trip:** 1 mile

**Estimated Hiking Time:** 45 minutes

**Cautions:** Use mosquito repellant. The connecting trail crosses a highway, where traffic goes much faster than the posted speed limit. **Supervise children and cross this road with care.** Also, carry a leaflet from the Visitor Center as you walk, and you'll have information keyed to numbered posts.

**Trail Directions:** Access the trail at .67 mi. on the Lincoln Boyhood Loop **[1].** Turn left and follow the connecting trail to the nature preserve. Overhead, we could hear a chorus of insects in the forest canopy. Note that the forest has been relatively undisturbed since the time of the Lincolns. At .03 mi. **[2],** cross a highway; you'll see the nature loop trailhead beside a sumac tree. We walked right and followed this route counterclockwise.

Throughout the Lincoln Boyhood National Memorial, you'll see red flags tagging research experiments in the forest; these are part of a program to return the forest to a wilderness state much like what Thomas Lincoln found. At .13 mi., note the log benches **[3]** to the left of the bark mulch trail. At .18 mi., there's a rail fence on the right. Ahead, you'll encounter an intermittent stream, where stone slabs have been placed as a crude bridge.

Look for wildflowers; the path winds left at .26 mi. through meadow grasses **[4].** Indiana has more than 150 species of grasses; here, we noted little bluestem, burdock, and prairie dock, along with a tiny, pale, red-violet flower with five petals growing near the ground. Come back in spring, and you'll find even more wild-flowers, encouraged by the combination of moisture and sunlight reaching past the unfurled leaves.

By .33 mi. **[5],** you'll be passing through younger forest, where slim saplings have begun to cast the shade that encourages shade-tolerant trees during the process of plant succession. The path is crushed stone the color of clay. Because this route is less traveled than the park's main trail, you have a greater chance to see woodland birds. We spotted a bright male cardinal and heard a woodpecker drilling for insect

larva beneath some tree bark. Soon, the path becomes mossy; continue counterclockwise around the loop. Notice evidence of the cycle of life around you. As logs decay, fungi thrive. Decomposing logs and leaves return nutrients to the soil, while providing habitat for small mammals, insects, mosses, and lichen.

At .41 mi. **[6],** we came upon log benches, a possible picnic site. Look for oak, hickory, sycamore, and tulip trees in the upper canopy and dogwood and redbuds in the understory. By .47 mi., you'll be walking on gravel again. Then by .56 mi. **[7],** we could hear traffic on the road to the right, behind the trees. Here, a tiny, red-headed woodpecker and a chattering blue jay added color to the scene. Startled by approaching footsteps, a young rabbit froze midtrail, then scampered off into tall grasses.

At .65 mi. **[8],** turn right—you'll see the road—and walk south on the connecting path to the Lincoln Boyhood Loop. Although the sign by the road says the speed limit is 15 miles per hour, vehicles were going much faster. Across the road, we could hear the rooster from the living history farm. Continue walking; you can return to the Visitor Center via the Trail of 12 Stones on the left.

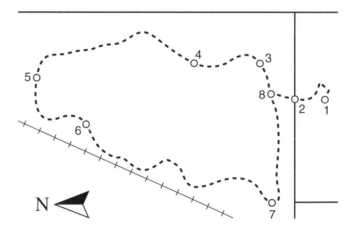

1. Trailhead
2. Highway
3. Log benches
4. Meadow grasses
5. Younger forest
6. Log benches
7. Sounds of traffic
8. Right turn

# Lake Lincoln Loop (Trail 1) 🥾🥾

**Distance Round-Trip:** 1.5 miles

**Estimated Hiking Time:** 1 hour

**Trail Directions:** Follow the park road; then park at the Lakeside Shelter **[1]**. Begin hiking beyond the boat ramp to the right. You'll make a counterclockwise loop around the lake. Look for a narrow dirt track that skirts the lake and crosses the dam **[2]**. At the edge of the water, large, fragrant water lilies bloom in July. At .04 mi., you'll be walking across the dam, with the lake on your left, as the squeals of children drift toward you from the beach.

Below on the right is the Nature Center; the naturalist has a fascinating collection of skins and bones, so visit the center before you leave the park. At .08 mi., you approach a red metal bridge **[3]** over the spillway, where the water surges through a channel on the right, and there are more water lilies on the lakeside. At .09 mi., the trail goes into the forest, thick with cottonwood trees, left of the bridge.

The path of small rocks and clay follows the lake. At .2 mi., there's a circle of logs and wooden benches on the right **[4]**, sometimes used by campers. Continue walking forward over a wide gravel path; we saw no signs or markers for the trail. However, the lake will be on your left. Although the woodland scene is lovely, the path may occasionally be covered by pools of water; when this happens, follow a bypass trail around. From .25 mi., you can see a log cabin beside the beach; ahead, we encountered another mud hole just before a wooden bridge.

The path heads uphill at .29 mi., where we could hear a turtle plop into a marshy arm of the lake as we passed. Just beyond, ignore the path to the right; instead, continue walking on the gravel as it curves left, goes downhill, and crosses another wooden bridge. At .34 mi. **[5]**, the trail to the fire tower heads to the right. Continue walking on Trail 1, and you'll walk through mixed pine forest on this loop around the lake.

At .37 mi., the path becomes level, as you come to a flat peninsula at the lake's east end. From a wooden bridge, you can see more lilies and other marsh plants on the left edge of the lake. At .43 mi. **[6]**, you'll be standing on pine needles, shaded by tall trees, enjoying a lakeside view. Continue along the path as it veers away from the lake, into the forest, and passes yellow poplar, maple, beech, and cottonwood trees.

At .57 mi., we saw the first marker for this trail: a wooden stake with a number 1 and a directional arrow. Here and there, the ground is covered with amazing light green plants with leaves organized around a circular center. Farther on, forest debris has blocked the flow of water to form a pond at left. Marshy grasses and flowers attract wonderful butterflies in July. We encountered another wooden bridge at .63 mi. **[7]**, where the path is mostly gravel.

At .69 mi., there's a Y in the trail, but nothing was marked, so we followed the branch to the right. This route took us past a cluster of handsome cabins before we picked up the lakeside trail again beyond them. At .83 mi., there's a small fishing dock on the left **[8]**. Take a right at the lily pond (an inlet from the lake), and you'll come to a long, wooden boardwalk that leads through the wetland and curves to the left.

When the boardwalk ends, at .92 mi., follow the path toward the lake and walk between the water on the left and an RV campground on the right **[9]**. There's soon another boardwalk, where our steps echoing in the woodland startled a flock of birds into flight. We noted cattails on the left. Continue walking and you'll cross the concrete walk that skirts the pedal boat rental, before coming to another wooden bridge. Keep walking around the lake, and you'll return to the Lakeside Shelter at 1.5 mi., or do what we did, and end the walk at the concession stand **[10]**!

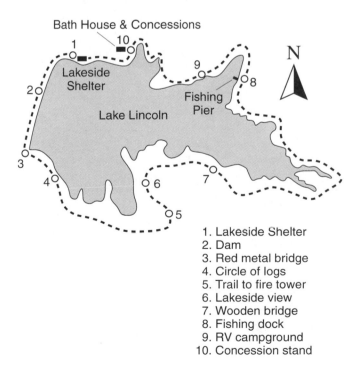

1. Lakeside Shelter
2. Dam
3. Red metal bridge
4. Circle of logs
5. Trail to fire tower
6. Lakeside view
7. Wooden bridge
8. Fishing dock
9. RV campground
10. Concession stand

# Pigeon Creek Historic Walk 🥾

**Distance Round-Trip:** .64 mile

**Estimated Hiking Time:** 45 minutes

**Trail Directions:** Follow park signs to the Pigeon Creek Church **[1]**, and park beside it. Before you walk, examine the historic cemetery **[2]** behind the church. Sarah Lincoln Grigsby, who was Abraham Lincoln's sister, is buried here. Begin hiking left (walk west) of the entrance road. You'll go over an early road **[3]**, no longer used, and pass pine trees on the left and an abandoned farm field on the right. By .08 mi., you'll be moving along a wide, grassy path through a mixed forest with scattered sweet gum trees.

At .25 mi. **[4]**, we came to the Noah Gordon Homesite; Gordon, you may recall, owned a mill where the young Lincoln bought grain. At the site, we couldn't find much evidence of the early home, only a clearing, a few black walnut trees, and an old well.

A sign on the right marks a spur trail to the amphitheater, where performances of the outdoor drama "Young Abe Lincoln" are held. Behind the theater, where the trail comes out, are plantings of coneflowers and other native species, as well as convenient rest rooms.

Return to the Noah Gordon Homesite; then walk straight ahead over the mowed-grass clearing. At .35 mi., you'll enter the woods again on a gravel path that turns promptly left **[5]**. Soon, a wooden bridge heads right and slopes downhill. From this vantage point, we could see a wonderful mix of sycamores, maples, beech, and walnut trees. Another slim tree, with large, pointed, oval leaves, which seemed out of proportion to the size of its trunk, we later learned was a pawpaw.

Continue walking, now on gravel. At .43 mi., a tiny creek has banks bordered by ferns. Follow the path left, and you pass fallen trees that have been cut through, then left for wildlife habitat. The trail crosses another creek over a bridge **[6]**. At .49 mi. **[7]**, you'll enter mixed forest dominated by conifers. Soon after, you'll encounter a larger creek, where there's a mixture of deciduous trees and some small, symmetrical evergreens we thought might be balsam fir. At .6 mile, the forest has changed to predominantly oak trees. Between these oaks and sycamores, you'll see the old cemetery again and the Pigeon Creek Church. At .64 mi. **[8]**, a spur to the right will take you to the park road, picnic shelters, boat ramp, and beach. On the left, walk toward the parking lot, where this hike ends.

1. Pigeon Creek Church
2. Cemetery
3. Early road
4. Noah Gordon Homesite
5. Left turn
6. Bridge
7. Mixed forest
8. Spur to road

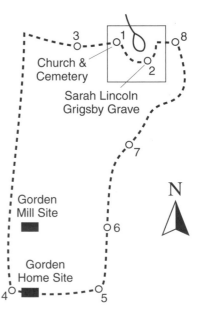

# 32.  Patoka Lake

- Wander over a 1,000-acre peninsula where a network of hiking trails leads to rock formations, wildlife habitats, a pine plantation, and a scenic overlook.

- Visit a rock shelter where archaeologists have found evidence of use for about 4,000 years.

- Within a solar-powered Nature Center, see wildlife up close—and behind glass—at a 26,000-acre recreation area developed beside a sprawling, recreational lake.

## Area Information

In the opinion of some geologists, a ridge of sandstone just beyond the Visitor Center at Patoka Lake was formed when a river dropped sand and silt into a shallow, inland sea. You can still see rock outcroppings from this Wickliffe Formation. Nearer to Totem Rock, an impressive outcropping of Mansfield sandstone deposited during the Pennsylvanian Age, indigenous people who inhabited the Patoka River valley camped here seasonally during hunting and food-gathering expeditions. The home villages of these people were thought to be the White, Wabash, and Ohio Rivers. Flint points, stone tools, scrapers, pottery, and other early artifacts found at the site offer clues to the lifestyle of these early people.

The first white settlers in the area found petroglyphs on rocks that depicted three turtles heading in the same direction. Although assumed to be totems, symbols that represented a family, the full meaning of the totems has never been discovered. Settlers divided some of the land into small family farms, built a schoolhouse, and used the scenic rock settings on the peninsula for social gatherings and picnics. For a time, saltpeter was extracted from a cave at Totem Rock, which was also a source of gypsum.

Constructed during the 1970s, the Patoka Lake reservoir was built for flood control and not primarily for recreation. Created by building a dam across the Patoka River, the lake supplies water to at least four counties. Patoka Lake is 25 miles long, forming a pattern that resembles a tree branch extending east of Jasper. There are 8,880 acres of water on the surface.

Including the surrounding 17,000 acres of land, this is the largest property managed by Indiana's Department of Natural Resources. Enhancing wildlife habitat and providing quality recreational activities are two of the park's goals.

**Directions:** Patoka Lake's hiking trails, bicycle trails, and campgrounds are located in the Newton-Stewart State Recreation Area. Drive 17 miles east of Jasper on SR 164; turn north at the sign for Newton-Stewart to reach the entrance. Follow the park road north, past the campground, to the Nature Center to reach the hiking trails.

**Hours Open:** You can hike the trails during daylight hours. Allow enough time and energy to return to the Visitor Center (also called the Nature Center or the Interpretive Center).

**Facilities:** Patoka Lake has marinas and launch ramps for boating on many sections of the lake. The Newton-Stewart area has several hundred campsites, modern and primitive, plus picnic tables and shelters. Many of the sites have scenic overlooks. Outside the entrance to Newton-Stewart are several food concessions. Jasper has an excellent selection of motels and restaurants.

**Permits and Rules:** Observe federal regulations, including speed limits on the water and along park roads. Do not litter; carry out any trash you generate. Do not feed wildlife; do not damage or remove any natural features or structures in the park.

**Further Information:** Contact Patoka Lake at RR 1, Birdseye, IN 47513; 812-685-2464. Call 812-482-9115 for Jasper and Dubois County tourism information.

## Other Areas of Interest

**Sultan's Run Wildlife Trail** (see park #30), east of Jasper, at 1490 North Meridian Road, is a fascinating nature trail that has been built by golf course maintenance supervisor Craig Healey. An appealing 1.25-mile loop trail that winds in and around the fairways and greens gives hikers access to an amazing variety of wildlife. Call 812-482-1009.

The **Yellow Birch Ravine Nature Preserve** near Taswell has an unusual mixture of hemlock, mountain laurel, and yellow birch trees on a 441-acre site with ridges, cliffs, and ravines. Call the Department of Natural Resources, Division of Nature Preserves; 317-232-4052.

# Patoka Lake

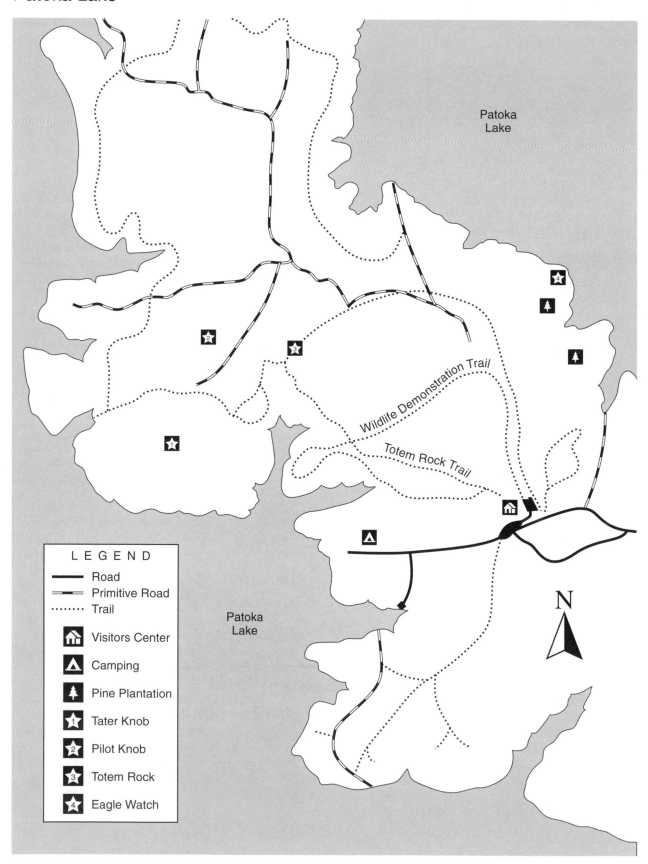

LEGEND
— Road
⊨ Primitive Road
⋯ Trail

🏠 Visitors Center

⛺ Camping

🌲 Pine Plantation

⭐1 Tater Knob

⭐2 Pilot Knob

⭐3 Totem Rock

⭐4 Eagle Watch

Patoka Lake

Patoka Lake

Wildlife Demonstration Trail

Totem Rock Trail

N

# Totem Rock Trail 👢👢👢

**Distance One-Way:** 2.15 miles

**Estimated Hiking Time:** 2 hours plus a 45-minute return using the maintenance road shortcut

**Cautions:** This route is not well marked; orient yourself to the Visitor Center before you leave, so you can return in that direction. Consider using a compass. Plan to leave the area before dark.

**Trail Directions:** Begin hiking on the main trail that starts behind the Visitor Center and beside a park bulletin board **[1]**. You'll walk a clay path overgrown with roots that descends into a maple forest. Along the trail, we noticed little violet flowers with green, stacked centers. Can you identify them?

At .1 mi., the Wildlife Management Demonstration Area Interpretive Trail goes to the left **[2]**. Continue walking to the right on the main trail toward Totem Rock. The trail follows a ridge covered with thin maples, and the forest floor is strewn with fallen branches and packed, brown leaves. Note the moss-covered rock formations in the ravine below, on the left. This mossy carpet extends over part of the path.

At .2 mi., a rock outcropping **[3]**, thought to be formed from early deposits of sand and silt, is covered with odd, little orange plants and luminous green mosses. The main trail continues forward, then descends steep, rocky steps. Occasionally, the trail is marked with white and orange blazes in the form of paint rings around dead trees. The trail crosses a tiny stream, before the route curves right. Then it curves left, before going over a low hill and narrows as it descends toward another rocky stream.

At .49 mi., cross the stream **[4]**; then follow the trail past clumps of ferns as it curves back into the forest. We noticed fungi with horizontal stripes radiating like a fan; later, we identified this as turkey tail fungus. The trail crosses another creek and ascends a low hill; we found it covered with young maple trees. After another creek, at .75 mi. the path goes uphill and turns right, just beyond another blaze. The leafy tops of slim maple trees filter the light. At .91 mi. **[5]**, the path crosses the wildlife management trail; soon, you encounter another creek and follow the rocky path uphill.

At 1.29 mi., the path curves left; we spotted toadstools of a light, pinky red, near mosses that glowed in various shades of green. Were you aware that ferns and mosses have chlorophyll, and lichen do not?

At 1.48 mi. **[6]**, walk on a ridge above a ravine filled with slim, young maples. You'll then cross a creek, walking across piled-up rocks to reach the other side. We noted a tree stump there, full of small holes made by woodpeckers. You'll see a ridge, and when you walk up it, the reward is a splendid view looking down into a ravine on the left. Then, at 2.11 mi., you've reached the impressive Totem Rock formations **[7]**, molded of Mansfield sandstone. Imagine the much earlier visitors who camped here, sometimes using the low caves as shelter. A majestic stand of maple and beech trees, flanked by moss-covered boulders and enhanced by ferns, guards the rock and cave formations.

This hike ends at 2.15 mi. Although we might have returned over the same route we came, it was getting dark, so we followed a rough, narrow access trail to the right that took us above the rocks to a utility access road **[8]**. Turn right, follow this grassy, rutty road, and you'll eventually return to the parking lot and the Visitor Center.

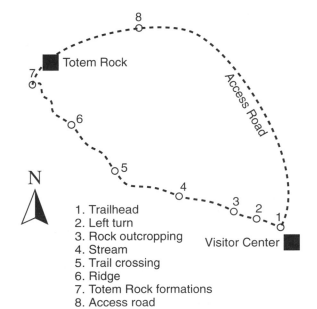

1. Trailhead
2. Left turn
3. Rock outcropping
4. Stream
5. Trail crossing
6. Ridge
7. Totem Rock formations
8. Access road

# Wildlife Management Demonstration Trail 👢👢

**Distance One-Way:** 1.71 miles

**Estimated Hiking Time:** 1 hour

**Cautions:** There are lots of stones, roots, and forest debris; wear boots or closed shoes.

**Trail Directions:** Begin walking on the main trail that begins by the bulletin board and behind the Visitor Center **[1]**. At .08 mi. **[2]**, take a left fork at the sign for Wildlife Management. This specialized route will show you interpretive examples of Indiana Department of Natural Resources wildlife management practices at Indiana reservoirs. You'll walk past a layered rock formation on the right, with some sandstone that has honeycomb patterns. The sandy clay trail passes skinny young trees and a great deal of underbrush.

At .31 mi., you'll be walking through a field that was farmed until the mid-20th century. By reestablishing the earlier forests, diverse kinds of wildlife can live here again. At .44 mi. **[3]**, you'll encounter a rocky creek clogged with forest debris. This intermittent stream only provides water for wildlife during certain times of the year. Deer and smaller mammals may not travel far from their homes; therefore, wildlife managers sometimes provide additional sources of water. Continue walking and you'll see ferns pushing up through a thick cover of leaves in this maple and beech forest.

At .71 mi. **[4]**, turn left, where you'll hike a wide, grassy path. Through an arrangement with local farmers, they leave 10 percent of their crops as wildlife food. They grow field corn, clover, sunflowers, sorghum, and other crops in rotation for this purpose. At .75 mi., you'll notice another access lane on the hiking peninsula. These openings allow access for equipment used in wildlife maintenance and, if needed, fire-fighting vehicles. Continue walking past a tangle of greenbrier and other plants. You'll soon see a meadow on the left. A three-acre area on the peninsula is deliberately burned every three years to control plant succession. Burning thick ground cover gives large young birds better access to insects, and the new plants that grow after the burning produce more seeds for wildlife food.

Continue walking past the lake on the left and a blackberry patch on the right. By .93 mi. **[5]**, you'll be hiking on a wide, grassy path. Beyond the post keyed to No. 10, you'll see boxes that have been provided for wood ducks, which normally prefer to make nests in trees. These alternative houses enable the once-threatened wood duck to breed near the lake. Continue walking and you'll pass selected species of lespedeza being grown for wildlife food and nesting cover.

By 1.0 mi., you'll be able to look across the water at the changes wrought by succession. Note that trees have replaced grasses and shrubs. The area you walk through gets mowed once or twice a year to set back this natural progression of changes. The trail then leads out of the woods and into a lower area. At 1.09 mi., you'll see an early hand-dug well and notice a mineral lick. Wildlife, as well as humans, require salt and other minerals. At 1.14 mi. **[6]**, the Wildlife Management Demonstration Trail crosses the main trail. Continue along the trail, and you'll see girdled trees being removed to release nut-producing trees from competition with them.

At 1.29 mi. **[7]**, you might see an old tire, one of several along the trail, that has been placed up high as a squirrel nesting box. Beyond it, you'll walk past a forest opening, made to create a smaller, sunlit ecosystem within the larger, shadier forest. The new plants that grow where more sunlight penetrates increase the diversity available to wildlife. Continue walking and you'll see a grassy maintenance road at 1.71 mi. **[8]**. Turn right, for the hike ends here; follow this wide, rutty road back to the Visitor Center and parking lot.

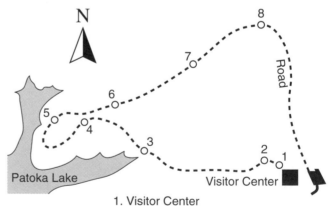

1. Visitor Center
2. Left turn
3. Creek
4. Left turn
5. Wide, grassy path
6. Trail crossing
7. Old tire
8. Maintenance road

# 33.  Hoosier National Forest

- Hike through vast tracts of forestland where you'll see occasional signs of human habitation over a period of 11,000 years.
- Choose from about 200 miles of trails.
- Follow trails through steep hills and ravines.

## Area Information

When the glaciers that surrounded this region were receding, bands of indigenous people found excellent hunting as they chased elk, bear, and mastodon across forests and meadows. During this period, these early people hunted in bands and gathered wild foods from the rich supply in the forests.

As the region's first people developed a settled lifestyle, they cultivated maize, squash, and other foods in village gardens. Nature supplied material for tools, and the clay they found enabled them to make pottery. Buffalo and white-tailed deer became an important part of the people's lifestyle, with the carcasses from these animals yielding not only meat, but also bones for tools and skins for clothing.

The Buffalo Trace, the route made by migrating buffalo, provided early settlers with a route through the forest. Although the hardwood forests in southern Indiana were in some ways an obstacle, they were also an asset. From the mid-19th century into the early 20th, more efficient equipment made it possible to harvest timber from the rugged areas in what is now the Hoosier National Forest.

Early records show that white oak, black walnut, tulip poplar, and black cherry were highly valued for their timber—and the first to be cut down. Young couples and families worked hard to raise crops and livestock or to sell timber; eventually, many moved elsewhere, leaving the land eroded and the soil depleted. During the economic depression of the 1930s, many landowners were unable to pay their taxes. In 1935, new legislation enabled the federal government to acquire such land for national forests. Using workers from the Civilian Conservation Corps program, the National Forest Service began rehabilitating portions of eroded southern Indiana land.

Eventually, as the population grew and the employment pattern in Indiana shifted from rural agricultural to urban manufacturing, the Forest Service became aware of people's need for recreation. Today, Hoosier National Forest lands extend from Monroe and Brown counties south to the Ohio River. Of the 200 miles of hiking trails, some are multiuse. Others have been developed for hikers and bikers or for hikers only. Some areas, like Hardin Ridge, have been developed with paved roads and elaborate campground facilities. Others are backcountry areas, where you must pack in all supplies and the only accommodation will be the tent you carry.

**Directions:** You can reach the smaller section of Hoosier National Forest, east of Bloomington and Bedford, by following SR 446 southeast of Bloomington or SR 58 southwest of Columbus. You can reach the larger, long sections that extend south to the Ohio River via SR 450 southwest of Bedford, US 150 southeast of Shoals, SR 64 west of Marengo, or via sections of SR 37.

**Hours Open:** You can use the trails year-round. At various times, however, hunters are allowed access to certain types of wildlife; plan your hiking with the hunting season in mind.

**Facilities:** For more details about facilities along the 13 trails and trail systems in the Hoosier National Forest, as well as the Charles C. Deam Wilderness, contact one of the offices during business hours (see phone numbers below). Generally, primitive camping is allowed in the backcountry; some sections have modern campgrounds, swimming lakes, and boat ramps, but others do not.

**Permits and Rules:** Mountain bikers yield to horses and hikers. Hikers yield to horseback riders, and riders should keep horses under control. Carry out any trash you bring in. Motorized vehicles are not permitted on trails.

**Further Information:** Hoosier National Forest, 811 Constitution Avenue, Bedford, IN 47421; 812-275-5987. Tell City Ranger District, 248 15th Street, Tell City, IN 47586; 812-547-7051.

## Other Areas of Interest

**The Adventure Hiking Trail,** a 27-mile backcountry loop through Harrison-Crawford State Forest and the Wyandotte Woods State Recreation Area, is a challenging route over natural escarpments, past caves and sinkholes, and through the habitats of a variety of wildlife. Call 812-738-8232, Department of Natural Resources office, Corydon, for Harrison-Crawford State Forest information. Call Department of Natural Resources, Wyandotte Woods State Recreation Area, 812-738-8232, for Wyandotte Woods information.

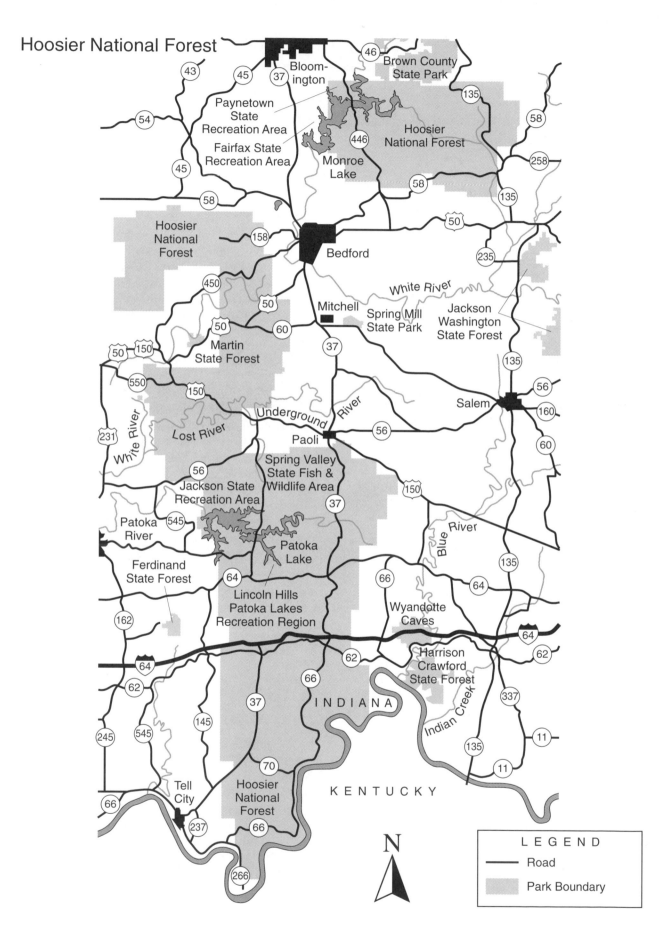

Hoosier National Forest

# Pioneer Mothers' Memorial Forest Trail 👢👢

**Distance One-Way:** 1.25 miles

**Estimated Hiking Time:** 45 minutes

**Trail Directions:** Drive 2 mi. south of Paoli on SR 37, then park in the lot beside the road. Enter the forest on a white stone path about three feet wide and pass a segment of wooden fence **[1]**. You'll hike through an 88-acre tract, the last area of old-growth forest of this size in the state of Indiana. The forest became a national natural landmark in 1974. The path soon becomes dirt, as it descends into an open area with low, green shrubs. We noticed pale, yellow touch-me-not flowers, also known as jewelweed, and scattered ferns. At .06 mi., a spur trail on the left leads to a giant black walnut tree **[2]**; crows caw and other birds chatter high in the canopy. Walnut trees 40 inches in diameter and 130 feet tall were once common in Indiana, but it took a major effort by many people to preserve this tract of forest.

We passed ash trees, violets, and more ferns before coming to another spur to the left at .16 mi. **[3]**. Follow the spur and you'll reach several large, ancient sycamores. Then return to the main path, now about three feet wide. We also noticed ancient oak trees, many maples, and shagbark hickory on this beautiful forest trail. At .24 mi., we saw the intricate pattern made by mosses and lichen on a stately black oak on the right and enjoyed delicate shell lichen on fallen logs. Soon, we were walking among hickory nuts, along a path past great oak and hickory trees that shaded much younger, slim maples and sassafras trees.

Unfortunately, a tall beech tree on the left at .36 mi. had been initialed by passing carvers. Continue walking downhill on a clay path strewn with twigs and leaves. Forest debris is everywhere; we passed a massive, decaying trunk, then walked around a tree that blocked the trail. By .51 mi. **[4]**, we had come to an open area; yet, the branches of the trees closed in overhead. One giant black walnut tree had been decapitated, perhaps by lightning. Broken tree trunks are favored by some animals as habitat, but this one was too high to see what might have been nesting there.

At .58 mi. **[5]**, a stone wall marks the Indiana Pioneer Mothers' Memorial. The trail passes between sections of the wall. Beyond it, we noticed brown toadstools and vibrant, green mosses on a fallen log. At .68 mi., the path curves right and descends. By .67 mi., we were walking beneath a lot more sky and could see evergreens ahead. Here and there were exquisite wildflowers; some of the smallest blossoms looked like large, purple bonnets above smaller, white doll dresses. By .74 mi., we had come to a parking lot **[6]** with a wooden bench. Here, continue walking ahead on a road that cuts through pine and maple forest. By .98 mi., we could hear traffic on SR 150 ahead. Beside the trail, we continued to see regal specimens of American beech and sycamore trees.

At 1.11 mi., the trail crosses a creek on a solid concrete bridge **[7]**; here, we could see water spilling over the rocks in the streambed, beneath the great arching branch of an ancient sycamore. To the right at 1.17 mi. was the creek and an expanse of meadow, bordered by small houses. By 1.25 mi., we had reached the other end of the trail, located along SR 150, 1.5 mi. southeast of Paoli. We returned the way we had come.

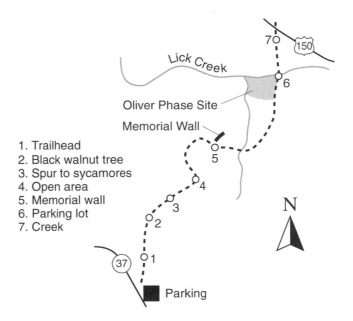

1. Trailhead
2. Black walnut tree
3. Spur to sycamores
4. Open area
5. Memorial wall
6. Parking lot
7. Creek

# Two Lakes Loop Trail 👢👢👢

**Distance Round-Trip:** 4 miles

**Estimated Hiking Time:** 2 to 3 hours

**Cautions:** Trail is not marked very well. If you lose the track, keep in mind the lake is on the left. Or take along a compass.

**Trail Directions:** Entrance to the park is 1.5 mi. south of I-64. Follow the park road west to the trailhead for Two Lakes Loop Trail **[1]**, and park south of the road. Begin walking south down a wide, clay path into a forest of mixed pine and oak. This route follows a most interesting segment of the 12-mile Two Lakes Loop, exploring hills and hollows before following the southwest shore of Lake Celina and passing rock shelters used by early inhabitants.

The route soon becomes open and grassy, as you descend left through pine trees. At .1 mi., look for wildlife around Deer Pond **[2]**. Beyond it, the West Trail of the Two Lakes Loop **[3]** heads toward Indian Lake. Continue walking forward, toward Lake Celina on the left. The trail you walk, marked in white, uses black directional arrows. You'll walk uphill over a grassy path. At .25 mi. **[4]**, a segment of the American Discovery Trail heads to the right.

Continue walking forward, descend a rocky, clay slope, and you'll hear water gurgling. At .34 mi., you'll ford a creek; then the trail heads left and uphill, but soon drops down again. You'll see Lake Celina between the maple and tulip trees as the route comes closer to the lake. At .61 mi., you'll cross a mowed-grass path on the dam for Winding Branch **[5]**. A town was once platted in this location, but we saw no signs of it when we passed. To the right is an open view, where, my companion claims, "You can almost see forever."

Continue uphill on the grassy path; by .88 mi., you'll have reached the crest of a ridge **[6]**. Look behind you for a great view of the lake, sometimes used for sailing. Continue walking into the upland forest of maple and beech. Ahead, you can begin to see the peninsulas where the trail will skirt the shore. The route winds through forest, then at 1.46 mi. curves left and down. At 1.52 mi., you'll encounter a branch that flows over rocks. Soon after, we saw a box turtle resting on the trail, its coloring blending amazingly with the surroundings.

By 2.0 mi., we were walking downhill again, then across another stream **[7]**—this one with a shale bottom. We forded the creek, then stepped across a smaller stream as the route came closer to Lake Celina (on the left). At 2.63 mi., we were walking through forest of mostly pine, with scattered ash and

other hardwoods. The trail curves right to pass through lowlands, then goes right and downhill.

At 3.25 mi., we could hear trucks on SR 37 to the right **[8]**. We soon forded a rocky creek before making our way through wetlands and crossing another rocky branch. The distinctive, rough terrain in this part of Perry County is credited to the lack of glaciation; thus, the trail is interesting and scenic.

At 3.64 mi., we took the Celina Lakes Interpretive Trail to the left **[9]**, rather than continuing on the Two Lakes Loop Trail on the right.

We walked along a foot-wide dirt path, passing a marshy pond on the left, before encountering the first of several rocky outcroppings at 3.83 mi. **[10]**. These sandstone rocks were formed millions of years ago from the soft mud and sand in an ancient sea. Some outcroppings have honeycombed indentations; we could see the older layers of these sedimentary rocks at the bottom, covered with mosses and lichen. Rock shelf outcroppings here make improvised seating; early indigenous people used the shallow caves and occasional rock overhangs as shelter. In some low boulders, we could see distinctive holes formed centuries ago by the stone tools they used for grinding grain. At 3.9 mi., we could still see sandstone formations on the right. Below, on the left, is 164-acre Lake Celina. At 4.0 mi., this hike ends at the historic Rickenbaugh-Celina House **[11]**, built in Pennsylvania Dutch style in 1874.

To return to the trailhead—and nearby parking—take the park road north, then follow the park entrance road west to the Two Lakes Loop Trail.

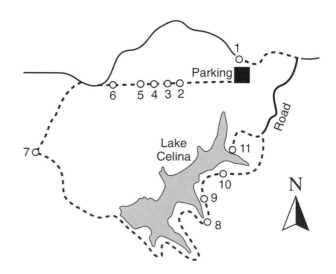

| | | |
|---|---|---|
| 1. Trailhead | 5. Dam | 9. Interpretive Trail |
| 2. Deer Pond | 6. Ridge | 10. Outcroppings |
| 3. West Trail | 7. Stream | 11. Rickenbaugh-Celina |
| 4. Trail | 8. SR 37 | House |

# Hemlock Cliffs 🥾🥾🥾

**Distance Round-Trip:** 1.44 miles

**Estimated Hiking Time:** 1 hour

**Cautions:** The USDA Forest Service sketch map of this area is distorted and misleading; the wormy figures do not represent the canyon walls accurately.

**Trail Directions:** Follow SR 37 south of English; turn west at the sign and drive 2.6 mi. Turn right, then go north 2.2 mi. to a gravel parking area. The trail begins as a two-foot-wide strip of gravel beyond the parking lot **[1]**. Follow this trail into an oak and hardwood forest; then descend into a box canyon. You'll see layered sandstone **[2]** at the right of the formed gravel path.

At .16 mi., there's a great view of a narrow waterfall with a 40-foot drop **[3]** splashing onto the cliffs below. From an overlook, framed by maples, you'll see ferns and mosses on the upper layers of rock and begin to feel the coolness of the canyon's microclimate. Continue walking along a creek **[4]**; at .16 mi., you'll cross it and see more cliffs rising on the right. Much of the sandstone here comes from the Tar Spring Formation.

At .4 mi., there's a pool of sand and rocks with the creek running through it. Begin looking for wintergreen; this is one of three places in Indiana where it grows. You can also find wild geranium, shooting star, and mountain laurel here. Take a right turn at the Y **[5]**; then follow a loop around the canyon. You'll come out at .48 mi. on the far side of the creek.

Continue walking on a major ledge, past shelter caves and a jutting beech tree **[6]**. Evidence of human habitation in the canyon has been dated to about 10,000 years ago. You'll pass honeycomb rock formations on the right, the pattern formed by iron ore weathering. At .77 mi., take an angled right turn **[7]** onto a narrow, dirt path in the valley. You'll cross a creek, then walk beside it. Watch for butterflies—we saw a spicebush swallowtail here—amid the lush grasses and wildflowers. Cross another section of creek and a few moss-covered, low rocks as you explore the canyon floor **[8]**.

By 1.12 mi., you'll be walking uphill again, on a wide, rocky trail. Ahead, another waterfall leaps over layers of gray slate **[9]**. Notice the occasional hemlock trees, evergreens with short needles and small cones, which thrive in this microclimate. You'll continue walking uphill on a white gravel path.

The trail follows the creek as it leaves the canyon and loops through oak-hickory forest over a mainly uphill route before returning to the parking area at 1.44 mi.

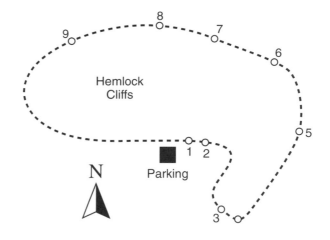

Hemlock Cliffs

Parking

N

1. Traihead
2. Sandstone layers
3. Waterfall
4. Creek
5. Right turn
6. Caves
7. Right turn
8. Canyon floor
9. Waterfall

# Mogan Ridge East Trail

**Distance Round-Trip:** 5 miles

**Estimated Hiking Time:** 3 hours

**Cautions:** There is a thriving population of ticks in the area—be prepared. Also, be especially alert during hunting season. Deer hunters may be near the trail in the fall (beginning in November), and turkey hunters in the spring.

**Trail Directions:** The trail is located near Derby, Indiana (a small community on the Ohio River). Turn on CR 370 off of SR 66 at the bridge near mile marker 104. Continue on CR 370 for .6 mi. The trailhead [1] is directly across from the parking lot. The trail is marked by white USFS markers, usually nailed to a tree. The other marker on the trail is that of the American Discover Trail (ADT). The ADT is part of the trail system across America.

Take the old roadbed from the trailhead for .3 mi., and go right at the intersection [2]. Soon you will cross a small stream. During heavy rains, the stream may be up, but it usually recedes quickly after a storm. The trail continues on the old roadbed, and you will soon ascend a hill. At .8 mi. from the intersection, the trail will leave the road [3].

Bear left, following the trail up a steep incline to the top of the ridge. The forest opens up into a small open space for wildlife. You may not see the animals, but on the trail you will see an abundance of their tracks. Continue along the ridge trail until you come to a trail leading off to the left.

At 1.3 mi. [4], you may continue on the main trail to the right or take the trail to the left on a side trip into the upper section of the Clover Lick Barrens (.25 mi.). Return on the same trail back to the main trail, and go left. At 1.8 mi. [5], you will pass through a United States Forest Service gate and hike on a gravel road to the intersection at 2.3 mi. [6].

Here you leave the gravel road and go left on the trail. You will climb up a hill to Kuntz Ridge for

.75 mi. Once on the ridge, you will be able to view the Clover Lick Barrens [7], a large area where trees have never grown, to your left. It is the habitat for many native grasses. As you hike down the trail to the 3.5-mi. point [8], there will be places along the ridge to your right to view the Ohio River. The views are at their best during the early spring and late fall, or in the winter, when the leaves are off the trees. At the second narrow passage on the ridge at 4.25 mi., there is a small cave [9] off to the left and actually under the trail.

Leaving the ridge, go left at [10]. The trail has been changed. Go right at the intersection at 4.5 mi. [11] or you may go into the lower Clover Lick Barrens. Continue on to the old road again. Go right and return to the parking lot.

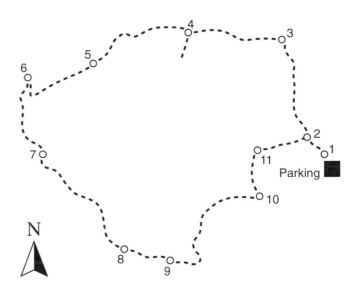

N

| | |
|---|---|
| 1. Trailhead | 6. Intersection |
| 2. Intersection | 7. Clover Lick Barrens |
| 3. Trail leaves road | 8. View of Ohio River |
| 4. Side trail to | 9. Cave |
| barrens | 10. Left turn |
| 5. USFS gate | 11. Intersection |

# 34. Avoca State Fish Hatchery

- Walk past ponds stocked with largemouth bass, bluegill, redear sunfish, black crappie, walleye, and rainbow trout.
- Learn how the hatchery produces from 200,000 to 1,000,000 fish a year.
- Enjoy a lovely setting. Water from a spring-fed pool flows past a grassy hill with picnic tables, shaded by great, gnarled black walnut trees.

## Area Information

In 1819, a grist mill powered by water from a spring-fed pool began operating on what became the first state-operated fish hatchery in Indiana. The Hamer brothers, who were the community's first residents, bought the mill and, in 1823, built the two-story residence where the property manager now lives.

As the village of Avoca grew, the large residence found uses as an inn, grocery store, and post office. Other families built homes near the junction of Spring Creek and Goose Creek, receiving supplies once a month by an oxen-drawn wagon overland from Louisville. Mail came by horseback; the average person received six letters per year, paying 25¢ to receive each one.

Early in the 20th century, Hayden Bridwell owned the house and grounds when the Department of Conservation (which became the Department of Natural Resources) bought the property and began building fishponds in 1923. Because harvesting the fish here has been done by draining the ponds, the water from Avoca Cave spring has been critical to successful operation. Filling or refilling a half-acre fish pond requires about 400,000 gallons of water.

The Avoca State Fish Hatchery today has 13 ponds that range in size from .24 acre to 1.28 acres. There is a total of 5.66 acres of water in the ponds, with most of it coming from an extensive cave more than 700 feet long. Thus, the water temperature stays around 52 to 54 degrees Fahrenheit year-round.

Brood stock for the ponds may come from other hatcheries. In producing largemouth bass, females and males are kept separate until the pond water reaches 60 degrees Fahrenheit. Nest building, mating, and spawning are followed by an incubation period for the eggs. During this period, the water temperature is critical. In early summer, adults are separated from fingerlings, which are eventually hauled to Hoosier lakes, reservoirs, and streams.

**Directions:** Drive to Avoca on SR 37; then turn west onto SR 54. Go .2 mile and turn south at the sign for Avoca State Fish Hatchery.

**Hours Open:** The hatchery is open daily, year-round, from 7:30 A.M. to sunset. Watch fish feeding each day at 8:15 A.M. and 4:15 P.M.

**Facilities:** Picnic tables, a shelter, and rest rooms are available on the site.

**Permits and Rules:** No fishing! Supervise young children with care. Place trash in proper receptacles. Do not feed the fish. No swimming or wading in the fishponds.

**Further Information:** Call Avoca State Fish Hatchery at 812-279-1215.

## Other Points of Interest

**The Green Hill Cemetery** in nearby Bedford has a grassy lawn, scattered shade trees, and some of the most interesting gravestones anywhere. Limestone from the area has been used in buildings across the nation. Talented local stone carvers have turned out intricately carved monuments over the years. Winged angels mark the graves of children. Married couples who died have been placed side by side, their graves marked with intertwined trees. For more information about one of the most memorable walks anywhere, call Lawrence County Tourism Commission; 812-275-7637.

## Area Trails

The mixed hardwood forest at Avoca, southwest of the fishponds, has a network of footpaths that run from the spring pool overlook past an early cemetery and various sinkholes to the shelter house. However, we found the trail poorly marked and maintained. Call the fish hatchery office at 812-279-1215 during business hours on weekdays to determine the condition of the trail before hiking.

# Avoca Fish Hatchery Pond Walk 🥾

**Distance Round-Trip:** 1 mile

**Estimated Hiking Time:** 20 minutes (plus return)

**Trail Directions:** (*Note:* The pond numbers serve as the numbered points of interest along this trail.) Park near the picnic grounds. Check the bulletin board at the start of a gravel road for notices before walking. You'll walk down a gravel road to the ponds. The stream channel on the right carries water from a spring pool, the source of most water used in the ponds. As you pass Ponds 1 and 2 on the right, you may see moving water or surfacing fish, depending on the season. Once the fish reach a minimum size, they are removed, then shipped to stock Indiana's lakes, rivers, and streams. At .08 mi., cross a culvert carrying water below the road.

Framed by the branches of a pine tree, you'll see Pond 3. Notice the water that may be spouting from a standpipe at the left. The flow through this white tube is used to maintain water levels and facilitate drainage. Look toward the left and you'll see the colonial-style residence of the hatchery manager, Garold Spoonmore. Built by the owners of a grist mill, the house is one of the oldest in Lawrence County. Continue walking and at .1 mi., the trail turns right; you'll see Goose Creek on the left.

At .11 mi., we saw the exposed clay and mud at the bottom and edges of partially drained Pond 4, on the right. You'll see that the ponds vary in size; Pond 5, on the right, is .53 acres and takes 400,000 gallons of water to fill. Continue walking along the maintenance road. Beyond Pond 6, the dense edge of the forest stretches in both directions. At .2 mi., there's a bridge across the creek, which widens and becomes more stagnant downstream. Continue walking on a dike that separates the sluggish, gray-green water of the stream at right from Pond 7, at left. Largemouth bass, bluegill, and redear sunfish fingerlings are produced here; some species mature at other hatcheries before reaching their ultimate destinations.

At .25 mi., we could hear the stream rushing over a dam on the right. To the right of Pond 9, we saw twin spillways on the right where water, not held back by the dam, flowed into a rocky channel. On the left, at .3 mi., you'll see the end of the park loop road that circles the four remaining ponds. Continue walking forward. On the right is a constructed, rocky cliff above the now-clear water of the stream. Thick and shadowy, the mixed hardwood forest beyond contains specimens of hop hornbeam, pignut hickory, buckeye, green ash, and other trees. Beyond Ponds 10, 11, and 12, Pond 13, at 1.28 acres, is the largest in the hatchery. Notice the way plants growing at the edge may be either covered by water or have their roots exposed, as the water level shifts. On the right, water rushes over rocks like some mountain stream.

At .43 mi., you'll see the back lawns of local residents, where mowed grass comes down to Pond 13. Someone had placed a plywood figure of a black bear here beneath a black walnut tree; although it resembles a target, black bears have not lived in rural Indiana for more than a century. At .48 mi., you'll complete the loop as you walk around Pond 13, ending the hike. Return to the parking lot over the road, the same way you came.

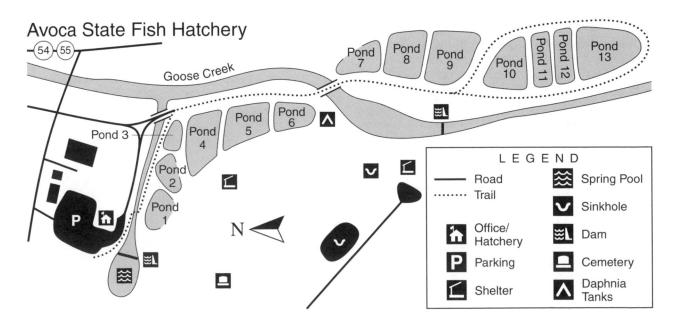

## Avoca State Fish Hatchery

Goose Creek

Pond 3

Pond 4

Pond 5

Pond 6

Pond 2

Pond 1

Pond 7

Pond 8

Pond 9

Pond 10

Pond 11

Pond 12

Pond 13

P

N

LEGEND

— Road

···· Trail

🏠 Office/ Hatchery

P Parking

🏕 Shelter

〰 Spring Pool

∨ Sinkhole

🌊 Dam

▭ Cemetery

🔺 Daphnia Tanks

# 35. Bloomington/Monroe County

- Explore 78,000 acres of forestland, much of it near the 10,750-acre reservoir Lake Monroe.
- Visit the Charles C. Deam Wilderness, the only nationally recognized wilderness tract in the state of Indiana.
- Choose from an array of nature, rails-to-trails, state park, and national forest trails in scenic Monroe County.

## Area Information

The rugged hills and hollows that characterize parts of Monroe County were among the last places in Indiana to be settled. Bands of indigenous people hunted mastodon, musk oxen, and bison in the area as the great glaciers receded. Eventually, these early inhabitants lived in settled villages, but left little impact on the land.

Because of the rugged terrain, the land was not easily cleared for farming. At one time, an acre of valuable hardwood forest could be bought for one dollar. Although pioneers cut and cleared land for small farms, survival was difficult, especially for children. Over the years, several dozen small farming businesses were attempted; however, many landowners lost their parcels through nonpayment of taxes during the depression of the 1930s.

After the Hoosier National Forest acquired some of this land, the government worked to control erosion, repair damage, and prevent or control forest fires. Civilian Conservation Corps workers cleared fire lanes, built fire towers, and planted trees on the hillsides in reforestation programs.

Charles C. Deam, a Hoosier native and self-educated botanist, was the author of important guides to Indiana trees and flowers. He became the state's first forester and helped lead what was then called the conservation movement. Some National Forest Service land within what is now the Charles C. Deam Wilderness was acquired in 1935. The wilderness was officially designated by the U.S. Congress in 1982.

**Directions:** Drive to Bloomington via SR 37 or SR 46. Follow SR 46 east through the town of Bloomington. Turn south on SR 446 to reach Lake Monroe, the Hoosier National Forest, and the Charles C. Deam Wilderness within the HNF.

**Hours Open:** Unless you are prepared to camp, plan to complete each hike and leave the wilderness before dark.

**Facilities:** Lake Lemon, Griffy Lake, and Lake Monroe all have boating facilities. In addition to state-run campgrounds at Allen's Creek and Paynetown, and a federally operated campground at Hardin Ridge, there are private campgrounds at Lake Monroe. The Charles C. Deam Wilderness contains a few primitive campsites that are not accessible by road. The Brooks cabin at the western entrance to the Deam Wilderness serves as an information center.

**Permits and Rules:** Camp only in designated areas. Only reusable or burnable packaging is allowed in the wilderness area. Cans and glass bottles are prohibited. Carry out whatever trash you bring in; do not bury garbage. Wheeled or motorized vehicles are prohibited in the wilderness reserve.

**Further Information:** For Bloomington and Monroe County Parks, contact Convention and Visitors' Bureau, 2855 Walnut Street, Bloomington, IN 47404; 812-334-8900. For Charles C. Deam Wilderness, contact Hoosier National Forest, 811 Constitution Avenue, Bedford, IN 47421; 812-275-5987.

## Other Areas of Interest

**Griffy Lake,** north of Bloomington, is a 200-acre nature preserve with two hiking trails and a nature trail, developed around a 109-acre lake. You may rent or launch canoes here for early- or late-day wildlife viewing. You may also arrange tours led by a naturalist; 812-349-3700.

The **Clear Creek Rail Trail** is 6.7 miles long and begins at Country Club Road. You may use it for hiking, jogging, or mountain biking; 812-349-3700.

The **Hardin Ridge Recreation Area** southeast of Lake Monroe has 200 campsites, 62 picnic sites, boat-launching facilities on Lake Monroe, a swimming beach, and bathhouse. Hiking trails run along Hardin Ridge Road and northwest of the amphitheater; 812-275-5987.

# Bloomington/Monroe County

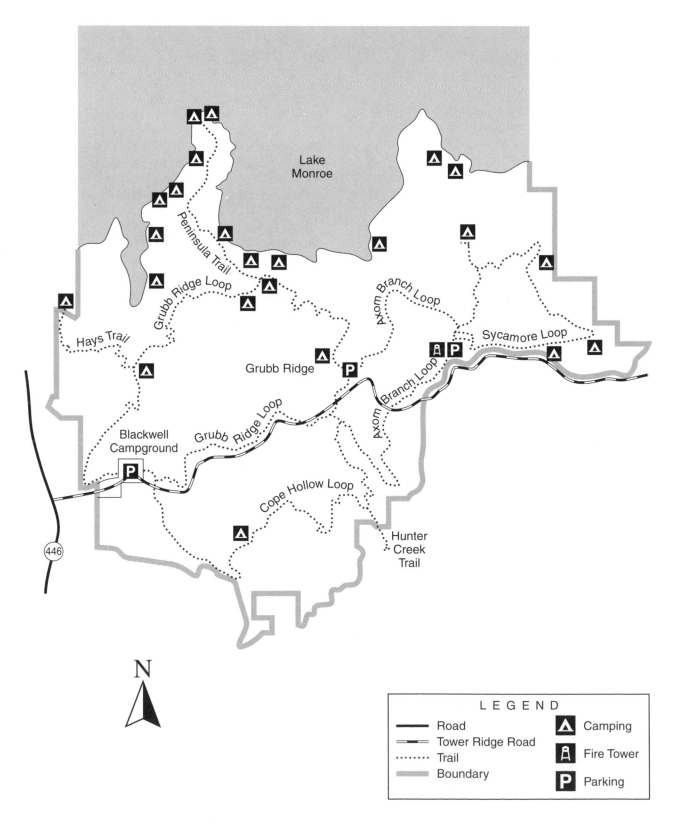

Lake
Monroe

Peninsula Trail

Grubb Ridge Loop

Hays Trail

Axom Branch Loop

Sycamore Loop

Grubb Ridge

Grubb Ridge Loop

Axom Branch Loop

Blackwell
Campground

Cope Hollow Loop

Hunter
Creek
Trail

446

N

### LEGEND

| | |
|---|---|
| —— Road | ▲ Camping |
| —■— Tower Ridge Road | 🛱 Fire Tower |
| ······· Trail | P Parking |
| ▬▬ Boundary | |

# Deam Wilderness—Axom Branch Experience 👢👢👢👢

**Distance Round-Trip:** 2 miles

**Estimated Hiking Time:** 3 hours

**Cautions:** Timber rattlers and copperheads inhabit the area. Do not disturb them. Just walk away.

**Trail Directions:** Enter the wilderness via Tower Ridge Road. Park at the space for Grubb Ridge Trail/Loop **[1]**. Walk .05 mi. north along Grubb Ridge. The trailhead for Axom Branch Loop is marked with a post on the right behind a tree. Follow this dirt path—one to two feet wide—right, left, and down. There's a steep slope into the ravine at the left. By .33 mi., you'll have descended into the ravine; the trail crosses a creek at .38 mi. **[2]**, then follows a tributary downstream to Axom Branch.

Already you've reached a lovely isolated place. Look 50 feet downstream and you'll see a black slate wall. Birds chirp high in the canopy. Listen for woodpeckers and owls; watch for hawks and herons in this maple-beech forest. At .5 mi. **[3]**, the trail crosses a wet, rocky creek bed with no bridges. The route follows the creek bed. You'll hear the water trickling on the right. At .57 mi. **[4]**, there's a marker beside the narrow dirt path.

Soon another creek joins the one you follow. You'll see slabs of broken bedrock in the water and can use these rocks to cross the creek. The path begins again beyond the end of a log on the other side. Note the clarity of the water and take time to look around. We found several rocks with geodes in the middle—and left them there.

At .7 mi. **[5]**, the rough dirt path runs through forested bottomland. The trail veers away from the creek, passing through a grassy meadow with wildflowers and butterflies. We especially enjoyed the black and spicebush swallowtails.

Beyond the trail marker at .76 mi. **[6]** was nature's equivalent of a fern garden. Notice the various shades of green—some ferns are evergreen, others deciduous.

The trail crosses the creek again. (This creek was dry in July.) Although we saw no other hikers, a pair of horses with riders came up the trail toward us.

At .88 mi., you'll still be walking on bottomland. The trail gets rougher as you walk through wilderness where there's no maintenance, combined with nature's periodic stormy rearrangement of anything in sight. We climbed over or walked around trees that lay across the path. The water on the right makes an S-shaped curve around the land—it's nearly an oxbow island.

At .94 mi. **[7]**, standing on a beach formed of shale, you have a good view of the scenic creek as it meanders downstream. There's a meadow on the left and a forested ridge behind you. At .99 mi. the trail came to a pond **[8]**, the water clear and still. At this point, we ended the hike and returned over the route we came.

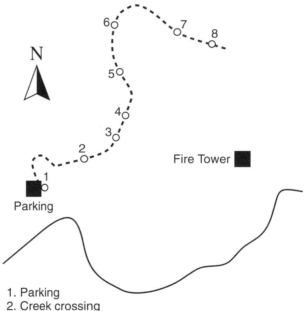

1. Parking
2. Creek crossing
3. Creek bed crossing
4. Trail marker
5. Grassy meadow
6. Fern garden
7. Shale beach
8. Pond

# Deam Wilderness—Grubb Ridge Trail 🥾🥾

**Distance Round-Trip:** 4.14 miles

**Estimated Hiking Time:** 1.5 hours

**Cautions:** This trail is shared with horseback riders; watch where you step. Carry drinking water. Allow enough time to return to parking before dark.

**Trail Directions:** Park in the space for Grubb Ridge **[1]**. The trail is a wide, earthen path that follows the ridge past occasional picnic areas and campsites. At .05 mi., ignore the narrow path for Axom Branch; keep walking ahead.

At .7 mi. **[2]**, you cross an old service road and see a marker for this trail. You'll be hiking on clay through forest. When we hiked, there were many downed trees. If one has fallen, look for a minitrail around it. In addition to the common maple and oak trees, look for white and yellow poplar (the tulip tree) and young sassafras trees. The roots of the sassafras were once used to make tea.

At .89 mi. **[3]**, the trail passes a campsite with a fire ring set in a grove of pine trees. Pines were often planted by early settlers and later by foresters to create windbreaks. Continue walking ahead. Notice the cavities in dead or dying trees. Look for squirrels, raccoons, opossums, chipmunks, foxes, and white-tailed deer. When I heard a serious rustling, it was my companion who glimpsed the tawny skin of a deer. You might also see scarlet tanagers, red-eyed vireos, or pileated woodpeckers.

At 1.3 mi. **[4]**, you follow the trail as it loops back to the right, but you're still hiking on the ridge. Stop occasionally to examine the forest floor for wildflowers. We found an exquisite lavender blossom that was possibly lopseed. We also noticed coral mushrooms and another one called scarlet cup.

At 1.48 mi. **[5]**, we passed more white pines and took another side trail around natural obstacles. We then rejoined the main trail. Soon, we were hiking through pine forest again, over a wide path of pine needles. The combination of rain and horses' hooves has formed rough, wet areas of mud across the trail, creating the need for another bypass. Even so, there were lovely patches of ferns.

At 2.07 mi. **[6]**, we encountered more mud, forest debris, and tiny bypass trails. It was getting late, so we retraced the route back to Tower Road and ended the hike.

1. Parking
2. Service road
3. Campsite
4. Loop to the right
5. White pines
6. Trail deteriorates

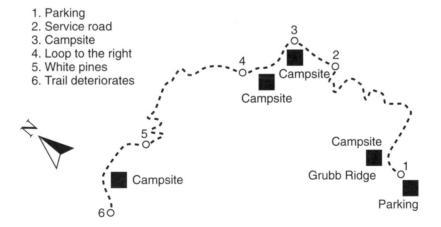

# 36. Spring Mill State Park

- Walk around an authentic pioneer village.
- Hike past small creeks and old-growth trees.
- Explore a large cave with side rooms.

## Area Information

Representative of the karst topography that under-lies much of Southwest Indiana, Spring Mill offers the visitor a wide choice of diversions. Explore caves—the park boasts two major systems—wonder at some of the largest old-growth trees the state has to offer, or simply relax along a tree-shaded stream. But natural history is only a part of the park's attraction. Here you'll find the authentic Pioneer Village, including a working grist mill among its dozen buildings, dating back to around 1814. Regardless of what trails you choose (Trail 4 passes through), plan to spend some time exploring the village.

**Directions:** The park entrance is located on the north side of SR 60, three miles east of the town of Mitchell. The nearest reference points are the cities of Bedford, to the northwest, and Salem, to the southeast.

**Hours Open:** The park is open all year from 7:00 A.M. to 11:00 P.M. (campers and lodge guests allowed in all hours).

**Facilities:** Boat rentals, camping, cave trips, fishing, hiking, inn and dining room, Nature Center, picnic areas, pioneer village, saddle horses, store, swimming pool (seasonal).

**Permits and Rules:** Fishing license required. Do not injure or damage any plant, animal, or structure in the park. Dogs or cats must be on leashes. Camp only in the campground; build a fire or park only in designated areas. Keep motorized vehicles on park roads; snowmobiles are prohibited.

**Further Information:** Spring Mill State Park, P.O. Box 376, Mitchell, IN 47446; 812-849-4129.

## Other Areas of Interest

Spring Mill is within easy driving time of both the north and south tracts of the **Hoosier National Forest** (see park #33) and its many recreational opportunities. Also worth a visit are the historic resort areas of **French Lick** and **West Baden Springs.**

# Spring Mill State Park

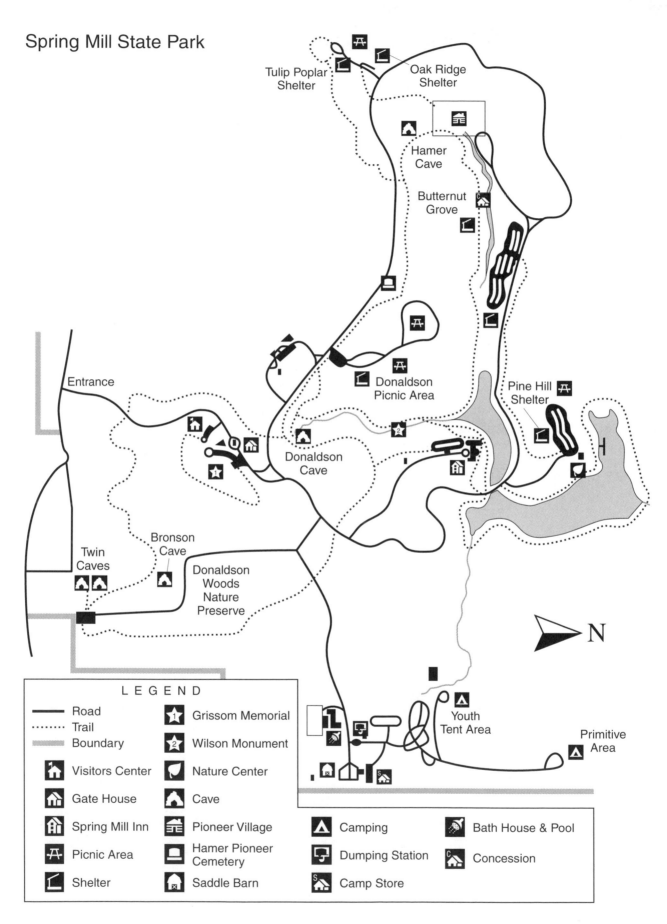

Tulip Poplar Shelter

Oak Ridge Shelter

Hamer Cave

Butternut Grove

Pine Hill Shelter

Entrance

Donaldson Picnic Area

Donaldson Cave

Bronson Cave

Twin Caves

Donaldson Woods Nature Preserve

Youth Tent Area

Primitive Area

N

## LEGEND

| | | | |
|---|---|---|---|
| —— Road | Grissom Memorial | Camping | Bath House & Pool |
| ···· Trail | Wilson Monument | Dumping Station | Concession |
| ▬▬ Boundary | Nature Center | Camp Store | |
| Visitors Center | Cave | | |
| Gate House | Pioneer Village | | |
| Spring Mill Inn | Hamer Pioneer Cemetery | | |
| Picnic Area | Saddle Barn | | |
| Shelter | | | |

# Pioneer Village/Donaldson Cave Loop (Trail #4) 🥾🥾

**Distance Round-Trip:** 2 miles

**Estimated Hiking Time:** 2 hours

**Cautions:** Take a flashlight for exploring the caves.

**Trail Directions:** This trail presents a great opportunity to sample both the human and natural histories of the park. You'll pass through the park's Pioneer Village and along meandering brooks, and you'll even have the opportunity to explore a large cave. From the parking lot at the Donaldson Picnic Area **[1]**, look for the trailhead to the southwest adjacent to the parking area. Take the trail in a clockwise direction. As you leave the picnic area, look for a large dead tree on your left and note the pileated woodpecker holes. The trail heads through a mix of old- and new-growth hardwoods with generally open understory, parallels the park road, and begins a gradual descent. At about .2 miles, one skirts the backside of the Hamer Cemetery **[2]**. Unfortunately, there is no entrance on the back end. Dating back to the 1830s, the graveyard is well worth a visit. Either walk around or plan a return at hike's end.

As the trail continues down its gentle slope, the surrounding forest becomes predominantly old-growth beech and maple. At about .3 mi. you'll come to an obvious but poorly marked trail leading off to your left **[3]**. Stay on the main trail, which drops down the edge of the ravine and picks up the sound of running water. In quick succession you'll come to the ruins of an old lime kiln, where crushed limestone was reduced to quick lime, and a quarry where stone was hand cut to build the mill, which gives the park its name. At about .61 miles a side trail leads to Hamer Cave **[4]**. With a significant spring-fed stream issuing from its mouth, Hamer supplied the water for the mill (when the mill was operating). Today, the cooling waters provide a welcome respite on a hot summer's afternoon.

Returning to the cutoff, you'll find that the main trail bears to the right and continues along the millrace, ultimately reaching a wooden aqueduct that carries the spring waters to the mill within Spring Mill Park's Pioneer Village (.8 miles into the hike) **[5]**.

The village itself dates back to 1814. It prospered, or, toward its end, existed, until the late 1800s, when the changes to more efficient mechanization spelled its doom. The Spring Mill operation was shut down in 1892. Happily, the buildings still remain and provide a window to the past. Indeed, during one weekend in September and in early December, the state park conducts candlelight tours—a highly recommended experience. (Check with the park office for exact dates and times.) Winding through the handful of buildings that make up the village, the scene becomes downright civilized, with picnic grounds and even a concession stand—still pleasant nonetheless.

But back to our hike: keep the stream on your left and you'll soon be back in a more natural setting. The trail climbs slowly as it reenters the woods, continuing to flank the stream. Shortly thereafter it leaves Hamer Creek and skirts a small lake, which, in season, offers good waterfowl viewing. Trail 1 intersects just above the water and leads to the Spring Mill Inn **[6]**.

Continuing along the trail, which now follows Donaldson Creek, you'll encounter a gentle rise through mixed hardwoods and, at the 1.75-mi. mark, offers a short side trail to Donaldson Cave **[7]**. Bring a flashlight. The cave, at least a portion of it, is open to visitors. Its main chamber is approximately 100 feet by 300 feet, and a side room off the rear of the main chamber allows another 200 to 300 feet of exploration.

From the cave it is approximately a quarter-mile, most of it uphill and up a series of wooden stairways, to the parking lot at trail's end.

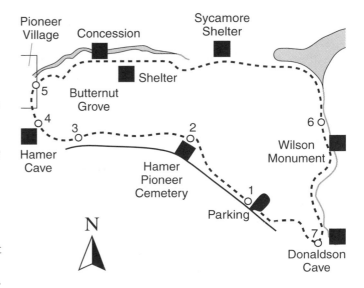

1. Parking area
2. Hamer Cemetery
3. Trail junction
4. Hamer Cave
5. Pioneer Village
6. Spring Mill Inn
7. Donaldson Cave

# Donaldson Nature Preserve Trail (Trail #3) 🥾🥾

**Distance Round-Trip:** 2 miles

**Estimated Hiking Time:** 1.5 hours

**Cautions:** Watch for traffic before crossing the roads.

**Trail Directions:** Park in the Twin Caves parking area [1] and follow the trail in a clockwise direction. You'll find the trailhead at the southwest corner of the parking area. A short tenth of a mile from the start you'll come to a short boardwalk on the right leading to the mouth of Bronson Cave [2]. Closed to visitors, the mouth of Bronson is at the far end of a sink.

After leaving the cave, you begin a gradual ascent of a quarter-mile through an old-growth mixed hardwood forest. At the .35-mi. mark you'll find a large downed oak on the right [3]. Notice the shallow root system indicative of the shallow soil covering the understory. As you walk by downed logs and other decaying duff on the forest floor, note the variety of fungi: some colorful, some edible—but make certain of your selections—others simply interesting in form. About a half-mile into the walk, just short of your first road crossing, note the huge oak propped precariously against other trees [4].

Here the trail swings off in a northerly direction. At .6 mi. [5], a bench appears offering a good spot to pause and enjoy the beauty that surrounds you. A short distance farther on your right you'll find the start of a sinkhole, a place where a tree's roots once held firm. Now tree and roots are gone, and the water is beginning to carve a larger depression into the subsurface limestone.

At 1.05 mi. you cross your second road [6]. As you proceed, watch for the sinkhole on your right, one of sizeable proportions, now supporting old-growth timber in its floor. At 1.1 mi. you'll encounter a juncture with a short side trail to the mouth of Donaldson Cave [7], certainly worth the trip if you do not intend to hike trail 4. At the very least, pause to enjoy the overlook high above the backside of the cave and the valley its spring-fed stream has produced. The caves in this area are the result of rainwater combining with decaying vegetable matter to form a weak acid which, over time, is strong enough to dissolve significant portions of limestone. It was at Donaldson in 1896 that Indiana University's Dr. Karl Eigleman first discovered the northern blind cavefish.

At the 1.3 mi. mark, just beyond the halfway point, another side spur off Trail 3 [8] leads to the Spring Mill Inn. A short distance later you cross a park road, the third of four, which also leads to the inn, a pleasant, rustic place to tarry after a day of hiking. As you continue on the far side of the road, you will note that the surrounding trees are significantly larger.

At 1.6 mi., the trail makes its fourth road crossing and brings you to the boundary of the Donaldson Preserve [9]. Named after George Donaldson, a Scotsman who lived in the area in the late 1800s, the woods is both a 67-acre state nature preserve and a slightly larger (104 acres) national natural landmark. Donaldson was a preservationist, a rarity in his day. Although an avid hunter, he allowed no hunting on his property. Indeed, he strove for total preservation of both animals and plants. Many of the trees here have lived for three to four hundred years.

The remaining half-mile of the hike is through the towering giants that make this small corner of Indiana unique. At approximately 1.7 mi., note the trio of behemoths, a pair of oaks and a beech, standing tall and silent as if to guard the trail. At about the 1.8-mile mark you'll encounter an unusual, significant stand of fern [10]. Throughout this portion of the walk the process of regeneration is evident. The living trees, the downed hulks of former giants in various stages of decay, and the young saplings, here primarily sugar maple and beech, all vie for a place in the sun.

As you near the end of the trail, two landmarks are evident. One is a large sinkhole to the left, the other a huge beech "protected" by a rail fence. It is a signal that the parking lot is just a few more yards down the trail.

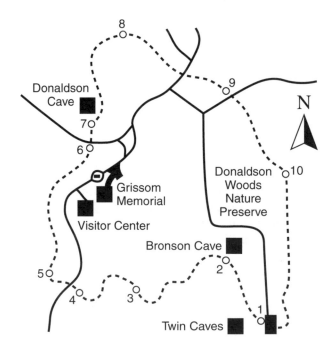

1. Parking area
2. Bronson Cave
3. Downed oak
4. Oak
5. Bench
6. Park road
7. Trail to cave
8. Spur to inn
9. Donaldson Preserve
10. Ferns

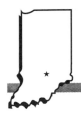

# 37.  Brown County State Park

- Explore one of Indiana's most scenic areas. The lack of glaciation has left rugged hills and hollows enhanced by forests and lakes.
- Scenic vistas abound. Bring a camera, especially in fall, to capture picture-postcard scenes.
- Find rare yellowwood trees in Ogle Hollow Nature Preserve, along with redbud and dogwood, lovely in spring.

## Area Information

The rugged nature of this unglaciated area in southern Indiana made it less appealing for farming, delaying settlement. Bears, deer, wolves, and cougars roamed the forests into the mid-19th century. Small game abounded and snakes were often found. In the early days of settlement, this was the wild west. Adventurers panned for gold and highwaymen (i.e., bandits) hid in the dense forests before robbing stagecoaches that passed over the rough dirt roads. Timber cut from the forests found countless uses—log cabins, boardwalks, wagons, furniture, boxes, barrels, and even water pails.

Early in the 20th century, T.C. Steele and other artists discovered the area. It is now a popular location for summer cabins; tourism peaks in the fall when visitors overrun Nashville's 300 or so shops and stores.

Outside the state, Brown County has become perhaps the best known county in Indiana. The 15,696-acre Brown County State Park is the largest in the state. Much of the park's development took place in the 1930s with the Civilian Conservation Corps workers. Black locust, black walnut, pine, and other trees were planted to counter erosion. Although the park now has 70 miles of bridle trails and more than 12 miles of hiking trails, there are large forested areas beyond these trails that few visitors ever see. The park shares boundaries with sections of Yellowwood State Forest and the Hoosier National Forest, forming a large area where wildlife can roam over forested hills and drink from bubbling streams.

**Directions:** Brown County State Park lies south of Nashville, which you can reach via SR 46 or SR 135. Follow 135/46 east of Nashville to reach the park's north gatehouse, or take SR 46 southeast of Nashville to reach the park's west gatehouse.

**Hours Open:** The park is open year-round. Hours are between 7:00 A.M. and 11:00 P.M.

**Facilities:** The Abe Martin Lodge within the park is open all year and the dining room is open to the public. Reserve far in advance for autumn weekends and major holidays. Rental cabins, campground, swimming pool, saddle barn, Nature Center, and picnic shelters are also available.

**Permits and Rules:** Do not damage any plant or animal in the park. Do not gather dead wood for fires. Dogs and cats must be leashed. Camp, build fires, or swim only in designated areas. Do not feed wildlife. Pull off the roads when observing wildlife.

**Further Information:** Call Brown County C&V Bureau, 812-988-7303; Abe Martin Lodge at 812-988-4418; Brown County State Park, Box 608, Nashville, IN 47448; 812-988-6406.

## Other Areas of Interest

The **Hickory Ridge** area of the Hoosier National Forest (south of Brown County State Park) contains 42 miles of multiuse hiking trails that access remote stretches of dense forests. Contact Hoosier National Forest at 812-275-5987. Be sure to ask about hunting seasons before making your plans.

You can access **Yellowwood State Forest** west of Brown County State Park and another section west of Nashville by SR 46 between Bloomington and Nashville. There is good bird and wildlife watching at Yellowwood Lake (northern section) and at North Fork Marsh (west of southern section). The **T.C. Steele State Historic Site** features the artist's former home and many of his paintings. The scenic historic site also has several short hiking trails.

## Park Trails

**Trail 5** 👢👢👢👢👢—.75 mile—Follow this self-guided nature trail through Ogle Hollow Nature Preserve to view rare yellowwood trees. The trail is short and rugged, but rewarding.

**Trail 6** 👢👢—1.75 miles—Follow this trail that begins behind the Nature Center and forms a loop around Strahl Lake. The lake was made soon after the park opened in 1929.

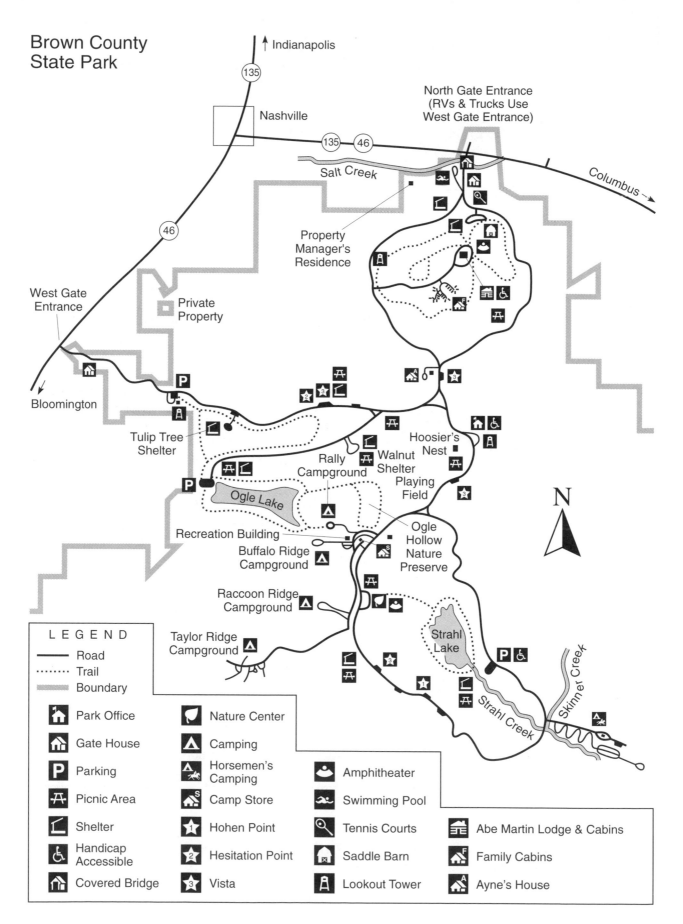

# Brown County
# State Park

↑ Indianapolis

(135)

Nashville

(135)(46)

Salt Creek

North Gate Entrance
(RVs & Trucks Use
West Gate Entrance)

Columbus →

(46)

Property
Manager's
Residence

West Gate
Entrance

Private
Property

Bloomington

Tulip Tree
Shelter

Hoosier's
Nest

Ogle Lake

Rally
Campground

Walnut
Shelter

Playing
Field

N

Recreation Building

Ogle
Hollow
Nature
Preserve

Buffalo Ridge
Campground

Raccoon Ridge
Campground

Strahl
Lake

Skinner Creek

Taylor Ridge
Campground

Strahl Creek

## LEGEND
— Road
⋯ Trail
▬ Boundary

| | | |
|---|---|---|
| 🏠 Park Office | 🍃 Nature Center | |
| 🏠 Gate House | ⛺ Camping | |
| P Parking | 🐎 Horsemen's Camping | 🔭 Amphitheater |
| 🍴 Picnic Area | 🏪 Camp Store | 🏊 Swimming Pool |
| 🏕 Shelter | ★1 Hohen Point | 🎾 Tennis Courts | 🏨 Abe Martin Lodge & Cabins |
| ♿ Handicap Accessible | ★2 Hesitation Point | 🏠 Saddle Barn | 🏠 Family Cabins |
| 🏠 Covered Bridge | ★3 Vista | 🗼 Lookout Tower | 🏠 Ayne's House |

152

# Tulip Tree Loop (Trail 8)

**Distance Round-Trip:** 2.5 miles

**Estimated Hiking Time:** 1.75 hours

**Cautions:** Wear sturdy shoes or boots. Be prepared for mud.

**Trail Directions:** Enter the park through the west gate. Park beside the West Lookout Tower **[1]**, a two-story stone and log structure with a great view of forested hills and ravines. Trail markers identify a grassy swath (Trail 8) that leads east of the tower. You'll walk downhill as the trail becomes packed earth, leading you through upland forest and along the park road.

The lack of glaciation—with its consequent smoothing over time—in this part of the state has made possible some fascinating and challenging hiking trails. You walk through a dense mixture of deciduous trees—maple, beech, elm, and many tulip trees. At .14 mi., the trail slopes downhill. The road at your left is flanked by forest.

Ignore a narrow downhill path to the right; your trail is roughened by rocks and roots and strewn with brown leaves. At .33 mi. **[2]**, the end of the Trail 8 loop comes back on the right. Continue walking forward—you'll go clockwise. At .4 mi. **[3]**, there's a large grassy clearing; continue walking along the grassy ruts and across a wash of red clay. You'll see a picnic area with parking on the left. Ignore a path going down on the right. Walk straight ahead and you'll go back into the forest.

The narrow dirt path dips downward. At .51 mi. **[4]**, there's a wooden bridge over a leafy runoff. On the left slope you'll see a natural fern garden; on the right the ridge drops sharply into a ravine. You'll walk uphill and cross two wooden bridges as the path ascends the hill, then veers gradually right and away from the road.

At .75 mi., you're still hiking along the ridge and near the road. Park maintenance has put gravel on the path we found strewn with hickory nuts. At 1.0 mi. **[5]**, the trail enters the clearing with the Tulip Tree Shelter and rest rooms. The trail curves back into the woods, beyond the rest rooms, and again follows the road. Continue on the grassy track, pass another roadside picnic area, and follow the trail into the forest again. You'll walk uphill on a sloping clay path that washes out during heavy rains.

At 1.25 mi. **[6]**, we noticed mushrooms that resembled pita bread with some bites taken out. You'll see how root steps along the path help hold back the soil. At 1.3 mi., there's a sign for Trail 8, Ogle Lake **[7]**. For the view from Hesitation Point, cross the road, then return to the trail.

As you begin the descent, you will walk through forests that were formerly inhabited by black bears, eastern timber wolves, and passenger pigeons. This is a steeper trail than before.

At 1.4 mi. begin descending a series of stepped, wooden bridges that lead into a wonderful ravine, filled with tulip trees (yellow), poplar, and oak. If you choose, there's a great spot to relax on a wooden bench and listen for birds. The trail continues over clay and down steps. At 1.45 mi., a sharp right path goes downhill; there's a wooden fence at the left. The trail makes a sharp right turn at 1.48 mi. **[8]**, then crosses a wooden bridge. You walk over fallen logs as the trail begins winding through the valley.

At 1.52 mi. you'll notice a bed of shale along the creek at the right, with an array of mosses on fallen logs. After you cross a wooden bridge, the character of the ravine changes as you pass through bottomland with spindly trees and low, green ground cover. A wooden bridge crosses a rocky creek that only dribbles water in July.

At 1.75 mi. **[9]**, beyond another wooden bridge, ferns have spread along the slope to the left. Then, at just under 2.0 mi. **[10]**, Trail 8 turns right for another half-mile to complete the loop. At left is a spur trail to Ogle Lake. You'll go right over a bridge—the sign says "West Lookout." The trail follows the streambed through a ravine, then heads gradually upward, crosses another bridge, and goes up a clay path onto a ridge. The wide track was strewn with mashed leaves.

At 2.25 mi. **[11]**, we were following the ridge, with ravines dropping off on both sides. When you reach an L-shaped wooden fence, continue along the ridge—don't take the downhill path to the left. The trail descends into a ravine again, crosses a streamlet, then runs along the other side.

At 2.5 mi. **[12]**, where a sign confirms Trail 8, take a left turn. Off to the right is the start of the loop you just hiked. The trail ends at West Lookout Tower.

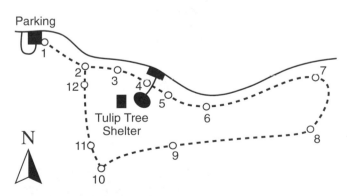

1. West Lookout Tower
2. End Trail 8 loop
3. Grassy clearing
4. Wooden bridge
5. Picnic shelter
6. Root steps
7. Trail 8 sign
8. Sharp right turn
9. Wooden bridge
10. Right turn
11. Ridge
12. Left turn

# Ogle Lake Loop (Trail 7) 👢👢👢

**Distance Round-Trip:** 1.5 miles

**Estimated Hiking Time:** 1 hour

**Trail Directions:** Park at Ogle Lake [1]. Cross the end of the park road and you'll see a sign marked "Trailhead" at the edge of the forest. Begin walking over a dirt path that follows a gravel road uphill, passes a stone shelter, and enters the woods again. The trail descends wooden steps, then goes across a wooden bridge before turning into a wide sylvan path, skirting a mucky inlet from the man-made lake where bass and bluegill await people who fish.

You'll follow Trail 7 clockwise around this lake, bordered with maple trees—gorgeous in the fall. As you walk, you'll see reflections of the surrounding forest in the still, shimmering water. The trail goes up and down the ridges that extend into the lake.

At .4 mi. [2], take the fork to the left; the trail on the right leads to the shore. Trail 7 stays wide and now makes shallower ups and downs. You have the occasional assistance of railroad-tie steps. Notice how the exposed roots and grasses help hold the clay in place. One aim of park officials soon after the park opened was to check erosion.

At .5 mi. [3], through an opening in the forest, you'll see light green pond grasses along the shallow eastern end of the lake. The path ahead will curve around through this marshy border. At .6 mi. [4], Trail 4 heads left toward the nature preserve. Continue walking right along a dirt path. A boardwalk leads through a patch of low, bushy plants with pink stems whose pointed leaves have serrated edges. Can you identify them? When we walked, the trail had narrow, mucky sections, usually bypassed by a higher, drier path that returned to the main trail.

This east-end forest, a lovely stretch of maple and beech, has patches of ferns among the ground cover of leaves. At 1.0 mi. [5], we encountered more wooden steps and bridges as we continued walking through forest with occasional views of fishermen and picnicking families across the lake. At 1.3 mi. [6], a bench and an observation platform have great views of the lake and forest. Then, at 1.4 mi. [7], you'll see the entire expanse of the lake at the right as you complete the hike by walking across the dam and back to the parking lot.

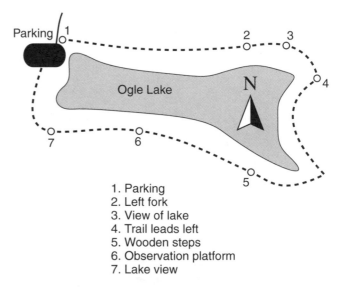

1. Parking
2. Left fork
3. View of lake
4. Trail leads left
5. Wooden steps
6. Observation platform
7. Lake view

# 38.  Wyandotte Cave State Recreation Area

- Walk through a cool, shadowy series of caverns featuring outstanding huge rock formations and fascinating miniature ones.
- Visit underground rooms where evidence shows the Adena and Hopewell people once lived.
- Follow a tree identification trail where you no longer have to guess which tree you see—you know for sure.

## Area Information

There are 200 or more caves in Indiana, most of them in the southern part, yet only a few are of any size. Indiana's caves, which typically form in limestone bedrock, undergo a series of four complex steps as they gradually develop. The series of caverns at Wyandotte have the greatest vertical relief of any in the state; the system has 23 miles of passageways that have been explored.

Thousands of years ago, tribes of indigenous people inhabited this area and found shelter in these caves. Archaeologists have found evidence that they gathered flints from the cave, as well as aragonite. The cave's earliest inhabitants once stored meat in a cool enclosure known as the Animal Pit, making their way in and out by the light of shagbark hickory torches.

The rugged terrain and dense forests around Wyandotte Cave meant the area was slow to be settled. Yet, those southern Indiana residents who knew of the cave found many creative ways to use it. In 1814, epsomite, the natural source of a laxative known as epsom salts, was found growing in the cave. In the mid-19th century, the Rothrocks began giving guided tours. In 1978, state geologist E.T. Cox explored Big Wyandotte extensively and had an associate produce a map of the passages he found. He summarized the various distances of routes taken, a total of 23.5 miles.

Some early guides through the cave left their names on a 35-ton rock. Various cairns of stones were built over the years, with the intention of showing visitors the way out of the cave. At one time, nearby residents stored barrels of onions in this natural refrigerator. Later, local residents held meetings in one cave room, calling it the Odd Fellows Hall.

Explore the forests around the cave to find native and introduced tree species. You'll find the official state tulip tree, along with the sassafras, whose roots were boiled by pioneers to make a tea. You can also see red cedar, persimmon, black cherry, white ash, honey locust, black walnut, shagbark hickory, and several kinds of oaks and maples here, although the forest is mainly shade-tolerant climax maple and beech.

Walking, hiking, and spelunking inside Wyandotte take place on guided tours. The easiest walk is a brief tour of Little Wyandotte Cave, in the same area, but not a part of the much larger Big Wyandotte system. The most difficult walk into Big Wyandotte is an all-day spelunking tour that requires extraordinary stamina and a combination of walking, climbing, and crawling through passageways that could be dry, or might be wet.

**Directions:** Wyandotte Caves lie north of SR 62 between Leavenworth and Corydon. From Leavenworth, drive east over scenic SR 62 for about three miles, then turn north at the sign. From Corydon, follow SR 62 west for about six miles, then turn north at the sign.

**Hours Open:** The caves are open between 9:00 A.M. and 5:00 P.M. year-round, with several exceptions. The park closes Mondays in the off-season (September through May) and during the four major holidays. Note that the park operates on Louisville time.

**Facilities:** Wyandotte Caves State Recreation Area has a Nature Center, gift shop, rest rooms, showers and changing areas, and picnic shelters and tables.

**Permits and Rules:** Do not damage the fragile cave environment. Do not litter. Flash photography is permitted, but tripods are not allowed. Children 12 and under must be accompanied by a parent or another adult on all cave tours.

**Further Information:** Wyandotte Caves State Recreation Area, 7315 South Wyandotte Cave Road, Leavenworth, IN 47131; 812-738-2782.

## Other Areas of Interest

From Wyandotte Caves, go east on SR 62, then south on SR 462 to reach the **Wyandotte Woods State Recreation Area.** Here are more than a dozen trails, many of them multiuse. The area also has a swimming pool, playgrounds, picnic grounds, and shelter houses.

**Marengo Cave,** near the town of Marengo, on SR 64, was discovered much later than Wyandotte. Now a national natural landmark, this cave has more stalagmites (formations that grow from the cave floor) than any other cave in the state.

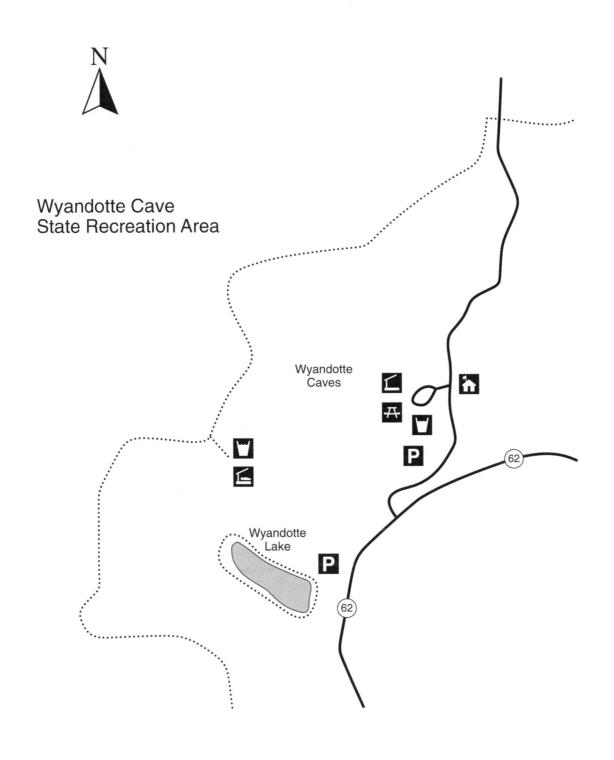

# Wyandotte Cave
## State Recreation Area

Wyandotte Caves

Wyandotte
Lake

62

62

L E G E N D

| | | | |
|---|---|---|---|
| —— Road | 🏠 Property Office | 🪣 Water Supply | Shelter House |
| ···· Trail | P Parking | 🪑 Picnic Area | Overnight Shelter |

# Monument Mountain Hike

👢👢👢

**Distance Round-Trip:** 1.6 miles

**Estimated Hiking Time:** 2 hours

**Cautions:** This hike can only be done with a guide. Much of the walk takes place on the rough surface of the cave floor. Wear sturdy footgear and a sweater or jacket to offset the cool, damp environment of the cave. Also, organize your belongings in a waist bag or day pack so you can use your hands and arms to climb the ladders. Damp portions of the walkway are slippery.

**Trail Directions:** This guided hike through Big Wyandotte begins about .2 mi. from the Nature Center at the cave entrance.

The hike begins in a large entrance cave that serves as a lobby [1]. You'll walk along the rough, rocky cavern floor. Note the historical graffiti on the ceiling—it dates from 1853. At this level, you'll see St. Genevieve limestone, one of three types in the Blue River group. Continue walking on broken rock along Washington Avenue, the longest dry passage in the cave.

At .14 mi., you'll pass a crevasse that serves as the entrance to the Animal Pit. By .22 mi., you'll be walking between the massive boulders of Bandits Hall [2] to reach a large room of Paoli limestone. At .28 mi., you'll duck under a low ceiling, then pass an old bat cave as you climb wooden steps. One room at Wyandotte has become a federally protected hibernation area for these creatures; this tour does not go there. At .34 mi., we passed a stone cairn, topped by a pointer, built in 1877 to help cave visitors return to the entrance.

We noticed a gray vein of flint (also called chert) just below the ceiling, then followed a sandy path through a long room. At .46 mi., the room had several rock stacks. These early cairns were built by visitors—with the encouragement of their guides—whose job it was to clear the path of rocks. Continue walking and you'll see a crystal called epsomite on the ceiling.

At .54 mi., you're walking between huge boulders in a vast room 180 feet below the ground [3]. Descend steps and enter a twisting passageway, and you'll soon see translucent calcite formations. At .62 mi., the route passes delicate helictite formations, not much thicker than soda straws. Don't touch! It takes hundreds of years for these to grow one inch.

Note the path below you has been dug out as a way to give visitors more head room without damaging cave formations. We could see dripping stalactites hanging from the ceiling and occasional pillars, formed when stalactites (growing down) and stalagmites (growing up) join together. Notice the helictites extending from fissures in the ceiling.

The route curves right through a passage used by early explorers; here, we saw gypsum needles growing in the dirt. By .8 mi., we were walking along a narrow, dark passage with a cobbled floor; soon, the trail became a ditch, which placed the wonderful, miniature helictites and other formations at eye level—at least for grown-ups. At .88 mi., there's a turnaround passage enabling donkeys brought down by cave explorers to return the way they came.

The highlight of the tour, for us, was the Monument Room and Rothrock Cathedral [4]. You'll see wonderful formations on the massive rock stack in the center, an underground mountain. By 1.08 mi., you've walked down to 350 feet underground. Be aware that the loose, shifting rocks on the uphill path can be slippery. Continue walking and you'll enter a small, winding passage at 1.2 mi. that opens to the Odd Fellows Hall [5]. Note the symbol of this organization—three links of a chain—on the ceiling of the cave room. Descend stairs and walk through another low passageway. At 1.4 mi. [6], you'll see a rock formation that resembles an eagle. Pass through one more massive room and another long, narrow passageway with a high ceiling before returning to the entrance over a cobblestone path. The hike ends here at 1.6 mi. at the cave entrance.

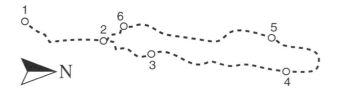

1. Cave entrance
2. Bandits Hall
3. Underground room
4. Rothrock Cathedral
5. Odd Fellows Hall
6. Stone eagle

# Twigs to Timber Trail 👢👢

**Distance Round-Trip:** .5 mile

**Estimated Hiking Time:** 30 minutes

**Trail Directions:** Park at the lot for cave visitors. Locate the trailhead by walking west of the parking lot into a picnic area; the trail begins left of the playground **[1]**. Carry a leaflet from the Nature Center, and you'll have detailed information about these trees.

At .04 mi., the tulip tree, with its gray bark, tulip-shaped leaves and large flowers, blooms in May or June. Continue walking through the maple-beech forest on a dirt path strewn with twigs and leaves. You'll also pass a large-tooth aspen on the left. Note that the quaking aspen, named for its characteristic movements, has rounder leaves on long stems that allow this motion.

At .1 mi. **[2]**, you'll learn more about Virginia pine, a tree commonly used during the 1930s to form windbreaks and counter erosion. Next, there's a wooden bench; continue walking and you'll see a dogwood tree, easier to recognize in spring with its lovely white blossoms or in fall, when it sports clusters of red berries. You'll also see a persimmon tree, which bears a tart, orange fruit used by southern Indiana cooks in puddings and pies.

The path descends into a gully **[3]**, where you walk through a muddy channel, covered with leaves. Ahead, you'll see specimens of white ash, honey locust, and slippery elm. The trail then passes another bench and heads downhill. The next trio of specimen trees are nut bearing: black walnut, shagbark hickory, and yellow buckeye. The path curves uphill, past fallen timbers. At .31 mi. **[4]**, examine the two types of oak tree, planted near one another, so

you can compare them. Note the shiny, leathery look of the leaves on the black oak and the bristles on the tips.

The hillside beyond is covered with violets **[5]**—see the blooms in spring. You'll next pass specimen beech and sugar maple trees before climbing a hill with tree-root steps. At .41 mi., turn left, go around another bench, and you'll see a spur trail **[6]** that leads to Little Wyandotte Cave. The door to the cave is set into boulders; it is opened only for tours. At .48 mi., you'll continue along a paved path **[7]** that leads to the Nature Center, or take a wooded, uphill path that leads directly to the parking lot.

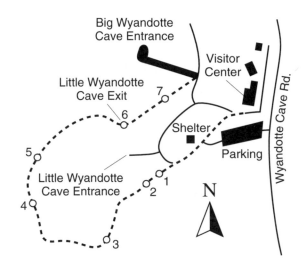

1. Trailhead
2. Virginia pine
3. Gully
4. Oak trees
5. Violets
6. Spur to Little Wyandotte
7. Paved path

# 39. Columbus

- Walk through a city known for quality architecture and distinguished designers for many of its public and private buildings.
- Pass carefully restored historic buildings from several periods.
- Hike a network of city trails used by local people and visitors.

## Area Information

The American Institute of Architects ranks the town of Columbus sixth in the nation for innovation and quality of architecture. Only the large cities of Chicago, Washington, New York, Boston, and San Francisco rank higher. Community leaders in Columbus—aided by major industries—have created a showcase for the work of acclaimed architects in some 50 public and private buildings. Creative designs used in buildings, parks, and gardens and a network of People Trails have improved the quality of life for all.

Like many other rural Indiana cities, Columbus grew outward, while the downtown deteriorated. During the late 1960s, the city's leaders developed a plan to renew the central 53-acre area. Unlike other towns, Columbus hired architects from Skidmore, Owings, and Merrill to do the planning.

Using talented architects was not new to Columbus. Eliel Saarinen had designed a First Christian Church building in 1942. Eero Saarinen and Harry Weese had been involved with designing Irwin Union Bank and Trust Company in the 1950s, setting the stage for renovation and renewal, not only downtown but throughout the community.

Now, the city's downtown shopping mall, churches, schools, banks, public library, industrial plants, and even the picnic shelters in public parks show the results of innovative design.

**Directions:** You can reach Columbus by I-65 and SR 46.

**Hours Open:** The self-guided architectural walk takes place over the public sidewalks. The Clifty Park Loop is a paved public path. Mill Race Park is open from sunrise to 11:00 P.M.

**Facilities:** The Columbus Inn (lodging) operates in a renovated city hall building. Restaurants occupy renovated downtown buildings and space in the Commons, an enclosed downtown mall. Mill Race and Clifty Parks have picnic tables and rest rooms.

**Permits and Rules:** Respect the privacy of local residents as you walk past their homes. Do not litter; put trash in proper containers.

**Further Information:** Columbus Area Visitors Center, 506 Fifth Street, Columbus, IN 47201; 812-378-2622.

## Other Areas of Interest

**Anderson Falls County Park,** 8.5 miles east of Columbus, south on CR 925E, then east on CR 1140E for 2.1 miles, has a scenic waterfall, hiking trails, picnic areas, and rest rooms.

## Park Trails

**People Trails** 🥾—9.4 miles—These trails link the riverfront, Mill Race Park, Donner Park, Westenedge Park, and Lincoln Park. Limited to walking, jogging, and bicycling, local residents use some trail segments to commute to work. The loop path around Clifty Park is also a People Trail.

**Bicycle Route** 🥾—22 miles—This trail links Columbus with Anderson Falls.

Columbus

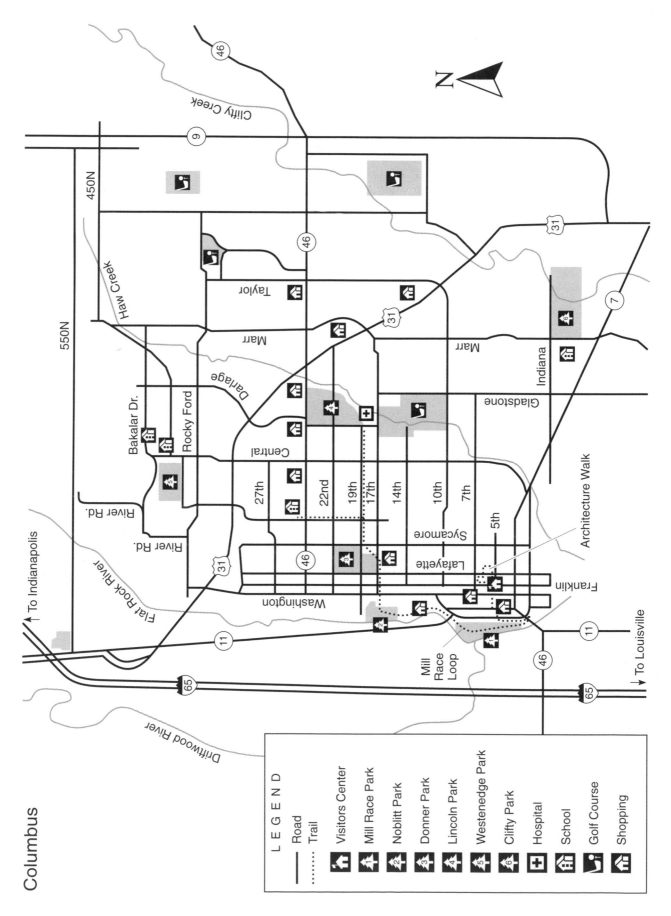

LEGEND

Road

Trail

Visitors Center

Mill Race Park

Noblitt Park

Donner Park

Lincoln Park

Westenedge Park

Clifty Park

Hospital

School

Golf Course

Shopping

# Architecture Walk 🥾

**Distance One-Way:** 1 mile

**Estimated Hiking Time:** 1 hour

**Cautions:** Be careful of traffic when crossing local streets. Watch especially for vehicles turning right on a red light.

**Trail Directions:** Begin walking at the Visitor Center **[1]** at the northeast corner of 5th and Franklin. Housed in a renovated private residence, the center has an art gallery on the second floor. The Yellow Neon Chandelier With Persians, an artwork by Dale Chihuly, hangs in the stairwell, and you can see it from outside the building. Walk along the east side of Franklin Street past scattered, renovated historic buildings and parking lots. The neighborhood has been on the National Register since 1982.

At .11 mi. **[2]**, turn right on 7th Street. Follow the sidewalk for one block and you'll note an intricately designed iron fence in front of an early brick house across the street. At the corner of Lafayette and 7th Street, you'll see charming homes on a street lined with trees, which are remnants of an earlier era. Turn right and go one block. At .23 mi. **[3]**, at the corner of Lafayette and 6th Street, turn left and follow the sidewalk along 6th Street for one block.

At .3 mi. **[4]**, turn right and cross 6th Street. You'll see a playground on the left and the low, brick structure of the Lincoln Elementary School across the street. Built in 1967, the structure has received awards for its design. Beyond it, you'll notice the startling spire of St. Peter's Lutheran Church ahead. Both buildings were designed by the architect Gunnar Birkerts. Continue walking to the corner of 5th Street and Pearl for a closer look at the church. Turn right and follow the sidewalk along 5th Street for one block. On the right, you'll pass the elaborate gardens, screened by an iron fence that formerly belonged to the Irwin family.

At .41 mi. **[5]**, from the corner of 5th and Lafayette, you'll see the spire of the First Christian Church on the left. This dramatic structure of brick and limestone, designed by Eliel Saarinen, was one of the first contemporary-style churches in the United States. Keep walking and you'll pass the Cleo Rogers Memorial Library on the right **[6]**. The plaza, with its striking, large arch sculpture by Henry Moore, is the setting for concerts and art shows. The Bartholemew County library building, a brick and glass pavilion, was designed by I.M. Pei.

Continue walking west along 5th Street for one more block. At .48 mi., you'll see the Columbus Inn, known for its afternoon tea, across on the left. Continue ahead along 5th Street. Note the stained glass in bay windows in the building on the right. At the corner of Washington and 5th, you'll see the Irwin Union Bank and Trust Company building across the street. Eero Saarinen designed the original building. Note the three-story addition built in 1973. There's a tree-lined brick street to your left. We craved an ice cream sundae, but—sorry—Zaharako's Ice Cream Parlor was closed.

At .61 mi. **[7]**, continue walking and you'll pass the entrance to the Commons Mall. Rather than pull shoppers from a deteriorating downtown core to the city's edge, planners envisioned a vital city center that offers much more. Parking facilities for the city center cover three square blocks. Continue walking west on 5th Street.

On the right, you'll see the Cummins Engine Company, Inc. corporate office building, designed by Roche Dinkeloo and Associates, built in 1983. An impressive landscaped walkway with a lattice roof screens the building's front parking lot. Just inside the entrance is an industrial sculpture, Exploded Engine, by Rudolph de Harak. Across the street, the Columbus Post Office was made of unusual materials and designed for low maintenance. Walk two more blocks on 5th Street and you'll reach the entrance to Mill Race Park at 1.0 mi. **[8]**, which is the end of this hike.

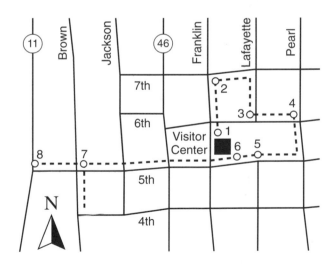

1. Visitor Center
2. Right turn
3. Left turn
4. Right turn
5. Corner of 5th and Lafayette Streets
6. Library
7. Commons Mall
8. Mill Race Park

# Mill Race Loop 🥾

**Distance Round-Trip:** 1.33 miles

**Estimated Hiking Time:** 45 minutes

**Trail Directions:** Begin at the entrance to Mill Race Park **[1]** at the west end of Fifth Street. You'll see a tower rising above the greenery as you walk toward it to start a clockwise loop. At .18 mi., you'll walk through what was the early town. Grist and wool mills, a tannery, and a brickyard were once located on this riverside site.

At .24 mi. **[2],** the large, grassy mound that appears on the right is the back of an amphitheater. The Columbus Symphony Orchestra plays here in the summer. Follow the sidewalk west, cross a park road, and walk to the tower. A contemporary structure of concrete and steel, the tower has open staircases and a distinctive platform at the top. Caution signs abound. Supervise children well, and do not let them throw objects from the platform. No horseplay is allowed.

At .27 mi. **[3],** continue walking right along a sidewalk that angles toward trees. To the left is the greenish tan, hammered-looking surface of the east fork of the White River. The paved path curves closer to the trees at river's edge. Note that the shaggy, unmowed grass at left has been left untended as an animal habitat.

At .36 mi. **[4],** there's a boat-launch ramp on the left. Continue on the River Walk, part of a network of People Trails throughout the community. Just beyond, note the painted steel, punched metal, and concrete picnic shelter on the right. In the distance, there's a wooden covered bridge. As you walk between the park road and the river, the view opens, framed by maple trees on the left.

At .45 mi. **[5],** we noticed a wooden bench, the first of several donated by a group known as the River Rats. Continue walking along the river. At .51 mi., you'll see the large, circular pond that reflects the weathered gray wood of the bridge. On the left, near the woods, we watched a half-dozen red-winged blackbirds take flight. Follow the path into the woods. Parts of the trail may be flooded after heavy rains. In summer, you can enjoy the shade of tall cottonwood trees.

At .7 mi. **[6],** you'll pass rest rooms with doorless curved entrances. This and other park structures were

designed by Stanley Saitowitz. You must go inside to appreciate the unusual design.

At .77 mi. **[7],** on the left, is the Lookout, a metal and concrete overlook. From the platform you can see the junction of the Driftwood and the Flatrock Rivers. Combined they form the east fork of the White River. At .93 mi., the paved path enters a tangle of forest. You'll walk past ancient trees covered with Virginia creeper and other vines. Wildflowers bloom here in season. A marshy area at left is strewn with rocks. The trail becomes slippery with mud whenever the lagoon on the left overflows.

At 1.02 mi. **[8],** climb some steps and you can walk through the covered bridge. From the east end of it, you'll see the paved path again on your right across the road. Follow this path around some huge locust trees that were flowering when we walked by. At 1.16 mi. **[9],** there's an open view across a wide, mowed-grass area. Note the oriental look of the amphitheater roof on the left. Even the fence repeats the bright orange of the other park structures. Continue walking and at 1.33 mi., you'll have completed the loop trail and made an architectural tour of the park.

| | |
|---|---|
| 1. Park entrance | 6. Rest rooms |
| 2. Amphitheater | 7. The Lookout |
| 3. View of White River | 8. Steps to covered bridge |
| 4. Boat-launch ramp | 9. View across grassy area |
| 5. River Rats bench | |

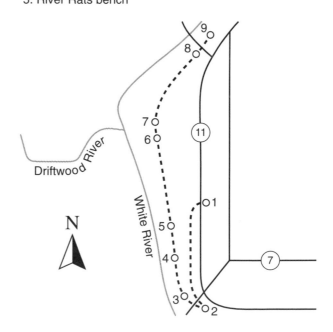

# 40. Jackson-Washington State Forest

- Hike challenging wooded trails through dense forests to explore curious bald knobs.
- Find tough trails that lead to rewarding scenic views.
- Explore 15,000 acres of state forest with hills and ravines bordering the shores of several lakes.

## Area Information

This area was once covered with dense forests, cut through by rivers and streams. By the time the state acquired this land in the 1930s, farmers had planted row crops on the hillsides or used the land for pasture. Erosion had formed ruts and gullies, and property owners had nailed fencing to living trees. Trees had been cut and sold for timber without replanting.

With the help of the Civilian Conservation Corps (CCC), eroded fields and pastureland were planted with black locust and pine trees. As these species died out naturally, native species grew in their places. The federally sponsored CCC program created work for the unemployed while helping preserve Indiana's rich, natural heritage.

Lakes, rivers, streams, and ponds add to the experience of forest trails. Five lakes in Jackson and Washington counties have been stocked with fish. Two of the hiking trails are self-guided, interpretive trails. Other trails loop through remote sections of forest where you will seldom see anyone else.

**Directions:** You can find these forest parks between Brownstown and Salem. To reach the Knob Lake area of the Jackson-Washington State Forest, follow SR 250 southeast of Brownstown. Turn northeast at the sign and follow the park road. To reach Starve Hollow Lake, take SR 135 to Vallonia. Turn south on CR 300 West, which becomes Lake Road. You'll see a sign for the park entrance beyond the intersection with Starve Hollow Road.

**Hours Open:** The parks are open between 7:00 A.M. and 11:00 P.M.

**Facilities:** Knob Lake has picnic shelters and camping.

**Permits and Rules:** Stay on marked trails. Fish only with the proper license.

**Further Information:** Jackson-Washington State Forest, 1278 East State Road 250, Brownstown, IN 47220; 812-358-2160.

## Other Areas of Interest

Southwest of Knob Lake, a rugged section of the Jackson-Washington State Forest accessed by Skyline Drive North has even more **remote hiking trails** into wildlife habitat areas. Climb a fire tower for a sweeping view of surrounding hills and hollows. Call 812-358-2160 for more information.

The **Muscatatuck National Wildlife Refuge** near Seymour has a Visitor Center, boating facilities, and hiking trails in a 7,802-acre property.

## Park Trails

**Trail 8** 🥾🥾🥾🥾—5.6 miles—This challenging route begins and ends at the Vallonia Tree Nursery. The long loop passes over hills and through hollows, offering access to wildlife habitats in a remote area. Allow four hours for hiking.

**Trail 6** 🥾🥾🥾—1.75 miles—With the park's brochure in hand, follow this interpretive route to learn about forest management.

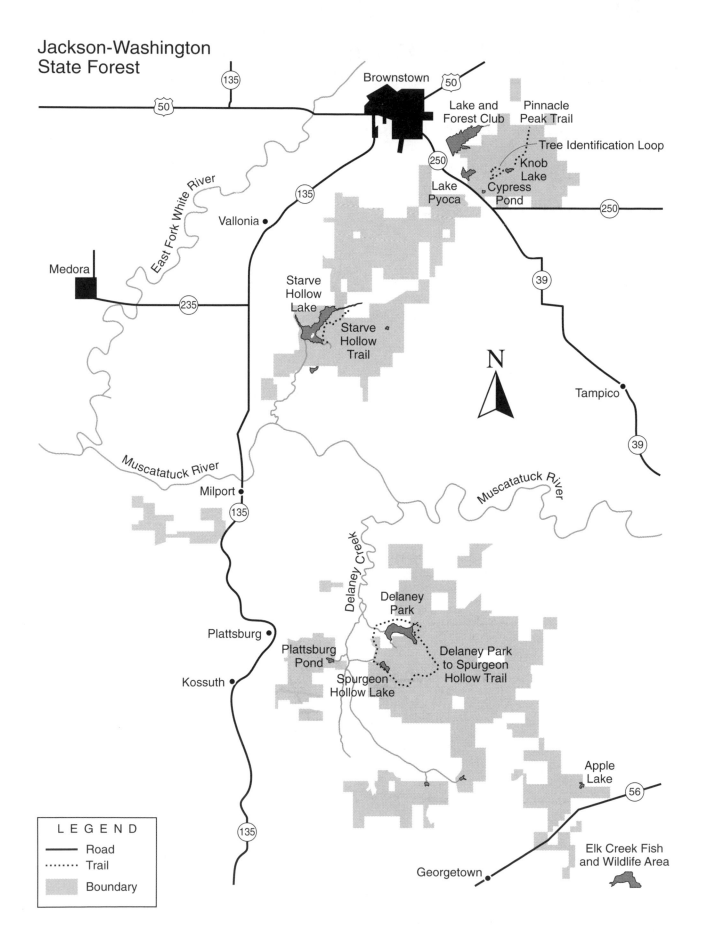

Jackson-Washington
State Forest

Brownstown

Lake and
Forest Club

Pinnacle
Peak Trail

Tree Identification Loop

Knob
Lake
Cypress
Pond

Lake
Pyoca

East Fork White River

Vallonia

Medora

Starve
Hollow
Lake

Starve
Hollow
Trail

N

Tampico

Muscatatuck River

Muscatatuck River

Milport

Delaney Creek

Delaney
Park

Plattsburg

Plattsburg
Pond

Delaney Park
to Spurgeon
Hollow Trail

Kossuth

Spurgeon
Hollow Lake

Apple
Lake

L E G E N D

——— Road

········ Trail

Boundary

Elk Creek Fish
and Wildlife Area

Georgetown

# Pinnacle Peak Trail (Trail 1) 👢👢👢👢

**Distance One-Way:** .73 mile

**Estimated Hiking Time:** 1 hour

**Cautions:** Avoid skidding on the loose shale on the steep slope below the peak. The clay segments of the trail can be slippery when wet.

**Trail Directions:** Follow the park road northeast. Park at the loop end of the road **[1]**. The trailhead for No. 1 marked "Pinnacle Peak" begins at the stone water fountain beside the parking lot. Climb steps, pass a picnic shelter and tables, and turn left onto a packed-dirt path about three feet wide. You'll walk uphill and, in fact, it's uphill much of the way as you ascend toward 966-foot Pinnacle Peak.

At .13 mi., walk past hickory trees as you make your way toward the site of an early tower at the crest of the first hill. At .2 mi. **[2]**, you can examine the stacked stone and iron supports—the bolts are still there. From this point, you see the forested hill sloping away on all sides. Continue left along Trail 1. Note the rocky, clay slope downward, which is slippery at times.

At .29 mi. the path crosses a ridge. You continue along a wide packed-clay path, strewn with small stones and twigs. At .32 mi., a segment of newly cut trail goes around a hill—not over it.

At .36 mi. **[3]**, there's a great view of low ravines on the right with forested knobstone hills on the left. Soon after, a sign confirms Trail 1. Continue walking right over a path, 9 or 10 feet wide, that resembles a dirt road without the ruts often made by wheels.

At .43 mi. **[4]**, you walk along another ridge with views of dramatic, deep ravines on both sides. Trail 1 then goes to the right. Although Trail 10 heads to the left, it's a wide path. You'll follow a trail two to three feet wide that becomes narrower as you cross a backbone.

At .56 mi. **[5]**, descend some tree-root steps as you encounter another ridge. There's a lovely ravine on the left; then by .66 mi., you'll see what, from a distance, looks like a patch of sand amid the trees. This is the bare-rock face of the knob. Continue climbing; the slope is steep. By .73 mi. **[6]**, you'll be sitting on top of the knob known as Pinnacle Peak. Another nearby peak known as High Point is actually 19 feet higher. However, you can't fault this one for the view, forested hills at the left and a valley framed by craggy, windblown trees. You've earned this. The hike ends here, except that you'll need to make your way back the way you came.

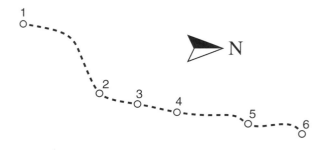

1. Parking
2. Early tower site
3. View of knobstone hills
4. Ridge
5. Tree-root steps
6. Pinnacle Peak

# Tree Identification Loop 🥾

**Distance Round-Trip:** .75 mile

**Estimated Hiking Time:** 1 hour

**Trail Directions:** The trail begins and ends across from the gatehouse **[1]**. You'll enter a forest of mixed pine and hardwoods and begin walking on a pine needle path. Carry the park's brochure titled "The Tree I.D. Trail" so you'll have information keyed to each of 40 stations along the way. Walk the loop clockwise to pass the stations in sequence.

You'll pass eastern cottonwoods and the official state tulip tree. It's remarkable that the leaves and the blossoms of the tulip poplar have the shape of the tulip flower. The leaves of the sweet gum, however, are shaped like stars.

At .1 mi. **[2]**, you'll encounter the first of several wooden bridges and a restful bench. The native Indiana pawpaw tree has leaves that are strikingly large in proportion to its size. Continue walking and you'll notice white ash and black cherry trees, both valued for their wood. The wood of the shagbark hickory, farther along the trail, has historically been used to make hickory-smoked meats. Walk farther and learn how to differentiate between several kinds of oaks. Notice the pointed lobes of the red oak leaves. Compare them with the rounded lobes of the white oak leaves.

At .15 mi. **[3]**, the wheelchair-accessible trail loops to the left. Return to the trailhead over this shorter route to see specimens of beech, maple, oak, sycamore, dogwood, and tupelo trees. Continue walking ahead and you'll learn more about the process of succession. As one plant community succeeds another, sun-loving plants are eventually replaced by shade-tolerant beech and other trees in a climax forest.

At .2 mi. **[4]**, you'll cross another bridge, and the trail turns right. You'll notice hop hornbeam, green-brier, and persimmon trees along the trail, along with sugar maples, chestnut oaks, and red pines. Did you know that there are more than 6,000 useful items made of wood?

At .25 mi. **[5]**, the trail crosses another bridge before turning left. You'll pass the persimmon tree, whose wood is used for food, and the sassafras tree whose roots were once—and occasionally still are—used for food. Look for the eastern white pine, the largest conifer in regional forests, and black walnut, a tree so valuable that it's now being planted in plantations.

At .5 mi. **[6]**, the trail loops back to follow the main park road. Continue walking straight ahead. You'll hear an occasional car on your left or perhaps children squealing on the playground. The trail ends at .75 mi. where you began.

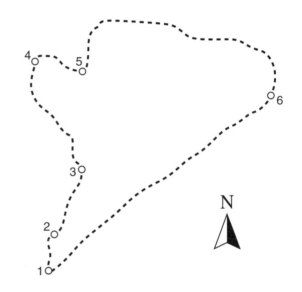

1. Trailhead
2. Wooden bridge
3. Wheelchair-accessible loop
4. Right turn
5. Wooden bridge
6. Continue straight

# Backcountry Fire Trail 👢👢👢

**Distance One-Way:** .73 mile

**Estimated Hiking Time:** 45 minutes (plus return)

**Cautions:** You have to walk through shallow water—a creek without a bridge.

**Trail Directions:** From the main entrance to Starve Hollow Lake State Recreation Area, head north on Lake Road. Turn east on Starve Hollow Road, and drive 1.3 mi. Turn right onto a grassy, gravel road, and park in a clearing. The trail begins **[1]** south of the parking area. Walk south to a clear-water creek, where you must go through water. On the left is a farmer's field and some abandoned buildings; on the right is forest. Ahead lies a fine walk over a fire trail road, which we undertook after a stormy spring when the Oak Leaf Nature Trail and the Vista Loop were said to be barely passable.

At .06 mi., a long, heavy metal bar across the road (i.e., the trail) barricades motor vehicles. Walk around it; then take the right fork ahead. You'll walk on coarse, small stones and see parallel ruts before you. At .16 mi., ignore the yellow marker for the Lakeside Trail at the right **[2]**. Continue walking ahead and uphill, through maple forest, the woods so quiet we could hear a cacophony of birds as the trail skirted a hill. At .22 mi., we found a ravine on the right, along with teasing glimpses of Starve Hollow Lake. High in the forest canopy, we could hear squirrels breaking twigs and dropping nuts.

At .25 mi., it looked as if someone had cut squared-off stones from the rock outcropping at the base of a hill on the left. On a hot day, the forest was cool and damp, and we wondered whether daily rains had turned every forest mesic. All around, the forest floor was covered with decaying leaves. At .32 mi., there was a long, wooden bench where the Vista Loop crosses the road **[3]**. Continue on the road and you'll follow the ruts downhill. Here, you can see between trees to the edge of the lake. At .46 mi. **[4],** we noted stagnant, brown water on the forest floor on the left and saw water lilies floating on the lake at the right. In season, you'll also get a view of campers' tents on the opposite shore, one wee bit of civilization!

Butterflies flitted about the occasional wildflowers; we spotted a tiger swallowtail. Continue walking on the road and you'll pass through a ravine where a sometimes-dry creek enters the lake. Walk uphill past decorative ferns on the shady slope at left. We found trees from recent windstorms across the road, so we went around them. The trail descends a hill, then heads straight and past more butterflies. This time, we saw a monarch. As we walked farther through lowlands, we crossed a creek; vines dangled from tall trees on both sides of the trail. We passed a hollow in a sycamore tree, walking over muddy ruts, and enjoyed the red-orange blooms of a trumpet vine. At .73 mi. **[5],** another section of the Vista Loop crosses the Backcountry Fire Trail. At this point, we ended the hike and returned over the route we had come.

1. Trailhead
2. Lakeside Trail
3. Vista Loop
4. Water lilies
5. Vista Loop

# Knobstone Trail—Delaney Park to Spurgeon Hollow 👢👢👢

**Distance Round-Trip:** 3 miles

**Estimated Hiking Time:** 2 hours

**Cautions:** The trail goes through remote, forested hill country. Let park officials know when you leave and when you expect to return. If you don't check back in, they may go look for you. If you get lost, stay where you are.

**Trail Directions:** Park at the boathouse, where park officials can see your car. To reach the trailhead **[1]**, walk straight east on the park road, which soon turns to gravel, then dead ends. At the signs, take the right fork; however, this hike does not include the Spurgeon Hollow Loop. Walk to the Spurgeon Hollow trailhead and return on the road. You'll enter an upland forest of mixed hardwoods; the trail is marked with white blazes on trees. Two blazes together alert you to a change ahead. Find the next white blaze before continuing along an uncertain path. The Knobstone Trail is marked with yellow KT on posts.

At .1 mi., the trail veers slightly left; you'll see the lake with its tree stumps on the right. Along the trail, we noticed three tulip trees that had grown together. The first reassuring white blaze was painted at eye level. We passed ferns and evergreens as we followed a pine needle path that led left, away from the lake. Beyond a dry creek bed, a patch of tall weeds covered the path. At .15 mi. a sign **[2]** directs hikers to the Spurgeon Hollow trailhead; we took the right fork and were soon following a creek that runs through Clay Hill Hollow. At .2 mi., the trail veers left and heads uphill. Another white blaze marks the trail at the edge of a ridge. The trail heads left, then follows a ridge above a tremendous ravine **[3]**; from that height, the ravine appeared to be bottomless.

At the top of the ridge **[4]**, about 1 mi., ignore the path to the left; that's the long Spurgeon Hollow Loop. Instead, you'll walk past a pond on the left; we heard frogs jumping and saw basking turtles. At the next white blaze, you'll head down the ridge. Two blazes alert you to another shift in direction. We noticed a faint, white blaze at the left—that turned

out to be the wrong way. Instead, continue going straight downhill. At 1.2 mi., the trail follows a narrow, rocky clay channel of a runoff creek; follow this downward (it was dry in July). You'll soon cross a creek bed and the route curves gently through the valley. At the next T in the trail, take a right; the sign says "To Spurgeon Hollow" **[5]**. Continue walking and by 1.7 mi., you'll see a pond ahead with tree stumps sticking above the water **[6]**. Floating lilies with big green leaves bloomed near the edge. Yellow daisies brightened the trail.

As we continued, we passed a recently used campsite underneath pine trees **[7]**. What a beautiful place to be. Continue walking, ignoring any mud, logs, or weeds that get in your way. Soon, the trail ends, and so does the hike, at the gravel parking lot for the Spurgeon Hollow trailhead.

Return to Delaney Creek Park by walking north on the county road **[8]**; turn east at the sign for the park.

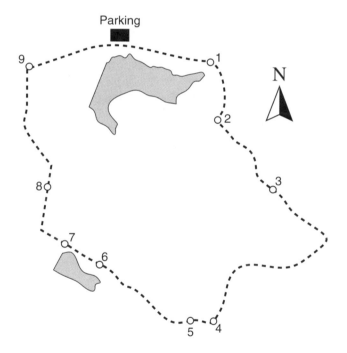

1. Trailhead
2. Sign
3. Ravine
4. Top of ridge
5. Sign
6. Pond
7. Campsite
8. County road
9. Turn east

# 41.  Falls of the Ohio State Park

- Discover fossils formed by ancient marine creatures.
- Walk past distinctive riverside plant communities.
- Explore bedrock islands when they're not under water.

## Area Information

Why should more than 175 acres of Ohio River bedrock—much of it underwater a significant part of the year—be designated an Indiana State Park? In the case of Falls of the Ohio, it's because that acreage is unique along the entire 981-mile course of the Ohio River. The bedrock here results from an ancient tropical sea. It is also exposed, and so are the geologic treasures it contains. Here visitors will find fossil remains of sea life—corals, shellfish, and other creatures—literally by the millions. Scientists have listed more than 600 fossil species at the Falls, and more than two-thirds of those were catalogued for the first time.

But it isn't only the fossils that bring visitors to the area. The state park is relatively small, just 68 acres of land. But that acreage is surrounded by another 1,404 acres making up the Falls of the Ohio National Wildlife Conservation Area, an area rich in living specimens. More than 265 species of birds and another 125 of fish have been recorded here.

There's no shortage of human history here. It was near here that George Rogers Clark established a fort and assembled a rag-tag army of frontiersmen who won what was then the "West" for the fledgling United States. A short distance downstream, Clark's younger brother William teamed with Meriwether Lewis and set off on the epic "Voyage of Discovery" that would eventually lead them to the Pacific Ocean. Aaron Burr trained troops here, and John James Audubon lived in the area while sketching birds.

**Directions:** Getting there can be a problem. The easiest and most direct route is from I-65. Take exit "0" to Market Street. Follow signs as you take Market toward the river (south) to Riverside Drive. Turn right (west) on Riverside and follow signs to the Interpretive Center (not the Visitors Center).

**Hours Open:** Interpretive center open 9:00 A.M. to 5:00 P.M. Monday through Saturday; Sunday, noon to 5:00 P.M. $2.00 fee for museum. Phone: 812-280-9970.

**Facilities:** Boat ramp, fishing, hiking, Interpretive Center, and picnic area.

**Permits and Rules:** Fishing license required. Indiana State Park rules apply.

**Further Information:** Falls of the Ohio State Park, P.O. Box 1327, Jeffersonville, IN 47131; 812-280-9970.

## Other Areas of Interest

With the city of **Louisville** just across the river, take a riverboat ride, visit the Louisville Slugger bat factory, or go to Churchill Downs. **Charlestown State Park** (see park #43), less than a half-hour northeast on route 62, works well in combination with Falls of the Ohio. Allow a half-day for each.

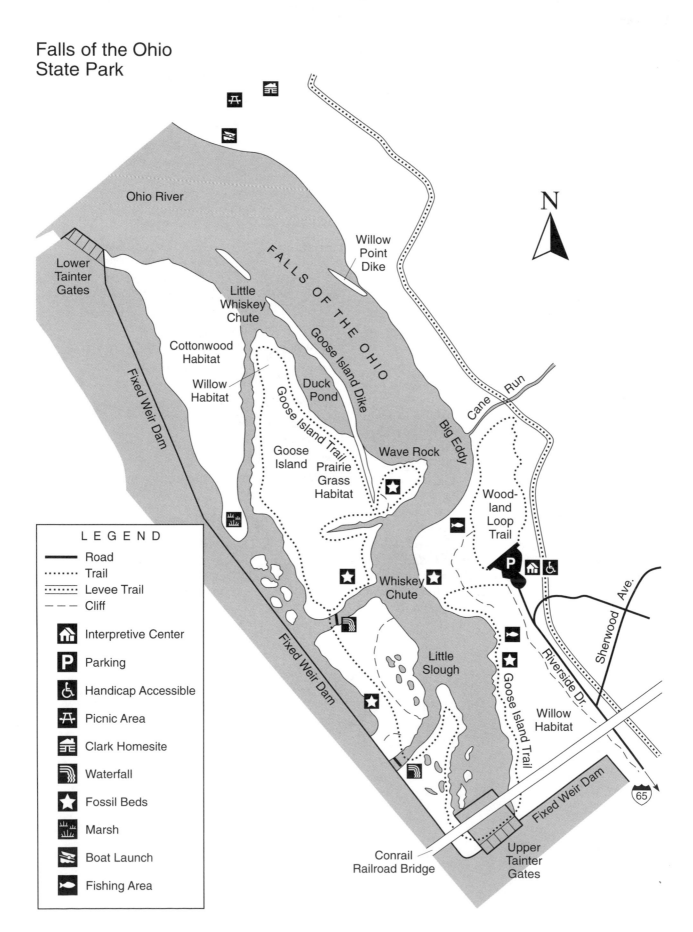

Falls of the Ohio
State Park

Ohio River

FALLS OF THE OHIO

N

Willow
Point
Dike

Lower
Tainter
Gates

Little
Whiskey
Chute

Cottonwood
Habitat

Goose Island Dike

Willow
Habitat

Duck
Pond

Cane Run

Big Eddy

Goose Island Trail

Goose
Island

Prairie
Grass
Habitat

Wave Rock

Wood-
land
Loop
Trail

Whiskey
Chute

LEGEND

——— Road
········· Trail
▥▥▥ Levee Trail
– – – Cliff

🏠 Interpretive Center

**P** Parking

♿ Handicap Accessible

🎪 Picnic Area

🏚 Clark Homesite

💦 Waterfall

⭐ Fossil Beds

🌾 Marsh

🚣 Boat Launch

🐟 Fishing Area

Fixed Weir Dam

Little
Slough

Goose Island Trail

Willow
Habitat

Riverside Dr.

Sherwood Ave.

65

Fixed Weir Dam

Conrail
Railroad Bridge

Upper
Tainter
Gates

# Goose Island Trail 👢👢

**Distance Round-Trip:** 3.5 miles

**Estimated Hiking Time:** 3.5 hours

**Cautions:** Take drinking water and wear hats and sunscreen; the rocks reflect heat. Do not hike when the water flows through the gates. Wear shoes with good traction—the rocks can be slippery and are surrounded by water. Supervise children well.

**Trail Directions:** Note that the Goose Island Trail is not a formal, marked trail. It is instead a route, one that will take you across a series of world-class fossil beds and allows plenty of opportunity for improvisation. Note, too, that the trek is not possible during periods of high water or gate releases by the Army Corps of Engineers. It is strongly suggested that you check with a park naturalist at the Interpretive Center before beginning the hike. Phone the center at 812-280-9970. You might also take time to view the center's movie detailing the formation of the area and pick up a copy of the brochure "Discovering Fossils at Falls of the Ohio State Park." Both will add significantly to your enjoyment of the hike.

Begin at the Interpretive Center **[1]** and follow either the stairs or the ramp to the fossil cliffs and the beds **[2]** below. Head upstream (east) past the fishing area to the next significant fossil area (approximately a quarter-mile from the start). Take time to explore.

Proceed through the willow habitat **[3]**, a typical gravel bar plant community, then under the railroad bridge and to the Army Corps of Engineers weir dam **[4]**. Turn toward the Kentucky shore and proceed along the dam to the upper tainter gates **[5]** a half-mile into the hike. Exercise extreme caution; the area can be very slippery. If the gates are closed, you can cross on the downstream portion of the gate structure. Should you find any of the gates open, **DO NOT** attempt a crossing! Current and turbulence are extremely dangerous.

At this point, the half-mile mark, you have reached the series of islands and islets that make up one of the most fascinating areas of the park. Fossils pepper the bedrock on both sides of Little Slough **[6]** and continue across Whiskey Chute **[7]** on the shores of Goose Island **[8]**. Both Little Slough and Whiskey Chute can be forded safely during periods of low water. Try just above the waterfall on Whiskey.

As noted earlier, there are no marked trails on the islands. Take time to explore and you'll be well rewarded. By working your way to Goose Island and hiking its perimeter, you'll cover 3.5 miles. Do justice to the fossil beds and you'll add both time and distance. But remember that the beds offer little shade. Wide-brimmed hats, sunscreen, and plenty of drinking water are the order of the day. With reflective heat, temperatures on the beds can be up to 20 degrees higher than on the surrounding tree-shaded shores.

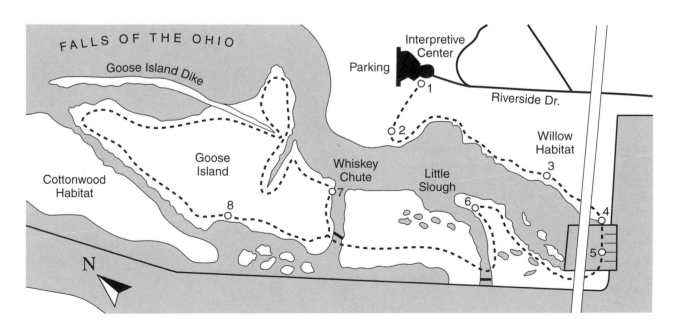

| | |
|---|---|
| 1. Interpretive Center | 5. Tainter gates |
| 2. Fossil beds | 6. Little Slough |
| 3. Willow habitat | 7. Whiskey Chute |
| 4. Weir dam | 8. Goose Island |

# Woodland Loop Trail 🥾

**Distance Round-Trip:** .75 mile

**Estimated Hiking Time:** 45 minutes

**Cautions:** Watch your footing when exploring the large rocks and fossils near the river. Carry a plastic bag and you can help pick up—and dispose of—trash deposited by high water.

**Trail Directions:** The trail, a self-guiding nature trail (pick up a brochure and a fossil leaflet at the Interpretive Center), begins at the northeast corner of the Visitor Center parking area and serves as a good introduction to the ecology of the Ohio River banks, both high and low. You will traverse a narrow strip of woodland between a grass-covered levee immediately to the east and the river itself to the west. Of the well-marked features identified in the trail guide, nine come in quick succession on the first half of the walk.

The first stop along the trail finds you in a stand of tall bamboo-like river cane [1], an important Native American building material. In quick succession you come to honey locust [2] with its king-sized spines, hackberry [3], and cottonwood trees [4], all typical of the riverside plant community. Note the sharp drop to the riverside. Not a natural feature, the excavation supplied dirt for the earthen levee that now protects the town of Clarksville. A pair of trees producing edible berries are next on the list. An elderberry tree is at marker five [5] and a white mulberry at six [6]. A short distance farther and the trail skirts a drain and quickly brings you to a stand of Jerusalem artichoke [7]. A staple of Native American populations, the tuberous root is still prized today and adds a crispy nut-like flavor to salads and other dishes. A short distance farther you'll find wild ginger [8] and pawpaw, sometimes called "Hoosier banana" [9]. Many consider its fall fruit a delicacy.

Note that at this juncture you have an alternative. You can climb the nearby levee and continue in a generally westerly direction along the levee top to the Clark homesite, a distance of approximately 1.3 miles. Frankly, the grass-covered levee, some of it abutting a residential area, makes for dull hiking, and the site itself is a disappointment. Neither buildings nor foundations exist, only a historic marker to commemorate the spot, plus a shaded picnic area and a boat launch.

If you opt to continue on the Woodland Loop Trail, you quickly drop to a shelf making up the lower woodland [10]. As you skirt Cane Run, be on the lookout for fresh beaver workings. The size of the trees the large-toothed critters can drop is amazing. You will also note evidence of the Ohio's power. Much of the area is littered with debris from the river's fluctuations.

From [11] on back to the parking lot and your starting point, you'll be on what many consider the most interesting part of the trail. These are the fossil beds, or at least a small part of them. It's time to get out your fossil brochure. The fossils are divided roughly into three types: colonizing animals such as corals and sponges; shellfish, including clams, snails, and brachiopods; and other sea animals, including trilobites and crinoids. The beds themselves are also divided into upper and lower. At this point you are on the upper beds, which boast smaller but more diverse fossils.

Continue along the shoreline—be careful, footing can be tricky—back to the parking area, the Visitor Center, or, if the experience has whetted your appetite, to the lower fossil beds. (See preceding entry on Goose Island Trail.)

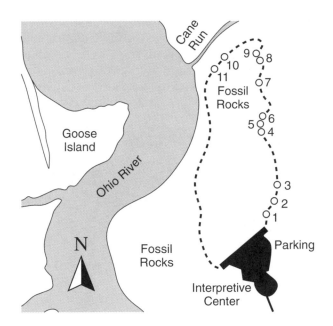

1. River cane
2. Honey locust
3. Hackberry
4. Cottonwood
5. Elderberry
6. White mulberry
7. Jerusalem artichoke
8. Wild ginger
9. Pawpaw
10. Lower woodland
11. Return trail

# 42. Clifty Falls State Park

- Climb an observation tower for a view of the rugged terrain.
- View rugged topography formed in the Ice Age.
- Photograph cool canyons and streambeds.

## Area Information

In an area where the actions of human beings and nature sometimes work together and sometimes compete for attention, it is nature that has made the major contribution. The area that now makes up Clifty Falls State Park is a prime example. The park's namesake, the falls, came into being during the last Ice Age, when the Ohio River was new and glacial waters cascaded down Clifty Creek to a final plunge to the larger river, a drop estimated at 200 feet. Today, the creek barely flows during later summer and fall. But topography, the lasting contribution of the Ice Age, remains rugged and spectacular. If you need quick proof, simply drive the park road to the SR 56 exit. Leave your car and hike the trails, and the effects become even more spectacular: deep valleys, rock outcroppings, fossil-laden stream beds, all within a stone's throw of the city of Madison.

And that brings us to the contributions of human beings. Madison's historic district is well preserved and well worth exploring. Less creditable was the ill-fated Madison and Indianapolis Railroad. Born in 1852, the project's main contributions to the park include stonework and a 600-foot tunnel, which provides flashlight-equipped hikers an inside look at the past. On the outside, it is nature, with exposed bedrock, streams, flora and fauna, which provides a better view.

**Directions:** The park is located on the west side of Madison between SR 62 and 56. There is an entrance station on each of the two state roads. From Indianapolis, Madison is 95 miles via I-74 south and US 421 east, or via I-65 south to SR 256 and then east. From Cincinnati, OH, it is 75 miles via I-71 west and US 421 west. From Louisville, KY, and Jeffersonville, IN, it is 55 miles via I-71 east and US 421.

**Hours Open:** The park is open all year from 7:00 A.M. to 11:00 A.M. (campers and lodge guests allowed in all hours).

**Facilities:** Camping, lodge with dining room, hiking, Nature Center, picnic areas, swimming pool, tennis courts.

**Permits and Rules:** Do not injure or damage any plant, animal, or structure in the park. Dogs or cats must be on leashes. Camp only in the campground; build a fire and park only in designated areas. Keep motorized vehicles on park roads; snowmobiles are prohibited.

**Further Information:** Clifty Falls State Park, 1501 Green Road, Madison, IN 47250; 812-265-1331.

## Other Areas of Interest

The city of **Madison** (see park #44) and its historic district, and the beautiful New England-like campus of **Hanover College** overlooking the Ohio River, just off State Roads 56 and 62, 5 miles southwest of town.

**Clark State Forest, Hardy Lake State Recreation Area,** and **Deam Lake State Recreation Area** are all within a 45-minute drive of Clifty Falls.

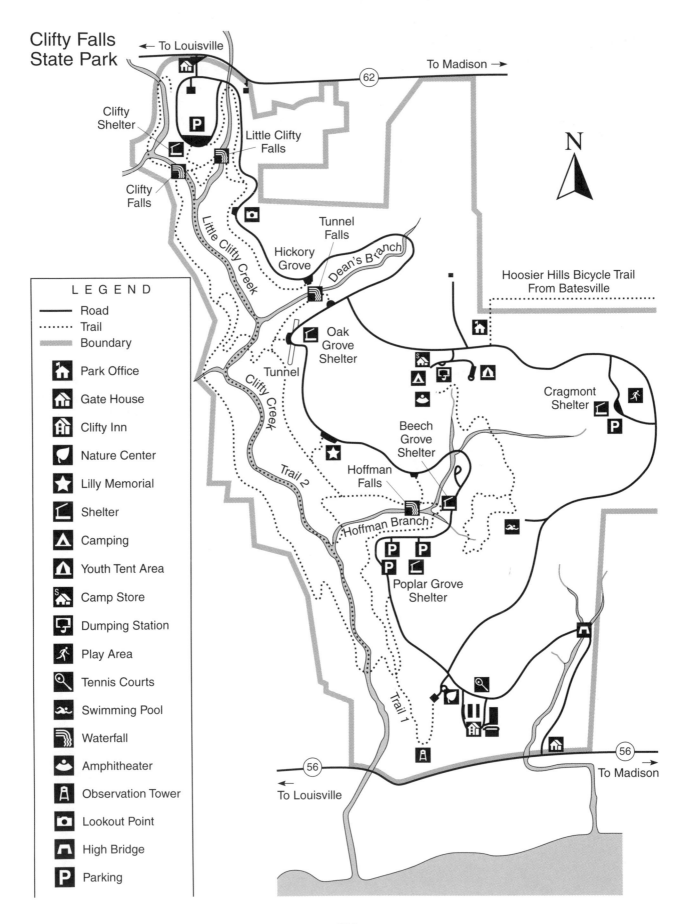

# Clifty Falls State Park

← To Louisville

To Madison →

62

To Madison →

N

Clifty Shelter

Little Clifty Falls

Clifty Falls

P

Little Clifty Creek

Little Clifty Falls

Tunnel Falls

Hickory Grove

Dean's Branch

Hoosier Hills Bicycle Trail From Batesville

LEGEND

| | |
|---|---|
| —— | Road |
| ···· | Trail |
| ▬▬ | Boundary |
| 🏠 | Park Office |
| 🏠 | Gate House |
| 🏠 | Clifty Inn |
| 🍃 | Nature Center |
| ★ | Lilly Memorial |
| ⌂ | Shelter |
| ⛺ | Camping |
| ⛺ | Youth Tent Area |
| 🏪 | Camp Store |
| 🚽 | Dumping Station |
| 🏃 | Play Area |
| 🎾 | Tennis Courts |
| 🏊 | Swimming Pool |
| 💧 | Waterfall |
| 🎭 | Amphitheater |
| 🗼 | Observation Tower |
| 📷 | Lookout Point |
| 🌉 | High Bridge |
| P | Parking |

Oak Grove Shelter

Tunnel

Clifty Creek

Trail 2

Cragmont Shelter

P

Beech Grove Shelter

Hoffman Falls

Hoffman Branch

P   P

P

Poplar Grove Shelter

Trail 1

56

To Louisville

56

To Madison

174

# Overlook Loop (Trail #1) 👢👢

**Distance Round-Trip:** 1.8 miles

**Estimated Hiking Time:** 1.5 hours

**Trail Directions:** This trail serves as a good test to see if you're up to the much more difficult Trail 2. Pick up the trailhead **[1]** at the parking area adjacent to the park's Nature Center. At .18 mi. you will reach an observation tower **[2]**. Although trees screen much of your view out over the Ohio River valley and the town of Madison, this spot still provides a good indication of the rugged surrounding terrain. The dull roar at this point is the Madison power plant, happily largely screened by the trees. As you exit the tower, the trail swings to the right and begins a descent through mixed hardwoods toward Clifty Creek far below.

At .4 mi., a small footbridge **[3]** spans an equally small creek falling off toward the valley floor. Look for papaw trees on your right. If it is late fall and the animals haven't gotten them first, you might be treated to the taste of what some term "Hoosier bananas."

After crossing a second small feeder stream, you'll find a quantity of loose limestone on your right. Take time to check for fossils. On a hot, humid evening, the woods are pleasantly cool. A little over a half-mile into the hike one comes to a trail junction **[4]**. Trails 2 and 8 lead off to the bottom of the valley and Clifty Creek, while Trails 1, 2, and 3 begin a moderately steep climb back up toward the road. Up to this point, Trail 1 has been a pleasant walk through the woods calling for little effort.

With virtually no switchbacks to break the climb, those who are out of condition will find themselves doing some huffing and puffing. Aside from the beauty of the surrounding woods, the rewards include some good examples of limestone outcroppings adorned by a variety of ferns and other plant life. On this particular evening, two white-tailed deer in fast retreat passed nearby. Two-tenths of a mile short of the full distance, you'll reach the road **[5]**. Turn right to return to the Nature Center parking lot.

Note that the same climb up from near the creek bottom to the road will be required at the conclusion of Trail 2, which is probably the most rugged trail in the park but also the most rewarding. If you have difficulty with Trail 1's climb, you might want to skip Trail 2.

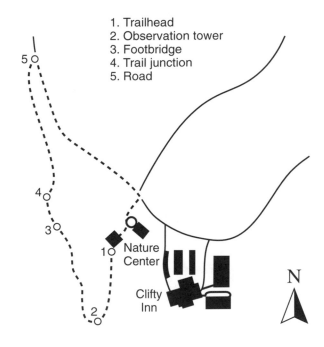

1. Trailhead
2. Observation tower
3. Footbridge
4. Trail junction
5. Road

Nature Center

Clifty Inn

N

# Falls/Clifty Creek Trail (Trail #2) 👢👢👢👢

**Distance One-Way:** 3 miles

**Estimated Hiking Time:** 3 hours

**Cautions:** The streambed section of the trail may not be passable when water is high. Trail includes sections of loose rubble and large boulders—watch your step. Wear sturdy footgear—which will probably get wet.

**Trail Directions:** Trail 2 begins just to the rear of the pavilion at the Clifty Falls parking area **[1]** and immediately begins a steep descent via boardwalks, steps, and ladders to the base of the falls. Note that a third of the way down a short side trip will take you to Little Clifty Falls **[2]**. Both Little and Big tumble some 60 feet to their respective creek bottoms and are well worth viewing, particularly earlier in the season when there is an increased water flow.

After returning to the main trail, work your way to the creek bed near the base of the larger of the two falls. Be aware, also, that this hike uses the streambed for 2 miles and may not be passable when the water is high. Check with park personnel if there is any question.

Having reached the creek, be prepared for the next .2 mi., which, arguably, makes up the most difficult portion of the hike. Here the creek bed is a rubble field made up of large boulder-sized pieces of limestone. Shoes that have good traction and provide good ankle support are highly recommended, but plan on getting that footwear wet. And concentrate on your footing. You'll spend a lot of time looking down, but there is a reward. Almost every boulder and every rock at this point is laced with fossils. Be sure to remember to leave them for the next hikers to admire.

After that initial test, the bed becomes considerably more uniform and provides easier footing. Still, pay attention. It's a long hike out, particularly with a sprained ankle. The creek bed itself is often lined by limestone bluffs on one side or the other, sometimes both. In the latter case, you will usually find a side path through the surrounding forest to rejoin the creek below the obstruction.

Progress here is measured in distance between feeder streams. The first of these, Little Clifty Creek **[3]**, comes in from your left about .2 mi. into the hike. Dean's Branch **[4]** is next, at the .7-mi. mark, followed by Hoffman's Branch **[5]**. At that point you're about 1.8 mi. into the hike and .7 mi. from intersecting with Trail 8.

Throughout the portion of the hike in the streambed, outcroppings and ledges—some with the start of shallow caves—add to the beauty of the setting. Depending on the time of year, the frequent small, clear pools are cooling and irresistible. We were there on a particularly hot August morning, but 15 minutes spent sitting chest-deep in conveniently placed pools sent us on our way cooled and refreshed.

At approximately the 2.25-mi. mark a sign suspended over the creek announces the junction of Trails 2 and 8 **[6]**. Here you have two options. You can take a right and follow Trail 8, which climbs to the top of the ravine on the west side and then follows the high road **[7]** back to the starting point. That adds an additional 2 miles to the total. The other option, providing you've been able to leave a car at the Poplar Grove picnic Shelter **[8]**, is to continue on Trail 2, which makes a long and moderately steep climb through pretty but not spectacular woods to the road. At the top, a left turn and several hundred yards will bring you to the picnic area.

1. Pavilion
2. Little Clifty Falls
3. Little Clifty Creek
4. Dean's Branch
5. Hoffman's Branch
6. Trail junction
7. Road
8. Picnic area

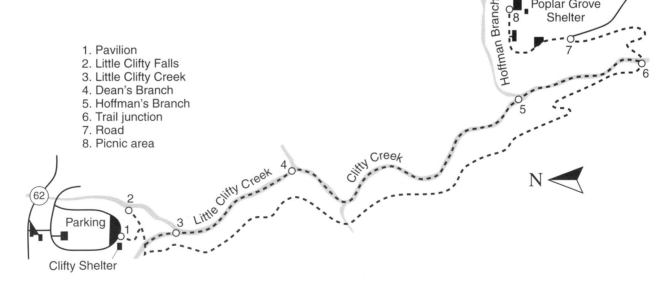

# 43.  Charlestown State Park

- Hike through hardwood forest and river bottom-lands.
- Find wildflowers in spring, summer, and fall.
- Pass a natural spring area where wildlife congregate.

## Area Information

Except for small valleys cut by the wanderings of Fourteenmile Creek and the steep hillsides leading down to the Ohio River floodplain, much of the area including and surrounding Charlestown State Park was farm and pasture land as recently as 1940. At that time what is now the state park became part of the sprawling Charlestown Army Ammunition Plant. And so it remained until 1990 when it was deeded to the state and officially designated a state park. Fortunately for today's park visitors, the Army allowed the land to return to its natural state. Farmlands and pastures began a natural progression, and aside from meadows, an occasional rusted piece of farm machinery, and a broken fence row, today's visitor sees little evidence of the world that was.

Charlestown, one of the newest and least developed in Indiana's state park system, offers a pleasant respite for the visitor.

**Directions:** The park entrance is located along the south side of SR 62, just northeast of the town of Charlestown. From the Louisville/Jeffersonville area route 62 itself provides the best access. From points north, exit I-65 at exit 19 (Henryville) and proceed south on route 160 to its junction with 62, approximately 11 miles. A left turn on 62 will lead you to the park entrance.

**Hours Open:** The park is open all year from 7:00 A.M. until sunset daily.

**Facilities:** Fishing in creek, picnicking, and hiking.

**Permits and Rules:** Do not injure or damage any plant, animal, or structure in the park. Dogs or cats must be on leashes. Camp only in the campground; build a fire or park only in designated areas. Keep motorized vehicles on park roads; snowmobiles are prohibited.

**Further Information:** Charlestown State Park, P.O. Box 38, Charlestown, IN 47111; 812-256-5600.

## Other Areas of Interest

With the **Louisville** metropolitan area less than a half-hour away, take a riverboat ride or visit the Louisville Slugger bat factory or Churchill Downs.

Charlestown State Park works well in combination with **Falls of the Ohio State Park** (see park #41) in Clarksville. Allow a half-day for each.

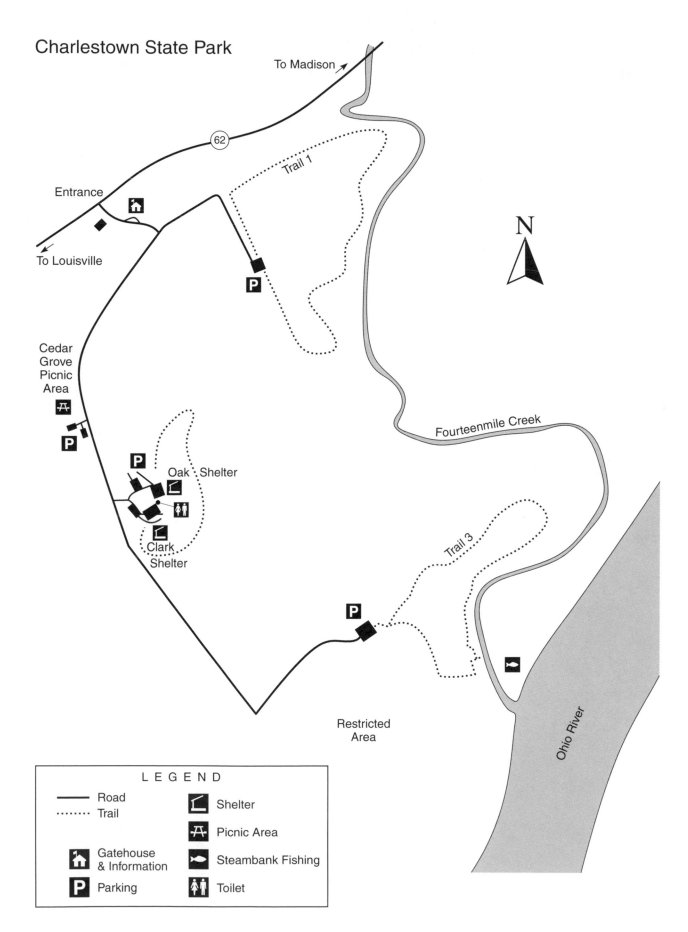

# Charlestown State Park

To Madison ↗

62

Entrance

To Louisville ↙

Trail 1

Cedar Grove Picnic Area

N

Oak Shelter

Clark Shelter

Fourteenmile Creek

Trail 3

Restricted Area

Ohio River

**L E G E N D**

| | | | |
|---|---|---|---|
| —— Road | | Shelter | |
| ···· Trail | | Picnic Area | |
| Gatehouse & Information | | Steambank Fishing | |
| P Parking | | Toilet | |

# Fourteenmile Creek Trail (Trail #3) 👢👢

**Distance Round-Trip:** 1.8 miles

**Estimated Hiking Time:** 2 hours

**Trail Directions:** From the parking area **[1]** at the far south end of the park, the trail follows a gravel road, skirting a portion of the huge, but now closed, Charlestown Army Ammunition plant. Approximately .15 mi. into the hike and with the Ohio River visible in the distance, the trail swings away from the military installation and heads into the woods **[2]**. Sycamores, beech, maple, and hardwoods typical of Southern Indiana provide a cooling canopy as the path, still wide and graveled, heads toward the bottomlands some 250 feet below. At the .4-mi. mark, the trail swings left, hugging the hillside. Straight ahead, Fourteenmile Creek **[3]** flows another .2 mi. south to its confluence with the Ohio. The mouth is an easy walk along flat lowlands.

If you retrace your steps from the Ohio and continue on the main trail, the path again drops to creek level (after a brief uphill climb) and quickly crosses a small tributary which, assuming enough water, cascades down a series of rock shelves. Another .2 mi. sees the trail narrow. Note the clumps of wild ginger in the area. As you approach the 1-mi. mark the trail crosses a small ravine **[4]**. Here the limestone outcroppings (on your left) add character to the topography. With the creek on your right, the trail widens into what appear to be wagon tracks and moves farther from the water.

About 1.25 mi. into the hike, rock outcroppings (on your left) add more character. You'll quickly arrive at a trail marker and a small clearing which, on a late summer afternoon, offers a display of wild sunflowers. At this point the trail leaves the river bottom and begins a gradual climb toward the ridge top. The climb steepens but is still moderate. Occasional rock outcroppings continue to add interest. The ridge narrows as the trail continues through mixed hardwoods with an occasional cedar. At 1.4 mi. you'll find a natural seep or spring area **[5]** adjacent to the trail on your right. The abundance of animal tracks indicates that it is a popular watering spot for wildlife.

With glimpses of Fourteenmile Creek now far below and the Ohio River valley in the distance, the trail breaks out into an open meadow, once farmland but now gradually reverting to Mother Nature's domain. The trail continues to skirt the open area for another .25 mi. before completing its loop and returning you to the parking area.

1. Parking area
2. Enter woods
3. Fourteenmile Creek
4. Small ravine
5. Spring

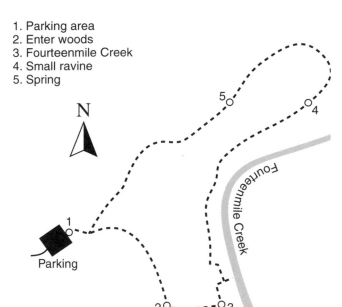

# Oak/Clark Shelter Loop (Trail #2) 🥾

**Distance Round-Trip:** 1 mile

**Estimated Hiking Time:** 1 hour

**Trail Directions:** Accessed from the picnic area at the Oak and Clark Shelters, Trail #2 offers a pleasant and easy walk through a combination of long-abandoned farmland and both new- and old-growth hardwood forest. A descriptive brochure completed as an Eagle-Scout project is available at the park entrance station. Unfortunately, a number of the corresponding markers along the trail are missing, but the written material still provides useful information. Join the trail **[1]** to your left and proceed clockwise. You'll cross what once was a cultivated field but now has reverted to meadow . . . good wildflower displays in season. In late summer the meadow boasts a good stand of ragweed and butterfly bush.

About a tenth of a mile from the start you leave the open area and enter the woods **[2],** primarily mixed hardwoods. The trail quickly begins a gentle dissent hugging hillsides into old growth woodlands. At about the halfway mark you'll parallel a small stream and find an overlook **[3]** that provides a good resting place above a small, cool pool. A spring on the opposite bank sends water over moss-covered rock, and a drop of about seven feet creates a natural shower that is extremely tempting on a warm summer's day. From the rest stop, a steady but gentle uphill climb leads to the completion of the loop.

As you near the top of the ridge, you'll cross an open area, apparently an abandoned power line right-of-way. Note that the surrounding forest is younger and oak, maple, and beech are interspersed with occasional hedge apple trees, mute testimony to the land's early agricultural use. Indeed, the woods quickly give way to open meadow, which the trail skirts in returning you to your starting point.

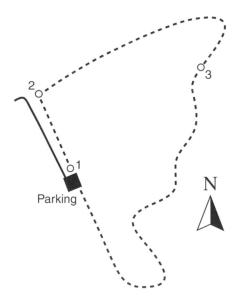

1. Trailhead
2. Enter woods
3. Overlook

N

# 44. Madison

- Enjoy Madison's historic downtown area.
- Pass the dock where riverboats sometimes land.
- Find shops, restaurants, and even bed-and-breakfast lodging along the trail.

## Area Information

Located on the banks of the Ohio River, Madison was born in the heyday of river traffic. The town prospered in the mid-1800s, and to its credit, much of that early history has been preserved and/or restored. Today, walking tours are the best way to experience the historic district. Pick up a map at the Madison Convention and Visitor's Bureau at 301 East Main. You'll find parking nearby and you can start your tour virtually as soon as you leave your car. In a comfortable two-hour walk you'll encounter some two dozen historic structures, most dating from the early to mid-1800s.

From the riverfront, which once welcomed steamboats to the Lanier Mansion and gardens, the district's homes speak of a slower, more genteel way of life. Many of the buildings are open to the public during the season, usually mid-April through October. Most charge a small admission fee.

**Directions:** From Indianapolis, it's 95 miles via I-74 south and US 421 east or via I-65 south to SR 256 and then east. From Cincinnati, OH, it's 75 miles via I-71 west and US 421 west. From Louisville, KY, and Jeffersonville, IN, it's 55 miles via I-71 east and US 421.

**Further Information:** Madison Area Convention and Visitor's Bureau, 301 E. Main St., Madison, IN 47205; 812-265-2956 or 800-559-2956.

## Other Areas of Interest

**Clifty Falls State Park** (see park #42), just west of Madison, and the beautiful New England-like campus of **Hanover College** overlook the Ohio River, just off SRs 56 and 62, five miles southwest of town.

# Historic District Walking Tour 🥾

**Distance Round-Trip:** 1.3 miles

**Estimated Hiking Time:** 2 hours

**Cautions:** Watch for traffic before crossing the streets.

**Trail Directions:** Madison, Indiana, and Clifty Falls State Park are a natural pair; at least the park is natural. Virtually adjacent to each other, the city and the park provide both sharp contrast and solid complements. Hike the wooded trails of the park, and for a change of pace, spend an afternoon or more amidst the charm of Madison's historic district. The town lends itself to a far more leisurely walk than does the park.

Begin with a stop at the local Convention and Visitor's Bureau. You'll find it at 301 E. Main, and it offers a handy brochure with route and descriptive material. We repeat that route here not to duplicate the bureau's efforts, but to allow you to take the tour should you arrive at a time when they are closed. Most of the important buildings have plaques that, although they don't replace descriptions in the brochure, do provide basic information.

Your walking tour begins at a city parking lot at W. Main Street and Poplar [1]. The route will take you south on Poplar Street to First Street, then west two blocks to Elm. From there it is two blocks north to Main and two and a half blocks west. Cross the street and return to Elm. Then it's north for one block, east on Third to Broadway, south to Main, and one block east to your starting point.

Among the treasures that await you along the way: the Jeremiah Sullivan House [2], 304 W. Second, built in 1818; the Masonic Schofield House [3], 217 W. Second, circa 1816; the Shrewsbury-Windle House [4], 301 W. First, built between 1846 and 1849; the Lanier Mansion and grounds [5], 511 W. First, completed in 1844; and the Francis Costigan House [6], 408 W. Third, built in 1851.

To complete your day "on the town," the downtown area offers good shopping and good eating to fit a variety of tastes. And a detour of a couple of blocks will take you to the river, where it's standard Indiana practice to sit for a spell and watch the Ohio flow by. If you're lucky, you may even catch the Delta Queen on one of its voyages along the historic waterway.

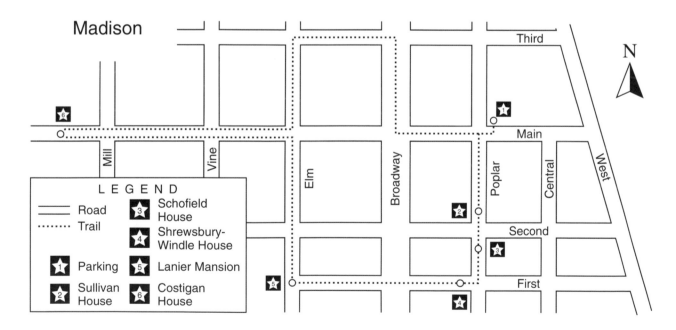

1. Parking lot
2. Jeremiah Sullivan House
3. Masonic Schofield House
4. Shrewsbury-Windle House
5. Lanier Mansion
6. Francis Costigan House

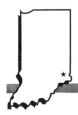

# 45. Versailles State Park

- This is a gorgeous park in the fall.
- Small creeks wander through the forests.
- Fossils can be observed in the streambeds.

## Area Information

Most of the area within and around the park was once farmland. As evidenced by the rolling hills, ravines, shallow soils, and frequent rock outcroppings, the land offered at best a meager living. In Indiana's park system since 1943, Versailles today comprises just over 5,900 acres. Two creeks, Laughery and Fallen Timber, traverse the property, with the former eventually joining the Ohio River to the south and east. Forests, typical of the area, include oak, hickory, tulip poplar, beech, maple, and walnut. All in all, Versailles and its surrounding area offer pleasant, if not spectacular, scenery.

**Directions:** Located just east of the junction of US 50 and 421 on 50, the park entrance will be on the north, approximately midway between the town of North Vernon and the Ohio state line.

**Hours Open:** The park is open all year from 7:00 A.M. to 11:00 P.M. (campers and those wishing to fish allowed in all hours).

**Facilities:** Boat rentals, camping, fishing, hiking, Nature Center, picnic areas, saddle horses, store, swimming pool (seasonal).

**Permits and Rules:** Fishing license required. Do not injure or damage any plant, animal, or structure in the park. Dogs or cats must be on leashes. Camp only in the campground; build a fire or park only in designated areas. Keep motorized vehicles on park roads; snowmobiles are prohibited.

**Further Information:** Versailles State Park, P.O. Box 205, Versailles, IN 47042; 812-689-6424.

## Other Areas of Interest

Versailles State Park is among the more isolated in the state. However, attractions within a relatively short driving distance include **Clifty Falls State Park** (see park #42) and the Ohio River city of **Madison** (see park #44), some 25 miles south via US 421, and the **Muscatatuck National Wildlife Refuge,** about 35 miles west on US 50.

Also of interest is the **Hoosier Hills Bicycle Route,** which begins at the state park and runs 27 miles to Batesville. There, it connects to the Whitewater Valley route, which eventually wends its way to Richmond.

# Versailles State Park

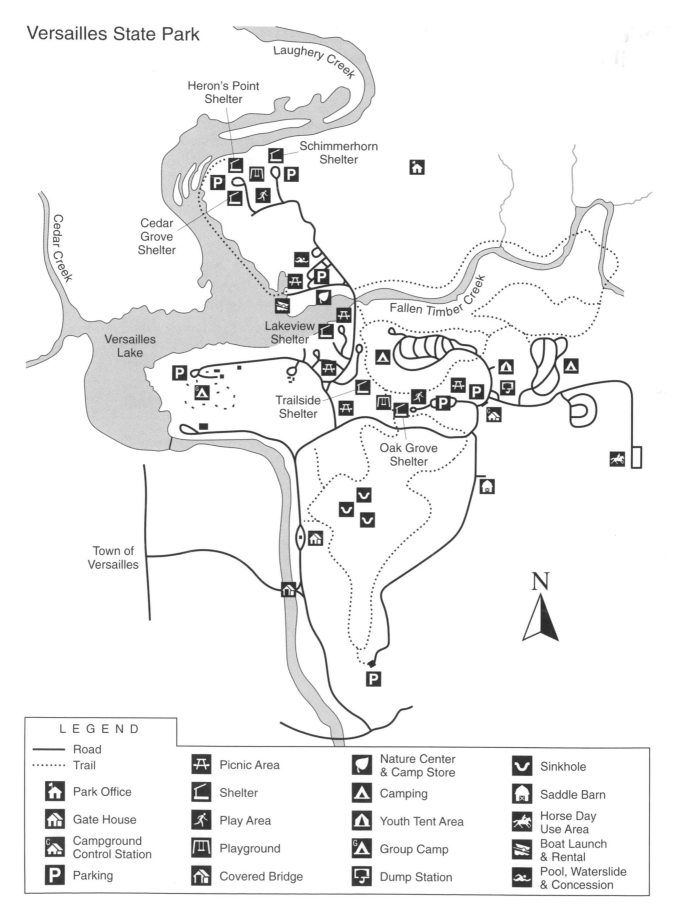

Laughery Creek

Heron's Point Shelter

Schimmerhorn Shelter

Cedar Grove Shelter

Cedar Creek

Versailles Lake

Fallen Timber Creek

Lakeview Shelter

Trailside Shelter

Oak Grove Shelter

Town of Versailles

N

## LEGEND

—— Road

········ Trail

Park Office

Gate House

Campground Control Station

P Parking

Picnic Area

Shelter

Play Area

Playground

Covered Bridge

Nature Center & Camp Store

Camping

Youth Tent Area

Group Camp

Dump Station

Sinkhole

Saddle Barn

Horse Day Use Area

Boat Launch & Rental

Pool, Waterslide & Concession

# Fallen Timber Creek Trail (Trail #3) 👢👢

**Distance Round-Trip:** 1.5 miles

**Estimated Hiking Time:** 1 hour

**Trail Directions:** Three creek crossings on the first half of the trail are among this trail's highlights. The trailhead **[1]** is found on the park's main road at its crossing of Fallen Timber Creek (near the Nature Center and camp store). Initially wide and obviously a service road, the trail leads up a gentle slope through a predominantly hardwood forest typical of southern Indiana. Note the cedar trees interspersed with the more common maple, oak, and beech. At about .1 mi., the trail dips to bring you close to the bank of Fallen Timber Creek **[2]**. Here the creek is, at least on this August afternoon, sluggish, muddy, and interspersed with small islands as it broadens near its confluence with Versailles Lake.

The trail continues along the edge of a narrow and heavily wooded valley. A few wildflowers, predominantly sunflowers, hold on against the heat and humidity of midsummer in southern Indiana. At .4 mi. you reach the first crossing of the creek **[3]**. Assuming low water, pay particular attention to the limestone, which makes up the 25-yard-wide bed. In that bed, as in a number of other southern Indiana stream bottoms, the fossil remains of ancient marine life are found in amazing number. The rule is look, touch, photograph . . . but do not take.

After the first crossing, the trail continues across gentle rises and dips through the stream-side forest to a second crossing at the .5-mi. mark **[4]**. Here there is slightly more flow, but no need to wet one's feet unless it is intentional. Again, the fossil material in the streambed limestone is the chief attraction. A short distance farther and the stream bank, easily visible from the trail, begins to take on more interest. Stratification is evident where the water has cut down to present levels. At some points the cliff-like sides reach 50 feet in height. At the same time, the width of the valley narrows.

At about .75 mi., you reach your third and final creek crossing **[5]**. At this point you have two options: either continue on the marked trail as it leaves the stream; or, if water levels permit, return to the starting point via the streambed. The latter option is clearly the choice if you have become fascinated by the fossils of Fallen Timber Creek.

For those who choose to continue on the trail, immediately after the third creek crossing the path doubles back on itself and proceeds up the steeper right bank, beginning to head back in the general direction of the trailhead. At approximately .9 mi., the trail crosses a small feeder stream with a series of interesting limestone ledges. With higher water levels, the ledges provide a series of cascades. A short distance later, Trail 3 intersects with Trail 2 **[6]**. It too will lead you back to the bridge over the creek and the starting point. Cross a small footbridge and go a few yards farther and you have reached the highest elevation on the trail. Then you begin a slow descent through old-growth forest with predominantly open understory.

At the 1.25-mi. mark, Trail 2 branches. Here you have the option of skirting the campground **[7]** and adding additional distance or turning right and taking the shorter route back to the starting point. The shorter route (the right turn) follows the stream. At 1.3 mi. the trail again branches, and again it is the right-hand branch that you follow. You'll briefly parallel a small feeder stream in the middle stages of cutting a ravine down to the main branch of Fallen Timber. At the small footbridge you'll find good examples of limestone ledges on your left.

At 1.4 mi., the trail skirts the edge of the campground and offers several shortcuts for those overnighting at the park. A short distance later, Trail 2 dips away from the campground and begins a descent down uneven steps—keep the kids in tow here—to a boardwalk **[8]** and the starting point near the lake, beach, and Nature Center.

In the early spring, the woods are alive with wildflowers—Dutchman's-breeches, trillium, bloodroot, and twin leaf. A bit later, you'll see wild ginger, poppies, columbine, and dwarf larkspur. In summer and fall, tall bellflower, snake root, wild sunflowers, black-eyed Susans, tall ironweed, with its purple display, teasels, thistles, and goldenrod are in abundance.

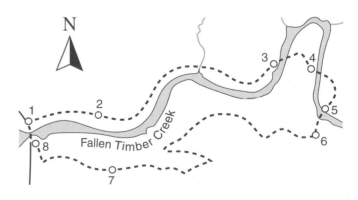

1. Trailhead
2. Fallen Timber Creek
3. First creek crossing
4. Second creek crossing
5. Final creek crossing
6. Trail junction
7. Campground
8. Boardwalk

# Laughery Creek Canoe Trail 🥾

**Estimated Paddling Time:** 2 hours

**Trail Directions:** All right, it's not a hiking trail, but for those who have an extra hour or so and want to give their feet a rest, the Laughery Creek Canoe Trail is a welcome change. Inexpensive rental canoes are available near the Nature Center [1] on Versailles Lake, and the mouth of the creek is but a short paddle to the north. Remember to pick up a self-guiding brochure at the center.

The first stop is just above the put-in. Cross the mouth of a small bay and look to your right. You'll see the work of the original dam builders, the beavers. It was human beings, however, and not the beavers, who were responsible for the state park's lake.

The trail brochure points out a variety of both flora and fauna you're likely to encounter along the water's edge. And make certain to stop on one of the three islands [2] formed in the mouth of the creek. There are almost always plenty of animal and bird tracks to test your identification skills.

The third and final listed stop along the trail provides the opportunity to experience vegetation—particularly water plants—up close [3].

From there it is up to you. You can continue to paddle upstream in the hopes of making new discoveries, or turn around and head back to the lake and the takeout.

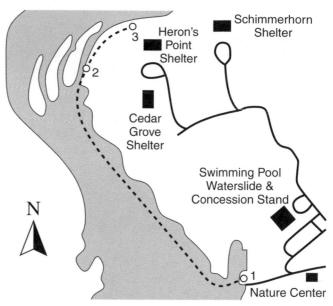

1. Nature Center
2. Three islands
3. Cattails